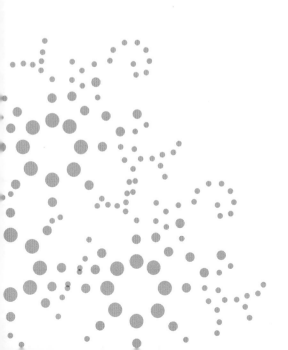

essential
ASIAN

essential
ASIAN

MURDOCH BOOKS

Published in 2011 by Murdoch Books Pty Limited

Murdoch Books Australia
Pier 8/9
23 Hickson Road
Millers Point NSW 2000
Phone: +61 (0) 2 8220 2000
Fax: +61 (0) 2 8220 2558
www.murdochbooks.com.au

Murdoch Books UK Limited
Erico House, 6th Floor
93–99 Upper Richmond Road
Putney, London SW15 2TG
Phone: +44 (0) 20 8785 5995
Fax: +44 (0) 20 8785 5985
www.murdochbooks.co.uk

Publisher: Kylie Walker
Project Editor: Melody Lord
Food Editor: Anneka Manning
Editor: Melissa Penn
Designer: Susanne Geppert

Photographer: Jared Fowler
Stylists: Cherise Koch, Emma Ross
Food preparation: Julie Ray, Alan Wilson

Text copyright © Murdoch Books Pty Limited 2011
Based on The essential Asian cookbook, first published by Murdoch Books 1997.
Recipes developed in the Murdoch Books Test Kitchen.
Design copyright © Murdoch Books Pty Limited 2011

National Library of Australia Cataloguing-in-Publication Data

Title: Essential Asian.
ISBN: 978-1-74266-088-2 (pbk.)
Series: New essential.
Notes: Includes index.
Subjects: Cooking, Asian.
Dewey Number: 641.595

A catalogue record for this book is available from the British Library.

Printed by 1010 Printing International Limited, China

IMPORTANT: Those who might be at risk from the effects of salmonella poisoning (the elderly, pregnant
women, young children and those suffering from immune deficiency diseases) should consult their doctor
with any concerns about eating raw eggs.

CONVERSION GUIDE: Cooking times may vary depending on the oven you are using. For fan-forced ovens, as a
general rule, set the oven temperature to 20°C (35°F) lower than indicated in the recipe. We have used 20 ml (4 teaspoon)
tablespoon measures. If you are using a 15 ml (3 teaspoon) tablespoon add an extra teaspoon for each tablespoon
specified. We have used 60 g (Grade 3) eggs in all recipes.

unique asia

Although it's been around for thousands of years, Asian food is suddenly the smart new food. Restaurant chefs from Vancouver to London are introducing Asian ingredients and cooking techniques into their repertoire, suburban greengrocers and supermarkets are stocking fresh coriander and lemongrass, and no wonder ... Asian food is fresh and colourful, full of flavour, and never boring or bland. With its emphasis on grains and vegetables, it is also healthy, cheap and often quick to prepare. Yet it's dangerous to generalise. Asian food is as multifaceted and diverse as European food. While neighbours share some common ingredients and cooking styles, Asian countries have developed cuisines that are uniquely their own. Sampling the food of each is truly an adventure. Selamat makan.

contents

prawn laksa (page 77)

your asian kitchen

Although the countries of Asia are spread over nearly half the globe, the various Asian cuisines have many things in common. Spices and herbs are used extensively, rice is a staple, and many ingredients, such as noodles, soy sauce and tofu, have crossed borders from one country to another and continue to do so. Stir-frying, deep-frying and steaming are techniques used in most Asian countries and there is one utensil, the wok, that is found, in various forms and with different names, throughout Asia.

the wok

No-one contemplating cooking a range of Asian dishes should be without a wok. With its large surface area and high sides it is ideal for stir-frying, and for deep-frying it requires less oil than a straight-sided pan. A wok is also ideal for steaming. Its sloping sides allow bamboo and metal steamers to fit firmly in place.

There are many types of woks available today. They vary in size, shape and the materials from which they are made. The traditional wok has a round base and is made from rolled steel. Woks are also made from stainless steel, cast iron and aluminium, and some have non-stick surfaces. A wok with a flat base is the best one to use on an electric stove because it will sit more directly and securely on the heating element, allowing a more even conduction of heat. Round-based woks work best on gas stoves; however a wok trivet may be necessary to provide stability. Choose a trivet which is open because this allows sufficient air to flow through, thus providing optimum heat. Gas stoves are ideal for wok cooking as the heat is delivered instantly and can be more easily controlled than it can with electric stoves.

seasoning and cleaning a wok

Rolled steel woks — the standard inexpensive ones available from Chinese and Asian stores — are coated with a thin film of lacquer to stop them rusting while they are being shipped and stored before being sold. This film has to be removed before the wok can be used. The best way to do this is to place the wok on the stove top, fill it with cold water and add 2 tablespoons of bicarbonate of soda. Bring the water to the boil and boil rapidly for 15 minutes. Drain, scrub off the varnish with a plastic scourer, and repeat the process if any lacquer remains. Then rinse and dry the wok.

The wok is now ready to be seasoned. This is done to create a smooth surface which stops the food sticking to it or discolouring. Place the wok over low heat. Have a small bowl of oil, preferably peanut oil, nearby and scrunch a paper towel into a wad. When the wok is hot, wipe it with the wadded paper that has been dipped into the oil. Repeat the process with fresh paper until it comes away clean and without any trace of colour.

A seasoned wok should not be scrubbed. To wash a wok after cooking, use hot water and a sponge, or soak the wok in warm water and detergent if food is stuck to it. Dry it well after washing by heating it gently over low heat, and rubbing it all over with an oiled paper towel. Store the wok in a dry, well-ventilated place. Long periods in a dark, warm, airless cupboard can cause the oil coating to turn rancid. Using the wok frequently is the best way to prevent it from rusting.

essentials for grinding

No Asian kitchen would be without some sort of grinding apparatus, usually a mortar and pestle. Ground spices quickly lose their flavour and aroma, so it is best to grind small amounts of whole spices when needed. While it is generally considered that a mortar and pestle gives the best results, an electric coffee grinder is ideal for this task: the motor, designed for hard beans, is strong enough to take the strain of grinding spices, the blades are low down and the bowl is appropriately small in size. If you cannot set aside a coffee grinder just for spices, grind a little rice to remove coffee flavours, and again after spices have been processed to remove their aromas.

Pounding the ingredients using a mortar and pestle is the best way to make curry and spice pastes, but if the paste is wet enough, a blender or food processor can be used.

essentials for cutting

Sharp, good-quality knives are essential as so much Asian cooking involves cutting up raw ingredients. For most jobs, a Western chef's knife is the easiest to handle. A medium-weight cleaver is useful when chopping a chicken Chinese-style. If preferred, a heavy-bladed chef's knife can be used. However, once you are used to the feel of it, a cleaver can be a very versatile instrument.

steaming tips

Food that is steamed is cooked by the moist heat given off by steadily boiling water. To get the best results:

■ Fill your wok or saucepan about one-third full with water. Place the steamer over the water to check that it is the correct level before you bring the water to the boil. It is important that you have enough, but not too much water, in your wok or pan. If there is too much water, it will boil up into the food and if you have too little water, it will quickly boil dry during cooking.

■ When the water is boiling, arrange the food in the steamer and place it carefully in the wok.

■ Cover the wok and maintain the heat so the water boils rapidly, allowing the steam to circulate evenly around the food.

■ When lifting the lid on a wok while steaming is in progress, always lift it up and away from you like a shield so the skin on your wrist is not exposed to a blast of scalding steam.

Bamboo steamers placed over water in a wok are ideal for steaming dishes such as won tons and fish parcels.

Whole fish can be steamed on a serving plate placed on a wire rack in a wok.

stir-frying tips

Stir-frying involves cooking small pieces of food over medium to high heat for a short period of time. To get the best results:

■ Prepare all the ingredients before you start to cook. The meat is often cut into even, paper-thin slices, fast-cooking vegetables are evenly sliced or cut into small pieces, and slower-cooking vegetables are cut thinly or blanched before being added to the stir-fry. Once the slicing and cutting is done, all the ingredients for the sauce should be measured out. If rice or noodles are part of the dish, these should be ready to be added as well.

■ Heat the wok before adding the oil.

■ Heat the oil before adding the food. This ensures that the cooking time will be short and that the ingredients, especially meat, will be seared instantly, sealing in the juices and the flavour.

■ Toss and turn food carefully while it cooks. Keeping it moving constantly ensures even cooking and prevents burning. Stir-fried vegetables should be crisp and meat tender and succulent.

deep-frying tips

It is important to make sure that the wok or pan you are using for deep-frying is stable and secure on the stovetop, and you should never leave the kitchen while the oil is heating as it can quickly overheat and ignite. To get the best results:

■ Add the oil, never filling the pan or wok more than half full, and heat over high heat. When the oil is the required temperature for deep-frying (180°C/350°F), it will start to move and a 3 cm (1¼ inch) cube of bread lowered into it will brown in just 15 seconds. Lower the heat to medium if that is all that is needed to maintain the right temperature.

■ Carefully add the food to the oil with tongs and move small pieces around, gently turning them to ensure even cooking.

■ When ready, carefully lift out the food with tongs, a wire mesh strainer or a slotted spoon and drain on a tray of paper towels.

■ If you are frying in batches, keep the cooked food warm in a 180°C (350°F/Gas 4) oven.

■ When frying food in batches, make sure you reheat the oil to the required temperature after each batch. Use a slotted spoon to remove any small fragments of food left in the oil as these will burn.

curry pastes

In Thai and Indian markets, mounds of colourful curry pastes, made fresh each day, await the home cook. Red (from fresh or dried red chillies), yellow (turmeric) and green (fresh green chillies and fresh green herbs), they come in a range of strengths and blends. Ready-made curry pastes are available in jars and cans, but making your own will give you the best results. Make a batch of each of your favourite pastes and store them in the refrigerator. This will save time when you are preparing a meal. Fresh paste will keep for up to three weeks in an airtight container in the refrigerator. Alternatively, place tablespoons of paste in an ice cube tray, cover and freeze. When the paste is frozen, release the cubes into a freezer bag, and store in the freezer until required. Allow the cubes to defrost for 30 minutes at room temperature before using them. Frozen paste will keep for up to four months.

spices and blends

It is best to grind small amounts of whole spices when needed as ground spices quickly lose their flavour and aroma. Dry-roasting whole spices brings out the flavour and makes them easier to grind. You can dry-roast each spice individually or, if doing small quantities, together. Heat a clean, dry, heavy-based frying pan over low heat. Add the spices, stir constantly until aromatic and lightly browned, then turn onto a plate to cool. Ground spices can also be dry-roasted to make them more aromatic, but they will burn quickly and so need the very lowest heat. While freshly prepared spices produce the best results, it may often be convenient to prepare a quantity of spice blends (see page 114) such as Garam masala or Ceylon curry powder. These will last well if stored in airtight glass jars away from sunlight and heat.

basic stocks

A number of recipes in this book include stock in the ingredients. The list of ingredients in a basic stock recipe can be modified to produce beef, chicken or seafood stock by varying the type of carcasses, bones or trimmings used and by following the cooking instructions for the type of stock. For chicken stock use chicken necks, feet or wings; for seafood stock, use fish heads or prawn heads and shells or lobster shells; and for beef stock, use bones, oxtail or shanks. Stock can be stored in the refrigerator for up to a week and in the freezer for up to six months.

1 kg (2 lb 4 oz) carcasses, bones or trimmings with fat removed
1 carrot, roughly chopped
3 red Asian shallots or 3 spring onions (scallions),
    roughly chopped
2 litres (70 fl oz/8 cups) cold water
5 cm (2 inch) piece fresh ginger, sliced
5 black peppercorns
2 garlic cloves, sliced

BEEF STOCK

1. Bake the beef bones in a baking dish, at 230°C (450°F/Gas 8) for 40 minutes, adding the carrots and shallots to the dish halfway through the cooking time.
2. Deglaze the baking dish with a little of the water and transfer the contents to a stockpot or large saucepan, with the remaining ingredients, including the remaining water, and bring to the boil. Remove any scum that has risen to the surface of the liquid.

3. Reduce the heat and simmer gently for 3 hours (or longer if you prefer a more concentrated stock). Occasionally remove any scum that rises to the top during simmering.
4. Strain the stock through a fine sieve, pressing the solids to extract all the liquid and then allow to cool. Remove any fat from the surface.

CHICKEN STOCK

1. Place the carcass or bones in a stockpot or large saucepan with the remaining ingredients and bring to the boil. Remove any scum that has risen to the surface of the liquid.
2. Reduce the heat and simmer for 1 hour. Occasionally remove any scum that rises to the top during simmering.
3. Strain the stock through a fine sieve and allow to cool. Remove any fat from the surface.

FISH STOCK

1. Cut the bones and fish trimmings into pieces, discard the eyes and gills. Soak the bones and trimmings in cold salted water for about 10 minutes to remove any blood. Break up prawn or lobster shells.
2. Place bones, trimmings or shells in a stockpot or large saucepan with the water and other ingredients and bring to the boil.
3. Simmer 20 minutes, skimming off the surface scum as it rises.
4. Strain the stock through a fine sieve and allow to cool.

VEGETABLE STOCK

For vegetable stock, increase the number of red Asian shallots to eight and use two extra carrots.
1. Put the chopped vegetables in a stockpot or large saucepan with the water and remaining ingredients. Bring to the boil and simmer for up to 1 hour.
2. Strain the stock through a fine sieve, pressing the vegetables with a ladle to extract all the liquid. Set aside to cool.

Our star rating:

When we test recipes, we rate them for ease of preparation. The following cookery ratings are used in this book:

❁ A single star indicates a recipe that is simple and generally quick to make, perfect for beginners.

❁❁ Two stars indicate the need for a little more care or a little more time.

❁❁❁ Three stars indicate special dishes that need more investment in time, care and patience, but the results are worth it. Even beginners can make these dishes as long as the recipe is followed carefully.

useful preparation techniques

chopping a chicken or duck, chinese-style

When cutting the chicken, bring the cleaver or knife down sharply in one clean stroke. With a dense bone mass, you may need to lift the blade with the food attached to it and bring it down sharply on the board again until the food is cleanly cut.

Cut the chicken in half by cutting along the breast bone, continuing down through the backbone.

Remove the wings, drumsticks and thighs. If you don't have a cleaver, use a heavy-bladed chef's knife.

Chop each large segment, such as the breasts or legs, into two or three pieces. The pieces must be a manageable size for handling with chopsticks.

preparing meat

Many Asian dishes call for the meat to be very thinly sliced. If the meat is partially frozen, this makes it firmer and much easier to slice.

Trim all the fat and sinew from the meat and cut it across the grain.

peeling prawns

Don't throw prawn heads and shells away but reserve them for use in stocks. They can be stored in the freezer for up to six months.

To peel prawns, break off the head then snap the shell away from the underbody. Depending on the recipe, either leave the tail intact or remove it by gently squeezing it off the body.

Cut down the back of the prawn with a sharp knife, then gently remove the vein.

handling chillies

Take great care when chopping or seeding chillies. Capsaicin, the pungent substance that gives chillies their hot taste, can cause severe skin irritation and remains active even in dried chillies. Wear disposable rubber gloves and handle the chilli, especially the membrane and seeds, as little as possible. Don't touch your eyes or any other sensitive part of your body. Immediately after preparing chillies, dispose of the gloves, wash your hands, the board and utensils. If you like a hot flavour, leave the seeds and membrane (the hottest parts) in, but for a milder flavour, remove them.

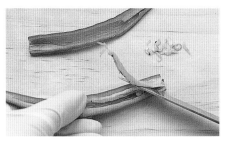

To seed a chilli, use a sharp knife to cut off the stalk, slit open the chilli lengthways and scrape out the central membrane and seeds.

preparing fresh herbs and spices

A number of herbs and spices are used time and time again in Asian recipes. The way they are prepared depends on the dish. Some common methods are shown here. Many fresh herbs are essential in Asian cooking. Wrap any leftover herbs in a damp paper towel and refrigerate them in a sealed plastic bag in the vegetable crisper for up to a week.

asian pantry

Today many of the herbs, spices, vegetables and other items needed to create authentic Asian dishes are readily available, often in local supermarkets. The more unusual ingredients can be found in Asian food stores.

asian greens

Bok choy (pak choy), also known as Chinese chard and Chinese white cabbage, has fleshy white stems and leaf ribs and green flat leaves. It has a slightly mustardy taste. Separate the leaves and wash well. The stems can be sliced thinly and eaten raw. Look for firm stems and unblemished leaves. A smaller type is baby bok choy or Shanghai bok choy.

Chinese broccoli (gai larn), also known as Chinese kale, has smooth, round stems sprouting large dark green leaves and small, white flowers. The juicy stems, trimmed of most of their leaves, are the piece of the plant which is most commonly eaten. Chinese broccoli has a similar flavour to Western broccoli, but without the large flower heads.

Chinese cabbage (wong bok), also known as celery cabbage and napa cabbage, has a long shape and closely packed broad, pale green leaves with wide white stems. It has a delicate mustard-like flavour. This is the vegetable which is always used in cabbage rolls and Kimchi.

Choy sum, also known as Chinese flowering cabbage, is slimmer than bok choy and has smooth green leaves and pale green stems with clusters of tiny yellow flowers on the tips of the inner shoots. The leaves and flowers cook quickly and have a light, sweet mustardy flavour; the stems are crunchy and juicy.

bamboo shoots

Crunchy in texture and with a subtle, refreshing taste, these are the edible young shoots of certain types of bamboo. Spring bamboo shoots are pale, fibrous and chunky; winter shoots are thinner with a finer texture and more pronounced flavour. Fresh bamboo shoots are hard to get and, if not already prepared, must be peeled then parboiled to remove toxic hydrocyanic acid — boil whole or in chunks for five minutes or more until they no longer taste bitter. Tinned and bottled bamboo shoots are the ones most often used.

banana leaves

The large flexible leaves of the banana plant are used throughout Asia to wrap foods for steaming or baking. They keep the food moist and impart a mild flavour. Remove the thick central stalk, rinse the leaves well and blanch in boiling water to soften. Foil can be used instead.

basil

Three varieties of basil are used in Asian cooking, all of which are very aromatic. If any are unavailable, substitute fresh sweet basil or fresh coriander in cooked dishes and fresh mint in salads.

Thai basil (bai horapha) has slightly serrated green leaves on purple stems. It has a sweet anise flavour and is used in stir-fries, red and green curries, shredded in salads and as a garnish for soups.

Lemon basil (bai manglaek) has small green leaves with a lemony scent and peppery flavour. It is usually sprinkled over salads or used in soups. Its seeds (luk manglak) are used in desserts and drinks.

Purple or holy basil (bai kaphrao) has narrow, dark, purple-reddish tinged leaves with a pungent, clove-like taste. It is added to stir-fries and strong-flavoured curries.

black beans

One of the most popular flavours in the cooking of southern China, black beans are dried soy beans that have been cooked and fermented with salt and spices. They are soft with a sharp, salty taste. Wash before use and lightly crush or chop to release the aroma. Black beans are available in tins or packets; once opened, refrigerate in an airtight container.

black fungus

Also known as cloud ear, this tree fungus has little flavour of its own, but is valued for its crunchy texture. It is most commonly available in its dried form, which looks like wrinkled black paper. Before use, soak in warm water for 15–30 minutes, until the fungus swells to about five times its size.

candlenuts

These hard, waxy, cream-coloured nuts are similar in shape to macadamia nuts, but have a drier texture. Roasted, then ground, they are used to thicken and enrich curries and sauces. They should be stored in the freezer to prevent them becoming rancid. Candlenuts should not be eaten raw as the oil is thought to be toxic. They are quite safe once cooked.

cardamom

This very aromatic spice of Indian origin is available as whole pods, whole seeds or ground. The pale green oval pods, each up to 1.5 cm (⅝ inch) long, are tightly packed with sweetly fragrant brown or black seeds. When using whole pods, lightly bruise them before adding them to the dish.

chinese barbecued pork

Also known as char siu, these are strips of pork fillet which have been marinated in five spice powder, soy sauce, sugar and red colouring (usually from annatto seeds) then barbecued over charcoal.

chillies, dried

Chilli flakes are dried red chillies that have been crushed, usually with the seeds (leaving in the seeds increases the hotness). Store in a cool, dark place in an airtight container.

Common dried red chillies will vary in size and degree of heat, depending on which type has been dried (it is not usually specified). Soak in hot water until soft, then drain well before adding to dishes. If preferred, remove the seeds before soaking to reduce the fieriness. The tiny chillies are very hot.

Chilli powder is made by finely grinding dried red chillies and can vary in hotness from mild to fiery. Chilli flakes can be substituted, but not Mexican chilli powder, which is mixed with cumin.

chillies, fresh

Bird's eye chillies are the hottest chillies of all. Measuring from 1–3 cm (½–1¼ inches) long, they are available fresh, dried or pickled in brine.

Small red chillies, approximately 5 cm (2 inches long) and also very hot, are the chillies used to make chilli powder and chilli flakes.

Medium chillies, 10–15 cm (4–6 inches) long, are the most commonly used in Indonesian and Malaysian cooking. Long thin chillies, these are hot but not overpowering.

Large red and green chillies, 15–20 cm (6–8 inches) long, are thicker than medium chillies. The ripened ones are very hot.

14

coconut cream and milk

Coconut cream, also known as thick coconut milk, is extracted from the flesh of fresh coconuts and has a thick, almost spreadable consistency. It is very rich.

Coconut milk is extracted from fresh coconut flesh after the cream has been pressed out and has a much thinner consistency. Once opened, the milk or cream does not keep, so freeze any that is left over. (Coconut milk is not the clear, watery liquid found in the centre of fresh coconuts — this is coconut water or coconut juice.)

coriander (cilantro)

Also known as cilantro and Chinese parsley, all parts of this aromatic plant — seeds, leaves, stem and root — can be eaten. The leaves add an earthy, peppery flavour to curries, and are used in salads and as a garnish, and the stems and roots are ground for curry pastes. Dried coriander is not a suitable substitute.

crisp fried garlic and onion

These are very thin slices of garlic cloves and onions or red Asian shallots that have been deep-fried until they are crisp. They are used as a crunchy, flavoursome garnish, and can be added to peanut sauce. Available in packets or they can be prepared at home.

cumin

These small, pale brown, aromatic seeds have a warm, earthy flavour. In its ground form cumin is an essential component of curry pastes and many other spice mixes. Black cumin is smaller and darker than common cumin and sweeter in taste.

curry leaves

These small, shiny, pointed leaves from a tree native to Asia have a spicy aroma and are used in southern India, Sri Lanka and Malaysia to impart a distinctive flavour to curries and vegetable dishes. Use as you would bay leaves, and remove before serving. Bay leaves are not a substitute.

daikon

Much used in Japanese and Chinese cooking, this carrot-shaped white radish can be up to 30 cm (12 inches) long, depending on the variety, and has a similar taste and texture to ordinary radish. It is added to stewed dishes, grated and mixed with finely chopped chillies as a relish, pickled in a solution of soy sauce, or thinly sliced as a garnish. The leaves can also be eaten raw in a salad or sautéed.

dashi

Made from dried kelp (kombu) and dried fish (bonito), this is the basic stock used in Japanese cooking. It is available as granules or a powder which are dissolved in hot water to make up the stock (page 174).

eggplant (aubergine)

Native to Asia, eggplants come in a variety of shapes, sizes and colours. Tiny *pea eggplants* are small, fat, green balls which grow in clusters, and can be bitter in flavour. They are used whole in Thai curries or raw in salads. *Slender eggplants*, also called baby and Japanese eggplants, are used in Indian curries and vegetarian cooking, where they readily absorb the flavours; the common eggplant used in Western cooking can be substituted.

fenugreek

An important ingredient in Indian cooking, the dried seeds from this plant of the pea family are small, oblong and orange-brown. They are usually gently dry-fried, then ground and added to a curry paste; in Sri Lanka a few seeds are often used whole in seafood curries. Use sparingly, as the flavour can be bitter. Pungently flavoured fenugreek leaves are cooked in vegetable dishes or ground as part of a tandoori marinade.

fish sauce

This thin, clear, brown, salty sauce with its characteristic 'fishy' smell and pungent flavour is an important ingredient in Thai, Vietnamese, Laotian and Cambodian cooking. It is made from prawns (shrimp) or small fish that have been fermented in the sun. Its strong flavour diminishes when cooked with other ingredients. It is also used as a base for dipping sauces. There is no substitute.

five-spice

This fragrant, ready-mixed ground spice blend is used extensively in Chinese cooking. It contains star anise, sichuan peppercorns, fennel, cloves and cinnamon. Use sparingly, as it can overpower lesser flavours.

flours

Asian rice flour is ground from medium-grain rice. It has a fine, light texture and is used in noodles, pastries and sweets, and gives a crunch to fried foods if used in a batter or as a coating.

Atta flour, also known as chapatti flour, is a finely milled, low-gluten, soft-textured, wholemeal wheat flour used for making Indian flatbreads, especially parathas and chapattis. Plain wholemeal (whole-wheat) flour can be used instead — sift first and discard the bran — but may result in heavier, coarser bread.

Besan is a pale yellow, finely milled flour made from dried chickpeas. Used in Indian cooking to make batters, doughs, dumplings and pastries, it has a slightly nutty aroma and taste.

galangal

This root is similar in appearance to its close relative, ginger, but it is a pinkish colour and has a distinct peppery flavour. Use fresh galangal if possible. When handling take care not to get the juice on your clothes or hands, as it stains. Dried galangal, sold in slices, must be soaked in hot water before use. It can also be bought sliced and bottled in brine. Galangal powder is also known as Laos powder.

garam masala

This is a mixture of ground spices which usually includes cinnamon, black pepper, coriander, cumin, cardamom, cloves and mace or nutmeg, although it can sometimes be made with mostly hot spices or with just the more aromatic spices. Commercially made mixtures are available, but garam masala is best freshly made (page 114).

garlic

Garlic is used in large quantities in all Asian cooking except Japanese. Asian varieties are often smaller and more potent than those used in Western cooking. The pungent flavour is released when a clove is cut; crushing releases maximum flavour. The strength diminishes with cooking. Pickled garlic is used as a garnish and relish.

garlic chives

Also known as Chinese chives, these thick, flat, garlic-scented chives, stronger in flavour than the slender variety used in Western cooking, are particularly prized when topped with the plump, edible flowerbud.

ginger

This spicy-tasting root, used fresh, is an indispensable ingredient in every Asian cuisine. Look for firm, unwrinkled roots and store them wrapped in foil in the refrigerator. The brown skin is usually peeled off before use. Ground ginger cannot be substituted for fresh.

golden mountain sauce

This thin, salty, spicy sauce made from soy beans is used as a flavouring in Thai cooking. It is available from Asian food stores.

hoisin sauce

From China, this thick, red-brown sauce is made from soy beans, garlic, sugar and spices and has a biting, sweet-spicy flavour. It is used in cooking and as a dipping sauce, usually with meat and poultry dishes.

kaffir lime (makrut) leaves

Native to Southeast Asia, this variety of lime tree has fragrant double-lobed green leaves and bears a dark green, knobbly fruit. The leaves and fruit zest are added to curries and other dishes to give a citrus tang (the fruit is not very juicy and is seldom used). Remove the coarse central vein from the leaves and tear or shred; pare or grate zest from limes. Leaves and limes are available fresh from Asian food stores; leftover fresh leaves can be frozen in airtight plastic bags. Also available are dried leaves and dried zest; these must be soaked in water before use. Fresh young lemon leaves and strips of zest from a standard lime can be substituted, but the flavour will not be quite the same.

kecap manis

Also known as sweet soy sauce, this thick, dark sauce is used in Indonesian cooking as a seasoning and condiment, particularly with satays. A substitute can be made by gently simmering 250 ml (9 fl oz/1 cup) dark soy sauce with 6 tablespoons treacle and 3 tablespoons soft brown sugar until the sugar has dissolved.

lemongrass

This long, grass-like herb has a citrus aroma and taste. Trim the base, remove the tough outer layers and finely slice, chop or pound the white interior. For pastes and salads, use the tender, white portion just above the root. The whole stem, trimmed, washed thoroughly and bruised with the back of a knife, can be added to simmering curries and soups (remove before serving). Dried lemon grass is rather flavourless so it is better to use lemon zest, although this will not duplicate the flavour of lemongrass.

miso

A staple of the Japanese diet, this is a protein-rich, thick, fermented paste made from soy beans and other ingredients, including wheat, rice or barley. It has a pungent, wine-like taste. Varieties include red, brown, light brown, yellow and white, each having a distinctive flavour and varying in texture from smooth to chunky. Lighter coloured miso is usually milder and sweeter. .

mushrooms

Dried Chinese mushrooms, also called Chinese black mushrooms, grow on fallen trees. Their distinctive woody, smoky taste is intensified by the drying process, and they are rarely eaten fresh.

Shiitake mushrooms are closely related to the Chinese black mushroom and are the most commonly used mushrooms in Japan. They have a rich smoky flavour, are grown on the bark of a type of oak tree, and are used fresh and dried. The fresh mushroom has a fleshy, golden-brown cap and a woody stem.

Straw mushrooms are named for their growing environment — straw — and are cultivated throughout Asia. They have globe-shaped caps, no stems and a musty flavour. They are available in tins; drain and rinse before use.

noodles

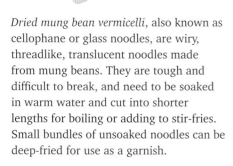

Dried mung bean vermicelli, also known as cellophane or glass noodles, are wiry, threadlike, translucent noodles made from mung beans. They are tough and difficult to break, and need to be soaked in warm water and cut into shorter lengths for boiling or adding to stir-fries. Small bundles of unsoaked noodles can be deep-fried for use as a garnish.

Dried rice stick noodles are short, translucent flat noodles made from rice. They need to be soaked in hot water until soft, then cooked briefly in boiling water until just tender. They are then ready for use in stir-fries, soups and salads.

Dried rice vermicelli are thin translucent noodles. They need to be soaked in hot water until tender, then drained thoroughly before being used in stir-fries and soups. Small bundles of unsoaked noodles quickly deep-fried until they expand can be used as a garnish.

Dried soba (buckwheat) noodles, a speciality of northern Japan, these are beige-coloured noodles made from a mixture of buckwheat and wheat flours; some are lightly flavoured with green tea or beetroot. They are cooked in simmering water, then rinsed in cold water to cool before use. The noodles are served either hot in a broth or cold in a salad with a dipping sauce.

Fresh egg noodles are made from egg and wheat flour and are pale yellow. Before use they need to be shaken apart and cooked in boiling water until tender and then drained well. In addition to their traditional use in chow mein, Chinese stir-fries and short soups, they are now used in recipes from many other parts of Asia. Fresh egg noodles are sold in a range of widths. The noodles are dusted lightly with flour before packing to stop them sticking together. Store in the refrigerator.

Fresh rice noodles are made from a thin dough of rice flour. This is steamed, giving it a firm, jellylike texture, then lightly oiled and packaged ready for use — the pearly white noodles need only to be rinsed in hot water to loosen and separate, then drained. They come in thick or thin varieties, or in a sheet that can be cut to the desired width. Rice noodles are used in stir-fries or added to simmered dishes near the end of cooking. Store in the refrigerator.

Harusame noodles are very fine, white, almost translucent Japanese noodles. They are made from mung bean flour and are very similar to dried mung bean vermicelli — use in the same way.

Hokkien noodles, also known as Fukkien and Singapore noodles, are thick, yellow, rubbery-textured noodles made from wheat flour. They are packaged cooked and lightly oiled and need no preparation before use — simply stir-fry or add to soups or salads. Store them in the refrigerator.

Potato starch noodles, also known as Korean vermicelli, are long, fine, green-brown, translucent dried noodles. Cook in rapidly boiling water for about 5 minutes or until plump and gelatinous; overcooking will cause them to break down and become gluggy.

Shanghai noodles are white noodles made from wheat flour and water, similar to the somen noodles of Japan. They can be thick or thin. Cook in boiling water before use. Fresh noodles are dusted lightly with flour before packing to stop them sticking together. Store in the refrigerator. Dried wheat flour noodles are also available.

Shirataki noodles are a basic ingredient in the Japanese dish sukiyaki. Thin, translucent and jellylike, they are made from the starchy root of a plant known in Japan as devil's tongue. They have a crunchy texture, but little flavour. They are available fresh or dried. Store the fresh noodles in the refrigerator.

Somen noodles are fine, white, dried wheat flour noodles used in Japanese cooking. Before use cook in boiling water for 1 to 2 minutes, then rinse in cold water.

Udon noodles are white, wheat flour noodles used in Japanese cooking. They may be round or flat. Cook in boiling water or miso soup before use. Udon noodles are used in Japanese soups and simmered dishes, or can be braised and served with a sauce.

nori

This is the most common form of dried seaweed used in Japanese and Korean cooking. It comes in paper-thin sheets, plain or roasted. Before use it can be toasted lightly over a naked flame to freshen and produce a nutty flavour. Keep in an airtight container at room temperature or in the freezer.

okra

Also known as ladies' finger, this vegetable of African origin is a narrow, five-sided seed pod, pointed at one end and containing small white seeds; it has a gelatinous quality when it is cooked. It is much used in Indian cooking where it is added to curries and stir-fries, stuffed with spices and deep-fried, or pickled. It is available fresh in summer, and it is also sold frozen, dried and in tins.

oyster sauce

This is a thick, smooth, deep brown sauce with a rich, salty, slightly sweet flavour. Although it is made from oysters and soy sauce, it does not have a fishy taste.

palm sugar (jaggery)

Made from the boiled-down sap of several kinds of palm tree, including the palmyra palm and the sugar palm of India, palm sugar ranges in colour from pale golden to deep brown. It is sold in block form or in jars. Palm sugar is thick, crumbly or solid and can be melted or grated before adding to sauces or dressings. Soft brown sugar can be substituted.

pawpaw, green

Green pawpaw is an underripe pawpaw. It is commonly used in Asian salads and some soups, or as a snack with sugar and chilli. To shred green pawpaw, peel and slice finely. It is sometimes lightly blanched before shredding.

plum sauce

This sweet-sour, jam-like sauce is used in Chinese cooking and as a dip with fried meats and snacks. It is made from plums, garlic, ginger, sugar, vinegar and spices.

rice vinegar

This clear, pale yellow, mild and sweet-tasting vinegar is made from fermented rice. Diluted white wine vinegar or cider vinegar can be substituted.

rice wine

Mirin is a golden-coloured, sweetened rice wine. In Japanese cooking it is added to salad dressings and marinades, mixed with soy sauce to make teriyaki sauce, or used as a seasoning in long-simmered dishes. Sweet sherry can be substituted.

Sake is a clear-coloured Japanese liquor made from fermented rice. In cooking it is combined with soy sauce and sugar to make rich-tasting sauces, added to water for steaming or simmering, or used as a tenderiser. It should be used within a year of manufacture and, once a bottle is opened, the sake begins to lose flavour.

Shaoxing rice wine, also known as Chinese rice wine, is amber-coloured with a rich, sweetish taste. It adds flavour and aroma to a variety of Chinese dishes and is also used in marinades and sauces. Dry sherry can be substituted, but grape wines are not suitable.

saffron powder and threads

Made from the dried, thread-like stigmas of the saffron crocus, this costly spice adds a vivid yellow colour and subtle flavour to food. It is available as bright orange threads (sealed in small glass jars or tiny plastic packets) or ground into powder (the powder is often adulterated and of inferior quality).

Saffron threads are usually soaked in a little warm water before use to release the colour into the water. The threads and liquid are then both added to the dish to give the characteristic saffron colouring.

sambal oelek

This is a hot paste made from fresh red chillies mashed and mixed with salt and vinegar. It is used as a relish in Indonesian and Malaysian cooking, and can be used as a substitute for fresh chillies in most recipes. Covered, it will keep for months in the refrigerator. Available ready-made or see recipe on page 114.

sesame oil

This dark amber, very aromatic oil is pressed from toasted white sesame seeds and has a strong, rich, nutty flavour. It is used as a flavouring in Chinese, Korean and Japanese dishes. It is not used for frying. Store in a cool dark place, but not in the refrigerator where it will turn cloudy. Cold-pressed sesame oil, pressed from the raw seed, has little flavour and cannot be used as a substitute.

sesame seeds

The tiny, oval, oil-rich seeds of an annual herb, sesame seeds are used throughout Asia for their flavour and their high protein content.

Black sesame seeds have a more earthy taste. They are used in sesame and seaweed sprinkle, a Japanese condiment, and in some Chinese desserts.

Japanese sesame seeds are plumper and have a nuttier flavour than other sesame seeds.

White sesame seeds are most common. Toasted and crushed, they are an essential ingredient in Japanese and Korean dressings, dipping sauces and marinades. Whole seeds are used as a garnish for many dishes and breads, and pressed seeds are made into a variety of pastes.

shallots, red asian

Small reddish-purple onions, these grow in bulbs, like garlic, and are sold in segments that look like large cloves of garlic. They have a concentrated flavour and are easy to slice and grind. If unavailable, substitute French shallots (eschalots) or brown or red onions.

shrimp paste

Also known as blachan, this type of shrimp paste, used in the cooking of Thailand, Malaysia and Indonesia, is made from prawns or shrimps that have been dried, salted and pounded. Sold in blocks, it has a very pungent odour and when opened should be wrapped in plastic, sealed in an airtight container and stored in the refrigerator or freezer (this is to reduce the smell as the paste itself does not require refrigeration). Use sparingly; always roast or fry before adding to a dish.

Bagoong, also known as shrimp sauce, is a soft, thick paste made from shrimps or prawns that have been salted and fermented in earthenware pots. It has a strong odour and taste, and is used in cooking and as a condiment, particularly in the Philippines.

snake beans

Also called long beans and yard-long beans, this legume grows wild in tropical Africa, where it probably originated. Growing to 38 cm (15 inches) and longer, with a crunchy texture and similar taste to green beans, it comes in two varieties: pale green with slightly fibrous flesh, and darker green with firmer flesh. Use as fresh as possible; snip off the ends and cut into bite-sized lengths. Stringless green beans can be substituted.

soy sauce

Soy sauce is made from fermented soy beans, roasted grain (usually wheat, but sometimes barley or rice) and salt. Dark-coloured with a rich, salty flavour, it is widely used in Asian cooking, and is essential for flavour and colour in many dishes.

Light soy sauce is thinner, lighter in flavour, but saltier and pale golden in colour. It is suitable for soups, seafood, vegetable dishes and dipping sauces.

Japanese soy sauce, also known as shoshoyu, is less salty and much lighter and sweeter than standard soy sauce, but not thick, like kecap manis. It is used in cooking and as a condiment. Because it is naturally brewed, it must be refrigerated after opening.

spring onions (scallions)

Also called green onions, these are immature onions which are pulled before the bulb has started to form and sold in bunches with the roots intact. Discard the roots and base of the stem, and wash stem leaves well before use. Spring onions add colour and a mild onion flavour and they need little, if any, cooking.

star anise

The dried, star-shaped seed pod of a tree native to China, star anise adds a distinctive aniseed taste to long-simmered meat and poultry dishes and is one of the components of five spice powder. Available whole or ground.

tamarind

The tropical tamarind tree bears fruit in pods like large, brown beans. The fruit is tart-tasting and has fibrous flesh and a flat stone at the centre. An essential flavour in many Asian dishes, tamarind is available in bottles as tamarind concentrate (also known as tamarind purée), a rich brown, ready-to-use liquid, and as blocks of compressed pulp that has to be soaked, kneaded and seeded (page 101).

tofu

Also called bean curd, tofu is a processed extract of soy beans. It is an excellent source of protein, and is available fresh or deep-fried.

Fresh tofu comes in two forms: a soft, white variety, also known as silken tofu, which is cut into cubes and used in Japanese dishes; and a firmer variety which is cut into cubes, wedges or slices and deep-fried. Both are available in blocks sealed in plastic; once opened, store in the refrigerator in water that is changed daily and use within a few days. Fresh tofu has little flavour when uncooked, but absorbs other flavours.

Tofu pouches, also known as inari, are deep-fried, thin slices of tofu, crisp on the outside and dry on the inside, that can be cut open to form bags. In Japan inari are stuffed with vegetables or vinegar-seasoned rice; they can also be added whole or shredded to soups and other dishes.

Tofu puffs are cubes of tofu that have been deep-fried until they are puffed and golden. They can be cooked in their own right with a strongly flavoured sauce, used in vegetarian cooking and braised dishes, added to salads or used as garnish for soups, or cut open and filled.

turmeric

This is a bitter-tasting spice which comes from the root of a plant related to ginger. It is used for its intense, bright yellow-orange colour and, dried and ground, it is the main ingredient in many curry powders. The fresh root is used in the same way as fresh ginger root — peel away the skin and finely slice, chop or grate the flesh. Store in a plastic bag in the refrigerator.

vietnamese mint

Also called laksa leaf and Cambodian mint, this trailing herb with narrow, pointed, pungent-tasting leaves does not belong to the mint family, despite its common name. It has a flavour resembling coriander but slightly sharper, and is eaten raw in salads, or as an accompaniment to most Vietnamese dishes.

wasabi paste

Also known as Japanese horseradish, this is a pungent paste made from the knobbly green root of the wasabi, a plant native to Japan. It is used as a condiment with seafoods and is extremely hot, so use it sparingly.

water chestnuts

These white-fleshed roots of a variety of water grass are prized for their semi-sweet taste and crisp texture, which is retained when cooked. They are used throughout China and Southeast Asia in both savoury and sweet dishes. Available tinned and sometimes fresh; cut off the woody base, peel away the papery skin, and cover in water to stop discolouring.

watercress

Watercress was introduced into Asia by the British. Its peppery flavour is added to soups and steamed vegetables in Chinese cooking, and it is used in salads in Thailand, Laos and Vietnam and as a garnish in Japan.

wrappers

These are thin pieces of dough used to wrap bite-sized savoury fillings. They are available fresh and frozen; defrost before use. When filling, work with one at a time and keep the others covered with a damp cloth to prevent them from drying out.

Dried rice paper wrappers are paper-thin, round, square or triangular, and are made from a dough of rice flour, water and salt. Soak them in water before use so they soften and become pliable.

Gow gee wrappers are round and made from a wheat flour and water dough.

Spring roll wrappers are square or round, and made from a wheat flour and egg dough.

Won ton wrappers are thin squares of a wheat flour and egg dough.

china

Chinese cuisine uses the freshest meats and vegetables in an endless variety of ways to create dishes in perfect balance. The Cantonese cooking of the south makes use of the abundant fresh ingredients, steamed or stir-fried over high heat and flavoured with just a little soy sauce, ginger or spring onion. Peking cuisine struggles with the harsher climate and geography of the north, but the result is wonderfully warming hotpots, dumplings and the famous Peking duck. Sichuan food is flavoured with vibrant chillies and spices, while ingredients in Shanghai are braised slowly to create rich meat and fish dishes.

prawn omelette with oyster sauce

✳ ✳ ✳

Preparation time: 30 minutes
Cooking time: 25 minutes
Serves 4

2 dried Chinese mushrooms
400 g (14 oz) raw prawns (shrimp)
3 tablespoons oil
5 cm (2 inch) piece fresh ginger, finely grated
125 g (4½ oz/½ cup) drained, tinned bamboo shoots, roughly chopped
6 spring onions (scallions), chopped
5 eggs
½ teaspoon ground white pepper
3 tablespoons oyster sauce
2 tablespoons soy sauce
2 tablespoons shaoxing rice wine (Chinese rice wine)
2 teaspoons cornflour (cornstarch)
spring onion (scallions), thinly sliced, extra, to garnish

1 Soak the mushrooms in hot water for 20 minutes. Drain, then squeeze to remove any excess liquid. Discard the stems and chop the caps finely.

2 Meanwhile, peel the prawns and gently pull out the vein from each prawn back, starting at the head end. Roughly chop the prawn meat.

3 Heat 1 tablespoon of the oil in a wok and stir-fry the ginger and prawn meat over very high heat for 2 minutes; transfer to a plate. Add the bamboo shoots, spring onion and mushroom and stir-fry for 1 minute. Transfer to a plate and wipe the wok clean with paper towels.

4 Whisk the eggs, 2 tablespoons of water and ½ teaspoon of salt and pepper in a bowl until foamy. Add the remaining oil to the wok, swirling it around to coat the base and side. Heat the wok until it is extremely hot and the oil is slightly smoking. Give the egg mixture a quick whisk again and immediately pour it into the very hot wok, swirling the wok a little so that the egg mixture coats the

side to about 5 mm (¼ inch) thickness. Cook for 2–3 minutes, swirling the wok to form an even omelette, until the mixture is just cooked through. Transfer carefully to a board.

5 Use a slotted spoon to drain away any juices from the prawn and bamboo shoot mixture and spoon down one side of the omelette. Roll up the omelette to enclose

the filling. Cut into portions and place on a serving platter.

6 Add the oyster sauce, soy sauce and rice wine to the wok. Mix the cornflour and 1 tablespoon of water and add to the wok, stirring constantly until the sauce boils and thickens slightly. Spoon over the omelette, garnish with spring onion and serve.

Finely slice the soaked mushrooms. (Everything should be ready before you begin cooking.)

Swirl the wok so the egg mixture coats the sides. (Make sure the wok is extremely hot before adding the egg as the heat produces the traditionally lacy appearance of the omelette.)

Divide the omelette into 4 or 5 sections with a spatula, and turn each section over to cook the other side.

cantonese lemon chicken

✹ ✹

Preparation time: **15 minutes**
Cooking time: **25 minutes**
Serves **4**

500 g (1 lb 2 oz) boneless, skinless
    chicken breasts
1 egg yolk, lightly beaten
2 teaspoons soy sauce
2 teaspoons dry sherry
3 teaspoons cornflour (cornstarch)
60 g (2¼ oz/½ cup) cornflour
    (cornstarch), extra
2½ tablespoons plain (all-purpose) flour
oil, for deep-frying
4 spring onions (scallions), thinly sliced,
    to garnish

LEMON SAUCE
80 ml (2½ fl oz/⅓ cup) lemon juice
2 tablespoons sugar
1 tablespoon dry sherry
2 teaspoons cornflour (cornstarch)

1 Cut the chicken into long strips, about
1 cm (½ inch) wide, and then set aside.
Combine the egg, 1 tablespoon water,
soy sauce, sherry and cornflour in a small
bowl and mix until smooth. Pour the egg
mixture over the chicken, mixing well,
and set aside for 10 minutes.
2 Sift the extra cornflour and plain flour
together onto a plate. Roll each piece of
chicken in the flour, coating each piece
evenly, and shake off the excess. Place the
chicken in a single layer on a plate.
3 Fill a wok one-third full of oil and heat
to 180°C (350°F), or until a cube of bread
dropped into the oil browns in 15 seconds.
Carefully lower the chicken pieces into the
oil, in batches, and cook for 2 minutes,
or until golden brown. Remove the
chicken with a slotted spoon and drain on
paper towels. Repeat with the remaining
chicken. Set aside while preparing the
sauce. Reserve the oil in the wok.
4 To make the lemon sauce, combine
2 tablespoons water, the lemon juice,

sugar and sherry in a small saucepan.
Bring to the boil over medium heat,
stirring until the sugar has dissolved. Mix
the cornflour and 1 tablespoon water and
add to the lemon juice mixture, stirring
constantly until the sauce boils and
thickens. Set aside.
5 Just before serving, reheat the oil in
the wok to very hot, add all the chicken
pieces and deep-fry for 2 minutes, or
until very crisp and a rich golden brown.
Remove the chicken with a slotted spoon
and drain well on paper towels. Pile the
chicken onto a serving plate, drizzle over
the sauce, sprinkle with the spring onion
and serve immediately.

NOTE: The first deep-frying of the
chicken pieces can be done several
hours in advance.

shaoxing rice wine

China's best known rice wine
is shaoxing, from Chekiang
(Zhejiang) province in the
northeast of the country, where
for more than 2000 years it
has been made from a mixture
of glutinous rice, millet, yeast
and local spring water. In China
it is known as 'carved flower',
for the pattern on the urns in
which it is stored, and also
as 'daughter's wine', because
traditionally some is put away
at the birth of a daughter to be
drunk at her wedding. Shaoxing
is aged for at least 10 years
and sometimes as long as 100
years. As a drink to accompany
food it should be served warm
in small cups without handles.

dried mandarin and tangerine peel

The dried fruit of these closely related Asian fruit trees is used in Chinese cooking to add a rich, fruity flavour. The peel is added dried to long-simmered dishes; otherwise it is either soaked in warm water to soften, or very finely chopped. It is available in packets from Asian food stores, or the peel of the fresh fruit can be slowly dried until hard in a very slow oven or in the sun.

beef with mandarin

❋

Preparation time: 30 minutes
Cooking time: 5 minutes
Serves 4

2 teaspoons soy sauce
2 teaspoons dry sherry
1 teaspoon chopped fresh ginger
1 teaspoon sesame oil
350 g (12 oz) rib eye steak, thinly sliced
1 tablespoon peanut oil

¼ teaspoon ground white pepper
2 teaspoons finely chopped dried mandarin or tangerine peel
2 teaspoons soy sauce, extra
1½ teaspoons caster (superfine) sugar
1½ teaspoons cornflour (cornstarch)
80 ml (2½ fl oz/⅓ cup) beef stock
steamed rice, to serve

1   Combine the soy sauce, sherry, ginger and sesame oil in a bowl. Add the beef and stir to coat in the marinade. Set aside for 15 minutes.

2   Heat the peanut oil in a wok, swirling gently to coat the base and side. Add the beef and stir-fry over high heat for 2 thinly sliced minutes, or until the beef changes colour. Add the white pepper, peel, extra soy sauce and sugar and stir-fry briefly.
3   Mix the cornflour and a little of the stock and add to the wok. Add the remaining stock and stir until the sauce boils and thickens. Serve with steamed rice.

chicken and sweet corn soup

❋

Preparation time: 30 minutes
Cooking time: 10 minutes
Serves 4

200 g (7 oz) boneless, skinless
    chicken breast
2 egg whites
750 ml (26 fl oz/3 cups) chicken stock
250 g (9 oz/1 cup) creamed corn
1 tablespoon cornflour (cornstarch)
2 teaspoons soy sauce
2 spring onions (scallions), thinly sliced,
    to garnish

1 Wash the chicken under cold water
and pat dry with paper towels. Place the
chicken in a food processor and process
until finely chopped. Add 1 teaspoon salt.
2 Lightly beat the egg whites in a small
bowl until foamy. Fold the egg whites into
the chopped chicken.
3 Bring the stock to the boil and add
the creamed corn. Mix the cornflour in
1 tablespoon water and add to the soup,
stirring until the mixture thickens.
4 Reduce the heat and add the chicken
mixture, breaking it up with a whisk.
Allow to heat through, without boiling,
for about 3 minutes. Season to taste with
soy sauce. Serve immediately, sprinkled
with the spring onion.

won ton soup

❋ ❋

Preparation time: 40 minutes
Cooking time: 5 minutes
Serves 4–6

4 dried Chinese mushrooms
250 g (9 oz) raw prawns (shrimp)
250 g (9 oz) minced (ground) pork
1 tablespoon soy sauce
1 teaspoon sesame oil
2 spring onions (scallions), finely chopped
1 teaspoon finely grated fresh ginger
2 tablespoons tinned drained, chopped
    water chestnuts
250 g (9 oz) won ton wrappers
cornflour (cornstarch), to dust
1.5 litres (52 fl oz/6 cups) chicken or beef
    stock
4 spring onions (scallions), extra, thinly
    sliced, to garnish

1 Soak the mushrooms in hot water
for 20 minutes. Drain, then squeeze
to remove any excess liquid. Discard
the stems and chop the caps finely.
Meanwhile, peel the prawns and gently
pull out the dark vein from each prawn
back, starting at the head end. Finely
chop the prawn meat and mix in a bowl
with the mushrooms, pork, soy sauce,
sesame oil, chopped spring onion,
ginger and water chestnuts.
2 Cover the won ton wrappers with a
damp tea towel (dish towel) to prevent
them drying out. Taking one wrapper at a
time, place a heaped teaspoon of mixture
on the centre. Moisten the edges with
water, fold in half diagonally, seal, and
then bring the two opposite points together
and seal again. Place on a tray dusted
with the cornflour. Cook the won tons in
a saucepan of rapidly boiling water for
4–5 minutes or until the filling is cooked.
3 In a separate saucepan bring the stock
to the boil. Remove the won tons with a
slotted spoon and place in serving bowls.
Scatter the sliced spring onion over the
top. Ladle the stock over the won tons.

won ton soup

fried and steamed scallops with ginger

✳ ✳

Preparation time: **10 minutes**
Cooking time: **10 minutes**
Serves **4 as an entrée**

12 scallops on the half shell
¼ teaspoon ground white pepper
2 tablespoons soy sauce
2 tablespoons dry sherry
2 tablespoons oil
8 cm (3¼ inch) piece fresh ginger, shredded
1 spring onion (scallion), white part only,
    sliced into long shreds

1 Sprinkle the scallops with the white pepper. Mix together the soy sauce and sherry in a bowl.
2 Heat the oil in a large, heavy-based frying pan until very hot. Carefully add several shells, scallop-side down, and cook for 30 seconds to sear. Turn face-up and place in a shallow dish. Repeat with the remaining scallops.
3 Sprinkle the scallops with the sherry and soy mixture and scatter a few shreds of ginger and spring onion over each of them.
4 Fill a wok about one-third full with water and bring to a simmer. Put a steamer lined with baking paper in the wok and place six scallops on it. Cover the steamer tightly and steam the scallops for 1 minute. If they aren't cooked, they may need about 30 seconds more. Remove and set aside to keep warm. Repeat with the remaining scallops. Serve immediately.

fried and steamed scallops with ginger

crystal prawns

✳ ✳

Preparation time: **15 minutes + 30 minutes
    marinating time**
Cooking time: **10 minutes**
Serves **4**

750 g (1 lb 10 oz) raw prawns (shrimp)
2 spring onions (scallions), roughly chopped
1 tablespoon cornflour (cornstarch)
1 egg white, lightly beaten
125 g (4½ oz) sugar snap peas or
    snow peas (mangetout)
1 small red capsicum (pepper)
1 tablespoon oyster sauce
2 teaspoons dry sherry
1 teaspoon cornflour (cornstarch), extra
1 teaspoon sesame oil
oil, for deep-frying
½ teaspoon crushed garlic
½ teaspoon finely grated fresh ginger

1 Peel the prawns and gently pull out the dark vein from each prawn back, starting at the head end. Place the prawn shells, heads and the spring onion in a saucepan with enough water to cover them. Bring the water to the boil; simmer, uncovered, for 15 minutes. Strain the liquid into a bowl, discarding the shells. Reserve 125 ml (4 fl oz/½ cup) of the prawn stock. Place the prawns in a glass bowl. Add 1 teaspoon salt and stir briskly for a minute. Rinse under cold, running water. Repeat the procedure twice, using ½ teaspoon salt each time. Rinse the prawns thoroughly the final time. Pat dry with paper towels.

2 Combine the cornflour and egg white in a bowl, add the prawns and place in the refrigerator, covered, for 30 minutes.

3 Wash and string the sugar snap peas. Cut the capsicum into thin strips. Combine the reserved prawn liquid, oyster sauce, sherry, extra cornflour and sesame oil in a small bowl. Heat the oil in a wok over medium-high heat until hot, and deep-fry the prawns in batches for 1–2 minutes or until lightly golden. Carefully remove from the oil with tongs or a slotted spoon. Drain on paper towels and keep warm.

4 Carefully pour off all but 2 tablespoons of the oil (if you are keeping it to re-use, only use it for seafood, as the prawn flavour will have permeated). Add the garlic and ginger to the wok and stir-fry for 30 seconds. Add the peas and capsicum and stir-fry over high heat for 2 minutes. Add the combined sauce ingredients and cook, stirring, until the sauce boils and thickens. Add the prawns and stir to combine. Serve immediately.

crispy fried crab

crispy fried crab

✹ ✹ ✹

Preparation time: 30 minutes + 2 hours
    freezing + overnight marinating time
Cooking time: 15 minutes
Serves 4 as an entrée

Pull back the apron from the underbelly and snap it off. Pull the body apart.

Remove the feathery gills and internal organs.

Use the back of the cleaver to crack the claws, or you may break the blade.

1 kg (2 lb 4 oz) live mud crab
1 egg, lightly beaten
1 red chilli, thinly sliced
½ teaspoon crushed garlic
¼ teaspoon ground white pepper
oil, for deep-frying

SEASONING MIX
4 tablespoons plain (all-purpose) flour
4 tablespoons rice flour
3 teaspoons caster (superfine) sugar
1 teaspoon ground white pepper

1 Place the crab in the freezer for 2 hours or until it is absolutely immobile and dead

(this is the most humane way to kill crab or lobster).

2 Scrub the crab clean of any mossy bits. Pull back the apron from the underbelly and snap off. Twist off the legs and claws. Pull the body apart and remove the feathery gills and internal organs. Using a cleaver, chop the body into four pieces. Crack the claws with a good hit with the back of the cleaver.

3 Combine the egg with the chilli, garlic, ½ teaspoon salt and the white pepper in a large bowl. Put the crab pieces in the mixture; cover and refrigerate overnight.

4 To make the seasoning mix, sift all the seasoning ingredients together on a large plate. Dip all the crab segments in the seasoning and dust off any excess.

5 Heat the oil in a wok and deep-fry the claws for 7–8 minutes, the body portions for 3–4 minutes and the legs for 2 minutes. Drain on paper towels and serve.

NOTE: Eat the crab with your fingers. This dish should be served on its own, without rice.

stir-fried beef and snow peas

✹

Preparation time: 15 minutes
Cooking time: 5 minutes
Serves 4

400 g (14 oz) rump steak, thinly sliced
2 tablespoons soy sauce
½ teaspoon grated fresh ginger
2 tablespoons peanut oil
200 g (7 oz) snow peas (mangetout),
    topped and tailed
1½ teaspoons cornflour (cornstarch)
125 ml (4 fl oz/½ cup) beef stock
1 teaspoon soy sauce, extra
¼ teaspoon sesame oil
steamed rice, to serve

1   Place the beef in a bowl. Mix the soy sauce and ginger and stir through the beef to coat it.
2   Heat the peanut oil in a wok or heavy-based frying pan, swirling gently to coat the base and side. Add the beef and snow peas and stir-fry over high heat for 2 minutes, or until the beef changes colour.
3   Mix the cornflour in a little of the stock and add to the wok with the remaining stock, extra soy sauce and the sesame oil. Stir until the sauce boils and thickens. Serve with steamed rice.

NOTE: If time allows, place the beef in the freezer for 30 minutes before slicing. This will firm it and make slicing it finely much easier.

chilli spare ribs

chilli spare ribs

✹ ✹

Preparation time: 20 minutes
Cooking time: 1 hour
Serves 4

750 g (1 lb 10 oz) pork spare ribs
1 tablespoon peanut oil
2 teaspoons finely chopped garlic
60 ml (2 fl oz/¼ cup) dry sherry
1 tablespoon chilli bean paste
    or sambal oelek
500 ml (17 fl oz/2 cups) water
2 teaspoons hoisin sauce
3 teaspoons caster (superfine) sugar
1 tablespoon soy sauce,
    preferably dark

1   Place the pork in a large saucepan with enough water to cover. Bring to the boil, reduce the heat, simmer for 5 minutes; drain well.

2   Place all the remaining ingredients and the pork in a wok or deep, heavy-based saucepan. Cover and simmer for 45 minutes. Drain, reserving 250 ml (9 fl oz/1 cup) of liquid. Heat a clean wok or heavy-based frying pan and sear the pork pieces to brown them.
3   Add the reserved cooking liquid and cook over medium heat until it forms a glazed coating for the pork.
4   Chop the pork into 3 cm (1¼ inch) pieces and pour the sauce over them.

noodles with prawns and pork

✻

Preparation time: 20 minutes
Cooking time: 10 minutes
Serves 4

10 raw large prawns (shrimp)
200 g (7 oz) Chinese barbecued pork
   (char siu)
500 g (1 lb 2 oz) shanghai noodles
60 ml (2 fl oz/¼ cup) peanut oil
2 teaspoons finely chopped garlic
1 tablespoon black bean sauce
1 tablespoon soy sauce
1 tablespoon white vinegar
60 ml (2 fl oz/¼ cup) chicken stock
1 stalk celery, cut into fine strips
1 carrot, cut into thin matchsticks
125 g (4½ oz) bean sprouts, trimmed
3 spring onions (scallions), finely shredded

1 Peel the prawns and gently pull out the dark vein from each prawn back, starting at the head end. Cut the pork evenly into thin slices.
2 Cook the noodles in a large saucepan of rapidly boiling water until just tender. Drain and set aside.
3 Heat the oil in a wok or heavy-based frying pan, swirling gently to coat the base and side. Add the garlic and cook, stirring, until pale gold. Add the prawns and pork, and stir for 3 minutes, or until the prawns are pink. Add the black bean sauce, soy sauce, vinegar and stock. Stir-fry over high heat until the mixture is heated through and the sauce is absorbed.
4 Add the celery and carrot and cook for 1 minute. Serve the noodles topped with the stir-fry and sprinkled with the bean sprouts and spring onions.

NOTE: Barbecued pork can be bought ready-cooked from speciality Chinese stores. If you enjoy a little 'fire' in your food, add a garnish of chopped chillies or a splash of chilli oil at the end of cooking.

chilli bean paste

A thick, red-brown sauce made from soy beans, dried red chilli, garlic and spices, chilli bean paste has a hot, nutty, salty taste and is much used in the fiery dishes of Sichuan and Hunan in central western China. Available in jars from Asian food stores and some supermarkets. Sambal oelek has a different flavour but can be used as a substitute.

stir-fried prawns with leeks

※

Preparation time: **15 minutes**
Cooking time: **5 minutes**
Serves **6**

800 g (1 lb 12 oz) raw king prawns (shrimp)
2 young leeks, white parts only
1 red chilli
3 cm (1¼ inch) piece fresh ginger
3 tablespoons oil
2 teaspoons light soy sauce
1 tablespoon mirin
80 ml (2½ fl oz/⅓ cup) chicken stock
1 teaspoon cornflour (cornstarch)
steamed rice, to serve

1 Peel the prawns and gently pull out the dark vein from each prawn back, starting at the head end.
2 Rinse the leeks well. Cut them first into 4 cm (1½ inch) lengths and then lengthways into fine shreds. Slit open the chilli, remove and discard the seeds and cut the flesh into fine shreds. Cut the ginger into fine shreds.
3 Heat a little of the oil in a wok over high heat and stir-fry the prawns in batches until just pink; remove from the wok. Add the remaining oil and stir-fry the leek, chilli and ginger over high heat for 40 seconds, then push to one side of the wok. Return the prawns to the wok and stir-fry for 1½ minutes, or until just cooked through.
4 Add the soy sauce and mirin to the wok. Mix the chicken stock and cornflour and pour in. Cook on high heat, stirring, until thickened. Serve immediately with steamed rice.

stir-fried prawns with leeks

chinese fried rice

※

Preparation time: **15 minutes**
Cooking time: **10 minutes**
Serves **4**

2 eggs, lightly beaten
1 onion
4 spring onions (scallions)
250 g (9 oz) piece ham
2 tablespoons peanut oil
2 teaspoons lard (optional)
270 g (9½ oz/1⅓ cups) long-grain rice, cooked and cooled (see Note)
40 g (1½ oz/¼ cup) frozen peas
2 tablespoons soy sauce
250 g (9 oz) cooked small prawns (shrimp), peeled

1 Season the eggs with salt and pepper.
2 Cut the onion into 8 wedges. Cut the spring onions diagonally into short lengths. Cut the ham into very thin strips.
3 Heat 1 tablespoon oil in a wok or large frying pan and add the egg, pulling the set egg towards the centre and tilting the wok to let the unset egg run to the edges. When the egg is almost set, break it up into large pieces so it resembles scrambled egg. Transfer to a plate and set aside.
4 Heat the remaining oil and lard, if using, in the wok, swirling to coat the base and side. Add the onion and stir-fry over high heat until it starts to turn translucent. Add the ham and stir-fry for 1 minute. Add the rice and peas and stir-fry for 3 minutes until the rice is heated through. Add the egg, soy sauce, spring onion and prawns. Heat through and serve immediately.

NOTE: If possible, cook the rice a day ahead and refrigerate it overnight. This makes the grains separate and means the fried rice is not gluggy.

soy sauce

Soy sauce, indispensable in the cooking of eastern Asia, has a long history. A mixture of brine and fermented soy beans was being made in China more than 3000 years ago. Known as shih, its original function was probably as a preservative for vegetables during the winter months. Over the centuries, techniques were developed for adding grain meal to the fermenting mash, ageing it and then straining off and bottling the liquid; by 1500 years ago, a sauce fairly similar to the modern version was being used. The darker sauce of the north is aged longer and is tinted and flavoured with molasses. The Japanese learned sauce-making skills from China about a thousand years ago and introduced their own refinements; Japanese soy sauce is lighter and less salty as it contains more wheat. In Indonesia, palm sugar, garlic, star anise and thickeners were added to produce kecap manis.

clay pot chicken and vegetables

✳

Preparation time: 20 minutes + 30 minutes marinating time
Cooking time: 35 minutes
Serves 4

500 g (1 lb 2 oz) boneless, skinless chicken thighs
1 tablespoon soy sauce
1 tablespoon dry sherry
6 dried Chinese mushrooms
2 tablespoons peanut oil
2 small leeks, white part only, sliced
5 cm (2 inch) piece ginger, finely grated
125 ml (4 fl oz/½ cup) chicken stock
1 teaspoon sesame oil

250 g (9 oz) orange sweet potato, halved lengthwise and sliced
3 teaspoons cornflour (cornstarch)
steamed rice, to serve

1 Cut the chicken into small pieces. Put it in a bowl with the soy sauce and sherry, cover and marinate for 30 minutes in the refrigerator.
2 Meanwhile, soak the mushrooms in hot water for 20 minutes. Drain, then squeeze to remove any excess liquid. Discard the stems and chop the caps finely.
3 Drain the chicken, reserving the marinade. Heat half the peanut oil in a wok, swirling gently to coat the base and side. Add half the chicken pieces and stir-fry briefly until seared on all sides. Transfer the chicken to a flameproof clay pot or casserole dish. Stir-fry the remaining chicken and add it to the clay pot. Heat

the remaining oil in the wok. Add the leek and ginger and stir-fry for 1 minute. Add the mushroom, reserved marinade, stock and sesame oil and cook for 2 minutes. Transfer to the clay pot with the sweet potato and cook, covered, on top of the stove over very low heat for 20 minutes or until the sweet potato is tender.
4 Mix the cornflour and 1 tablespoon water and add it to the pot. Cook, stirring over high heat, until the mixture boils and thickens. Serve the chicken and vegetables at once with the steamed rice.

NOTE: Like all stews, this is best cooked 1–2 days ahead and stored, covered, in the refrigerator to allow the flavours to mature. It can also be frozen, but omit the sweet potato. Steam or boil the potato separately and stir it through the reheated stew.

Remove the seeds from the cucumber and slice into matchsticks. Slice the spring onion sections and place in iced water to form brushes.

Roll the dough balls into circles. Lightly brush one circle with sesame oil and place another circle on top.

When cool enough to handle, peel the two halves of the double pancake apart.

peking duck with mandarin pancakes

✸ ✸ ✸

Preparation time: 1 hour + 30 minutes
　　standing time
Cooking time: 1 hour 15 minutes
Serves 6

1.7 kg (3 lb 12 oz) whole duck
3 litres (105 fl oz/12 cups) boiling water
1 tablespoon honey
12 spring onions (scallions)
1 Lebanese (short) cucumber
2 tablespoons hoisin sauce

MANDARIN PANCAKES
310 g (11 oz/2½ cups) plain
　　(all-purpose) flour
2 teaspoons caster (superfine) sugar
250 ml (9 fl oz/1 cup) boiling water
1 tablespoon sesame oil

1 Remove the neck and any large pieces of fat from inside the duck carcass. Hold the duck over the sink and very carefully and slowly pour the boiling water over it, rotating the duck so the water scalds all the skin. Drain well.

2 Put the duck on a rack in an ovenproof dish. Mix the honey and 125 ml (4 fl oz/½ cup) hot water and brush two coats of this glaze all over the duck. Dry the duck in a cool, airy place for about 4 hours. The skin is sufficiently dry when it feels papery.

3 Preheat the oven to 210°C (415°F/Gas 6–7). Cut an 8 cm (3¼ inch) section from the white end of each spring onion. Make fine parallel cuts from the top of the section towards the white end. Put the onion pieces in iced water — they will open into 'brushes'. Remove the seeds from the cucumber and slice into matchsticks.

4 Roast the duck for 30 minutes, then turn it over carefully without tearing the skin and roast it for another 30 minutes. Remove the duck from the oven and leave for a minute or two, then place it on a warm dish.

5 Meanwhile, to make the mandarin pancakes, put the flour and sugar in a bowl and pour in the boiling water. Stir the mixture a few times and leave until lukewarm. Knead the mixture, on a lightly floured surface, into a smooth dough. Cover and set aside for 30 minutes. Take two level tablespoons of dough and roll each one into a ball. Roll out to circles 8 cm (3¼ inches) in diameter. Lightly brush one of the circles with sesame oil and place another circle on top. Re-roll to make a thin pancake about 15 cm (6 inches) in diameter. Repeat with the remaining dough and oil to make about 10 'double' pancakes.

6 Heat a small cast iron frying pan over medium heat and cook the double pancakes one at a time. When small bubbles appear on the surface, turn the pancake over and cook the second side, pressing the surface with a clean tea towel (dish towel). The pancake should puff up when done. Transfer the pancake to a plate. When cool enough to handle, peel the two halves of the double pancake apart. Stack them on a plate and cover them at once to prevent them drying out.

7 To serve, thinly slice the duck. Place the pancakes and duck on separate serving plates. Arrange the cucumber batons and spring onion brushes on another serving plate. Put the hoisin sauce in a small dish. Each diner helps themselves to a pancake, spreads a little sauce on it and adds a couple of pieces of cucumber, a spring onion brush and, finally, a piece of duck. The pancake is then folded over into a neat envelope for eating.

yum cha

Meaning literally 'to drink tea', this morning ritual is accompanied in tea houses throughout China with tiny steamed or fried parcels of dim sum, stuffed with fresh seafood, meats and vegetables.

crabmeat dim sims

In a bowl, combine 200 g (7 oz) drained and flaked crabmeat, 250 g (9 oz) raw prawns (shrimp), peeled, deveined and chopped, 4 finely chopped spring onions (scallions), 3 chopped and soaked dried Chinese mushrooms, 3 tablespoons finely chopped bean sprouts, 1 tablespoon teriyaki sauce, 2 crushed garlic cloves and 2 teaspoons grated fresh ginger. Working with 1 won ton wrapper at a time (you will need about 20), place 1 tablespoon filling in the centre, gather up the corners and pinch together to seal. Keep the other won ton wrappers covered with a damp tea towel (dish towel) until needed. Line the base of a bamboo or metal steamer with a circle of baking paper. Arrange the dim sims on the paper, making sure they are not touching (you may need to cook them in batches). Cover and steam for 8 minutes. Serve immediately. Makes about 20.

chicken moneybags

In a bowl, combine 375 g (13 oz) minced (ground) chicken, 90 g (3¼ oz) finely chopped ham, 4 finely chopped spring onions (scallions), 1 finely chopped celery stalk, 3 tablespoons chopped bamboo shoots, 1 tablespoon soy sauce, 1 crushed garlic clove and 1 teaspoon finely grated fresh ginger. Working with 1 won ton wrapper at a time (you will need about 40), place 2 teaspoons filling in the centre, gather up the corners and pinch together to form a pouch, leaving a frill at the top. Cut 20 chives in half and place in a heatproof bowl. Cover with boiling water for 1 minute; rinse and drain. Deep-fry the moneybags in hot oil for 4–5 minutes until crisp and golden; drain on paper towels. Tie a chive around each moneybag. Serve immediately. Makes about 40.

prawn gow gees

In a bowl, mix 500 g (1 lb 2 oz) raw prawns (shrimp), peeled, deveined and chopped, 4 finely chopped spring onions (scallions), 1 tablespoon finely grated fresh ginger and 2 tablespoons chopped water chestnuts. Mix 3 teaspoons cornflour (cornstarch), 2 teaspoons sesame oil, 1 teaspoon soy sauce, ½ teaspoon caster (superfine) sugar and a little salt and pepper until smooth, and stir into the prawn mixture. Working with 1 gow gee (egg) dumpling wrapper at a time (you will need about 40), put 1 rounded teaspoon of mixture in the centre and press the edges together to form a semicircle. Twist the corners down to form a crescent shape. Line the base of a bamboo or metal steamer with a circle of baking paper. Arrange the gow gees on the paper, making sure they are not touching (you may need to cook them in batches). Steam, covered, for 8 minutes. Makes about 40.

stuffed capsicums (peppers)

Mix together 500 g (1 lb 2 oz) peeled, deveined and finely chopped raw prawns (shrimp), 300 g (10½ oz) minced (ground) lean pork, 1 teaspoon salt, 3 finely chopped spring onions (scallions), 3 tablespoons finely chopped water chestnuts, 3 teaspoons soy sauce and 2 teaspoons dry sherry. Cut 3 capsicums (peppers) lengthways into 3–4 segments and remove the seeds and membrane. Fill the capsicum wedges with filling and cut in half. Heat 1 tablespoon oil in a wok. Cook the capsicum pieces in two batches over medium–high heat for 3–4 minutes, or until well browned. Turn over and cook for a further 3 minutes. Repeat with the remaining pieces. Serve immediately. Makes about 24.

sichuan soup

sichuan soup

✺

Preparation time: 20 minutes
Cooking time: 15 minutes
Serves 6–8

4 dried Chinese mushrooms
50 g (1¾ oz) thick dried rice stick noodles
1 litre (35 fl oz/4 cups) chicken stock
175 g (6 oz/1 cup) cooked chicken, chopped
225 g (8 oz) tin bamboo shoots, drained
    and chopped
1 teaspoon finely grated fresh ginger
1 tablespoon cornflour (cornstarch)
1 egg, lightly beaten
1 teaspoon tomato sauce (ketchup)

1 tablespoon soy sauce
1 tablespoon shaoxing rice wine (Chinese
    rice wine)
2 teaspoons sesame oil
2 spring onions (scallions), finely chopped
spring onion (scallion) (optional), extra,
    thinly sliced, to garnish

1 Soak the mushrooms in hot
water for 20 minutes. Drain, then
squeeze to remove any excess liquid.
Discard the stems and chop the caps
finely. Soak the noodles in hot water
for 20 minutes. Drain and cut into
short lengths. Set aside.
2 Heat the stock in a large saucepan and
bring to the boil. Add the mushroom,
noodles, chicken, bamboo shoots and
ginger. Reduce the heat to a gentle simmer.
3 Mix the cornflour with 80 ml
(2½ fl oz/⅓ cup) water, add it to the
soup and stir until clear. Add the egg to
the soup in a fine stream, stirring the
mixture constantly. Remove the pan
from the heat. Add the tomato sauce, soy
sauce, rice wine, sesame oil and spring
onion. Season to taste. Serve topped with
extra spring onion, if desired.

black satin chicken

✺ ✺

Preparation time: 45 minutes
Cooking time: 1 hour
Serves 10

3 dried Chinese mushrooms
125 ml (4 fl oz/½ cup) dark soy sauce
3 tablespoons soft brown sugar
2 tablespoons shaoxing rice wine (Chinese
    rice wine)
1 tablespoon soy sauce
1 teaspoon sesame oil
¼ teaspoon ground star anise or 1 whole
    star anise
1.4 kg (3 lb 2 oz) whole chicken
4 cm (1½ inch) piece fresh ginger,
    finely grated
2 spring onions (scallions), thinly sliced,
    to garnish

1 Soak the mushrooms in hot water for
20 minutes. Drain and reserve the liquid.
Put the dark soy sauce, sugar, rice wine,
soy sauce, sesame oil, star anise and
reserved liquid in a small saucepan and
bring to the boil, stirring continuously.
2 Rub the inside of the chicken with
ginger and 1 teaspoon salt. Place the
chicken in a large saucepan. Cover with
soy marinade and mushrooms, turning the
chicken over so it is evenly coated. Cover
and cook over low heat, turning regularly,
for 55 minutes or until the juices run clear
when pierced with a skewer. Remove the
chicken and allow it to cool briefly.
3 Boil the sauce over high heat until
thick and syrupy. Discard the mushrooms.

4 Chop the chicken Chinese-style (see page 11). Arrange the chicken pieces on a serving platter, brush lightly with the syrupy sauce and sprinkle over the spring onion. Alternatively you could serve the sauce separately, for dipping.

honey prawns

※

Preparation time: 20 minutes
Cooking time: 12 minutes
Serves 4

16 raw king prawns (shrimp)
30 g (1 oz/¼ cup) cornflour (cornstarch)
40 g (1½ oz/¼ cup) white sesame seeds
oil, for deep-frying
90 g (3¼ oz/¼ cup) honey

BATTER
125 g (4½ oz/1 cup) self-raising flour
30 g (1 oz/¼ cup) cornflour
    (cornstarch)
¼ teaspoon lemon juice
1 tablespoon oil

1 Peel the prawns, leaving the tails intact. Gently pull out the dark vein from each prawn back, starting at the head end. Pat the prawns dry with paper towels, then lightly dust them with the cornflour.
2 Toast the sesame seeds in a dry frying pan over medium heat for 3–4 minutes, shaking the pan gently, until the seeds are golden brown; remove from the pan at once to prevent burning.
3 To make the batter, sift the flour and cornflour into a medium bowl. Combine 250 ml (9 fl oz/1 cup) water, the lemon juice and oil. Make a well in the centre of the flour and gradually add the liquid, beating well to make a smooth batter.
4 Heat the oil in a large, deep frying pan or wok until moderately hot. Working with a few prawns at a time, dip the prawns in the batter; drain any excess. Use tongs or a slotted spoon to place the prawns in the hot oil. Cook

sichuan cooking

The immense geographical and climatic diversity of China has led to the development of many distinct and varied regional cuisines. There are four major styles: Peking, Cantonese, Shanghai and Sichuan. The distinctive hot and spicy sichuan cuisine is a medley of many influences, one of the most important being the traders and Buddhist missionaries from India, who more than 2000 years ago brought cooking techniques, tangy spices and herbs, and a tradition of vegetarian dishes. Sichuan cooking makes liberal use of fiery chillies and most dishes include vinegar, sugar, salt and the unique spice, sichuan pepper (which has a numbing effect on the tongue, rather than a bite).

for 2–3 minutes or until the prawns are crisp and golden. Drain on paper towels and keep warm.
5 Place the honey in a large frying pan and warm over very low heat. (Don't overheat the honey or it will caramelise and lose some of its flavour.)
6 Place the cooked prawns in the pan with the warmed honey; toss gently to coat. Transfer to a serving plate and sprinkle over the sesame seeds. Serve immediately.

beef with capsicum and oyster sauce

✳

Preparation time: **15 minutes**
Cooking time: **10 minutes**
Serves **6**

500 g (1 lb 2 oz) rump steak
1 tablespoon soy sauce
1 egg white, lightly beaten
1 tablespoon cornflour (cornstarch)
2 tablespoons peanut oil
1 tablespoon finely grated fresh
    ginger
¼ teaspoon five-spice
1 small green capsicum (pepper),
    cut in diamond shapes
1 small red capsicum (pepper),
    cut in diamond shapes
2 celery stalks, thinly sliced
410 g (14½ oz) tin whole baby corn,
    drained
2 tablespoons oyster sauce
2 spring onions (scallions), thinly sliced,
    to garnish

1 Trim the beef of any fat and sinew, and slice it evenly across the grain into long, thin strips. Combine the soy sauce, egg white, cornflour and ¼ teaspoon ground black pepper in a bowl; add the beef, stirring to coat.
2 Heat 1 tablespoon of the peanut oil in a wok or heavy-based saucepan, swirling gently to coat the base and side. Add the ginger, five-spice, capsicum, celery and corn and stir-fry over high heat for 2 minutes or until just beginning to soften. Remove from the wok and keep warm.
3 Heat the remaining oil in the wok, swirling gently to coat the base and side. Cook the beef quickly in small batches over high heat until browned but not cooked through.
4 Return all the beef to the wok with the vegetables and add the oyster sauce. Stir-fry over high heat until the beef is cooked and the sauce is hot. Remove from the heat and serve immediately, sprinkled with the spring onion.

chinese barbecued pork

✳

Preparation time: **15 minutes + 30 minutes**
    marinating time
Cooking time: **35 minutes**
Serves **6**

60 ml (2 fl oz/¼ cup) tomato sauce
    (ketchup)
1 tablespoon hoisin sauce
2 tablespoons honey
1 tablespoon malt extract or molasses
1 tablespoon chopped garlic
2 tablespoons caster (superfine) sugar
1 teaspoon five-spice
2 teaspoons cornflour (cornstarch)
750 g (1 lb 10 oz) pork neck or fillet
steamed rice sprinkled with crisp fried
    onion, to serve

1 Combine the tomato sauce, hoisin sauce, honey, malt extract, garlic, sugar and five-spice in a small saucepan. Mix

chinese barbecued pork

the cornflour in 1 tablespoon water and add to the mixture. Bring to the boil, then reduce to a simmer and stir for 2 minutes. Allow to cool.

2 If using pork neck, cut it in half lengthways. Pork fillets do not need to be cut. Place the pork in the sauce, turning to coat; cover and marinate in the refrigerator for at least 30 minutes.

3 Preheat the oven to 210°C (415°F/ Gas 6–7). Lift the pork from the marinade with a slotted spoon and reserve the marinade. Place the pork on a wire rack over a baking tray half-filled with hot water and cook for 15 minutes.

4 Reduce the oven temperature to 180°C (350°F/Gas 4) and cook the pork for a further 15 minutes, basting it occasionally with the reserved marinade. Remove the pork from the oven and let it stand for 5 minutes before slicing and serving with steamed rice and crisp fried onion.

crispy skin chicken

✳ ✳ ✳

Preparation time: 40 minutes
Cooking time: 40 minutes
Serves 4

1.3 kg (3 lb) whole chicken
1 tablespoon honey
1 whole star anise
1 strip dried mandarin or tangerine peel
oil, for deep-frying
spring onions (scallions), thinly sliced,
    to garnish
2 lemons (optional), cut into wedges, to serve

FIVE-SPICE SALT
2 tablespoons salt
1 teaspoon white peppercorns
½ teaspoon five-spice
½ teaspoon ground white pepper

1 Put the chicken in a large saucepan and cover with cold water. Add the honey, star anise, mandarin peel and 1 teaspoon salt and bring to the boil. Reduce the heat to low and simmer for 15 minutes. Turn off the heat and leave the chicken,

crispy skin chicken

covered, for a further 15 minutes. Transfer the chicken to a plate to cool.

2 Cut the chicken in half lengthways. Place it on paper towels, uncovered, in the refrigerator for 20 minutes.

3 Fill a wok or deep heavy-based saucepan one-third full of oil and heat to 160°C (315°F), or until a cube of bread dropped into the oil turns golden brown in 30–35 seconds. Very gently lower in half of the chicken, skin side down. Cook for 6 minutes, then carefully turn the chicken over and cook for another 6 minutes, making sure all the skin comes in contact with the oil. Drain on paper towels. Repeat with the second chicken half.

4 To make the five-spice salt, put the salt and peppercorns in a small frying pan and dry-fry until the mixture smells aromatic and the salt is slightly browned. Crush the mixture using a mortar and pestle or wrap in foil and crush it with a rolling pin. Mix with the five-spice and white pepper and place in a small, shallow dish.

5 Use a cleaver or a large kitchen knife to chop the chicken halves into smaller pieces. Sprinkle over the five-spice salt and garnish with the spring onion. Serve with the lemon wedges, if desired.

NOTE: Any leftover five-spice salt can be stored in an airtight container for several months.

whole steamed fish with crisp finish

the capsicum into fine matchsticks 4 cm (1½ inches) long.

3 Place a pair of wooden chopsticks in a cross in the base of a large wok (to act as a rack) and fill the wok with about 7 cm (2¾ inches) water. Score the fattest part of the fish three times, place on a heatproof dinner plate and sit the plate on top of the chopsticks. Cover and bring the water to the boil over high heat. Cook for 15–20 minutes; turn off the heat, scatter over the vegetables and leave, covered, for 3 minutes.

4 Slide the steamed fish onto a warmed serving platter. Heat the oil in a small saucepan until it is very hot and slightly smoking, then carefully pour it over the vegetables. The vegetables or fish skin may crackle. Serve with small bowls of soy and chilli sauce and steamed rice.

NOTE: The oil must be very hot so it just crisps and brightens the vegetables. If desired, the oil can be poured over the fish at the table so the guests can watch; the crackling is quite spectacular.

sweet and sour pork

✹ ✹

Preparation time: 35 minutes
Cooking time: 25 minutes
Serves 4

350 g (12 oz) pork loin, cut into
    bite-sized pieces
2 eggs, lightly beaten
4 tablespoons cornflour (cornstarch)
oil, for deep-frying
1 carrot, very thinly sliced
1 onion, cut into thin wedges
160 g (5¾ oz/1 cup) chopped fresh
    pineapple
½ red capsicum (pepper), cut into bite-
    sized pieces
½ green capsicum (pepper), cut into bite-
    sized pieces
1 celery stalk, sliced
75 g (2½ oz/⅓ cup) sweet pickled Chinese
    vegetables, roughly chopped
60 ml (2 fl oz/¼ cup) white vinegar

whole steamed fish with crisp finish

✹ ✹

Preparation time: 25 minutes
Cooking time: 25 minutes
Serves 4

1 kg (2 lb 4 oz) whole snapper or bream,
    cleaned and scaled
½ teaspoon ground white pepper
3 cm (1¼ inch) piece fresh ginger,
    very finely sliced
1 tablespoon sesame oil
1 tablespoon soy sauce

3 spring onions (scallions)
1 celery stalk
½ red capsicum (pepper)
125 ml (4 fl oz/½ cup) oil
steamed rice, to serve

1 Thoroughly wash the fish inside the cavity and out and pat dry with paper towels. Sprinkle the fish with ½ teaspoon salt and the white pepper and place the ginger inside the cavity. Combine the sesame oil and soy sauce and lightly brush over the fish.

2 Cut the spring onions and celery into 4 cm (1½ inch) lengths, then finely shred them into long fine strips. Cut

60 ml (2 fl oz/¼ cup) soy sauce
2 tablespoons tomato paste (concentrated purée)
2 tablespoons caster (superfine) sugar
2 tablespoons orange juice
2 teaspoons cornflour (cornstarch), extra, mixed with 1 tablespoon water

1 Mix ½ teaspoon salt through the pork. Dip each piece of pork in the egg, then roll it in the cornflour. Place the pork on a plate in a single layer.
2 Heat the oil in a wok over medium heat, drop in 4 pieces of pork and cook for about 3 minutes or until golden brown. Remove the pork with a slotted spoon and drain it on paper towels. Repeat with the remaining pork.
3 Remove all but 1 tablespoon of the oil from the wok, reheat and stir-fry the carrot, onion and pineapple for 2 minutes or until the carrot is just tender. Add the capsicum, celery and pickled vegetables and stir-fry for a further 2 minutes.
4 Combine the vinegar, soy sauce, tomato paste, sugar and orange juice in a small bowl; stir in the cornflour mixture and mix well. Pour the sauce into the vegetables and stir constantly until the mixture boils and thickens slightly. Return the pork to the wok, stirring well to lightly coat the pork with the sauce. Arrange on a serving plate and serve immediately.

NOTE: Be sure to fry the pork quickly after coating it with the cornflour so it does not become sticky on standing.

smoked five-spice chicken

✵✵

Preparation time: 30 minutes + 4 hours marinating time
Cooking time: 40 minutes
Serves 6

1.7 kg (3 lb 12 oz) whole chicken
60 ml (2 fl oz/¼ cup) soy sauce
1 tablespoon finely grated fresh ginger
2 strips dried mandarin or tangerine peel
1 star anise
¼ teaspoon five-spice
3 tablespoons soft brown sugar
1 spring onion (scallion), thinly sliced, to garnish
1 small handful coriander (cilantro) sprigs, to garnish

1 Put the chicken in a large non-metallic bowl along with the soy sauce and ginger. Cover and marinate for at least 4 hours, or leave overnight in the refrigerator, turning occasionally.
2 Put a small rack in the base of a saucepan large enough to hold the chicken. Add water up to the level of the rack. Place the chicken on the rack. Bring the water to the boil, cover tightly, then reduce the heat and steam for 15 minutes. Turn off the heat and allow the chicken to rest in the pan, covered, for another 15 minutes. Transfer the chicken to a bowl.
3 Wash the pan and line it with three or four large pieces of foil. Use a mortar and pestle to pound the dried mandarin peel and star anise until the pieces are the size of coarse breadcrumbs, or process in a food processor. Add the five-spice and brown sugar. Spread the spice mixture over the foil in the pan.
4 Replace the rack in the pan and place the chicken on it. Put the pan over medium heat and, when the spice mixture starts smoking, cover tightly. Reduce the heat to low and smoke the chicken for 20 minutes. Test if the chicken is cooked by piercing the thigh with a skewer; the juices should run clear. (The heat produced in this final step is very intense. When the chicken is removed from the pan, leave the pan on the stove to cool a little before handling it.)
5 Remove the chicken from the pan and chop into smaller pieces using a cleaver or large knife. Transfer to a platter. Garnish with the spring onion and coriander.

smoked five-spice chicken

chinese vegetables

chinese vegetables

✳

Preparation time: **10** minutes
Cooking time: **5** minutes
Serves **4**

500 g (1 lb 2 oz) Chinese green vegetables
    (see Note)
2 teaspoons peanut oil
½ teaspoon finely chopped garlic
1 tablespoon oyster sauce
½ teaspoon caster (superfine) sugar
1 teaspoon sesame oil

1 Bring a large saucepan of water to
the boil.
2 Wash the Chinese greens. Remove any
tough leaves and trim the stems. Chop the
greens into three equal portions.
3 Add the greens to the pan of boiling
water. Cook for 1–2 minutes, or until just
tender but still crisp. Use tongs to remove
the greens from the pan, drain well and
place on a heated serving platter.
4 Heat the peanut oil in a small saucepan
and cook the garlic briefly. Add the oyster
sauce, sugar, 2 tablespoons water and
the sesame oil and bring to the boil.
Pour over the greens and toss to coat.
Serve immediately.

NOTE: Use choy sum, bok choy (pak
choy) or Chinese broccoli (gai larn), or a
combination of any two.

pork with
plum sauce

✳

Preparation time: **15** minutes
Cooking time: **15** minutes
Serves **4**

3 tablespoons oil
2 garlic cloves, finely chopped
1 large onion, cut into thin wedges
500 g (1 lb 2 oz) pork loin, sliced
2 tablespoons cornflour (cornstarch)
½ teaspoon sugar

adding cornflour

Cornflour (cornstarch) will thicken a sauce
without affecting the flavour. Mix the cornflour
with a little cold water or stock to make a thin,
smooth paste. Remove the wok or pan containing
the sauce from the heat for a minute or so, then
stir the cornflour mixture immediately before
adding it to the sauce, as the cornflour does not
stay in suspension for long. Return the wok to the
heat and, while stirring, quickly bring the sauce
to the boil.

60 ml (2 fl oz/¼ cup) plum sauce
1 tablespoon soy sauce
2 teaspoons hoisin sauce

1 Heat 1 tablespoon of the oil in a wok and cook the garlic and onion until softened. Transfer to a plate and remove the wok from the heat.
2 Coat the pork lightly in the cornflour and season well with salt and pepper. Add the remaining oil to the wok and return to the heat. When the wok is extremely hot, stir-fry the pork in two batches until dark golden brown, then return all the pork and its juices to the wok.
3 Add the plum sauce, soy sauce and hoisin sauce and return the onion to the wok. Toss well to coat the pork with the sauce and serve immediately.

stir-fried vegetables

✹

Preparation time: 5 minutes
Cooking time: 5 minutes
Serves 4

1 carrot
1 red capsicum (pepper)
125 g (4½ oz) green beans, trimmed
1 tablespoon oil
1 teaspoon finely chopped garlic
200 g (7 oz) straw mushrooms
1½ teaspoons cornflour (cornstarch)
80 ml (2½ fl oz/⅓ cup) chicken stock
1 teaspoon sesame oil
1 teaspoon caster (superfine) sugar
2 teaspoons soy sauce
steamed rice, to serve

1 Slice the carrot thinly. Seed the capsicum and cut it into 4 cm (1½ inch) pieces. Cut the beans in half.
2 Heat the oil in a wok or heavy-based frying pan, swirling gently to coat the base and side. Add the carrot and stir-fry it over high heat for 30 seconds. Stir in the garlic; add the remaining vegetables and stir-fry over high heat for 2 minutes — they should be very crisp and firm.

3 Dissolve the cornflour in a little of the stock; mix with the remaining stock, sesame oil, sugar and soy sauce. Add the cornflour mixture to the wok and stir until the sauce boils and thickens. Serve immediately with the steamed rice.

sweet garlic eggplant

✹

Preparation time: 5 minutes
Cooking time: 15 minutes
Serves 4

3 eggplants (aubergines)
140 ml (4½ fl oz/7 tablespoons) oil
1½ teaspoons finely chopped garlic
6 teaspoons caster (superfine) sugar
1½ tablespoons soy sauce
1½ tablespoons cider vinegar
1 tablespoon dry sherry
steamed rice, to serve

1 Cut the eggplants in half lengthways and then slice into wedges about 3 cm (1¼ inches) wide. Cut the wedges into pieces about 3 cm (1¼ inches) long.
2 Heat 3 tablespoons of the oil in a wok or heavy-based frying pan, swirling gently to coat the base and side. Add half the eggplant and stir-fry over high heat for 5 minutes, or until browned and all the oil is absorbed. Transfer to a plate. Repeat the cooking procedure with another 3 tablespoons of the oil and the remaining eggplant.
3 Heat the remaining oil in the wok, swirling gently to coat the base and side. Add the garlic and cook slowly until just golden. Add the sugar, soy sauce, vinegar and sherry. Bring to the boil, stirring. Add the eggplant and simmer for 3 minutes to allow it to absorb the sauce. Serve with the steamed rice.

NOTE: This dish can be cooked up to 2 days ahead and refrigerated until required. Serve it at room temperature.

chinese green vegetables

There are a number of Chinese green vegetables available in most fruit and vegetable markets. Choy sum, bok choy (pak choy) and Chinese broccoli (gai larn) are all easily prepared by cutting off the base, separating the leaves and rinsing in cold water. Roughly chop the vegetables into large pieces. The whole plant is used, including the stem — this requires longer cooking than the leaves, but don't overcook it or it will lose its lovely vibrant green colour.

indonesia

The cuisine of Indonesia is rich and varied, a reflection of the many diverse influences that have shaped the country's history. Indonesian cooking combines the spicy flavours of chillies, herbs and other aromatic seasonings with the sweetness of fresh coconut, palm sugar and peanuts, and the sourness of limes, lemongrass and tamarind. Meals are often served with small bowls of sambal: spicy relishes made from combinations of coconut, chilli and shrimp paste.

Remove the omelette from the pan with a spatula.

Process the garlic, onion, chilli, shrimp paste, coriander and sugar into a paste.

Stir-fry the steak and prawns until they change colour.

Stir-fry the rice, breaking up any lumps with a wooden spoon.

nasi goreng (fried rice)

✳ ✳

Preparation time: 35 minutes
Cooking time: 30 minutes
Serves 4

2 eggs
80 ml (2½ fl oz/⅓ cup) oil
3 garlic cloves, finely chopped
1 onion, finely chopped
2 red chillies, seeded and very finely chopped
1 teaspoon shrimp paste
1 teaspoon coriander seeds
½ teaspoon sugar
400 g (14 oz) raw prawns (shrimp)
200 g (7 oz) rump steak, thinly sliced
200 g (7 oz/1 cup) long-grain rice, cooked and cooled
2 teaspoons kecap manis
1 tablespoon soy sauce
4 spring onions (scallions), finely chopped
½ lettuce, finely shredded
1 Lebanese (short) cucumber, thinly sliced, to garnish
3 tablespoons crisp fried onion, to garnish

1 Beat the eggs and ¼ teaspoon salt until foamy. Heat a frying pan over medium heat and lightly brush with a little of the oil; pour about one-quarter of the egg mixture into the pan and cook for 1–2 minutes until the omelette sets. Turn the omelette over and cook the other side for 30 seconds. Remove the omelette from the pan and repeat three times with the remaining egg mixture. When the omelettes are cold, gently roll them up and cut them into fine strips; set aside.
2 Peel the prawns and gently pull out the dark vein from each prawn back, starting at the head end. Combine the garlic, onion, chilli, shrimp paste, coriander seeds and sugar in a food processor or mortar and pestle, and process or pound until a paste is formed.
3 Heat 1–2 tablespoons of the oil in a wok or large deep frying pan; add the paste and cook over high heat for 1 minute or until aromatic. Add the

prawns and beef and stir-fry for 2–3 minutes, or until they change colour.
4 Add the remaining oil and the cold rice to the wok. Stir-fry, breaking up any lumps, until the rice is heated through. Add the kecap manis, soy sauce and spring onion and stir-fry for another minute.
5 Arrange the lettuce around the outside of a large platter. Place the rice in the centre, and garnish with the omelette strips, cucumber slices and crisp fried onion. Serve immediately.

beef fillet in coconut

✳

Preparation time: 15 minutes + 1 hour marinating time
Cooking time: 10 minutes
Serves 4

2 garlic cloves, crushed
2 teaspoons finely grated lemon zest
1 teaspoon grated fresh ginger
2 teaspoons ground coriander
½ teaspoon ground turmeric
2 teaspoons grated palm sugar (jaggery) or soft brown sugar
3 tablespoons peanut oil
500 g (1 lb 2 oz) beef eye fillet, thinly sliced
45 g (1¾ oz/½ cup) desiccated coconut
3 spring onions (scallions), cut into thin strips
125 ml (4 fl oz/½ cup) coconut milk
steamed rice, to serve

1 Mix together the garlic, lemon zest, ginger, coriander, turmeric, palm sugar and 2 tablespoons of the oil; add the beef and toss well to coat. Cover and refrigerate for 1 hour.
2 Heat the remaining oil in a wok or frying pan; add the beef and stir-fry in batches until well browned. Add the coconut and spring onion and stir-fry for 1 minute. Return all the beef to the wok, add the coconut milk and stir until heated through. Serve with the steamed rice.

deep-fried spiced tofu

✳ ✳

Preparation time: **10 minutes**
Cooking time: **10 minutes**
Serves **4**

375 g (13 oz) firm tofu
90 g (3¼ oz/½ cup) rice flour
2 teaspoons ground coriander
1 teaspoon ground cardamom
1 garlic clove, crushed
vegetable oil, for deep-frying
lime wedges, to serve

1 Drain the tofu and cut it into 1 cm
(½ inch) thick slices, then halve the slices.
2 Combine the flour, coriander, cardamom
and garlic in a bowl; add 125 ml (4 fl oz/
½ cup) water and stir until smooth.
3 Heat the oil in a large saucepan. Dip
the tofu slices into the spice mixture and
coat thickly. Place the tofu slices into
the oil, three at a time, and cook over
medium heat for about 2 minutes, or until
crisp and golden brown. Drain on paper
towels. Serve with the lime wedges.

NOTE: Serve the tofu with stir-fried
vegetables and any sauce of your choice;
for example, peanut, chilli or soy sauce —
the tofu soaks up the flavours.

deep-fried spiced tofu

tofu

Tofu, or bean curd, is said to have been discovered
more than 2000 years ago by a Chinese emperor
who, while working with a group of scientists on
new medicines, discovered the art of coagulating
soy milk. In a region which has no tradition
of dairy product consumption, tofu has long
been valued for its high calcium and protein
content. In addition, it is cheap to produce and
extremely versatile.

chicken soup with vermicelli and vegetables

gado gado (vegetables with peanut sauce)

✻ ✻

Preparation time: 50 minutes
Cooking time: 25 minutes
Serves 4

250 g (9 oz) potatoes
2 carrots
200 g (7 oz) green beans, trimmed
¼ cabbage, shredded
3 hard-boiled eggs, peeled
200 g (7 oz) bean sprouts, trimmed
½ Lebanese (short) cucumber, sliced
150 g (5½ oz) firm tofu, cut into small cubes
80 g (2¾ oz/½ cup) unsalted roasted
   peanuts, roughly chopped, to garnish

PEANUT SAUCE
1 tablespoon oil
1 large onion, very finely chopped
2 garlic cloves, finely chopped
2 red chillies, very finely chopped
1 teaspoon shrimp paste, optional
250 g (9 oz) crunchy peanut butter
250 ml (9 fl oz/1 cup) coconut milk
2 teaspoons kecap manis
1 tablespoon tomato sauce (ketchup)

1   Cut the potatoes into thick slices; place in a medium saucepan, cover with cold water and bring to the boil. Reduce the heat and simmer for about 6 minutes or until just tender. Drain and allow to cool.
2   Cut the carrots into thick slices. Cut the beans into 4 cm (1½ inch) lengths. Bring a large saucepan of water to the boil, add the carrot and beans, and cook for 2–3 minutes. Remove the vegetables with a sieve and plunge briefly into a bowl of iced water. Drain well.
3   Plunge the shredded cabbage into the boiling water for about 20 seconds. Remove it from the pan and plunge it briefly into the iced water. Drain well.
4   Cut the eggs into quarters or halves. Arrange the eggs, potato, carrot, beans, cabbage, bean sprouts, cucumber and tofu in separate piles on a large serving platter.

Cover the platter with plastic wrap and refrigerate.
5   To make the peanut sauce, heat the oil in a heavy-based saucepan, add the onion and garlic and cook over low heat for 8 minutes, stirring regularly. Add the chilli and shrimp paste to the pan and cook for another minute. Remove the pan from the heat and mix in the peanut butter. Return the pan to the heat and slowly stir in the combined coconut milk and 250 ml (9 fl oz/1 cup) water. Bring the sauce to the boil, stirring constantly over medium heat, and being careful the sauce does not stick and burn. Reduce the heat, add the kecap manis and tomato sauce, and simmer for another minute. Allow to cool.
6   Drizzle a little of the peanut sauce over the salad, garnish with the chopped peanuts and serve the remaining sauce in a bowl.

NOTE: Fresh peanut butter, available from health food stores, will give the sauce the best flavour. Be sure not to overcook the vegetables — they should be tender yet still crisp.

chicken soup with vermicelli and vegetables

✻

Preparation time: 15 minutes
Cooking time: 35 minutes
Serves 4

1 kg (2 lb 4 oz) chicken pieces (such as
   drumsticks and thighs)
6 spring onions (scallions), chopped
2 cm (¾ inch) piece fresh ginger,
   very thinly sliced
2 bay leaves
2 tablespoons soy sauce
100 g (3½ oz) dried rice vermicelli
50 g (1¾ oz) spinach leaves,
   chopped
2 celery stalks, thinly sliced
200 g (7 oz) bean sprouts,
   trimmed

crisp fried onion, to garnish
chilli sauce, to serve

1   Combine the chicken and 1.5 litres (52 fl oz/6 cups) water in a saucepan and bring to the boil. Skim off any scum. Add the spring onion, ginger, bay leaves, soy sauce, ¼ teaspoon salt and ¼ teaspoon pepper, then reduce the heat and simmer for 30 minutes.
2   Meanwhile, cover the vermicelli with boiling water and leave to soak for 5 minutes or until soft; drain well.
3   Arrange the vermicelli, spinach, celery and bean sprouts on a platter. To serve, each diner places a serving of vermicelli and a selection of vegetables in large individual serving bowls. Pour the chicken soup, including a couple of chicken pieces, into each bowl. Sprinkle over the fried onion and season with the chilli sauce.

grow your own bean sprouts

To grow your own sprouts, place ¼–½ cup mung beans in a large glass jar (the sprouts will take up 10 times as much space as the beans). Rinse well, then soak the beans in cold water for 12 hours. Drain off the water, cover the top of the jar with a piece of muslin (cheesecloth) held in place with a rubber band, and leave it in a dark place. Twice a day fill the jar with water, swirl, and then drain well, as any remaining water could cause the sprouts to rot. By the fourth or fifth day the beans should be well sprouted — about 2.5 cm (1 inch) long. Rinse again, transfer to a plastic bag and refrigerate.

beef soup with rice noodles

✦ ✦

Preparation time: 30 minutes + 1 hour
marinating time
Cooking time: 1 hour
Serves 4

350 g (12 oz) fillet steak
2 teaspoons soy sauce
60 ml (2 fl oz/¼ cup) coconut milk
1 tablespoon crunchy peanut butter
1 tablespoon grated palm sugar (jaggery)
or soft brown sugar
2 teaspoons sambal oelek
1 teaspoon oil
125 g (4½ oz) dried rice vermicelli
1.5 litres (52 fl oz/6 cups) beef stock
2 tablespoons grated palm sugar (jaggery)
or soft brown sugar, extra

2 tablespoons fish sauce
1 small Lebanese (short) cucumber
90 g (3¼ oz/1 cup) bean sprouts, trimmed
2 iceberg lettuce leaves, cut into small
pieces
6 tablespoons finely chopped mint
80 g (2¾ oz/½ cup) unsalted roasted
peanuts, finely chopped

1 Trim the beef and slice it evenly across
the grain into thin slices.
2 Combine the beef, soy sauce, coconut
milk, peanut butter, palm sugar and
sambal oelek. Cover and marinate in the
refrigerator for 1 hour.
3 Heat the oil in a frying pan and cook
the beef in small batches over high heat
for 3 minutes, or until browned all over.
Remove from the heat and cover.
4 Cover the vermicelli with boiling
water and leave to soak for 5 minutes;
drain well.

5 Place the stock in a large saucepan and
bring to the boil. When the stock is boiling
add the extra palm sugar and fish sauce.
6 Cut the cucumber in quarters
lengthways and then into thin slices. Place
about 1 tablespoon of the cucumber slices
in each individual serving bowl; divide
the bean sprouts, pieces of lettuce and
mint leaves evenly between the bowls.
Place some vermicelli and then a ladleful
of stock in each bowl. Top with slices of
cooked beef, sprinkle with the peanuts
and serve immediately.

spicy roast chicken

✦

Preparation time: 20 minutes
Cooking time: 1 hour
Serves 4–6

1.6 kg (3 lb 8 oz) whole chicken
3 teaspoons chopped red chilli
3 garlic cloves
2 teaspoons peppercorns, crushed
2 teaspoons soft brown sugar
2 tablespoons soy sauce
2 teaspoons ground turmeric
1 tablespoon lime juice
30 g (1 oz) butter, chopped

1 Preheat the oven to 180°C (350°F/
Gas 4). Use a large cleaver to cut the
chicken in half by cutting down the
backbone and along the breastbone. To
prevent the wings from burning, tuck
them underneath. Put the chicken, skin
side up, on a rack in a roasting tin and
roast for 30 minutes.
2 Meanwhile, combine the chilli, garlic,
peppercorns and sugar in a food processor
or use a mortar and pestle and process or
pound until smooth. Add the soy sauce,
turmeric and lime juice, and process in
short bursts, or stir if using a mortar and
pestle, until combined.
3 Brush the spice mixture over the
chicken, dot it with the butter pieces and
roast for a further 25–30 minutes, or until
cooked through and a rich red colour.
Serve at room temperature.

beef soup with rice noodles

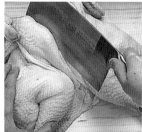

Cut the chicken in half by cutting down the backbone and along the breastbone.

Combine the chilli, garlic, peppercorns and sugar in a food processor.

Brush the spice mixture all over the chicken.

fiery prawn curry

dried red chillies in a food processor and process until just combined. Add the shrimp paste, coriander seeds, fresh red and green chilli, galangal and lemongrass and process until well combined, scraping down the sides of the bowl with a spatula. Add the candlenuts, turmeric and oil and process until a smooth paste is formed.

2 Peel the prawns, leaving the tails intact. Gently pull out the dark vein from each prawn back, starting at the head end. Cut the pineapple into bite-sized pieces. Cut the potatoes into slightly larger pieces.

3 Place the potato in a large saucepan with enough water to cover and cook for 5 minutes, or until just tender. Drain and set aside.

4 Heat the oil in a large frying pan or wok; add the spice paste and cook over medium heat for 5 minutes, stirring. Add the pineapple, potato, coconut milk and 125 ml (4 fl oz/½ cup) water and bring to the boil. Reduce the heat, add the prawns and simmer for 5 minutes. Add the tamarind, sugar and 1 teaspoon salt. Serve with the steamed rice.

baked spiced fish cutlets

✳

Preparation time: **15 minutes**
Cooking time: **30 minutes**
Serves **4**

1 tablespoon oil
1 onion, very finely chopped
2 garlic cloves, finely chopped
5 cm (2 inch) piece fresh ginger,
    finely grated
1 teaspoon ground coriander
1 lemongrass stem, white part only,
    finely chopped
2 teaspoons tamarind concentrate
2 teaspoons very finely grated lemon zest
4 small fish cutlets, such as blue eye
lime wedges, to garnish
steamed rice, to serve

fiery prawn curry

✳ ✳

Preparation time: **45 minutes**
Cooking time: **35 minutes**
Serves **4**

500 g (1 lb 2 oz) raw prawns (shrimp)
250 g (9 oz) fresh pineapple
250 g (9 oz) potatoes
1 tablespoon oil
250 ml (9 fl oz/1 cup) coconut milk
2 tablespoons tamarind concentrate
1 teaspoon sugar
steamed rice, to serve

SPICE PASTE
6 small dried red chillies
1 teaspoon shrimp paste
1 teaspoon coriander seeds
1 large red onion, roughly chopped
6 garlic cloves
4 small red chillies, roughly chopped
2 green chillies, roughly chopped
4 cm (1½ inch) piece fresh galangal, roughly
    chopped
1 lemongrass stem, white part only, sliced
6 candlenuts
½ teaspoon ground turmeric
1 tablespoon oil

1 To make the spice paste, soak the dried chillies in hot water until soft, then drain. Wrap the shrimp paste in a small piece of foil and cook under a hot grill (broiler) for 3 minutes each side. Dry-fry the coriander seeds in a small frying pan until aromatic. Place the onion, garlic and drained

1 Preheat the oven to 160°C (315°F/ Gas 2–3).

2 Heat the oil in a frying pan; add the onion, garlic, ginger, coriander and lemongrass, and stir over medium heat for 5 minutes or until aromatic.

3 Stir in the tamarind, lemon zest and season with black pepper, to taste. Remove from the heat and set aside until cool.

4 Line a baking dish with foil and grease it lightly to prevent the fish from sticking. Arrange the fish in the baking dish in a single layer and bake for 10 minutes. Turn the fish over gently, spread with the spice paste and bake for another 8 minutes, or until the flesh flakes when tested with a fork. Be sure not to overcook the fish or it will become dry. Garnish with the lime wedges and serve with the steamed rice.

NOTE: Adjust the cooking time if the cutlets are thick.

mee goreng (fried noodles)

❋ ❋

Preparation time: 45 minutes
Cooking time: 20 minutes
Serves 4

1 kg (2 lb 4 oz) raw prawns (shrimp)
1 large onion, finely chopped
2 garlic cloves, finely chopped
2 red chillies, seeded and very finely chopped
2 cm (¾ inch) piece fresh ginger, finely grated
60 ml (2 fl oz/¼ cup) oil
350 g (12 oz) hokkien (egg) noodles, gently
  pulled apart
250 g (9 oz) rump steak, thinly sliced
4 spring onions (scallions), chopped
1 large carrot, cut into 4 cm (1½ inch)
  matchsticks
2 celery stalks, cut into 4 cm (1½ inch)
  matchsticks
1 tablespoon kecap manis
1 tablespoon soy sauce
1 tablespoon tomato sauce (ketchup)
spring onions (scallions), extra, thinly sliced,
  to garnish

1 Peel the prawns and gently pull out the dark vein from each prawn back, starting at the head end.

2 Combine the onion, garlic, chilli and ginger in a food processor or use a mortar and pestle, and process in short bursts, or pound, until a paste is formed, adding a little of the oil if necessary. Set aside until needed.

3 Heat about 1 tablespoon of the oil in a large wok; add the noodles and stir-fry over medium heat until they are plump and warmed through. Place the noodles on a serving plate and cover to keep warm.

4 Add another tablespoon of the oil to the wok; add the paste mixture and stir-fry until golden. Add the prawns, beef, spring onion, carrot and celery, and stir-fry for 2–3 minutes. Add the kecap manis, soy and tomato sauces, and season well with salt and pepper. Spoon the mixture over the noodles and garnish with the extra spring onion. Serve immediately.

satays & kebabs

To prevent the wooden skewers used for satays and kebabs burning before the meat is cooked, soak them in water for at least 30 minutes. The ends can also be wrapped in foil.

chicken satays

Cut 500 g (1 lb 2 oz) chicken tenderloins in half lengthways. In a shallow non-metallic dish, combine 1 tablespoon honey, 60 ml (2 fl oz/¼ cup) soy sauce, 2 teaspoons sesame oil, 1 teaspoon ground coriander, 1 teaspoon ground turmeric and ½ teaspoon chilli powder. Thread the chicken lengthways onto soaked wooden skewers and place the skewers in the marinade. Cover and refrigerate for at least 2 hours. To make quick satay sauce, cook a small finely chopped onion in 1 tablespoon oil until softened and then stir in 125 g (4½ oz/½ cup) crunchy peanut butter, 2 tablespoons soy sauce, 125 ml (4 fl oz/½ cup) coconut cream and 2 tablespoons sweet chilli sauce. Cook gently until smooth and heated through. To cook the satays, cook the skewers under a preheated grill (broiler) for 5–7 minutes, turning and basting with the marinade frequently. Serve with the warm quick satay sauce. Makes 8 satays.

teriyaki steak kebabs

Cut 750 g (1 lb 10 oz) lean rump steak into thin strips, 15 cm (6 inches) long and thread onto skewers. Combine 125 ml (4 fl oz/½ cup) soy sauce, 125 ml (4 fl oz/½ cup) sherry or sake, 1 crushed garlic clove and 1 teaspoon each ground ginger and sugar. Place the beef with the mixture in a non-metallic dish and marinate it for at least 1 hour in the refrigerator. Drain and place skewers on a preheated, oiled grill (broiler) tray or barbecue flatplate and cook for 3–4 minutes each side. Makes 24 kebabs.

kofta on skewers

Combine 750 g (1 lb 10 oz) minced (ground) beef, 1 small grated onion, 30 g (1 oz/½ cup) chopped parsley, 2 tablespoons chopped coriander (cilantro) leaves, ½ teaspoon each ground cumin, nutmeg and cardamom, and ½ teaspoon each dried oregano and mint. Let stand for 1 hour. With wet hands, form the mixture into 24 sausage shapes; thread two koftas onto each skewer with a wedge of lime. Place the koftas on a preheated barbecue grill or flatplate, or under a hot grill (broiler) and cook for 10–12 minutes, turning frequently. Makes 12 skewers.

malaysian lamb satays

Trim any fat or sinew from 500 g (1 lb 2 oz) lamb fillets. Slice the lamb across the grain into very thin strips (if you have time, put the lamb in the freezer for 30 minutes as this will make it easier to thinly slice). In a food processor, combine 1 roughly chopped onion, 2 crushed garlic cloves, 2 cm (¾ inch) lemongrass stem (white part only), 2 slices fresh galangal, 1 teaspoon chopped fresh ginger, 1 teaspoon ground cumin, ½ teaspoon ground fennel, 1 tablespoon ground coriander, 1 teaspoon turmeric, 1 tablespoon soft brown sugar and 1 tablespoon lemon juice and process until a smooth paste is formed. Transfer the paste to a shallow non-metallic dish and add the lamb, stirring to coat well. Cover and refrigerate overnight. Thread the lamb onto skewers and cook under a preheated grill (broiler) for 3–4 minutes on each side, or until cooked. Brush regularly with the remaining marinade while cooking. Makes 8 satays.

chilli pork kebabs

Trim fat and sinew from 500 g (1 lb 2 oz) pork fillet and cut into small cubes. Combine 2 tablespoons sweet chilli sauce, 2 tablespoons tomato sauce (ketchup), 2 tablespoons hoisin sauce, 2 crushed garlic cloves, 60 ml (2 fl oz/¼ cup) lemon juice, 2 tablespoons honey and 2 teaspoons grated fresh ginger. Pour over pork and stir. Cover and refrigerate for several hours or overnight. Thread pork onto skewers; cook under a preheated, oiled grill (broiler) or barbecue flatplate for 3–4 minutes each side, until cooked. Brush with marinade while cooking. Serve with quick satay sauce (see Chicken satays). Makes 8 kebabs.

chicken satays and kofta on skewers

cold vegetable salad with spice dressing

❋

Preparation time: **15** minutes
Cooking time: **5** minutes
Serves **4**

300 g (10½ oz) green or snake (yard-long)
  beans, trimmed
10 English spinach leaves
80 g (2¾ oz) snow pea (mangetout) sprouts
1 red capsicum (pepper)
1 red onion
100 g (3½ oz) bean sprouts, trimmed

SPICE DRESSING
2 tablespoons peanut oil
1 garlic clove, crushed
1 teaspoon finely grated fresh ginger
1 small red chilli, chopped
2 tablespoons desiccated coconut
1 tablespoon brown vinegar

1 Cut the beans into 10 cm (4 inch) lengths. Remove the stems from the spinach leaves and slice the leaves thinly. Remove about 1 cm (½ inch) of the long stems from the snow pea sprouts. Cut the capsicum into thin strips. Thinly slice the onion.
2 Put the beans in a large saucepan of boiling water and cook for 1 minute to blanch, then drain. Combine the beans, spinach, snow pea sprouts, bean sprouts, capsicum and onion in a bowl.
3 To make the spice dressing, heat the oil in a small frying pan. Add the garlic, ginger, chilli and coconut, and stir-fry over medium heat for 1 minute. Add the vinegar and 80 ml (2½ fl oz/⅓ cup) water, and simmer for 1 minute. Allow to cool.
4 To serve, add the dressing to the vegetables, and toss until combined.

NOTE: Snow pea (mangetout) sprouts are the growing tips and tendrils from the snow pea plant. Any blanched vegetables can be used in this salad. Try to use a variety of vegetables which result in a colourful appearance. The spice dressing can be added up to 30 minutes before serving.

pork sambalan

❋

Preparation time: **10** minutes
Cooking time: **10** minutes
Serves **4**

400 g (14 oz) pork fillet
1–2 tablespoons Indonesian sambal paste
  (page 114)
1 tablespoon oil
375 ml (13 fl oz/1½ cups) coconut milk
spring onion (scallion), thinly sliced,
  to garnish
steamed rice, to serve

1 Slice the pork fillet into thin strips. Place the strips in a bowl with the sambal paste and oil, and toss until well combined.
2 Heat a wok to very hot; stir-fry the pork for about 2 minutes in two batches, until tender and lightly browned. Return all the pork to the wok.
3 Add the coconut milk and simmer, uncovered, for 2 minutes. Garnish with the spring onion and serve with the steamed rice.

NOTE: Two tablespoons of sambal paste will make this dish quite hot. Use less paste for a milder dish, if you prefer.

cold vegetable salad

baked fish with spices

✳

Preparation time: 15 minutes
Cooking time: 30 minutes
Serves 2

2 whole white fish (such as bream or
   snapper), each about 300 g (10½ oz),
   cleaned and scaled
1 onion, chopped
1 garlic clove, crushed
1 teaspoon chopped fresh ginger
1 teaspoon chopped lemon zest
2 tablespoons tamarind concentrate
1 tablespoon light soy sauce
1 tablespoon peanut oil
spring onion (scallion), thinly sliced, and
   coriander (cilantro) sprigs, to garnish

1 Preheat the oven to 180°C (350°F/
Gas 4).
2 Place the fish onto large pieces of foil.
Make three deep incisions with a sharp
knife on each side of the fish.
3 Process the onion, garlic, ginger, lemon
zest, tamarind, soy sauce and oil in a food
processor until a smooth paste forms.
4 Spread the onion mixture on the inside
of the fish and on both sides.
5 Wrap the foil around the fish and
secure it firmly. Place the fish in a baking
dish and bake for 30 minutes, or until the
fish is just cooked. Garnish with spring
onion and coriander.

baked fish with spices

tamarind chicken

✳

Preparation time: 15 minutes + 2 hours
   marinating time
Cooking time: 35 minutes
Serves 4

4 boneless chicken thighs
4 chicken drumsticks
80 ml (2½ fl oz/⅓ cup) tamarind
   concentrate
2 teaspoons ground coriander
1 teaspoon ground turmeric
2 garlic cloves, crushed
2 tablespoons peanut oil
2 red chillies, finely chopped
6 spring onions (scallions), finely chopped
oil, for deep-frying

1 Remove the skin from the chicken
drumsticks. Put all the chicken in a large
saucepan with enough water to cover it.
Cover and simmer for 15 minutes, or until
cooked through. Drain and cool.
2 Combine the tamarind, coriander,
turmeric and garlic. Add the tamarind
mixture to the chicken and toss to coat.
Cover and marinate in the refrigerator for
at least 2 hours, or overnight.
3 Heat the peanut oil in a frying pan;
add the chilli and spring onion, and stir-
fry over low heat for 3 minutes. Set aside.
4 Heat the oil in a large, deep frying
pan. Cook the chicken in three batches
over medium heat for 5 minutes, or until
the chicken is golden brown and heated
through. Drain on paper towels, and keep
warm while frying the remaining chicken.
Serve the chicken pieces with a spoonful
of the chilli mixture on the side.

grating coconut

To make grated fresh coconut, gently prise the flesh away from the shell using a flat-bladed knife. Use a vegetable peeler to remove the tough skin and then grate the flesh or use the vegetable peeler to flake it. Roast in a slow oven for 10–15 minutes to dry out before using.

vegetable coconut curry

☀

Preparation time: 40 minutes
Cooking time: 35 minutes
Serves 4 as part of a shared meal

300 g (10½ oz) pumpkin (winter squash)
200 g (7 oz) potatoes
250 g (9 oz) okra
1 onion
2 tablespoons oil

1 garlic clove, crushed
3 green chillies, seeded and very
   finely chopped
½ teaspoon ground turmeric
½ teaspoon fenugreek seeds
8 curry leaves
1 cinnamon stick
500 ml (17 fl oz/2 cups) coconut milk
steamed rice, to serve

1 Cut the pumpkin into 2 cm (¾ inch) cubes. Cut the potatoes into 2 cm (¾ inch) cubes. Trim the stems from the okra. Chop the onion.

2 Heat the oil in a large heavy-based saucepan. Add the garlic, chilli, turmeric, fenugreek seeds and onion, and cook over medium heat for 5 minutes, or until the onion is soft.

3 Add the pumpkin, potato, okra, curry leaves, cinnamon stick and coconut milk. Bring to the boil, then reduce the heat and simmer, uncovered, for 25–30 minutes, or until the vegetables are tender. Serve with the steamed rice.

baked fish cakes

❋

Preparation time: 20 minutes
Cooking time: 15 minutes
Serves 6 as an entrée

500 g (1 lb 2 oz) boneless white
    fish fillets
1 tablespoon Indonesian sambal paste
    (page 114)
2 tablespoons chopped lemongrass, white
    part only
2 cm (¾ inch) piece fresh ginger, finely
    grated
1 teaspoon ground cumin
3 spring onions (scallions), finely chopped
1 egg, lightly beaten
1 tablespoon chopped mint
lemon wedges, to serve

1 Preheat the oven to 180°C (350°F/
Gas 4).
2 Place the fish, sambal paste,
lemongrass, ginger, cumin and spring
onion into a food processor and process
until a smooth paste is formed.
3 Transfer the fish mixture to a bowl, and
mix through the egg and mint.
4 Divide the mixture into 6 equal
portions, and shape each portion into a
sausage. Wrap each portion in a 15 x
25 cm (6 x 10 inch) piece of baking paper
and bake for 15 minutes. Serve with a
squeeze of lemon juice.

indonesian rendang

❋

Preparation time: 15 minutes
Cooking time: 2 hours 30 minutes
Serves 6

1.5 kg (3 lb 5 oz) chuck steak, trimmed
2 onions, roughly chopped
4 teaspoons crushed garlic
420 ml (14½ fl oz/1⅔ cups) coconut milk
2 teaspoons ground coriander
½ teaspoon ground fennel
2 teaspoons ground cumin
¼ teaspoon ground cloves

4 red chillies, chopped
1 lemongrass stem, white part only, or
    4 strips lemon zest
1 tablespoon lemon juice
2 teaspoons grated palm sugar (jaggery) or
    soft brown sugar
steamed rice, to serve
red chilles, sliced, to serve
coriander (cilantro) sprigs, to garnish

1 Cut the beef evenly into small (about
3 cm/1¼ inch) cubes.
2 Place the onion and garlic in a food
processor and process until smooth,
adding water if necessary.
3 Place the coconut milk in a large
saucepan and bring it to the boil, then
reduce the heat to moderate and cook,
stirring occasionally, until the milk is
reduced by half and the oil is separated
out. Do not allow the milk to brown.
4 Add the coriander, fennel, cumin and

cloves, and stir for 1 minute. Add the beef
and cook for 2 minutes until it changes
colour. Add the onion mixture, chilli,
lemongrass, lemon juice and palm sugar.
Cook over moderate heat for 2 hours, or
until the liquid is reduced and the mixture
is quite thick. Stir frequently to prevent it
catching on the bottom of the pan.
5 Cook until the oil from the coconut milk
begins to emerge again, letting the curry
develop colour and flavour. This dish needs
constant attention to prevent it from
burning. The curry is cooked when it is
brown and dry. Serve with steamed rice,
chillies and coriander.

NOTE: Like most curries, this one benefits
from being made ahead of time. Prepare
2–3 days in advance and store, covered, in
the refrigerator. Reheat over low heat. The
curry can also be cooled in the refrigerator
then frozen for up to 1 month.

indonesian rendang

balinese fried rice

✳

Preparation time: 20 minutes
Cooking time: 20 minutes
Serves 6

500 g (1 lb 2 oz) raw prawns (shrimp)
2 teaspoons oil
2 eggs
2 onions, chopped
2 garlic cloves
3 tablespoons oil, extra

¼ teaspoon shrimp paste
125 g (4½ oz) rump steak, thinly sliced
1 cooked chicken breast, thinly sliced
300 g (10½ oz/1½ cups) long-grain rice,
    cooked and cooled
1 tablespoon soy sauce
1 tablespoon fish sauce
1 tablespoon sambal oelek
1 tablespoon tomato paste (concentrated
    purée)
6 spring onions (scallions), finely chopped
1 telegraph (long) cucumber sliced,
    to garnish

1 Peel the prawns and gently pull out the dark vein from each prawn back, starting at the head end; chop the prawn meat.
2 Heat the oil in a wok or heavy-based saucepan. Lightly beat the eggs and season with salt and pepper. Add the egg to the wok and cook over moderately high heat, pulling the cooked edges of the egg towards the centre. When set, transfer the omelette to a plate, cool, and cut into fine strips. Set aside.
3 Place the onion and garlic in a food processor and process until finely chopped.
4 Heat the extra oil in the wok; add the onion mixture and cook over medium heat, stirring frequently until it is reduced in volume and is translucent. Add the shrimp paste and cook a further minute. Add the prawns and beef and cook over high heat for 3 minutes. Add the chicken and rice and toss until heated.
5 Combine the soy sauce, fish sauce, sambal oelek, tomato paste and spring onion and add to the rice mixture. Mix well. Remove the rice from the heat and transfer to a serving platter. Top with the omelette strips and garnish with the sliced cucumber.

balinese fried fish

✳ ✳

Preparation time: 25 minutes
Cooking time: 30 minutes
Serves 4

750 g (1 lb 10 oz) firm white fish fillets
    (such as jewfish or ling)
oil, for shallow-frying
4 red Asian shallots, sliced lengthways
2.5 cm (1 inch) piece lemongrass, white part
    only, finely chopped
2 red chillies, finely chopped
2 cm (¾ inch) piece fresh ginger, grated
½ teaspoon shrimp paste
2 tablespoons kecap manis
1 tablespoon grated palm sugar (jaggery)
    or soft brown sugar
2 teaspoons lime juice
3 spring onions (scallions), finely chopped

balinese fried rice

feasts in bali

Feasts are an important feature of Balinese family and community life. For temple festivals an entire community prepares foods and offerings. Pork (a largely forbidden food in the rest of Indonesia, where the population is mostly Muslim) is festive food in Bali, with babi guling — roast suckling pig — the usual feast centrepiece.

1 Preheat the oven to 160°C (315°F/ Gas 2–3). Cut the fish into bite-sized pieces; sprinkle with ½ teaspoon salt and ½ teaspoon pepper.

2 Heat the oil, about 2 cm (¾ inch) deep, in a deep frying pan; add the fish 3–4 pieces at a time, and cook over moderately high heat for about 4 minutes, turning the pieces over, until they are light golden brown. Drain the fish on paper towels and place in the oven to keep warm.

3 In a small saucepan, heat 2 tablespoons of the fish frying oil; add the shallots, lemongrass, chilli, ginger and shrimp paste and cook for 3 minutes over low heat, stirring occasionally. Add 125 ml (4 fl oz/½ cup) water, the kecap manis and palm sugar, and stir until the sauce boils and thickens. Stir in the lime juice and spring onion. Drizzle the sauce over the fish and serve immediately.

NOTE: The fish must have a solid meaty texture or it will fall apart during the frying. Kecap manis is Indonesian soy sauce, and is slightly thicker and sweeter than Chinese soy sauce.

sweet kecap pork

☼ ☼

Preparation time: 20 minutes
Cooking time: 1 hour 30 minutes
Serves 4

500 g (1 lb 2 oz) diced pork
2 tablespoons oil
1 large onion, finely chopped
3 garlic cloves, finely chopped
5 cm (2 inch) piece fresh ginger, finely grated
3 red chillies, finely chopped
2 tablespoons kecap manis
250 ml (9 fl oz/1 cup) coconut milk
2 teaspoons lime juice
red chilli, thinly sliced, to serve
steamed rice, to serve
lime slices, to serve

1 Mix together the pork, oil, ¼ teaspoon salt and ¼ teaspoon pepper and leave to stand for 10 minutes.

2 Heat a wok or heavy-based frying pan and cook the pork in batches over medium heat, until well browned. Remove all the pork from the wok and set aside. Reduce the heat to low, add the onion, garlic, ginger and chilli and cook for 10 minutes, stirring occasionally until the onion is very soft and golden. Add the pork, kecap manis and coconut milk, and cook over low heat for 1 hour, stirring occasionally. Stir in the lime juice and serve with the chilli, steamed rice and lime slices.

stir-fried hot beef

☼ ☼

Preparation time: 25 minutes
Cooking time: 10 minutes
Serves 4

1 teaspoon coriander seeds
500 g (1 lb 2 oz) sirloin, fillet or topside steak, thinly sliced
1 tablespoon oil
2 tablespoons tamarind concentrate
2 teaspoons grated palm sugar (jaggery) or soft brown sugar
2 tablespoons coconut cream

sweet kecap pork

SPICE PASTE
5 red chillies
2 cm (¾ inch) piece fresh galangal, sliced
1 teaspoon shrimp paste
10 red Asian shallots, roughly chopped
4 garlic cloves
2 tablespoons oil

1 To make the spice paste, place all the paste ingredients in a food processor and process until a smooth paste forms, scraping down the sides of the bowl with a spatula regularly.

2 Dry-fry the coriander seeds over low heat for 1 minute in a frying pan, shaking the pan constantly. Grind the seeds using a mortar and pestle or food processor.

3 Combine the beef with the coriander and ½ teaspoon salt, mixing well. Set aside.

4 Heat the oil in a wok or frying pan; add the spice paste and cook over high heat for 3 minutes, or until very aromatic and a little oily. Remove the spice paste from the wok.

5 Reheat the wok to high: add the beef in two batches and stir-fry for 2–3 minutes or until just cooked. Add the spice paste, tamarind, palm sugar and coconut cream. Toss over very high heat for 1 minute and serve immediately.

1 Cut the squid into large pieces and score the tender inner flesh diagonally, in a criss-cross pattern, taking care not to cut all the way through. Place in a bowl with the lime juice and season to taste with salt and pepper. Cover and refrigerate.

2 To make the spice paste, place all the ingredients in a food processor and process until a smooth paste forms, scraping down the sides of the bowl with a spatula regularly.

3 Heat the oil in a wok and add the chilli and spring onion. Add the squid in

batches and cook over moderate heat for 2 minutes. Remove from the wok.

4 Heat the extra oil in the wok, add the spice paste, tamarind and lemongrass and cook over moderate heat, stirring, for 5 minutes.

5 Return the squid to the wok and add the stock. Season with pepper and add the basil. Bring to the boil, then reduce the heat and simmer for 20 minutes. Serve with the steamed rice.

balinese chilli squid

✳ ✳

Preparation time: **25 minutes**
Cooking time: **35 minutes**
Serves **4**

750 g (1 lb 10 oz) squid tubes
60 ml (2 fl oz/¼ cup) lime juice
2 tablespoons oil
1 large red chilli, seeded and
  sliced
3 spring onions (scallions), sliced
1 tablespoon oil, extra
1 tablespoon tamarind concentrate
1 lemongrass stem, white part only,
  thinly sliced
250 ml (9 fl oz/1 cup) chicken
  stock
5 Thai basil leaves, shredded
steamed rice, to serve

SPICE PASTE
2 large red chillies, seeded and
  chopped
2 garlic cloves, chopped
2 cm (¾ inch) piece fresh turmeric,
  chopped
2 cm (¾ inch) piece fresh ginger,
  chopped
3 spring onions (scallions), chopped
1 tomato, peeled, seeded and chopped
2 teaspoons coriander seeds
1 teaspoon shrimp paste

shrimp paste

Shrimp paste is always cooked before it is eaten. This transforms its acrid flavour into an aromatic seasoning. If it is not to be fried with the spice paste, wrap it in foil and dry-fry in a frying pan or roast in the oven or under the grill (broiler) — this will prevent its overpowering odour filling the entire house.

festive coconut rice

✳ ✳

Preparation time: 25 minutes
Cooking time: 40 minutes
Serves 6–8

3 tablespoons oil
1 onion, cut into thin wedges
4 cm (1½ inch) piece fresh ginger, finely grated
2 garlic cloves, finely chopped
500 g (1 lb 2 oz/2½ cups) long-grain rice
1 teaspoon ground turmeric
1 litre (35 fl oz/4 cups) coconut milk
6 curry leaves

GARNISHES
3 hard-boiled eggs, peeled, cut into quarters
35 g (1¼ oz/½ cup) crisp fried onion
1 Lebanese (short) cucumber, sliced into matchsticks
2 red chillies, thinly sliced
coriander (cilantro) sprigs

1   Heat the oil in a large heavy-based saucepan; add the onion, ginger and garlic and fry over low heat for 5 minutes. Add the rice and turmeric, and cook for 2 minutes, stirring well.
2   Place the coconut milk in a medium saucepan, and heat until nearly boiling.

Pour it over the rice, stirring constantly until the mixture comes to the boil. Add 1 teaspoon salt and the curry leaves. Cover with a tight-fitting lid, reduce the heat to very low and cook for 25 minutes or until all the coconut milk is absorbed.
3 Remove the lid, stir well and cool for 10 minutes. Remove the curry leaves and pile the rice onto a platter (traditionally lined with banana leaves). Serve the egg, cucumber, chilli, fried onion and coriander separately, or over the top.

fresh corn sambal

❋ ❋

Preparation time: **25 minutes**
Cooking time: **10 minutes**
Serves **8**

3 corn cobs
1 tablespoon coriander seeds
1 teaspoon shrimp paste, crumbled into pieces
1 garlic clove
1 onion, roughly chopped
3 red chillies
3 tablespoons tamarind concentrate
3 teaspoons sugar
steamed rice, to serve

1 Remove the husk and silks from the corn. Cut down the cobs with a sharp knife to remove the kernels. Dry-fry the corn kernels over medium heat for 5 minutes, in batches if necessary, shaking the pan regularly until the corn kernels turn golden but do not burn. Set aside.
2 Dry-fry the coriander seeds and shrimp paste in a frying pan for 3 minutes or until aromatic. Roughly grind the coriander and shrimp paste using a mortar and pestle.
3 Place the corn, ground coriander and shrimp paste, garlic, onion and chilli in a food processor and process until a rough paste forms. Add the tamarind, 2 tablespoons water, ½ teaspoon salt and the sugar and process again.
4 Serve the sambal as an accompaniment to curries, fish and vegetable dishes with the steamed rice.

mixed vegetables with tamarind

mixed vegetables with tamarind

❋

Preparation time: **25 minutes**
Cooking time: **30 minutes**
Serves **4**

250 g (9 oz) pumpkin (winter squash)
200 g (7 oz) potatoes
100 g (3½ oz) beans, trimmed
200 g (7 oz) cabbage
100 g (3½ oz) English spinach leaves
500 ml (17 fl oz/2 cups) vegetable stock
125 ml (4 fl oz/½ cup) tamarind concentrate
2 cinnamon sticks
2 bay leaves
4 garlic cloves, finely chopped
10 red Asian shallots, very thinly sliced
5 cm (2 inch) piece fresh ginger, finely grated
200 g (7 oz) baby corn
steamed rice, to serve
chilli, thinly sliced, to serve

1 Roughly chop the pumpkin. Cut the potato into thick slices. Shred the cabbage and spinach leaves.
2 Place the stock, tamarind, cinnamon, bay leaves, garlic, shallots and ginger in a large saucepan, and bring to the boil.
3 Add the pumpkin and potato and simmer for 5 minutes. Add the corn and beans and cook for another 5 minutes.
4 Add the cabbage and spinach and cook until just tender. Serve with the steamed rice as an accompaniment to a main meal, with thinly sliced chilli.

singapore & malaysia

Separated by only a narrow strip of water, peninsular Malaysia and the island state of Singapore have many dishes in common. The Indian, Muslim and Chinese heritage of both countries can be seen in Indian-hot curries, Middle Eastern-inspired satays and Chinese noodles, stir-fries and roasted meats. These influences come together in dishes such as laksa, a creamy curry of seafood or chicken simmered in coconut milk. In Singapore, the mix of Malays and Chinese has created Nonya food — an exciting blend of Chinese balance and Malaysian heat.

Hit the legs and larger front
nippers to crack the shells.

Turn the crab and hold it in oil until
the shell just turns red.

chilli crab

✳ ✳ ✳

Preparation time: 30 minutes
Cooking time: 45 minutes
Serves 2–4

2 fresh blue swimmer crabs,
    approximately 500 g (1 lb 2 oz) each
60 g (2¼ oz/½ cup) plain (all-purpose) flour
60 ml (2 fl oz/¼ cup) oil
1 onion, finely chopped
5 cm (2 inch) piece fresh ginger, finely grated
4 garlic cloves, finely chopped
3–5 red chillies, finely chopped
500 ml (17 fl oz/2 cups) tomato passata
    (puréed tomatoes)
2 tablespoons soy sauce
2 tablespoons sweet chilli sauce
1 tablespoon rice vinegar
2 tablespoons soft brown sugar
spring onion, thinly sliced, to garnish

1   Place the crabs in the freezer for
2 hours or until they are absolutely
immobile and dead (this is the most
humane way to kill crab or lobster).
2   Wash the crabs well and scrub the
shells using a scourer. Use a large cleaver
to cut the crabs in half and rinse well
under cold water, carefully removing the
yellow gills or spongy parts. Hit the legs
and larger front nippers with the flat side
of the cleaver to crack the shells (to make
it easier to eat the meat inside).
3   Lightly and carefully coat the shells
with a little flour. Heat about
2 tablespoons of the oil in a large wok,
cook one crab half at a time, carefully
turning and holding the crab in the hot oil
until the shell just turns red. Repeat with
the remaining crab halves.
4   Add the remaining oil to the wok; cook
the onion, ginger, garlic and chilli for
5 minutes over medium heat, stirring
regularly. Add the tomato passata,
250 ml (9 fl oz/1 cup) water, soy sauce,
sweet chilli sauce, vinegar and sugar.
Bring to the boil and cook for 15 minutes.
Return the crab to the wok and simmer,
turning carefully in the sauce for 8–10
minutes or until the crab meat turns

white. Do not overcook. Garnish with the
spring onion. Serve with steamed rice, if
desired, and provide finger bowls.

NOTE: It is essential that only fresh crabs
are used so order them from your
fishmonger the day before required, and
insist on having crabs that have been
freshly caught. Live crabs can be killed by
your fishmonger if you prefer. Don't buy
cooked crabs for this recipe.

singapore noodles

✳

Preparation time: 45 minutes
Cooking time: 15 minutes
Serves 2–4

300 g (10½ oz) dried rice vermicelli
600 g (1 lb 5 oz) raw prawns (shrimp)
2 tablespoons oil
2 garlic cloves, finely chopped
350 g (12 oz) pork loin, cut into strips
1 large onion, cut into thin wedges
1 tablespoon mild curry powder
150 g (5½ oz) green beans, trimmed, cut
    into 3–4 cm lengths
1 large carrot, cut into fine matchsticks
1 teaspoon caster (superfine) sugar
1 tablespoon soy sauce
200 g (7 oz) bean sprouts, trimmed
spring onion (scallion), thinly sliced,
    to garnish

1   Soak the vermicelli in boiling water for
5 minutes or until soft; drain well.
2   Peel the prawns and gently pull out the
dark vein from each prawn back, starting
at the head end. Chop the prawn meat.
3   Heat 1 tablespoon of the oil in a wok
over high heat. When hot, add the prawn
meat, garlic and pork. Stir-fry for 2 minutes
or until just cooked; remove from the wok.
4   Reduce the heat to medium and heat
another tablespoon of the oil; add the
onion and curry powder and stir-fry for
2–3 minutes. Add the beans, carrot, sugar
and 1 teaspoon salt, sprinkle with a little
water and stir-fry for 2 minutes.
5   Add the vermicelli and soy sauce to the
wok; toss with 2 wooden spoons. Add the
bean sprouts and pork mixture, season
with salt, pepper and sugar to taste, and
then toss well. Serve garnished with the
spring onion.

singapore noodles

mixed vegetable salad

✳ ✳

Preparation time: 40 minutes
Cooking time: 5 minutes
Serves 4–6

300 g (10½ oz) fresh pineapple, chopped
1 telegraph (long) cucumber, sliced
250 g (9 oz) cherry tomatoes, halved
155 g (5½ oz) green beans, trimmed,
 thinly sliced
150 g (5½ oz) bean sprouts, trimmed
80 ml (2½ fl oz/⅓ cup) rice vinegar
2 tablespoons lime juice
2 red chillies, seeded and very finely
 chopped
2 teaspoons sugar

30 g (1 oz) dried shrimp, to garnish
small mint leaves, to garnish

1 Toss together the pineapple, cucumber, tomatoes, beans and sprouts in a bowl. Cover and refrigerate until chilled. Combine the vinegar, lime juice, chilli and sugar in a small bowl and stir until the sugar has dissolved.
2 Dry-fry the shrimp in a frying pan, shaking the pan constantly until the shrimp are light orange and fragrant. Process the shrimp in a food processor until finely chopped.
3 Arrange the chilled salad on a serving platter, drizzle the dressing over the top and garnish with the shrimp and mint leaves. Serve immediately.

mixed vegetable salad

garlic prawns in chilli sauce

✳

Preparation time: 40 minutes
Cooking time: 10 minutes
Serves 4

1 kg (2 lb 4 oz) raw king prawns (shrimp)
2 garlic cloves, crushed
2 tablespoons peanut oil
3 teaspoons finely grated fresh ginger
1 celery stalk, diced
1 red capsicum (pepper), seeded and diced
1 tablespoon sweet chilli sauce
1 tablespoon hoisin sauce
2 tablespoons lime juice
1 teaspoon sugar
steamed rice, to serve

1 Peel the prawns, leaving the tails intact. Gently pull out the dark vein from each prawn back, starting at the head end. Place the prawns in a non-metallic bowl and mix in the garlic. Set aside.
2 Heat a wok over medium heat and add 1 tablespoon of the oil. Add the ginger, celery and capsicum and cook until softened. Remove from the wok. Heat the remaining oil and add the prawns. Cook over high heat until bright pink and cooked through. Spoon the celery and capsicum mixture back into the wok with the prawns and add the chilli sauce, hoisin sauce, lime juice and sugar. Season to taste with pepper. Heat through for a minute or so then serve with the steamed rice.

siamese noodles with spicy coconut sauce

✳ ✳ ✳

Preparation time: 1 hour 10 minutes
Cooking time: 30 minutes
Serves 6

1 tablespoon dried tamarind pulp
1.25 litres (44 fl oz/5 cups) coconut milk

300 g (10½ oz) dried rice vermicelli
400 g (14 oz) fried tofu
oil, for shallow frying
400 g (14 oz) bean sprouts, trimmed
500 g (1 lb 2 oz) cooked prawns (shrimp),
    peeled and deveined, tails intact
125 g (4½ oz/ 1 cup) garlic chives, snipped
3 hard-boiled eggs, peeled, cut into quarters
2 red chillies (optional), seeded and finely
    sliced
3 limes, quartered, to serve

SPICE PASTE
10 dried red chillies, soaked in hot water
    until softened
10 red Asian shallots, chopped
1 lemongrass stem, white part only, chopped
1 teaspoon shrimp paste
3 tablespoons peanut oil
1 tablespoon sugar

1 To make the spice paste, drain and
seed the soaked chillies, reserving the
water, and chop. Place the chillies in a
food processor or blender along with the
shallots, lemongrass and shrimp paste.
Process until finely chopped, adding a
little of the chilli water if necessary. Heat
the peanut oil in a small frying pan and
fry the paste over low heat for about
3 minutes. Add 1 teaspoon salt and the
sugar. Set aside.
2 Soak the tamarind in 125 ml
(4 fl oz/½ cup) warm water for about
10 minutes.
3 Take half the spice paste and place it in
a saucepan along with the coconut milk.
Strain the soaked tamarind and water
through a nylon sieve into the coconut
milk and discard any seeds and fibre.
Bring the mixture to the boil and simmer
for 3 minutes. Set aside.
4 Soak the vermicelli in boiling water for
5 minutes or until soft; drain well. Cut
the tofu into thick slices. Heat the oil in a
small frying pan and fry the slices of tofu
until golden on both sides. Remove and
drain on paper towels.
5 When ready to serve the dish, heat the
remaining spice paste in a large wok and
add the bean sprouts. Turn the heat up
high and cook for about a minute. Add

half the prawns and half the garlic chives.
Add the drained vermicelli to the wok;
toss until heated through. Reheat the
coconut sauce and keep it hot.
6 To serve, transfer the vermicelli
mixture to a large warm serving platter
and arrange the remaining prawns, the
egg quarters and slices of tofu on top.
Scatter over the sliced chilli, if desired,
and remaining garlic chives. Pour the
coconut sauce into a large warm soup
tureen. Provide deep bowls for diners to
fill with the vermicelli mixture, then
ladle over some coconut sauce and a
squeeze of lime juice.

spring rolls

Spring rolls were originally
eaten in China at festivities to
celebrate the Lunar New Year,
which heralds the coming of
spring. Because no work should
be done at this time, the rolls
— which traditionally contained
fresh bamboo shoots — were
made ahead. Many varieties of
spring roll are eaten throughout
Southeast Asia.

finger food

Asia has a delicious range of finger food, served with fragrant tea in the middle of the day, a cooling beer in the evening or bought piping hot from a street stall.

thai spring rolls

Soak 30 g (1 oz) dried rice vermicelli in boiling water for 5 minutes or until soft. Drain well and cut into shorter lengths. Heat 1 tablespoon oil in a wok or pan and add 3 chopped garlic cloves, 2 teaspoons finely grated fresh galangal or ginger, 3 finely chopped coriander (cilantro) roots and 3 chopped spring onions (scallions). Stir-fry for 2 minutes. Add 200 g (7 oz) minced (ground) pork and 2 finely sliced celery stalks and stir-fry for 3 minutes to brown the pork, breaking up any lumps. Add 155 g (5½ oz/1 cup) grated carrot, 25 g (1 oz) chopped coriander (cilantro) leaves, 45 g (1¾ oz/¼ cup) finely chopped Lebanese (short) cucumber, 1 tablespoon sweet chilli sauce, 2 teaspoons fish sauce, 1 teaspoon brown sugar and the noodles and mix well. Cool completely. Place 1 spring roll wrapper at a time (you will need about 14), with a corner towards you, on a damp tea towel (dish towel). Wet the edges with a little water. Spread about 1½ tablespoons of the filling in the centre of the wrapper. Fold the edges towards the centre, roll up the spring roll tightly and seal the edge with water. Repeat with the remaining wrappers and filling. Half fill a deep saucepan with oil and heat until moderately hot. Fry the rolls, in batches, for 2–3 minutes or until golden brown. Drain and serve with sweet chilli sauce and soy sauce. Makes 14.

prawn toasts

Peel and devein 350 g (12 oz) raw prawns (shrimp). Separate 2 eggs into small bowls and lightly beat the egg yolks. Place the prawn meat, egg whites, 1 garlic clove, 75 g (2¾ oz) drained, finely chopped tinned water chestnuts, 1 tablespoon chopped coriander (cilantro) leaves, 2 teaspoons grated fresh ginger, and ¼ teaspoon each ground white pepper and salt in a food processor. Process for 20–30 seconds, or until the mixture is smooth. Trim the crusts from 6 slices of white bread, cut in half diagonally then cut the halves in half again to form small triangles. Brush the top of each bread triangle with egg yolk, spread the prawn mixture evenly over the triangles and sprinkle each with white sesame seeds — you will need about 1 tablespoon. Half fill a deep saucepan with oil and heat until moderately hot. Fry the triangles in small batches, with the prawn mixture face down, for a few seconds, or until golden and crisp. Drain on paper towels. Serve hot. Makes 24.

vegetarian won tons

Heat 1 tablespoon oil in a wok or frying pan and cook 2 chopped garlic cloves, 4 chopped spring onions (scallions) and 3 teaspoons grated fresh ginger for 2 minutes. Add 2 finely sliced celery stalks, 150 g (5½ oz/2 cups) finely shredded cabbage, 310 g (11 oz/2 cups) grated carrot, 125 g (4½ oz) finely sliced fried tofu, 125 g (4½ oz/1 cup) chopped, trimmed bean sprouts and 2 tablespoons drained, chopped tinned water chestnuts. Cover the wok and steam for 2 minutes. Mix 3 teaspoons cornflour (cornstarch), 1 tablespoon water, 2 teaspoons sesame oil, 2 teaspoons soy sauce and ½ teaspoon each of salt and ground white pepper and mix until smooth. Add to the vegetable mixture and stir for 2 minutes, or until the sauce thickens. Cool completely. Place 1 tablespoon of filling in the centre of each won ton wrapper (you will need about 40). Brush the edges with a little water and gather around the filling to form a pouch; twist and pinch the sides together. Deep-fry in hot oil for 4–5 minutes or steam in a bamboo or metal steamer for 25–30 minutes. Makes 40.

seafood won tons

Make as for vegetarian won tons (above) but replace the celery, cabbage, carrot and tofu with 750 g (1 lb 10 oz) raw prawns (shrimp), peeled, deveined and chopped. After steaming, stir in 170 g (6 oz) drained tinned crabmeat and 2 tablespoons chopped coriander (cilantro) leaves. Makes 50.

malaysian coconut chicken

✳

Preparation time: **25 minutes**
Cooking time: **45–60 minutes**
Serves **4–6**

1.6 kg (3 lb 8 oz) chicken
1 tablespoon oil
2 onions, sliced
3 garlic cloves, crushed
2 red chillies, seeded and chopped
45 g (1¾ oz/½ cup) desiccated coconut
2 teaspoons ground turmeric
2 teaspoons ground coriander
2 teaspoons ground cumin
2 lemongrass stems, white part only,
   chopped
8 curry leaves
500 ml (17 fl oz/2 cups) coconut milk
cooked vermicelli noodles, to serve

1 Cut the chicken into 8–10 pieces.
2 Heat the oil in a large suacepan and
cook the onion until soft. Add the garlic,
chilli, coconut and turmeric. Stir the
mixture for 1 minute. Add the coriander,
cumin, lemongrass, curry leaves and
coconut milk. Stir until well combined.
3 Add the chicken pieces and stir until
well coated with the sauce. Simmer,
uncovered, for 45–60 minutes, or until the
chicken is tender and the sauce is
thickened. Serve with the noodles.

rotis with spicy meat filling

✳ ✳

Preparation time: **40 minutes + 2 hours
   resting time**
Cooking time: **1 hour 30 minutes**
Makes **12**

375 g (13 oz/3 cups) roti flour or plain
   (all-purpose) flour
2 tablespoons ghee or oil
1 egg, lightly beaten

rotis with spicy meat filling

oil, to brush
1 egg, extra, beaten
½ red onion, finely chopped
extra ghee or oil, for frying

SPICY MEAT FILLING
1 tablespoon ghee
1 onion, finely chopped
3 garlic cloves, crushed
2 teaspoons ground cumin
1 teaspoon ground coriander
1 teaspoon ground turmeric
250 g (9 oz) lean minced (ground) beef
   or lamb
1 teaspoon finely chopped, seeded red chilli
1 tablespoon chopped coriander (cilantro)
   leaves

1 Sift the flour into a large bowl and
stir in 1 teaspoon salt. Rub in the ghee or
pour in the oil. Add the egg and 250 ml

(9 fl oz/1 cup) water and mix with a
flat-bladed knife to form a moist mixture.
Turn the mixture out on to a well-floured
surface and knead for about 10 minutes
until you have a soft dough, sprinkling
with more flour as necessary. Form the
dough into a ball and brush it with oil.
Place it in an oiled bowl, cover with plastic
wrap and leave to rest for 2 hours.
2 To make the spicy meat filling, heat
the ghee in a large frying pan and add
the onion. Cook over low heat for about
5 minutes until soft and golden. Add the
garlic, cumin, coriander and turmeric and
cook for 1 minute. Turn up the heat, add
the minced meat and brown well, using
a fork to break up any lumps. Carry on
cooking until the meat is cooked through,
adding the chilli in the last few minutes of
cooking. Remove from the heat, stir in the
coriander and season with salt to taste.

3 Working on a floured work surface (use a clean bench top), divide the dough into 12 pieces and roll it into balls. Take one ball and, working with a little oil on your fingertips, hold the ball in the air and work around the edge pulling out the dough until a 15 cm (6 inch) round is formed. Lay the roti on a lightly floured surface and cover with plastic wrap so it doesn't dry out. Repeat with the other balls.

4 Heat a wide heavy frying pan or griddle and brush it with ghee or oil. Drape a roti over a rolling pin and carefully place the roti in the pan. Quickly brush the roti with some beaten egg and spoon over two heaped tablespoons of the meat filling. Cook until the underside of the roti is golden. This won't take long. Sprinkle the meat filling with some chopped onion, fold in two sides of the roti and then the other two sides, pressing to totally enclose the filling. Use a spatula to slide the roti onto a plate and brush the pan with some more ghee or oil. Return the roti to the heat to cook the other side. Cook until that side is golden. Cook the remaining rotis with the filling in the same way. Serve warm.

NOTE: Roti flour is a creamy-coloured flour available from Indian food stores. It is used in Indian unleavened breads. Plain flour can be used as a substitute.

prawn and noodle soup

☀

Preparation time: **40 minutes**
Cooking time: **25 minutes**
Serves **4**

200 g (7 oz) baby spinach leaves
500 g (1 lb 2 oz) shanghai noodles
1 tablespoon oil
1 large onion, finely chopped
5 cm (2 inch) piece fresh ginger, finely grated
2 red chillies, finely chopped
1.5 litres (52 fl oz/6 cups) chicken stock

2 tablespoons soy sauce
2 teaspoons soft brown sugar
6 spring onions (scallions), chopped
300 g (10½ oz) small cooked prawns (shrimp), peeled and deveined, tails intact

GARNISHES
2 tablespoons crisp fried garlic
2 tablespoons crisp fried onion
90 g (3¼ oz/1 cup) bean sprouts, trimmed
2 teaspoons chilli flakes
1 tablespoon garlic chives, snipped

1 Wash and drain the spinach and snap off any long stems; set aside. Add the noodles to a saucepan of boiling water and cook for 3 minutes, or until plump and tender. Drain and set aside.

2 Heat the oil in a large saucepan and cook the onion and ginger over medium heat, stirring regularly, for 8 minutes. Add the chilli, stock, soy sauce and sugar and bring to the boil. Reduce the heat and leave to simmer for 10 minutes. Add the spring onion.

3 Transfer the noodles to large soup bowls and top with the prawns and spinach leaves. Pour the boiling stock over the top and serve immediately. Place the garnishes in small bowls, along with salt, pepper and sugar, for the diners to add according to their taste.

prawn and noodle soup

fried rice noodles

✺

Preparation time: 20 minutes
Cooking time: 15 minutes
Serves 4

400 g (14 oz) raw prawns (shrimp)
2 Chinese dried pork sausages
   (see Note)
500 g (1 lb 2 oz) thick fresh rice noodles
2 tablespoons oil
2 garlic cloves, finely chopped
1 onion, finely chopped

3 red chillies, seeded and chopped
250 g (9 oz) Chinese barbecued pork
   (char siu), chopped
150 g (5½ oz) garlic chives, cut into short
   lengths, plus extra, to garnish
2 tablespoons kecap manis
3 eggs, lightly beaten
1 tablespoon rice vinegar
100 g (3½ oz) bean sprouts, trimmed,
   plus extra, to garnish

1 Peel the prawns and gently pull out the dark vein from each prawn back, starting at the head end. Slice the sausages on the diagonal into paper-thin slices. Use your fingertips to gently separate the noodles.

2 Heat the oil in a large wok or frying pan over high heat. Fry the sausage slices, tossing regularly, until they are golden and very crisp. Use a slotted spoon to remove from the wok and drain on paper towels.

3 Reheat the oil in the wok, add the garlic, onion, chilli and barbecued pork and stir-fry for 2 minutes. Add the prawns and toss constantly until they change colour. Add the noodles, chives and kecap manis and toss. Cook for 1 minute or until the noodles begin to soften. Pour the combined egg and vinegar over the top of the mixture and toss for 1 minute. Be careful not to let the egg-coated noodles burn on the base of the pan. Add the bean sprouts and toss.

4 Arrange the noodles on a large serving platter, scatter the drained pork sausages over the top and toss a little to mix a few slices among the noodles. Garnish with chives and bean sprouts and serve immediately.

NOTE: These spicy, dried pork sausages (lup chiang) are available from Asian food stores. They will keep for up to 3 months in the refrigerator.

prawn laksa

✺ ✺

Preparation time: 30 minutes
Cooking time: 35 minutes
Serves 4–6

750 g (1 lb 10 oz) raw prawns (shrimp)
1½ tablespoons coriander seeds
1 tablespoon cumin seeds
1 teaspoon ground turmeric
1 onion, roughly chopped
2 teaspoons roughly chopped
   fresh ginger
3 garlic cloves
3 lemongrass stems, white part only,
   sliced
6 candlenuts or macadamia nuts, roughly
   chopped

fish balls

These are small round balls made of finely minced fish, crab, prawns (shrimp) or scallops, and seasonings, bound with cornflour (cornstarch) or egg white, then kneaded, formed into balls and cooked. They are added to soups and braised dishes. Available ready-made from Asian food stores, they should be stored in the refrigerator and used within three days of purchase, or frozen.

4–6 small red chillies, roughly chopped
2–3 teaspoons shrimp paste
1 litre (35 fl oz/4 cups) chicken stock
60 ml (2 fl oz/¼ cup) vegetable oil
750 ml (26 fl oz/3 cups) coconut milk
4 kaffir lime (makrut) leaves
2½ tablespoons lime juice
2 tablespoons fish sauce
2 tablespoons grated palm sugar (jaggery)
   or soft brown sugar
250 g (9 oz) dried rice vermicelli
90 g (3¼ oz/1 cup) bean sprouts, trimmed
4 fried tofu puffs, cut into thin strips
3 tablespoons chopped Vietnamese mint
1 small handful coriander (cilantro) leaves
lime wedges, to serve

1 Peel the prawns, leaving the tails intact. Gently pull out the dark vein from each prawn back, starting at the head end. Dry-fry the coriander seeds in a small frying pan over medium heat for 1–2 minutes, or until aromatic, tossing constantly. Grind finely using a mortar and pestle or spice grinder. Repeat the process with the cumin seeds.
2 Put the ground coriander and cumin, turmeric, onion, ginger, garlic, lemongrass, candlenuts, chilli and shrimp paste in a food processor or blender. Add 125 ml (4 fl oz/½ cup) of the stock and blend to a fine paste. Heat a wok over low heat, add the oil and swirl to coat the base and side.

Cook the paste for 3–5 minutes, stirring constantly. Pour in the remaining stock and bring to the boil, then reduce the heat and simmer for 15 minutes, or until reduced slightly. Add the coconut milk, lime leaves, lime juice, fish sauce and palm sugar and simmer for 5 minutes. Add the prawns and simmer for 2 minutes, or until pink and cooked. Do not boil or cover.
3 Meanwhile, soak the vermicelli in boiling water for 5 minutes, or until soft. Drain well and divide among serving bowls along with most of the sprouts. Ladle on the hot soup then top with the tofu, mint, coriander and the remaining sprouts. Serve with lime wedges.

barbecued seafood

✷

Preparation time: **35 minutes**
Cooking time: **10 minutes**
Serves 4

4 squid tubes
2 boneless firm white fish fillets,
    each about 300 g (10½ oz)
8 raw king prawns (shrimp)
banana leaves, to serve
lime cheeks, to serve

SPICE PASTE
1 onion, grated
4 garlic cloves, chopped
5 cm (2 inch) piece fresh ginger, grated
3 lemongrass stems, white part only,
    chopped
2 teaspoons ground turmeric
1 teaspoon dried shrimp paste
80 ml (2½ fl oz/⅓ cup) oil

1 To make the spice paste, combine all the ingredients and ¼ teaspoon salt in a food processor or blender. Process in short bursts until a smooth paste forms.
2 Cut the squid in half lengthways. Hold a sharp knife at a slight angle and make shallow, close cuts in one direction across the underside of each piece, then cut in the opposite direction, taking care not to cut all the way through. Then cut the squid into pieces about 3 x 4 cm (1¼ x 1½ inches).
3 Wash all the seafood under cold running water and pat dry with paper towels. Brush the seafood lightly with the spice paste. Place the seafood on a tray and allow to stand for 15 minutes.
4 Lightly brush a barbecue hotplate with oil and heat gently. When the plate is hot, arrange the fish fillets and prawns side by side on the plate. Cook for about 3 minutes on each side, turning them once only, or until the fish flesh is just firm and the prawns turn bright pink to orange. Add squid pieces and cook for about 2 minutes or until the flesh turns

Process all the ingredients for the spice paste until smooth.

Score a fine honeycomb pattern into the soft underside of the squid.

white and becomes firm. Take care not to overcook the seafood.

5 Arrange seafood on a platter lined with banana leaves, add lime slices and serve.

spicy prawns in sarongs

☀

Preparation time: 30 minutes + 2 hours
    marinating time
Cooking time: 5 minutes
Serves 4 as an entrée

500 g (1 lb 2 oz) raw king prawns (shrimp)
1 tablespoon lime juice
2 teaspoons grated palm sugar (jaggery)
    or soft brown sugar

80 ml (2½ fl oz/⅓ cup) coconut milk
2 cm (¾ inch) wide strips of banana leaf
    (see Note), to wrap around each prawn
sweet chilli sauce (optional), to serve

SPICE PASTE
6 red Asian shallots, finely chopped
6 garlic cloves, crushed
3 candlenuts
2 teaspoons finely chopped fresh galangal
4 red chillies, seeded and finely chopped
1 teaspoon ground turmeric
1 teaspoon shrimp paste

1 To make the spice paste, place all the ingredients in a food processor or blender. Process until a rough-textured paste forms.
2 Peel the prawns and gently pull out the dark vein from each prawn back, starting at the head end. Place the prawns in a non-metallic bowl and sprinkle with the lime juice and ¼ teaspoon salt. Add the palm sugar and coconut milk and then stir through the spice paste. Combine well, cover and place in the refrigerator to marinate for 2 hours.
3 Preheat the grill (broiler) to as hot as it will go. Tie a strip of banana leaf around each prawn and cook under the hot grill for about 2 minutes on each side or until the prawns are cooked. Serve with sweet chilli sauce, if desired.

NOTE: Banana leaves are available from speciality fruit and vegetable shops or from a friend who has a banana tree!

coconut milk

Coconut milk is fundamental to Asian cooking and is made not from the liquid inside the coconut, but from the juice of the grated and pressed coconut flesh. The first extraction, which is the coconut cream, is very thick; the milk comes from a second pressing. Coconut milk is available in cans, tetra packs, or in powdered form.

malaysian fish curry

✳

Preparation time: 25 minutes
Cooking time: 25 minutes
Serves 4

1 tablespoon oil
1 tablespoon fish curry powder
250 ml (9 fl oz/1 cup) coconut milk
1 tablespoon tamarind concentrate

1 tablespoon kecap manis
350 g (12 oz) firm white fish fillets,
    cut into bite-sized pieces
2 ripe tomatoes, chopped
1 tablespoon lemon juice
steamed rice, to serve

SPICE PASTE
3–6 medium red chillies
1 onion, chopped
4 garlic cloves

3 lemongrass stems, white part only,
    sliced
4 cm (1½ inch) piece fresh ginger, sliced
2 teaspoons shrimp paste
1–2 tablespoons oil

1 To make the spice paste, put the
chillies, onion, garlic, lemongrass, ginger
and shrimp paste in a food processor and
roughly chop. Add enough oil to assist the
blending and process until a smooth paste
forms, regularly scraping down the sides
of the bowl with a spatula.
2 Heat the oil in a wok or heavy frying
pan; add the spice paste and stir for
3–4 minutes over low heat, until very
fragrant. Add the curry powder and stir
for another 2 minutes.
3 Add the coconut milk, 250 ml
(9 fl oz/1 cup) water, tamarind and
kecap manis. Bring to the boil, stirring
occasionally, then reduce the heat and
simmer for 10 minutes. Add the fish,
tomato and lemon juice and season to
taste with salt and pepper. Simmer for
about 5 minutes or until the fish is just
cooked. Serve with the steamed rice.

malaysian rendang

✳

Preparation time: 20 minutes
Cooking time: 1 hour 40 minutes
Serves 4–6

2 onions, chopped
4 garlic cloves, crushed
5 red chillies, seeded
1 tablespoon finely grated fresh ginger
500 ml (17 fl oz/2 cups) coconut milk
1 tablespoon oil
1 tablespoon ground coriander
1 tablespoon ground cumin
1 teaspoon ground turmeric
1 teaspoon ground cinnamon
¼ teaspoon ground cloves
¼ teaspoon chilli powder
1 large strip lemon zest
1 kg (2 lb 4 oz) chuck or skirt steak,
    cubed
1 tablespoon lemon juice

malaysian fish curry

fish curry powder

Fish curry powder is a blend of coriander, cumin,
fennel seeds, turmeric, peppercorns and chillies,
particularly suitable for using in fish curries.
Specific curry powders such as this one are
usually only found in Asian food stores. If fish

curry powder is not available, simply use a freshly
ground mixture of the spices above. Avoid curry
powders that are sold in cardboard packaging as
the packaging tends to absorb the flavour and
the aroma of the spice blend.

1 tablespoon soft brown sugar
1 teaspoon tamarind concentrate
steamed rice, to serve

1 Place the onion, garlic, chillies, ginger
and 2 tablespoons of the coconut milk in a
food processor, and process until a smooth
paste has formed.
2 Heat the oil in a large saucepan,
add the paste, coriander, cumin, turmeric,
cinnamon, cloves, chilli powder, lemon
zest and beef and stir until the beef is
well coated with the spice mixture. Add
the remaining coconut milk and bring
to the boil, then simmer over low heat,
stirring occasionally, for 1½ hours, or until
the beef is tender and the mixture
is almost dry.
3 When the oil starts to separate from
the gravy, add the lemon juice, sugar and
tamarind; stir until heated through.
Serve with the steamed rice.

NOTE: This recipe produces a 'dry' curry
which does not have much liquid. The
spicy flavours are absorbed by the beef as
it cooks. It tastes even better if it is made
a day in advance.

chicken kapitan

☀

Preparation time: 35 minutes
Cooking time: 30 minutes
Serves 4–6

30 g (1 oz) dried shrimp
80 ml (2½ fl oz/⅓ cup) oil
4–8 red chillies, seeded and finely chopped
4 garlic cloves, finely chopped
3 lemongrass stems, white part only,
    finely chopped
2 teaspoons ground turmeric
10 candlenuts
2 large onions, chopped
500 g (1 lb 2 oz) boneless, skinless chicken
    thighs, chopped
250 ml (9 fl oz/1 cup) coconut milk
125 ml (4 fl oz/½ cup) coconut cream
2 tablespoons lime juice
steamed rice, to serve

chicken kapitan

1 Put the shrimp in a clean frying pan
and dry-fry over low heat, shaking the
pan regularly, for 3 minutes, or until the
shrimp are dark orange and are giving
off a strong aroma. Transfer the shrimp
to a mortar and pound with a pestle until
finely ground. Set aside.
2 Put half the oil with the chilli, garlic,
lemongrass, turmeric and candlenuts in
a food processor and process in short
bursts until very finely chopped, regularly
scraping down the sides of the bowl with
a rubber spatula.
3 Heat the remaining oil in a wok or
frying pan, add the onion and
¼ teaspoon salt and cook over low heat
for 8 minutes, or until golden, stirring
regularly. Take care not to let the onion
burn. Add the spice mixture and nearly
all of the ground shrimp meat, setting a

little aside to use as a garnish. Stir
for 5 minutes. If the mixture begins
to stick to the bottom of the pan, add
2 tablespoons of the coconut milk to the
mixture. It is important to cook the
mixture thoroughly to fully develop
the flavours.
4 Add the chicken to the wok and stir
well. Cook for 5 minutes, or until the
chicken begins to brown. Stir in the
remaining coconut milk and 250 ml
(9 fl oz/1 cup) water, and bring to the
boil. Reduce the heat and simmer for
7 minutes, or until the chicken is cooked
and the sauce is thick. Add the coconut
cream and bring the mixture back to the
boil, stirring constantly. Add the lime juice
and serve immediately, sprinkled lightly
with the reserved ground shrimp meat.
Serve with the steamed rice.

spicy eggs and snake beans

or until the mixture is heated through. Serve with the steamed rice.

NOTE: Use any combination of mushrooms up to the weight given. Some suitable mushrooms are button, oyster, shiitake or enoki.

crunchy stuffed tofu puffs

※

Preparation time: 30 minutes
Cooking time: 5 minutes
Serves 6–8

12 deep-fried tofu puffs (see Note)
90 g (3¼ oz/1 cup) bean sprouts, trimmed
40 g (1½ oz/¼ cup) roasted peanuts, chopped
1 carrot, grated
1 tablespoon chopped coriander (cilantro) leaves

CHILLI SAUCE
2 small red chillies, finely chopped
2 garlic cloves, crushed
2 teaspoons soft brown sugar
1 tablespoon soy sauce
1 tablespoon white vinegar
125 ml (4 fl oz/½ cup) boiling water

1 To make the chilli sauce, combine all the ingredients in a small saucepan, bring to the boil, reduce the heat and simmer for 5 minutes, or until the sauce thickens slightly.
2 Cut the tofu puffs in half. Cut a small slit in each half and open it up carefully to form a pocket.
3 Place the bean sprouts, peanuts, carrot and coriander in a bowl, and toss until well mixed. Fill each pocket with a portion of the mixture. Serve drizzled with a little chilli sauce, and offer the rest of the sauce for dipping.

NOTE: Tofu puffs are cubes of tofu that have been deep-fried and are puffed and golden. They are available from Asian food stores.

spicy eggs and snake beans

※

Preparation time: 20 minutes
Cooking time: 10 minutes
Serves 4

4 spring onions (scallions)
300 g (10½ oz) snake (yard-long) beans, trimmed
1 teaspoon sesame oil
1 tablespoon oil
2 garlic cloves, crushed
200 g (7 oz) mixed mushrooms (see Note)
8 eggs, lightly beaten
1 tablespoon kecap manis
2 teaspoons sambal oelek

3 tablespoons chopped mint
3 tablespoons chopped coriander (cilantro) leaves
steamed rice, to serve

1 Chop the spring onions. Cut the snake beans into 5 cm (2 inch) lengths. Heat the combined oils in a wok or large frying pan, add the garlic and spring onion and cook over moderately high heat for 2 minutes.
2 Add the beans and mushrooms and stir-fry for 1 minute. Remove from the wok. Add the combined eggs, kecap manis, sambal oelek, mint and coriander to the centre of the wok. Allow to set for 2 minutes.
3 Return the vegetables to the wok and stir-fry, breaking up the egg, for 2 minutes

nonya lime chicken

✳ ✳

Preparation time: 20 minutes
Cooking time: 25 minutes
Serves 4–6

60 ml (2 fl oz/¼ cup) vegetable oil
1 kg (2 lb 4 oz) boneless, skinless chicken
   thighs, cut into 3 cm (1¼ inch) cubes
400 ml (14 fl oz) coconut milk
1 teaspoon finely grated lime zest
125 ml (4 fl oz/½ cup) lime juice
6 kaffir lime (makrut) leaves, finely
   shredded, plus extra, to garnish
2 tablespoons tamarind purée
steamed rice, to serve

CURRY PASTE
70 g (2½ oz/⅔ cup) red Asian shallots
4 garlic cloves
2 lemongrass stems, white part only,
   chopped
2 teaspoons finely chopped fresh galangal
1 teaspoon ground turmeric
2 tablespoons sambal oelek
1 tablespoon shrimp paste

1 Combine all the curry paste ingredients
in a food processor or blender and blend
until a smooth paste forms.
2 Heat a non-stick wok until very hot,
add the oil and swirl to coat the base
and side. Add the curry paste and stir-fry
for 1–2 minutes, or until aromatic. Add
the chicken and stir-fry for 5 minutes,
or until browned. Add the coconut milk,
lime zest and juice, lime leaves and
tamarind purée.
3 Reduce the heat and simmer for
15 minutes, or until the chicken is cooked
and the sauce has reduced and thickened
slightly. Season well with salt. Serve
with the steamed rice and garnish
with the extra lime leaves.

nonya food

Nonya food is a mixture of Chinese ingredients with Malay spices and flavourings. The blending of the two cuisines evolved because Chinese merchants who settled in trading centres on the Straits of Malacca (Penang, Malacca and Singapore) were unable to bring Chinese women with them, so they married Malay wives. Nonya recipes are hot and spicy and often based on a rempah, a paste of hot chillies, shallots, lemongrass, candlenuts, galangal and turmeric. Coconut, unused in China, is an ingredient in many dishes, such as laksa, and the creamy coconut gravies of the Malacca region. To the north, around Penang, Nonya cooking shows Thai influences in the use of lime and tamarind.

fish and
herb salad

✷ ✷

Preparation time: 40 minutes
Cooking time: 15 minutes
Serves 4–6

500 g (1 lb 2 oz) smoked cod
60 ml (2 fl oz/¼ cup) lime juice
30 g (1 oz/½ cup) flaked coconut
200 g (7 oz/1 cup) jasmine rice,
    cooked and cooled

25 g (1 oz) Vietnamese mint,
    chopped
3 tablespoons chopped mint
25 g (1 oz/½ cup) chopped coriander
    (cilantro) leaves
8 kaffir lime (makrut) leaves,
    very finely shredded

DRESSING
1 tablespoon chopped coriander
    (cilantro) root
2 cm (¾ inch) piece fresh ginger, finely
    grated
1 red chilli, finely chopped

1 tablespoon chopped lemongrass, white
    part only
3 tablespoons chopped Thai basil
1 avocado, chopped
80 ml (2½ fl oz/⅓ cup) lime juice
2 tablespoons fish sauce
1 teaspoon soft brown sugar
125 ml (4 fl oz/½ cup) peanut oil

1 Preheat the oven to 150°C (300°F/
Gas 2). Put the cod in a large frying pan
and cover with water. Add the lime juice
and simmer for 15 minutes, or until
the fish flakes when tested with a fork.
Drain and set aside to cool slightly before
breaking it into bite-sized pieces.
2 Meanwhile, spread the coconut onto
a baking tray and toast in the oven for
10 minutes, or until golden brown,
shaking the tray occasionally. Remove
the coconut from the tray immediately
to prevent it burning.
3 Put the fish, coconut, rice, Vietnamese
mint, mint, coriander and lime leaves in a
large bowl and mix to combine.
4 To make the dressing, put the
coriander root, ginger, chilli, lemongrass
and basil in a food processor and process
until combined. Add the avocado, lime
juice, fish sauce, sugar and peanut oil and
process until creamy. Pour the dressing
over the salad and toss to coat the rice
and fish. Serve immediately.

singapore
spare ribs

✷

Preparation time: 20 minutes + 4 hours
    marinating time
Cooking time: 50 minutes
Serves 6

2 teaspoons sesame oil
1 teaspoon finely chopped fresh ginger
3 garlic cloves, crushed
2 tablespoons soy sauce
2 tablespoons shaoxing rice wine (Chinese
    rice wine)
½ teaspoon five-spice

fish and herb salad

chinese food in singapore

The food of Singapore, while sharing a similar heritage to Malaysia, also reflects the strong influence of the island's now predominantly Chinese population. Singapore–Chinese food is mostly Cantonese-style, with chicken, seafood and vegetables in clear sauces — a hint of chilli, tamarind and shrimp paste give it a Singaporean touch. Pork is popular, in contrast to largely Muslim Malaysia (converted to Islam in the early fifteenth century), where it is not eaten.

2 tablespoons honey

1 teaspoon sambal oelek

1.5 kg (3 lb 5 oz) pork spare ribs, cut into individual ribs (ask your butcher to do this), trimmed of excess fat

1 tablespoon snipped garlic chives

2 lemons, cut into wedges, to serve

steamed rice, to serve

1 Combine the sesame oil, ginger, garlic, soy sauce, rice wine, five-spice, honey, sambal oelek and ½ teaspoon salt in a large non-metallic bowl. Mix well.

2 Add the pork spare ribs and stir until the ribs are totally coated in the marinade. Cover and refrigerate for at least 4 hours or overnight so they absorb the flavour of the marinade.

3 Preheat the oven to 180°C (350°F/ Gas 4). Place the ribs and marinade into an oiled baking dish and cook for 50 minutes, turning and basting with pan juices every 15 minutes. If the marinade begins to burn, add a few tablespoons of warm water to the dish during cooking.

4 Scatter the garlic chives over the spare ribs and serve with the wedges of lemon and steamed rice.

NOTE: Line the baking dish with thick foil to make the washing-up easier.

the philippines

The 7000 islands of the Philippines owe much of their exciting cuisine to the sea that surrounds them. An abundance of fresh fish is hauled to shore daily in wooden outriggers and cooked in clay pots; Chinese merchants arriving by sea brought spring rolls and sticky noodles; while the Spanish, who colonised and later named the islands after their king, introduced foods such as spicy chorizo and empanadas. Filipino cooking often has a tart sharpness, with its meats and fish being marinated in vinegar or citrus fruit.

bagoong

Bagoong is a form of shrimp paste used mainly in the Philippines. The shrimps are salted and fermented in earthenware pots rather than being dried, as in other parts of Asia, and the paste has a runnier consistency.

prawn fritters

☀

Preparation time: 30 minutes
Cooking time: 15 minutes
Serves 4–6

300 g (10½ oz) raw prawns
   (shrimp)
50 g (1¾ oz) dried rice vermicelli
1 egg
1 tablespoon fish sauce
125 g (4½ oz/1 cup) plain
   (all-purpose) flour
¼ teaspoon bagoong

3 spring onions (scallions), sliced
1 small red chilli, finely chopped
oil, for deep-frying
sweet chilli sauce, to serve

1 Peel the prawns and gently pull out the dark vein from each prawn back, starting at the head end. Place half the prawns in a food processor and process until smooth. Chop the remaining prawns, place them in a bowl with the processed prawns and mix to combine.

2 Soak the vermicelli in boiling water for 5 minutes, or until soft. Drain well and cut into short lengths.

3 In a small jug, beat the egg, 185 ml (6 fl oz/¾ cup) water and the fish sauce. Sift the flour into a bowl; make a well in the centre, gradually add the egg mixture and stir until smooth.

4 Add the prawn mixture, bagoong, spring onion, chilli and vermicelli to the bowl and mix to combine.

5 Heat the oil in a large saucepan or wok; add tablespoons of the mixture to the pan and deep-fry for 3 minutes, or until the fritters are crisp and golden. Drain on paper towels. Repeat with the remaining mixture. Serve with the sweet chilli sauce.

rice with chicken and seafood

✳ ✳

Preparation time: 30 minutes
Cooking time: 1 hour 5 minutes
Serves 4–6

500 g (1 lb 2 oz) black mussels
200 g (7 oz) squid tubes
500 g (1 lb 2 oz) raw prawns (shrimp)
¼ teaspoon saffron threads
2 tablespoons boiling water
4 large tomatoes
3 tablespoons oil
2 chorizo sausages, thickly sliced
500 g (1 lb 2 oz) chicken pieces
300 g (10½ oz) pork fillet, thickly sliced
4 garlic cloves, crushed
2 red onions, chopped
¼ teaspoon ground turmeric
440 g (15½ oz/2 cups) medium-grain rice
1.25 litres (44 fl oz/5 cups) chicken stock
125 g (4½ oz) green beans, trimmed, cut
    into 4 cm (1½ inch) lengths
1 red capsicum (pepper), cut into
    thin strips
155 g (5½ oz/1 cup) peas

1   Scrub the mussels thoroughly and remove the hairy beards. Cut the squid tubes into ½ cm (¼ inch) thick slices. Peel the prawns, leaving the tails intact. Gently pull out the dark vein from each prawn back, starting at the head end. Soak the saffron threads in the boiling water for 15 minutes.
2   Score a cross in the base of each tomato, place in a heatproof bowl, cover with boiling water and leave for 2 minutes. Plunge into cold water and then peel the skin away from the cross. Cut the tomatoes in half horizontally, scoop out the seeds with a teaspoon and chop the flesh.
3   Heat 1 tablespoon of the oil in a large, heavy-based saucepan; add the chorizo slices and cook over medium heat for 5 minutes, or until browned. Drain on paper towels. Add the chicken pieces to the pan and cook for 5 minutes, or until

golden, turning once. Drain on paper towels. Add the pork to the pan and cook for 3 minutes, or until browned, turning once. Drain on paper towels.
4   Heat the remaining oil in the pan; add the garlic, onion, saffron and soaking liquid and turmeric, and cook over medium heat for 3 minutes or until the onion is golden. Add the tomato and cook for 3 minutes or until soft. Add the

rice and stir for 5 minutes, or until the rice is translucent. Stir in the stock and bring to the boil; cover and simmer for 10 minutes.
5   Return the chicken pieces to the pan, cover and continue cooking for 20 minutes. Add the pork, prawns, mussels, squid, chorizo and vegetables; cover and cook for 10 minutes or until the liquid has been absorbed.

Drain the browned chorizo slices on paper towels.

Cook the pork slices until they are browned, turning once.

combination noodles with chorizo

☀ ☀

Preparation time: 25 minutes + 30 minutes
    drying time
Cooking time: 35 minutes
Serves 6

500 g (1 lb 2 oz) thin fresh egg noodles
500 g (1 lb 2 oz) raw prawns (shrimp)
3 tablespoons oil
4 garlic cloves, crushed
6 spring onions (scallions), thinly sliced
175 g (6 oz/1 cup) shredded cooked
    chicken
250 g (9 oz) chorizo sausage, sliced
75 g (2¾ oz/1 cup) shredded cabbage

3 tablespoons soy sauce
3 tablespoons coriander (cilantro)
    leaves
lemon wedges, to serve

1 Fill a large saucepan with salted water and bring it to the boil. Cook the noodles for 5 minutes or until tender. Rinse under cold water, drain and spread in a single layer on paper towels. Allow to dry for 30 minutes.

2 Peel the prawns, reserving the heads, tails and shells. Gently pull out the dark vein from each prawn back, starting at the head end. Dry-fry the prawn heads, tails and shells in a frying pan for about 5 minutes, until they turn bright orange. Add 250 ml (9 fl oz/1 cup) water to the pan, bring to the boil, reduce the heat slightly and cook until the liquid has reduced to about a quarter. Add another 125 ml (4 fl oz/½ cup) water, bring to the boil, then reduce the heat and simmer for 3 minutes. Strain the liquid and set it aside, discarding all the prawn heads, tails and shells.

3 Heat 1 tablespoon of the oil in a large wok. When the oil is very hot add a quarter of the noodles and fry until golden all over, turning when necessary. Remove the noodles from the wok and repeat three times with the remaining noodles, adding more oil when necessary.

4 Add another tablespoon of the oil and fry the garlic and spring onion over low heat until soft; remove from the wok. Add the prawns and chicken and fry until golden; remove from the wok. Add the chorizo and cook until brown. Add the cabbage, soy sauce and prawn cooking liquid, and cook over high heat, stirring all the time until the liquid has reduced by a third.

5 Return the noodles to the wok with the garlic, spring onion, chicken and prawns. Toss well until heated through. Season with salt and pepper, scatter over the coriander and serve immediately with the lemon wedges.

The chorizo used in the recipe on the opposite page gives an indication of the long-lasting impact the Spanish made on the people of the Philippines. Many of the traditional Spanish dishes they introduced — such as paella and empanadas — are popular to this day.

beef pot roast

✳ ✳

Preparation time: **15 minutes**
Cooking time: **3 hours**
Serves **6**

75 g (2½ oz) pork fat
1.5 kg (3 lb 5 oz) topside beef
3 onions, quartered
4 tomatoes, quartered
125 ml (4 fl oz/½ cup) white vinegar
2 tablespoons soy sauce
2 bay leaves
3 potatoes, peeled, halved lengthwise and thickly sliced
3 sweet potatoes, peeled, halved lengthwise and thickly sliced

1 Cut the pork fat into thin slivers. Use a sharp knife to make deep cuts evenly over the beef and then insert a sliver of the pork fat into each cut.

2 Place the beef in a large saucepan with a tight-fitting lid. Add the onion, tomato, vinegar, soy sauce and bay leaves. Bring the liquid to the boil, then reduce the heat to a gentle simmer, cover and cook for 2 hours, until the beef is tender. Season with salt and pepper. Remove the lid and simmer for a further 30 minutes.

3 Add the potato and sweet potato and simmer, uncovered, until tender. Remove the pan from the heat and remove the beef from the pan. Cut the beef into thin slices, drizzle with the gravy and serve with the potato and sweet potato. Garnish with the coriander and serve.

NOTE: Pork fat is available from butchers. If unavailable, lard can be used instead.

oxtail and vegetable stew

✳

Preparation time: **20 minutes**
Cooking time: **2 hours 15 minutes**
Serves **6**

1.5 kg (3 lb 5 oz) oxtail, cut into 2 cm
  (¾ inch) lengths (ask your butcher
  to do this)
60 g (2¼ oz/¼ cup) lard
2 tablespoons annatto seeds
  (see Note)
4 garlic cloves, crushed
2 onions, finely sliced
1 bay leaf
1 tablespoon soy sauce
2 tablespoons fish sauce
2 turnips, chopped
250 g (9 oz/2 cups) trimmed, sliced
  green beans
2 slender eggplants (aubergines), sliced
2 large sweet potatoes, peeled and chopped
110 g (3¾ oz/½ cup) medium- or long-grain
  rice
80 g (2¾ oz/½ cup) unsalted raw
  peanuts

1 Place the oxtail pieces into a large heatproof bowl, cover with salted boiling water and leave to stand for 5 minutes; remove and pat dry with paper towels.
2 Heat the lard in a large frying pan, add the annatto seeds and cook over medium heat until the lard turns red. Add the garlic and onion to the pan and cook for 5 minutes. Remove the garlic and onion mixture from the pan with a slotted spoon and drain on paper towels.
3 Heat a large deep saucepan, add the meat in batches and cook over medium heat for 5 minutes, or until brown on both sides. Return all the meat to the pan and add the onion and garlic mixture, 1.5 litres (52 fl oz/6 cups) water, the bay leaf, soy sauce and fish sauce. Bring to the boil, reduce the heat, cover and simmer for 1½ hours. Add the vegetables and simmer, covered, for 20 minutes, or until tender.

oxtail and vegetable stew

4 Meanwhile, preheat the oven to 180°C (350°F/Gas 4). Spread the rice on a baking tray and roast for 15 minutes or until golden. Spread the peanuts on a baking tray and roast for 5 minutes or until lightly browned. Remove from the oven, cool slightly and process both in a food processor until the mixture resembles fine breadcrumbs. Sift the mixture to remove any large pieces, then add it to the stew and stir until the sauce thickens.

NOTE: If annatto seeds are unavailable, substitute 1 tablespoon of paprika combined with ½ teaspoon turmeric. The annatto seeds can be left in the dish but they are too hard to eat.

fish with ginger and black pepper

✳

Preparation time: **10 minutes**
Cooking time: **35 minutes**
Serves **4**

2 whole firm white fish (such as snapper or
  bream), each about 500 g (1 lb 2 oz),
  cleaned and scaled
4 cm (1½ inch) piece fresh ginger, sliced
3 tablespoons oil
4 tablespoons finely chopped fresh ginger,
  extra
½ red onion, thinly sliced

1 tablespoon coriander (cilantro) leaves,
   to garnish
1 tablespoon thinly sliced spring onion
   (scallions), to garnish
steamed rice, to serve

1 Preheat the oven to 180°C (350°F/
Gas 4). Wash fish inside and out and pat
dry. Place the ginger slices inside the fish.
2 Heat the oil in a wok; add the chopped
ginger and cook over low heat for
1–2 minutes, or until soft and aromatic.
Stir in 1 teaspoon pepper.
3 Place the fish in a baking dish, scatter
over ½ teaspoon salt and pour in 250 ml
(9 fl oz/1 cup) water. Place onion slices
over the fish, cover the dish and bake for
approximately 30 minutes or until the fish
flakes when tested with a fork.
4 Carefully lift out the fish and place
it on a serving platter. Scatter over the
coriander and spring onion. Pour the
ginger mixture around the fish and serve
with the steamed rice.

chicken adobo

✳ ✳

Preparation time: 20 minutes + 2 hours
   marinating time
Cooking time: 1 hour
Serves 6

6 garlic cloves, crushed
250 ml (9 fl oz/1 cup) cider vinegar
375 ml (13 fl oz/1½ cups) chicken stock
1 bay leaf
1 teaspoon coriander seeds
1 teaspoon black peppercorns
1 teaspoon annatto seeds
3 tablespoons soy sauce
1.5 kg (3 lb 5 oz) chicken pieces
2 tablespoons oil
steamed rice, to serve
kaffir lime (makrut) leaves, to serve

1 Combine the garlic, vinegar, stock, bay
leaf, coriander seeds, black peppercorns,
annatto seeds and soy sauce in a large
bowl. Add the chicken, cover and leave to
marinate in the refrigerator for 2 hours.

2 Transfer the chicken mixture to a large
heavy-based saucepan and bring to the
boil. Reduce the heat, cover and simmer
for 30 minutes. Remove the lid from the
pan and continue cooking for 10 minutes,
or until the chicken is tender. Remove the
chicken from the pan and set aside. Bring
the liquid to the boil again and cook over

high heat for 10 minutes, or until the
liquid is reduced by half.
3 Heat the oil in a wok or large frying
pan, add the chicken in batches and cook
over medium heat for 5 minutes, or until
crisp and brown. Pour the reduced stock
mixture over the chicken, garnish with
lime leaves and serve with steamed rice.

chicken adobo

annatto seeds

Also known as achuete, these small red-brown
seeds are used in Filipino cooking for their strong
colour. They come from a small flowering tree
native to Central and South America, which
was introduced into the Philippines by Spanish
traders. Annatto seeds are also used by the
Chinese to colour barbecued pork.

rice

As the staple of all Asian cuisines, this grain is of huge importance — in Thailand an invitation to a meal is 'kin khao', literally 'come and eat rice'.

cooking methods

rapid boiling

Bring a large saucepan of water to a fast boil. The quantity of water should be six times the quantity of rice. Add the rice and cook, uncovered, for 12–15 minutes, or until the swollen grains are tender and opaque. Drain.

absorption

The most common method of cooking rice throughout Asia, it is easy to obtain good results if the water to rice ratio is correct. A quick and easy method is to place the quantity of rice required in a large saucepan and add enough water to reach the first joint of your index finger when the tip is on the top of the rice. For a more accurate measure, add 500 ml (17 fl oz/2 cups) water for the first 200 g (7 oz/1 cup) long-grain rice and 375 ml (13 fl oz/1½ cups) water for each additional 200 g of rice. For short-/medium-grain rice, add 375 ml water for the first 200 g rice and 250 ml (9 fl oz/1 cup) for each additional 200g of rice.
saucepan: Wash rice in a sieve until the water runs clear; place in a large saucepan with the water, bring to the boil and boil for 1 minute. Cover with a tight-fitting lid, then reduce the heat to as low as possible and cook for 10–15 minutes, or until all the water has been absorbed and the rice is tender. Steam tunnels will form holes on the surface. Turn off the heat and leave the pan, covered, for at least 10 minutes. Fluff the rice with a fork.
electric rice cooker: This appliance steams rice in the same way as the absorption method and is ideal for making large quantities. Wash rice in a sieve until the water runs clear, drain and add to the rice cooker with water. Follow the manufacturer's instructions for cooking times.

rice varieties

long-grain

Cultivated throughout Southeast Asia, this long slender grain is the favoured rice of the Chinese. When cooked, the grains separate easily and are non-starchy: perfect for fried rice.

jasmine

Originating in Thailand, this variety of long-grain rice is now popular throughout Southeast Asia. It is a lightly aromatic rice that goes well with all kinds of Asian dishes.

basmati

This aromatic, narrow, long-grain rice is grown in the foothills of the Himalayas. It is traditionally used for biryani and pilau dishes that utilise the firm texture of the cooked basmati rice.

short-/medium-grain

These small oval grains, which are high in starch, are preferred by the Japanese and Koreans. Best cooked by the absorption method, this rice is slightly sticky.

glutinous

white glutinous: This is the staple rice of the Laotians and northern Thais who use it as an accompaniment to savoury dishes. However, its main use is for leaf-wrapped snacks or Asian desserts. The grains are short and turn translucent when cooked. Ill-named because it contains no gluten, it has a high starch content and is commonly called 'sticky rice' or 'sweet rice'.
black glutinous: The layer of bran is left on this rice, giving it a dark colour, and it has a nutty flavour. It combines well with palm sugar (jaggery), coconut milk and sesame seeds, and is a popular dessert rice in Burma, Thailand, Indonesia and the Philippines. For best results, the rice should be soaked overnight.

prawn crepes

✵ ✵

Preparation time: 1 hour
Cooking time: 20 minutes
Serves 4–6

5 eggs
2 tablespoons oil
60 g (2¼ oz/½ cup) cornflour (cornstarch)
60 g (2¼ oz/½ cup) plain (all-purpose) flour
oil, extra, for brushing
lime wedges, to serve

PRAWN FILLING
500 g (1 lb 2 oz) raw prawns (shrimp)
1 tablespoon oil
300 g (10½ oz) tinned bamboo shoots, cut
    into matchsticks
90 g (3¼ oz/1 cup) bean sprouts, trimmed
80 g (2¾ oz/½ cup) unsalted roasted
    peanuts, roughly chopped
½ iceberg lettuce, shredded
30 g (1 oz/1 cup) coriander (cilantro) leaves

1 Beat the eggs, 375 ml (13 fl oz/ 1½ cups) water and oil in a bowl until combined. Whisk in the cornflour and plain flour and beat the batter until smooth. Cover and set aside for 20 minutes.
2 Brush a small non-stick frying pan or crepe pan with oil, heat over low heat, add 2 tablespoons of the batter and swirl the pan to ensure the base has a very thin covering of batter; pour any excess batter back into the bowl. Cook the crepe for 2 minutes or until lightly golden. Turn and cook the other side for 2 minutes. Repeat with the remaining batter.
3 To make the prawn filling, peel the prawns and gently pull out the dark vein from each prawn back, starting at the head end. Cut the prawns in half lengthways if large. Heat the oil in a non-stick frying pan; add the prawns and cook over medium heat for 3 minutes or until they are bright pink. Arrange the prawns, bamboo shoots, bean sprouts, peanuts, lettuce and coriander on a platter.
4 On each crepe place a little shredded lettuce, a few coriander leaves, prawns, bamboo shoots, bean sprouts and peanuts; fold in the sides and roll up the crepe to enclose the mixture. Serve with the lime wedges.

Drain the bamboo shoots and cut them into matchsticks.

Fold in the sides and roll up the crepe to enclose the mixture.

sour beef soup

✵ ✵

Preparation time: 30 minutes
Cooking time: 2 hours 30 minutes
Serves 6

500 g (1 lb 2 oz) chicken bones
500 g (1 lb 2 oz) lean stewing beef
250 g (9 oz) pork chops, fat removed
1 onion, finely diced
2 tomatoes, diced
1 tablespoon dried tamarind pulp
250 g (9 oz) sweet potato, peeled and
    cut into chunks
1 large daikon, thinly sliced
90 g (3¼ oz/2 cups) shredded Chinese
    cabbage (wong bok)
1 tablespoon fish sauce
1 lime, cut into wedges, to serve

1 Place chicken bones, beef, pork chops and 2.5 litres (87 fl oz/10 cups) water in a large saucepan. Stir in the onion, tomato and 1 teaspoon salt. Bring to the boil, then cover and simmer for 2 hours. Remove the chicken bones, beef and pork. Allow the beef and pork to cool and discard the chicken bones.

2 Pour 2 tablespoons boiling water over the tamarind pulp and soak it for 10 minutes. Stir and press the tamarind pulp with a spoon until it is fully dissolved, then strain it into the soup. Discard any seeds and fibre.

3 Dice the beef. Cut the meat from the pork chops, slice it thinly and discard the bones. Return the meat to the soup. Add the sweet potato and daikon and simmer for 20 minutes. Add the cabbage and fish sauce and serve immediately with the lime wedges.

empanadas

empanadas

✹ ✹

Preparation time: 30 minutes + 30 minutes standing time
Cooking time: 1 hour 15 minutes
Makes 24

FILLING
1 tablespoon oil
4 bacon slices, chopped
1 large onion, finely chopped
3 garlic cloves, chopped
150 g (5½ oz) minced (ground) pork and veal
150 g (5½ oz) minced (ground) chicken
2 tablespoons tomato paste (concentrated purée)
1 teaspoon soft brown sugar
2 hard-boiled eggs, chopped
4 gherkins (pickles) (optional), finely chopped
15 g (½ oz/½ cup) coriander (cilantro) leaves, chopped
1 egg white, beaten
oil, for shallow frying

PASTRY
560 g (1 lb 4 oz/4½ cups) plain (all-purpose) flour
2 eggs, beaten

2 teaspoons caster (superfine) sugar
100 g (3½ oz) butter, melted, plus extra, for brushing

1 To make the filling, heat the oil in a frying pan; add the bacon, onion and garlic and cook over medium heat for 5 minutes, stirring regularly. Add the pork and veal mince and the chicken mince and cook for another 5 minutes or until browned, breaking up any lumps with a fork or wooden spoon.

2 Add the tomato paste, sugar and 1 tablespoon water to the pan and bring the mixture to the boil, stirring constantly. Reduce the heat and simmer, uncovered, for 20 minutes. Add the egg, gherkin, if desired, and coriander. Set the mixture aside for at least 30 minutes to cool.

3 To make the pastry, combine the flour, 250 ml (9 fl oz/1 cup) water, the egg, sugar and butter in a food processor and process for 20–30 seconds or until the mixture comes together. Transfer the

pastry to a floured surface and gather together into a ball. Cover with plastic wrap and set aside for 10 minutes.

4 Roll the pastry into a 20 x 30 cm (8 x 12 inch) rectangle. Brush with some extra melted butter and tightly roll up into a long sausage. Cut into 3 cm (1¼ inch) slices and cover with a clean tea towel (dish towel) to stop the pastry drying out.

5 Place 1 slice of pastry flat on a lightly floured surface; roll it out to a 12 cm (4½ inch) circle. Place 1 heaped tablespoon of filling in the centre and lightly brush the edges with egg white. Bring 1 side over to meet the other and press the edges to seal. Decorate the edge with a fork, if desired. Repeat with the remaining filling and pastry.

6 Heat 2 cm (¾ inch) of the oil in a large saucepan; add the empanadas in batches and cook over medium heat for 2–3 minutes each side. Drain on paper towels and serve.

thailand

Every Thai meal is a delicate balancing act of bold flavours. The soups and curries are both tart and creamy sweet, flavoured with sour tamarind, scarlet-hot chillies, tangy lime leaves and handfuls of aromatic basil, coriander and mint. While the cooking of Thailand has borrowed from other countries — stir-fries and steamed dishes from China, spices from India — these influences have been shaped into a cuisine whose tastes and aromas are uniquely Thai.

using dried galangal

If fresh galangal is not available, use a similar amount of dried galangal. Cover the galangal with boiling water for 10 minutes; drain. The soaking water can be substituted for the stock in the recipe.

tom kha gai

❁

Preparation time: 20 minutes
Cooking time: 20 minutes
Serves 4

5 cm (2 inch) piece fresh galangal, thinly sliced
500 ml (17 fl oz/2 cups) coconut milk
250 ml (9 fl oz/1 cup) chicken stock
600 g (1 lb 5 oz) boneless, skinless chicken
   breasts, cut into thin strips
1–2 teaspoons finely sliced red chilli, plus
   extra slices, to garnish

2 tablespoons fish sauce
1 teaspoon soft brown sugar
10 g (¼ oz ⅓ cup) coriander (cilantro) leaves
coriander (cilantro) sprigs, to garnish

Combine the galangal, coconut milk and stock in a saucepan. Bring to the boil, then reduce the heat and simmer over low heat for 10 minutes, stirring occasionally. Add the chicken and chilli to the pan and simmer for 8 minutes. Add the fish sauce and sugar and stir to combine. Add the coriander leaves and serve immediately, garnished with coriander sprigs and chilli slices.

golden prawn puffs

❁

Preparation time: 15 minutes + 30 minutes
   resting time
Cooking time: 10 minutes
Serves 4–6

750 g (1 lb 10 oz) raw prawns (shrimp)
4 red chillies, finely chopped
15 g (½ oz/½ cup) coriander (cilantro)
   leaves
2 egg whites
1 tablespoon finely grated fresh ginger
2 garlic cloves, chopped
1 tablespoon fish sauce
60 g (2¼ oz/⅓ cup) rice flour
   or cornflour (cornstarch)
125 ml (4 fl oz/½ cup) oil
chilli sauce, to serve

1 Peel the prawns and gently pull out the dark vein from each prawn back, starting at the head end.
2 Place the prawns, chilli, coriander leaves, egg whites, ginger, garlic and fish sauce in a food processor and process for 10 seconds or until the mixture is well combined.
3 Transfer the mixture to a bowl and stir in the flour. Refrigerate the prawn mixture for at least 30 minutes, or until you are ready to fry the puffs.
4 Heat the oil in a heavy-based frying pan. Very gently drop rounded teaspoons

tom kha gai

tamarind pulp

If tamarind concentrate is not available, soak a piece of tamarind pulp in hot water — 3 tablespoons pulp to 125 ml (4 fl oz/½ cup) hot water — and work with your fingertips until soft. Strain, using the back of a spoon to force the liquid from the seeds and fibre. The liquid should have the consistency of a light sauce. Any leftover liquid can be frozen in convenient measures and stored in the freezer.

of the mixture into the hot oil and cook for 2 minutes, carefully turning them with tongs until golden brown on all sides. Drain the puffs on paper towels and serve immediately with the chilli sauce.

NOTE: Do not overprocess or overcook the mixture or it will become tough.

tom yum goong
※

Preparation time: 25 minutes
Cooking time: 45 minutes
Serves 4–6

500 g (1 lb 2 oz) raw prawns (shrimp)
1 tablespoon oil
2 tablespoons red curry paste (pages 102–3)
2 tablespoons tamarind concentrate
2 teaspoons ground turmeric
1 teaspoon chopped red chilli
  (optional)
4–8 kaffir lime (makrut) leaves,
  shredded
2 tablespoons fish sauce
2 tablespoons lime juice
2 teaspoons soft brown sugar
10 g (¼ oz ⅓ cup) coriander (cilantro)
  leaves, to garnish
red chilli, thinly sliced, to serve

1 Peel the prawns and gently pull out the dark vein from each prawn back, starting at the head end, leaving the tails intact. Reserve the shells and heads.
2 Heat the oil in a large saucepan, add the prawn shells and heads to the pan and cook for 10 minutes over high heat, tossing frequently, until the shells and heads are deep orange in colour.
3 Have 2 litres (70 fl oz/8 cups) water ready. Add 250 ml (9 fl oz/1 cup) of the water and the curry paste to the pan. Boil for 5 minutes, until the liquid is reduced slightly. Add the remaining water and simmer for 20 minutes. Drain the stock, discarding the prawn heads and shells.
4 Return the drained stock to the pan. Add the tamarind concentrate, turmeric, chilli and lime leaves, bring to the boil and cook for 2 minutes. Add the prawns to the pan and cook for 5 minutes or until the prawns turn pink. Add the fish sauce, lime juice and sugar and stir to combine. Serve immediately, sprinkled with the coriander leaves and chilli slices.

red vegetable curry

✹

Preparation time: 25 minutes
Cooking time: 30 minutes
Serves 4

1 tablespoon oil
1 onion, chopped
1–2 tablespoons red curry paste (see below)
    or ready-made paste

375 ml (13 fl oz/1½ cups) coconut milk
350 g (12 oz) potatoes, chopped
200 g (7 oz) cauliflower florets
6 kaffir lime (makrut) leaves
150 g (5½ oz) snake (yard-long) beans,
    trimmed, cut into 3 cm (1¼ inch) pieces
½ red capsicum (pepper), cut into strips
10 baby corn, cut in half lengthways
1 tablespoon green peppercorns, roughly
    chopped
15 g (½ oz/½ cup) Thai basil, finely chopped

2 tablespoons fish sauce
1 tablespoon lime juice
2 teaspoons soft brown sugar
green peppercorn stems or extra Thai basil
    leaves (optional), to garnish
steamed rice, to serve

1 Heat the oil in a large wok or frying
pan. Cook the onion and curry paste for
4 minutes over medium heat, stirring.
2 Add the coconut milk and 250 ml
(9 fl oz/1 cup) water, bring to the boil
and simmer, uncovered, for 5 minutes.
Add the potato, cauliflower and lime
leaves, and simmer for 7 minutes. Add
the snake beans, capsicum, corn and
peppercorns and cook for 5 minutes or
until the vegetables are tender.
3 Stir in the basil, fish sauce, lime juice
and sugar. Garnish as desired and serve
with the steamed rice.

red curry paste

✹

Preparation time: 20 minutes
Cooking time: 10 minutes
Makes approximately 250 ml (9 fl oz/1 cup)

1 tablespoon coriander seeds
2 teaspoons cumin seeds
1 teaspoon black peppercorns
2 teaspoons shrimp paste
1 teaspoon freshly ground nutmeg
12 dried or fresh red chillies, roughly
    chopped
20 red Asian shallots, chopped
2 tablespoons oil
4 lemongrass stems, white part only,
    finely chopped
12 small garlic cloves, chopped
2 tablespoons coriander (cilantro) roots,
    chopped
2 tablespoons coriander (cilantro) stems,
    chopped
6 kaffir lime (makrut) leaves, chopped
2 teaspoons finely grated lime zest
2 teaspoons salt
2 teaspoons ground turmeric
1 teaspoon paprika

red vegetable curry

1   Place the coriander and cumin seeds in a dry frying pan and roast over medium heat for 2–3 minutes, shaking the pan constantly.

2   Place the roasted spices and peppercorns in a mortar and use a pestle to pound until finely ground.

3   Wrap the shrimp paste in a small piece of foil and cook under a hot grill (broiler) for 3 minutes, turning the package twice.

4   Place the ground spices, shrimp paste, nutmeg and chilli in a food processor and process for 5 seconds. Add the remaining ingredients and process for 20 seconds at a time, scraping down the sides of the bowl each time with a spatula, until a smooth paste forms.

green chicken curry

✳

Preparation time: **20 minutes**
Cooking time: **30 minutes**
Serves **4**

1 tablespoon oil
1 onion, chopped
1–2 tablespoons green curry paste
    (pages 110–11) or ready-made
    paste
375 ml (13 fl oz/1½ cups) coconut
    milk
500 g (1 lb 2 oz) boneless, skinless
    chicken thighs, cut into bite-sized
    pieces
100 g (3½ oz) green beans, trimmed,
    cut into short pieces
6 kaffir lime (makrut) leaves
1 tablespoon fish sauce
1 tablespoon lime juice
1 teaspoon finely grated lime zest
2 teaspoons soft brown sugar
10 g (¼ oz/⅓ cup) coriander (cilantro)
    sprigs

1   Heat the oil in a wok or heavy-based saucepan. Add the onion and curry paste to the wok and cook for 1 minute, stirring constantly. Add the coconut milk and 125 ml (4 fl oz/½ cup) water to the wok and bring to the boil.

2   Add the chicken pieces, beans and lime leaves to the wok, stirring to combine. Reduce the heat and simmer for 15–20 minutes or until the chicken is tender.

3   Add the fish sauce, lime juice, lime zest and sugar to the wok; stir to combine. Sprinkle with coriander sprigs just before serving. Serve with steamed rice, if desired.

NOTE: Boneless, skinless chicken thighs are sweet in flavour and have a good texture for curries, but you can use boneless, skinless chicken breasts if you prefer. Do not overcook breasts or they will become tough.

larb (spicy pork salad)

※

Preparation time: 20 minutes
Cooking time: 10 minutes
Serves 4–6

1 tablespoon oil
2 lemongrass stems, white part only,
    thinly sliced
2 green chillies, finely chopped
500 g (1 lb 2 oz) lean minced
    (ground) pork or beef
60 ml (2 fl oz/¼ cup) lime juice
2 teaspoons finely grated lime zest
2–6 teaspoons chilli sauce
lettuce leaves, to serve
10 g (¼ oz) chopped coriander (cilantro)
    leaves
5 g (⅛ oz) chopped mint
1 small red onion, thinly sliced
50 g (1¾ oz/⅓ cup) unsalted roasted
    peanuts, chopped
25 g (1 oz/¼ cup) crisp fried garlic

1 Heat the oil in a wok and stir-fry the
lemon grass, chilli and mince over high
heat for 6 minutes, until the mince is
cooked, breaking up any lumps. Transfer
to a bowl; allow to cool.
2 Add the lime juice, zest and chilli sauce
to the mince mixture. Arrange the lettuce
leaves on a serving plate. Stir most of
the coriander, mint, onion, peanuts and
fried garlic through the mince, spoon over
the lettuce and sprinkle the rest of the
coriander, mint, onion, peanuts and garlic
over the top.

larb (spicy pork salad)

fish fillets in
coconut milk

※

Preparation time: 15 minutes
Cooking time: 15 minutes
Serves 4

2 long green chillies
2 small red chillies
400 g (14 oz) firm white fish fillets
2 lemongrass stems, white part only
2 coriander (cilantro) roots, finely chopped
4 kaffir lime (makrut) leaves
2 cm (¾ inch) piece fresh ginger,
    grated
2 garlic cloves, crushed
3 spring onions (scallions), white part
    only, thinly sliced
1 teaspoon soft brown sugar
250 ml (9 fl oz/1 cup) coconut milk
125 ml (4 fl oz/½ cup) coconut cream
1 tablespoon fish sauce
2–3 tablespoons lime juice
kaffir lime (makrut) leaves, extra,
    to garnish

1 Heat a wok until hot. Add the whole
chillies and roast until just beginning to
brown all over. Remove the green chillies,
cool and slice.
2 Cut the fish into cubes. Bruise the
lemongrass by crushing with the flat side
of a knife.
3 Add the lemongrass, coriander roots,
lime leaves, ginger, garlic, spring onion,
sugar and coconut milk to the wok. Bring
to the boil, then simmer for 2 minutes.
Add the fish pieces and simmer gently for
2–3 minutes, or until the fish is tender.
Stir in the coconut cream.
4 Stir through the sliced green chilli, fish
sauce, lime juice and salt to taste. Remove
the lemongrass and whole chillies to
serve. Sprinkle with the extra lime leaves.

watercress and duck salad with lychees

☀

Preparation time: **25 minutes**
Cooking time: **30 minutes**
Serves **4**

2 large duck breasts, skin on
1 tablespoon soy sauce
½ each red, green and yellow
    capsicum (pepper)
250 g (9 oz) watercress
12 fresh or tinned lychees
2 tablespoons pickled shredded ginger
1–2 tablespoons green peppercorns in brine
    (optional), rinsed and drained
1 tablespoon white vinegar
2 teaspoons soft brown sugar
1–2 teaspoons chopped red chilli
1 large handful coriander
    (cilantro) leaves

1 Preheat the oven to 210°C (415°F/
Gas 6–7). Brush the duck breasts with the
soy sauce and put on a rack in a roasting
tin. Bake for 30 minutes. Remove from
the oven and allow to cool.
2 Slice the capsicums into thin strips.
Discard any tough woody stems from the
watercress. Peel the fresh lychees and
remove the seeds. If you are using tinned
lychees, drain them thoroughly.
3 Arrange the capsicum strips,
watercress, lychees and ginger on a large
serving platter. Slice the duck into thin
pieces and toss gently through the salad.
4 In a small bowl, combine the
peppercorns, if using, vinegar, sugar,
chilli and coriander. Serve this on the
side for spooning over the salad.

hot pork curry with pumpkin

✳

Preparation time: 20 minutes
Cooking time: 25 minutes
Serves 4

1 tablespoon oil
1–2 tablespoons red curry paste
    (pages 102–3) or ready-made paste
500 g (1 lb 2 oz) lean pork, cut into thick
    strips or chunks
250 ml (9 fl oz/1 cup) coconut milk
350 g (12 oz) butternut pumpkin (squash),
    cut into small chunks
6 kaffir lime (makrut) leaves
60 ml (2 fl oz/¼ cup) coconut cream
1 tablespoon fish sauce
1 teaspoon soft brown sugar
2 red chillies, thinly sliced
basil leaves (optional), to serve
steamed rice, to serve

1 Heat the oil in a wok or heavy-based saucepan; add the curry paste and stir for 1 minute. Add the pork and stir-fry over moderately high heat until golden brown.
2 Add the coconut milk, 125 ml (4 fl oz/½ cup) water, pumpkin and lime leaves, reduce the heat and simmer for 20 minutes, or until the pork is tender.
3 Add the coconut cream, fish sauce and sugar to the wok and stir to combine. Scatter the chilli over the top. Garnish with sprigs of basil, if desired, and serve with the steamed rice.

prawns in lime coconut sauce

prawns in lime coconut sauce

✳

Preparation time: 20 minutes
Cooking time: 35 minutes
Serves 4

15 g (½ oz/¼ cup) shredded coconut
500 g (1 lb 2 oz) raw prawns (shrimp)
1 teaspoon shrimp paste

250 ml (9 fl oz/1 cup) coconut milk
2 lemongrass stems, white part only,
    finely chopped
2–4 kaffir lime (makrut) leaves
2 teaspoons chopped red chilli
2 tablespoons tamarind
    concentrate
2 teaspoons fish sauce
1 teaspoon soft brown sugar
2 limes, zest finely shredded
steamed rice, to serve

1 Preheat the oven to 150°C (300°F/ Gas 2). Spread the coconut on a baking tray and toast it in the oven for 10 minutes, or until it is dark golden, shaking the tray occasionally. Peel the prawns, leaving the tails intact. Gently pull out the dark vein from each prawn back, starting at the head end.
2 Meanwhile, wrap the shrimp paste in a piece of foil and cook under a hot grill (broiler) for 3 minutes, turning twice.

3 Combine the coconut milk and 250 ml (9 fl oz/1 cup) water in a wok or frying pan and cook over medium heat until just boiling. Add the lemongrass, lime leaves and chilli; reduce the heat and simmer for 7 minutes. Add the shrimp paste, tamarind, fish sauce and sugar and simmer for 8 minutes.

4 Add the prawns to the sauce and cook for 5 minutes or until they turn pink. Sprinkle with the coconut and long, thin shreds of lime zest just before serving with the steamed rice.

NOTE: The prawns can be cooked and served in their shells. If so, provide a finger bowl and napkin for each diner.

chicken and peanut penang curry

✳

Preparation time: 25 minutes
Cooking time: 30–40 minutes
Serves 4

1 tablespoon oil
1 large red onion, chopped
1–2 tablespoons ready-made penang
    curry paste
250 ml (9 fl oz/1 cup) coconut milk
500 g (1 lb 2 oz) boneless, skinless chicken
    thighs, cut into bite-sized pieces
4 kaffir lime (makrut) leaves
60 ml (2 fl oz/¼ cup) coconut cream
1 tablespoon fish sauce
1 tablespoon lime juice
2 teaspoons soft brown sugar
80 g (2¾ oz/½ cup) unsalted roasted
    peanuts, chopped
15 g (½ oz/¼ cup) Thai basil leaves
80 g (2¾ oz/½ cup) chopped fresh
    pineapple
basil leaves, to garnish
1 Lebanese (short) cucumber, sliced, to serve

1 Heat the oil in a wok or large frying pan; add the onion and curry paste and stir over medium heat for 2 minutes. Add the coconut milk and bring to the boil.

2 Add the chicken and lime leaves to the wok; reduce the heat and cook for 15 minutes. Remove the chicken with a wire mesh strainer or slotted spoon. Simmer the sauce for 5 minutes or until it is reduced and quite thick.

3 Return the chicken to the wok. Add the coconut cream, fish sauce, lime juice and sugar and cook for 5 minutes. Stir in the peanuts, basil and pineapple. Garnish with the basil leaves. Serve with the sliced cucumber on the side, as well as chilli sauce and steamed rice, if desired.

NOTE: Penang curry paste is based on ground nuts (usually peanuts). Penang curry originated in Malaysia but is now also found in both Thai and Indonesian cuisines.

stuffed prawn omelettes

✳

Preparation time: **25 minutes**
Cooking time: **15 minutes**
Makes **8**

500 g (1 lb 2 oz) raw prawns (shrimp)
1½ tablespoons oil
4 eggs, lightly beaten
2 tablespoons fish sauce
8 spring onions (scallions), chopped
6 coriander (cilantro) roots, chopped
2 garlic cloves, chopped
1 small red chilli, seeded and chopped
2 teaspoons lime juice

2 teaspoons grated palm sugar (jaggery)
  or soft brown sugar
3 tablespoons chopped coriander
  (cilantro) leaves
1 small red chilli, extra, finely sliced,
  to garnish
coriander (cilantro) sprigs, to garnish
sweet chilli sauce, to serve

1 Peel the prawns and gently pull out the dark vein from each prawn back, starting at the head end; chop the prawn meat.
2 Heat a wok over high heat, add 2 teaspoons of the oil and swirl to coat. Combine the egg with half of the fish sauce. Add 2 tablespoons of the mixture to the wok and swirl to a 16 cm (6¼ inch) round. Cook for 1 minute, then gently lift out. Repeat with the remaining egg mixture to make eight omelettes.
3 Heat the remaining oil in the wok. Add the prawns, spring onion, coriander root, garlic and chilli. Stir-fry for 3–4 minutes, or until the prawns are cooked. Stir in the lime juice, palm sugar, coriander leaves and the remaining fish sauce.
4 Divide the prawn mixture among the omelettes and fold each into a small firm parcel. Cut a slit in the top and garnish with the chilli and coriander sprigs. Serve with the sweet chilli sauce.

crisp fried whole fish with sour pepper and coriander sauce

✳

Preparation time: **20 minutes**
Cooking time: **15 minutes**
Serves **4**

1 kg (2 lb 4 oz) whole firm sweet fish
  (such as snapper or red emperor),
  cleaned and scaled
oil, for deep-frying
4 spring onions (scallions), chopped
5 cm (2 inch) piece fresh ginger, grated
2–4 teaspoons fresh green peppercorns,
  crushed
2 teaspoons chopped red chilli
125 ml (4 fl oz/½ cup) coconut milk
1 tablespoon tamarind concentrate
1 tablespoon fish sauce
iceberg lettuce leaves, to serve
30 g (1 oz) coriander (cilantro) leaves
sweet chilli sauce, to serve

1 Cut a shallow, criss-cross pattern on both sides of the fish. Use kitchen scissors or a sharp knife to trim the fins if they are very long.
2 Heat the oil in a large wok or heavy-based, deep frying pan. Place the whole fish in the oil and cook for 4–5 minutes on each side, moving it around in the oil to ensure the whole fish is crisp and cooked (including the tail and head). Drain the fish well on paper towels and keep warm.

stuffed prawn omelettes

3 Drain almost all the oil from the wok. Heat the wok over medium heat, add the spring onion, ginger, peppercorns and chilli and stir-fry for 3 minutes. Add the coconut milk, tamarind and fish sauce and cook for 2 minutes.

4 Place the fish on a bed of lettuce on a serving plate and pour over the sauce. Sprinkle with the coriander leaves and serve with the sweet chilli sauce.

NOTE: To serve, use tongs or a small spatula to lift pieces of fish away from the bones. Then remove the bones, or turn the fish over, and lift pieces of fish from the underside.

stir-fried cauliflower and snake beans

✻

Preparation time: **15 minutes**
Cooking time: **10 minutes**
Serves **4**

4 coriander (cilantro) roots, chopped, or
   1 tablespoon chopped leaves and stems
1 teaspoon soft brown sugar
½ teaspoon ground turmeric
2 garlic cloves, crushed
2 tablespoons fish sauce
400 g (14 oz) cauliflower
6 spring onions (scallions)
200 g (7 oz) snake (yard-long) beans, trimmed
2 tablespoons oil
4 garlic cloves, extra, sliced
   lengthways
20 spinach leaves, coarsely shredded
1 tablespoon lime juice

1 Use a mortar and pestle or a blender to blend the coriander, sugar, turmeric, crushed garlic and 1 tablespoon of the fish sauce to make a smooth paste.

2 Cut the cauliflower into florets. Cut the spring onions in half lengthways, then cut the white parts into short lengths, reserving some of the green tops for a garnish. Cut the snake beans into short lengths.

crisp fried whole fish

3 Heat half the oil in a large saucepan or wok, add the extra sliced garlic and stir-fry for 30 seconds or until just beginning to brown. Reserve some of the garlic for a garnish.

4 Add the spinach to the pan and stir-fry for another 30 seconds or until just wilted. Add ½ teaspoon pepper and the remaining fish sauce and mix well. Arrange on a serving plate; keep warm.

5 Heat the remaining oil in the same pan; add the paste and cook over high heat for 1 minute or until aromatic.

Add the cauliflower and stir-fry until well combined. Add 125 ml (4 fl oz/ ½ cup) water, bring to the boil, reduce the heat and simmer, covered, for 3 minutes. Add the beans, cover and cook for another 3 minutes. Add the spring onion and stir until just wilted. Spoon the vegetables over the spinach, drizzle with the lime juice and sprinkle over the reserved fried garlic and spring onion.

steamed fish cutlets with ginger and chilli

1 Line a bamboo steaming basket with banana leaves or baking paper (this is so the fish will not stick or taste of bamboo).
2 Arrange the fish cutlets in the basket and top with the ginger, garlic, chilli and coriander. Cover and steam over a wok or large saucepan of boiling water for 5–6 minutes.
3 Remove the lid and sprinkle the spring onion and lime juice over the fish. Cover and steam for 30 seconds, or until the fish is cooked. Serve immediately with the steamed rice and wedges of lime, if desired.

green curry paste

☀

Preparation time: **20 minutes**
Cooking time: **10 minutes**
Makes **approximately 250 ml (9 fl oz/1 cup)**

1 tablespoon coriander seeds
2 teaspoons cumin seeds
1 teaspoon black peppercorns
2 teaspoons shrimp paste
8 large green chillies, roughly
    chopped
20 red Asian shallots
5 cm (2 inch) piece fresh galangal, chopped
12 small garlic cloves, chopped
100 g (3½ oz) chopped coriander (cilantro)
    leaves, stems and roots
6 kaffir lime (makrut) leaves,
    chopped
3 lemongrass stems, white part only,
    finely chopped
2 teaspoons finely grated lime zest
2 teaspoons salt
2 tablespoons oil

1 Place the coriander and cumin seeds in a dry frying pan and roast over medium heat for 2–3 minutes, shaking the pan constantly.
2 Pound the roasted spices and peppercorns using a mortar and pestle until finely ground.
3 Wrap the shrimp paste in a small piece of foil and cook under a hot grill (broiler) for 3 minutes, turning the package twice.

steamed fish cutlets with ginger and chilli

☀

Preparation time: **15 minutes**
Cooking time: **10 minutes**
Serves 4

banana leaves (optional), for steaming
4 firm white fish cutlets (such as snapper),
    each approximately 200 g (7 oz)
5 cm (2 inch) piece fresh ginger, cut into
    fine shreds
2 garlic cloves, chopped
1 long red chilli, seeded and cut into thin
    strips
2 tablespoons finely chopped coriander
    (cilantro) stems
3 spring onions (scallions), cut into fine
    shreds each 4 cm (1½ inches) long
2 tablespoons lime juice
steamed rice, to serve

4 Place the ground spices and shrimp paste in a food processor and process for 5 seconds. Add the remaining ingredients and process for 20 seconds at a time, scraping down the sides of the bowl with a spatula each time, until a smooth paste forms.

coriander pork with fresh pineapple

☀

Preparation time: **25 minutes**
Cooking time: **15 minutes**
Serves **4**

400 g (14 oz) pork loin or fillet
¼ medium pineapple
1 tablespoon oil
4 garlic cloves, chopped
4 spring onions (scallions), chopped
1 tablespoon fish sauce
1 tablespoon lime juice
15 g (½ oz/½ cup) coriander (cilantro) leaves
15 g (½ oz/¼ cup) chopped mint
steamed rice, to serve
red chilli, sliced, to serve

1 Partially freeze the pork until it is just firm, then slice it thinly. Trim the skin from the pineapple and cut the flesh into bite-sized pieces.
2 Heat the oil in a wok or heavy-based frying pan over medium-high heat. Add the garlic and spring onion and cook for 1 minute. Remove from the wok.
3 Heat the wok to very hot; add the pork in two or three batches and stir-fry each batch for 3 minutes or until the pork is just cooked. Return the pork, garlic and spring onion to the wok and then add the pineapple pieces, fish sauce and lime juice. Toss well. Just before serving, sprinkle over the coriander leaves and mint and toss lightly. Serve with the steamed rice and red chilli on the side.

thai curry pastes

Thai curry pastes are traditionally made of fresh herbs that grow in the house gardens or nearby fields, rather than the dry spices (those of the spice trade — cumin, coriander seeds, cardamom, cinnamon and cloves) used in Indian cooking. Throughout Thailand, market stalls provide a variety of pastes, each freshly made, for the home cook. The deceptively cool-coloured green curry paste is the most searingly hot; the colour comes from fresh green chillies and coriander (cilantro) leaves. Red curry paste is only marginally milder; here, the colour is derived mainly from dried or fresh red chillies.

coriander pork with fresh pineapple

steamed mussels with lemongrass, basil and wine

☀

Preparation time: 30 minutes
Cooking time: 15 minutes
Serves 4–6

1 kg (2 lb 4 oz) black mussels
1 tablespoon oil
1 onion, chopped
4 garlic cloves, chopped
2 lemongrass stems, white part only, chopped
1–2 teaspoons chopped red chilli
250 ml (9 fl oz/1 cup) white wine or water
1 tablespoon fish sauce
30 g (1 oz/⅔ cup) Thai basil, chopped

1 Discard any open mussels. Scrub the outside of the mussels with a brush. Remove and discard the hairy beards. Soak the mussels in a bowl of cold water for 10 minutes; drain.
2 Heat the oil in a wok or large saucepan. Add the onion, garlic, lemongrass and chilli, and cook for 4 minutes over low heat, stirring occasionally. Add the wine and fish sauce and cook for 3 minutes.
3 Add the mussels to the wok and toss well. Cover the wok, increase the heat and cook for 3–4 minutes or until the mussels open. (Do not overcook or the mussels will become tough.) Discard any which have not opened after 4 minutes. Add the basil, toss well and serve with steamed rice, if desired.

mee grob

☀

Preparation time: 30 minutes
Cooking time: 15 minutes
Serves 4–6

4 dried Chinese mushrooms
8 raw prawns (shrimp)
oil, for deep-frying
100 g (3½ oz) dried rice vermicelli
100 g (3½ oz) fried tofu puffs, cut into thin strips
4 garlic cloves, crushed
1 onion, chopped
200 g (7 oz) boneless, skinless chicken breast, thinly sliced
8 green beans, trimmed, sliced on the diagonal
6 spring onions (scallions), thinly sliced
30 g (1 oz/⅓ cup) bean sprouts, trimmed
coriander (cilantro) leaves, to garnish

SAUCE
1 tablespoon light soy sauce
60 ml (2 fl oz/¼ cup) white vinegar
60 ml (2 fl oz/¼ cup) fish sauce
1 tablespoon sweet chilli sauce
110 g (3¾ oz/½ cup) sugar

1 Soak the mushrooms in hot water for 20 minutes. Drain, then squeeze to remove any excess liquid. Discard the stems and chop the caps finely.
2 Peel the prawns and gently pull out the dark vein from each prawn back, starting at the head end.
3 Fill a wok or heavy-based saucepan one-third full of oil and heat to 180°C (350°F), or until a cube of bread dropped into the oil browns in 15 seconds. Cook the vermicelli in batches for 5 seconds, or until puffed and crispy. Drain on paper towels.
4 Add the tofu to the wok in batches and deep-fry for 1 minute, or until crisp.

Drain on paper towels. Cool the oil slightly and carefully remove all but 2 tablespoons of the oil.

5 Reheat the wok over high heat until very hot. Add the garlic and onion and stir-fry for 1 minute. Add the mushrooms, chicken, green beans and half the spring onion and stir-fry for 2 minutes, or until the chicken is almost cooked through. Add the prawns and stir-fry for a further 2 minutes, or until the prawns just turn pink.

6 To make the sauce, combine all the ingredients, stirring to dissolve the sugar. Add to the wok and stir-fry for 2 minutes, or until the sauce is syrupy and the chicken and prawns are tender. Remove the wok from the heat and stir in the vermicelli, tofu and bean sprouts. Garnish with the coriander and the remaining spring onion.

pad thai

☀

Preparation time: **30 minutes**
Cooking time: **10 minutes**
Serves **4–6**

250 g (9 oz) dried rice stick
    noodles
1 tablespoon tamarind purée
1 small red chilli, chopped
2 garlic cloves, chopped
2 spring onions (scallions), sliced
1½ tablespoons sugar
2 tablespoons fish sauce
2 tablespoons lime juice
2 tablespoons oil
2 eggs, beaten
8 raw large prawns (shrimp)
150 g (5½ oz) pork fillet, thinly sliced
100 g (3½ oz) fried tofu puffs,
    cut into thin strips
90 g (3¼ oz/1 cup) bean sprouts
40 g (1½ oz/¼ cup) chopped unsalted
    roasted peanuts, to garnish
3 tablespoons coriander (cilantro) leaves,
    to garnish
1 lime, cut into wedges, to garnish
dried chilli flakes, to serve

pad thai

1 Put the noodles in a heatproof bowl, cover with warm water and soak for 15–20 minutes, or until soft and pliable. Drain well.

2 Combine the tamarind with 1 tablespoon water. Put the chilli, garlic and spring onion in a spice grinder or use a mortar and pestle and grind to a smooth paste. Transfer the mixture to a bowl. Stir in the tamarind mixture along with the sugar, fish sauce and lime juice, stirring until combined.

3 Heat a wok until very hot, add 1 tablespoon of the oil and swirl to coat the base and side. Add the egg, swirl to

coat and cook for 1–2 minutes, or until set. Remove, roll up and cut into thin slices.

4 Peel the prawns and gently pull out the dark vein from each prawn back, starting at the head end.

5 Heat remaining oil in the wok, stir in chilli mixture and stir-fry for 30 seconds. Add the pork and stir-fry for 2 minutes, or until tender. Add prawns and stir-fry for a further minute, or until pink and curled.

6 Stir in the noodles, egg, tofu and bean sprouts and gently toss together until heated through. Serve immediately topped with the peanuts, coriander, lime wedges and chilli flakes.

curry pastes & powders

The secret to making authentic Asian curries is to grind your own fresh spices into dry powder or wet pastes. Just a few minutes over high heat unlocks the aromas into the air.

ceylon curry powder

In a small frying pan, dry-fry 6 tablespoons coriander seeds, 3 tablespoons cumin seeds, 1 teaspoon fennel seeds and ½ teaspoon fenugreek seeds for 8–10 minutes, or until the spices are dark brown, stirring occasionally to prevent the spices from burning. Place the roasted spices with 3 small dried chillies, 3 cloves, ¼ teaspoon cardamom seeds, 1 crushed cinnamon stick and 2 dried curry leaves in a food processor and grind to a fine powder. Cool and transfer to an airtight jar. Store in a cool, dark place for up to 3 months.

indonesian sambal paste

Soak 12 large dried red chillies in hot water for 30 minutes; drain. Place the chillies, 2 roughly chopped large red onions, 6 garlic cloves, 1 teaspoon shrimp paste and 125 ml (4 fl oz/½ cup) oil in a food processor and mix into a smooth paste, scraping down the sides regularly. Heat a heavy-based saucepan over low heat and cook the paste for 10 minutes, stirring regularly, until very oily. Stir in 185 ml (6 fl oz/¾ cup) tamarind concentrate, 1 tablespoon grated palm sugar (jaggery) or soft brown sugar, 2 teaspoons salt and 1 teaspoon pepper. Bring to the boil and simmer for 2 minutes. Pour into warm sterilised jars, seal and cool. Store in the refrigerator for up to 2 weeks or freeze for up to 3 months.

garam masala

Put 4 tablespoons coriander seeds, 3 tablespoons cardamom pods, 2 tablespoons cumin seeds, 1 tablespoon whole black peppercorns, 1 teaspoon whole cloves and 3 cinnamon sticks in a frying pan and dry-fry over moderate heat until aromatic. Open the cardamom pods, retaining the seeds only. Put the fried spices in a food processor or blender with a grated whole fresh nutmeg and process to a powder. Store in an airtight jar in a cool, dark place for up to 3 months.

balti masala paste

Put 4 tablespoons coriander seeds, 2 tablespoons cumin seeds, 2 crumbled cinnamon sticks, 2 teaspoons each of fennel seeds, black mustard seeds and cardamom seeds, 1 teaspoon fenugreek seeds, 6 whole cloves, 4 bay leaves and 20 dried curry leaves in a small frying pan or balti. Dry-fry over moderate heat until the spices just start to become aromatic. Transfer to a mortar, then allow to cool before grinding to a powder using a pestle. Add 4 teaspoons each ground turmeric and garlic powder, 2 teaspoons ground ginger, 1½ teaspoons chilli powder and 250 ml (9 fl oz/1 cup) vinegar. Heat 250 ml (9 fl oz/1 cup) oil in the pan, add the paste and stir-fry for 5 minutes. Pour into warm sterilised jars, seal and cool. Store in the refrigerator for up to 2 weeks.

chilli paste

Remove the stalks from 200 g (7 oz) small red chillies. Place in a small saucepan with 250 ml (9 fl oz/1 cup) water and bring to the boil. Reduce the heat and simmer, partially covered, for 15 minutes, then cool slightly. Transfer the chillies and liquid to a food processor; add 1 teaspoon each of salt and sugar, and 1 tablespoon each of vinegar and oil. Process until finely chopped. Store in a sealed container in the refrigerator for up to 2 weeks.

chicken and vegetable salad

frying pan. Bring the mixture to the boil, reduce the heat slightly and simmer for 5 minutes.

2 Add the chicken to the pan and cook in the hot liquid for 5 minutes, stirring occasionally. Drain and allow to cool. Discard the liquid.

3 Bring a large saucepan of water to the boil and cook the broccolini, corn, snow peas, capsicum and spring onion for 2 minutes. Drain and plunge into iced water, then drain again.

4 Combine the sweet chilli sauce, honey, lime juice and zest in a small bowl and mix well. Arrange the vegetables and chicken in a serving bowl. Pour the sauce over the top and gently toss. Sprinkle with the coriander leaves.

NOTE: To trim snow peas, cut or break both ends off and then pull away any strings from along the sides.

curried rice noodles with chicken

✳

Preparation time: **25 minutes**
Cooking time: **10–15 minutes**
Serves **4–6**

200 g (7 oz) dried rice vermicelli
1½ tablespoons oil
1 tablespoon red curry paste (pages 102–3) or ready-made paste
450 g (1 lb) boneless, skinless chicken thighs, cut into fine strips
1–2 teaspoons chopped red chilli
2 tablespoons fish sauce
2 tablespoons lime juice
100 g (3½ oz) bean sprouts
80 g (2¾ oz) chopped unsalted roasted peanuts
20 g (¾ oz/¼ cup) crisp fried onion
25 g (1 oz/¼ cup) crisp fried garlic
25 g (1 oz/¾ cup) coriander (cilantro) leaves

1 Cook the vermicelli in a saucepan of rapidly boiling water for 2 minutes. Drain and then toss with 2 teaspoons of the

chicken and vegetable salad

✳

Preparation time: **30 minutes**
Cooking time: **20 minutes**
Serves **4**

3 slices fresh ginger
2 lemongrass stems, white part only, roughly chopped
2 tablespoons fish sauce
400 g (14 oz) boneless, skinless chicken breasts, cut into short, thin strips
250 g (9 oz) broccolini, cut into florets
150 g (5½ oz) baby corn
100 g (3½ oz) snow peas (mangetout), trimmed
1 red capsicum (pepper), cut into strips
3 spring onions (scallions), cut into strips
125 ml (4 fl oz/½ cup) sweet chilli sauce
2 tablespoons honey
2 tablespoons lime juice
2 teaspoons finely grated lime zest
1 handful coriander (cilantro) leaves, to garnish

1 Put the ginger, lemongrass, fish sauce and 250 ml (9 fl oz/1 cup) water in a

oil to prevent the strands from sticking together; set aside.

2 Heat the remaining oil in a wok. Add the curry paste and stir for 1 minute or until aromatic. Add the chicken in batches and stir-fry for 2 minutes or until golden brown. Return all the chicken to the pan.

3 Add the chilli, fish sauce and lime juice; bring to the boil and simmer for 1 minute. Add the bean sprouts and vermicelli and toss well. Arrange the mixture on a serving plate and sprinkle with peanuts, onion, garlic and coriander leaves. Serve immediately.

spicy roasted eggplant with tofu

☀

Preparation time: **15 minutes**
Cooking time: **15 minutes**
Serves 4

4 slender eggplants (aubergines) (about 400 g/14 oz)
250 g (9 oz) firm tofu
2–4 small red or green chillies
4 garlic cloves, crushed
4 coriander (cilantro) roots, chopped
1 small onion, chopped
3 teaspoons soft brown sugar
2 tablespoons lime juice
2 tablespoons fish sauce
1 tablespoon oil
15 g (½ oz/¼ cup) Thai basil
2 teaspoons dried shrimp (optional), finely chopped, to garnish

1 Heat a medium frying pan or wok until hot. Add the eggplant and cook until the skin begins to char, turning to cook all sides. Remove from the heat and cool. Slice the eggplant diagonally into 2 cm (¾ inch) thick slices. Drain the tofu and cut into 3 cm (1¼ inch) cubes.

2 Blend the chillies, garlic, coriander, onion, sugar, lime juice and fish sauce in a food processor or blender until smooth.

3 Heat the oil in the same frying pan or wok, add the paste and stir over high heat for 1 minute or until fragrant. Add the eggplant, stir to combine and cook, covered, for 3 minutes or until just tender.

4 Add the tofu and half the basil and gently stir through. Serve garnished with the remaining basil and dried shrimp, if desired.

NOTE: This dish can be eaten hot or as a cold accompaniment. If you prefer a milder, less spicy dish, use only 2 chillies.

storing fresh coriander

To store a bunch of fresh coriander (cilantro), stand it, unwashed, in a container of suitable size with the roots in 1 cm (½ inch) water. Enclose the leaves and stems with a large plastic supermarket carrier bag and tie the handles together around the container, then stand the whole thing in the refrigerator. It should keep for up to 2 weeks — break off leaves as you need them. The roots will also freeze well.

green pawpaw and peanut salad

☀

Preparation time: 25 minutes
Cooking time: 5 minutes
Serves 4

50 g (1¾ oz) dried shrimp
    (see Note)
100 g (3½ oz) green beans,
    trimmed
1 small iceberg lettuce
½ green pawpaw, peeled and grated
    (see Note)
60 ml (2 fl oz/¼ cup) lime juice
2 tablespoons fish sauce
2 teaspoons soft brown sugar
1–2 teaspoons chopped red chilli
80 g (2¾ oz/½ cup) unsalted roasted
    peanuts, chopped
1 red chilli, extra, finely chopped

1   Use a mortar and pestle to pound the shrimp, or chop finely. Cut the beans into short pieces and cook them in a saucepan of boiling water for 2 minutes. Drain, then plunge them into iced water and drain again. Shred the lettuce and arrange it on a serving plate. Top with the shrimp, beans and pawpaw.

2   Combine the lime juice, fish sauce, sugar and chilli in a small bowl and mix well. Pour over the salad and sprinkle the peanuts and extra chilli over the top.

NOTE: Dried shrimp and green pawpaw are available at Asian food stores.

fresh spring rolls

☀

Preparation time: 30 minutes
Cooking time: nil
Makes 8

16 cooked prawns (shrimp)
50 g (1¾ oz) dried mung
    bean vermicelli
8 dried rice paper wrappers
16 Thai basil leaves
30 g (1 oz/1 cup) coriander (cilantro)
    leaves
1 carrot, cut into short thin strips
1 tablespoon finely grated lime zest
2 tablespoons sweet chilli sauce

DIPPING SAUCE
1 teaspoon sugar
2 tablespoons fish sauce
1 tablespoon white vinegar
1 small red chilli (optional), finely chopped
1 tablespoon chopped coriander
    (cilantro) leaves and stems

1   To make the dipping sauce, place 80 ml (2½ fl oz/⅓ cup) cold water in a small bowl; add the sugar and stir until it has dissolved. Stir in the fish sauce, vinegar, chilli, if desired, and coriander leaves and stems.

2   Peel the prawns and gently pull out the dark vein from each prawn back, starting at the head end. Soak the vermicelli in 500 ml (17 fl oz/2 cups) hot water for 10 minutes and then drain. Dip a rice paper wrapper into lukewarm water until it softens and place it on a work surface. Place 2 prawns side by side in the centre of the wrapper and top with 2 basil leaves, 1 tablespoon coriander, a few carrot strips, a little lime zest and a small amount of vermicelli. Spoon a little sweet chilli sauce over the top.

3   Press the filling down to flatten it a little; fold in two sides, then roll up the parcel. Lay seam-side down on a serving plate and sprinkle with a little water; cover with plastic wrap. Repeat with the remaining ingredients. Serve with the dipping sauce and a little extra sweet chilli sauce.

NOTE: Rice paper wrappers must be kept moist or they become brittle. Continue to sprinkle cold water on them while rolling them up or if they are left for any length of time before serving.

Place 2 prawns side by side in the centre of the wrapper and top with the other ingredients.

Fold in the sides of the wrapper then roll it up to form a parcel.

steamed fish in banana leaves

❋

Preparation time: **45 minutes**
Cooking time: **10 minutes**
Makes **10**

2 large banana leaves
350 g (12 oz) firm white fish fillets,
    cut into thin strips
1–2 tablespoons red curry paste
    (pages 102–3) or ready-made paste
250 ml (9 fl oz/1 cup) coconut
    cream
banana leaves, extra, or cabbage
    leaves, for steaming
150 g (5½ oz/2 cups) finely
    shredded cabbage
2 tablespoons fish sauce
2 tablespoons lime juice
1–2 tablespoons sweet chilli sauce
1 red chilli (optional), chopped

1 Cut the banana leaves into squares
10 x 10 cm (4 x 4 inches) and make a
3 cm (1¼ inch) cut towards the centre
on each corner. Fold in the corners, then
staple and/or tie around with a piece of
string to form a cup. Trim the corners to
neaten, if necessary.
2 Put the fish in a bowl with the curry
paste and coconut cream and stir gently
to combine. Place spoonfuls of the fish
mixture in each banana leaf cup.
3 Line a large steaming basket with the
extra banana leaves or cabbage leaves
and place the prepared cups in the basket.
Top each piece of fish with shredded
cabbage and a little fish sauce. Place the
basket over a wok of simmering water
and steam, covered, for about 7 minutes.
Drizzle lime juice and sweet chilli sauce
over the top and serve immediately,
sprinkled with the chilli, if desired.

NOTE: The fish can be cooked in foil cups
instead of banana leaves.

spicy beef curry

✹

Preparation time: 20 minutes
Cooking time: 30–35 minutes
Serves 4

1 tablespoon oil
1 large onion, chopped
1–2 tablespoons green curry paste
   (pages 110–11) or ready-made paste
500 g (1 lb 2 oz) round or blade steak,
   cut into thick strips
185 ml (6 fl oz/¾ cup) coconut milk
6 kaffir lime (makrut) leaves
100 g (3½ oz) pea eggplants (aubergines)
2 tablespoons fish sauce
1 teaspoon soft brown sugar
2 teaspoons finely grated lime zest
15 g (½ oz/½ cup) coriander (cilantro) leaves
30 g (1 oz/½ cup) shredded basil
steamed rice, to serve

1   Heat the oil in a wok or large frying
pan. Add the onion and curry paste and
stir for 2 minutes over medium heat
until aromatic.
2   Heat the wok until it is very hot.
Add the beef in two batches and stir-fry
until brown. Return all the beef to the
wok. Add the coconut milk, 60 ml
(2 fl oz/¼ cup) water and the lime leaves.
Bring to the boil, reduce the heat, cover
and simmer for 10 minutes. Add the
eggplants and simmer, uncovered, for
another 10 minutes or until both the
beef and eggplants are tender.
3   Add the fish sauce, sugar and lime
zest to the wok and mix well. Stir in the
coriander and basil. Serve immediately
with the steamed rice.

NOTE: Use thinly sliced slender eggplants
if pea eggplants are not available.

son-in-law eggs

✹

Preparation time: 15 minutes
Cooking time: 20 minutes
Serves 4

son-in-law eggs

8 eggs
2 tablespoons oil
2 tablespoons grated palm sugar (jaggery)
   or soft brown sugar
1 tablespoon fish sauce
2 tablespoons tamarind concentrate
1 teaspoon chopped red chilli (optional)

1   Place the eggs in a saucepan of cold
water. Bring the water to the boil and cook
the eggs for 7 minutes (begin timing when
the water boils). Drain and run under cold
water until cool. Remove the shells.
2   Heat the oil in a wok or frying pan. Add
the eggs to the wok in batches and turn
frequently over medium heat. When they
are golden brown and blistered, remove
the eggs from the wok and keep warm.
3   Remove the excess oil from the wok
and add the palm sugar, fish sauce,
tamarind concentrate and chilli, if using.
Bring to the boil and boil rapidly for
2 minutes, or until the mixture resembles
a syrup. Serve the eggs with the syrup
poured over them.

thai fish cakes

Add the cornflour, fish sauce, egg, coriander, curry paste and chilli. Process for 10 seconds or until well combined.
2 Transfer the fish mixture to a large bowl. Add the beans and spring onion and mix well. Using wet hands, form 2 rounded tablespoons of the mixture at a time into fairly flat patties.
3 Heat the oil in a heavy-based frying pan over medium heat. Cook four fish cakes at a time until they are dark golden brown on both sides. Drain on paper towels and serve immediately with the dipping sauce.

NOTE: The fish cakes can be prepared ahead up to the end of Step 2 and stored, covered, in the refrigerator for up to 4 hours.

ginger chicken with black fungus

✺

Preparation time: **40 minutes**
Cooking time: **15 minutes**
Serves **4**

10 g (¼ oz/¼ cup) dried black fungus
1 tablespoon oil
3 garlic cloves, chopped
6 cm (2½ inch) piece fresh ginger, cut into fine shreds
500 g (1 lb 2 oz) boneless, skinless chicken breasts, sliced
4 spring onions (scallions), chopped
1 tablespoon golden mountain sauce
1 tablespoon fish sauce
2 teaspoons soft brown sugar
½ red capsicum (pepper), finely sliced
15 g (½ oz/½ cup) coriander (cilantro) leaves
25 g (1 oz) chopped Thai basil

1 Place the fungus in a heatproof bowl, cover with hot water, and leave for 15 minutes until it is soft and swollen; drain and chop roughly.

thai fish cakes

✺

Preparation time: **25 minutes**
Cooking time: **5–10 minutes**
Serves **4–6**

450 g (1 lb) firm white fish fillets
3 tablespoons cornflour (cornstarch) or rice flour
1 tablespoon fish sauce
1 egg, beaten

15 g (½ oz/½ cup) coriander (cilantro) leaves
3 teaspoons red curry paste (pages 102–3) or ready-made paste
1–2 teaspoons chopped red chilli (optional)
100 g (3½ oz) green beans, trimmed, very thinly sliced
2 spring onions (scallions), finely chopped
125 ml (4 fl oz/½ cup) oil
dipping sauce (page 118), to serve

1 Place the fish in a food processor and process for 20 seconds or until smooth.

2 Heat the oil in a large wok, add the garlic and ginger and stir-fry for 1 minute. Add the chicken in batches, stir-frying over high heat until it changes colour. Return all the chicken to the wok. Add the spring onion and golden mountain sauce and stir-fry for 1 minute.

3 Add the fish sauce, sugar and fungus to the wok. Stir thoroughly; cover and steam for 2 minutes. Serve immediately with the capsicum, coriander and basil scattered on top.

cucumber salad with peanuts and chilli

☀

Preparation time: 25 minutes + 45 minutes
marinating time
Cooking time: nil
Serves 4–6

3 Lebanese (short) cucumbers
2 tablespoons white vinegar
2 teaspoons sugar
1–2 tablespoons chilli sauce
½ red onion, chopped
1 large handful coriander (cilantro) leaves
160 g (5¾ oz/1 cup) unsalted roasted
peanuts, chopped
2 tablespoons crisp fried garlic
½ teaspoon chopped chilli
1 tablespoon fish sauce

1 Peel the cucumbers and slice in half lengthways. Remove the seeds with a teaspoon and slice thinly.

2 Combine the vinegar and sugar in a small bowl, and stir until the sugar has dissolved. Transfer to a large bowl and toss with the cucumber, chilli sauce, onion and coriander. Allow to marinate for 45 minutes.

3 Just before serving, add the peanuts, garlic, chilli and fish sauce. Toss lightly to combine.

a thai meal

A traditional Thai meal consists of a variety of dishes — usually a soup, a curry or stewed dish, a stir-fry and a salad. These dishes are selected for a balance of flavours (sweet, sour, hot, bitter and salty), as well as textures and colours. All dishes are served at the same time and eaten warm or at room temperature; diners help themselves and eat using a knife and fork. Rice is always served, and a number of tasty sauces and dips add even more flavour to the dishes. The main meal is sometimes followed by a platter of fresh tropical fruits and desserts made of mung bean flour, rice, palm sugar, coconut and eggs. Tea and water accompany the meal.

green curry with sweet potato and eggplant

※

Preparation time: **15 minutes**
Cooking time: **20 minutes**
Serves **4–6**

1 onion
1 eggplant (aubergine)
1 orange sweet potato
1 tablespoon vegetable oil

1–2 tablespoons green curry paste
 (see pages 110–11)
375 ml (13 fl oz/1½ cups) coconut milk
250 ml (9 fl oz/1 cup) vegetable stock
6 kaffir lime (makrut) leaves
2 teaspoons grated palm sugar (jaggery)
 or soft brown sugar
2 tablespoons lime juice
2 teaspoons finely grated lime zest
coriander (cilantro) leaves, to garnish
kaffir lime (makrut) leaves (optional), extra,
 to garnish
steamed rice, to serve

1 Chop the onion. Quarter and slice the eggplant and cut the sweet potato into cubes. Heat the oil in a large wok. Add the onion and green curry paste and cook, stirring, over medium heat for 3 minutes. Add the eggplant and cook for a further 4–5 minutes, or until softened. Pour in the coconut milk and stock, bring to the boil, then reduce the heat and simmer for 5 minutes. Add the lime leaves and sweet potato and cook, stirring occasionally, for 10 minutes, or until the eggplant and sweet potato are very tender.

2 Mix in the palm sugar, lime juice and lime zest until well combined with the vegetables. Season to taste with salt. Garnish with the coriander leaves and extra lime leaves, if desired, and serve with the steamed rice.

fried rice with coriander and basil

※

Preparation time: **20 minutes + overnight
 standing time**
Cooking time: **20 minutes**
Serves **4**

100 g (3½ oz) pork loin
300 g (10½ oz) boneless, skinless chicken
 thighs
2 tablespoons oil
3 cm (1¼ inch) piece pork fat, chopped
4 garlic cloves, chopped
4 cm (1½ inch) piece fresh ginger,
 finely grated
2 teaspoons chopped red chilli
500 g (1 lb 2 oz/2½ cups) jasmine rice,
 cooked and cooled (see Note)
1 tablespoon fish sauce
2 teaspoons golden mountain sauce
2 spring onions (scallions), chopped
30 g (1 oz/⅔ cup) Thai basil, chopped
15 g (½ oz/½ cup) coriander (cilantro)
 leaves, chopped

1 Dice the pork and the chicken.
2 Heat the oil in a wok or large heavy-based frying pan. When the oil is very

green curry with sweet potato and eggplant

hot, add the pork fat, garlic, ginger and chilli; stir for 2 minutes.

3 Add the diced chicken and pork to the wok and stir-fry for 3 minutes or until the meat changes colour. Break up any lumps in the rice and add it to the wok; toss well using two wooden spoons. When the rice is warmed, add the fish sauce and golden mountain sauce and toss through with the spring onion, basil and most of the coriander, reserving some for garnish. Serve immediately, garnished with the remaining coriander leaves.

NOTE: If possible, cook the rice a day ahead and refrigerate it overnight before making the fried rice so the finished dish is not gluggy.

thai beef salad

※

Preparation time: **20 minutes**
Cooking time: **5 minutes**
Serves **6**

500 g (1 lb 2 oz) lean beef fillet
2 tablespoons peanut oil
2 garlic cloves, crushed
1 tablespoon grated palm sugar (jaggery)
   or soft brown sugar
3 tablespoons finely chopped coriander
   (cilantro) roots and stems
80 ml (2½ fl oz/⅓ cup) lime juice
2 tablespoons fish sauce
¼ teaspoon ground white pepper
2 small red chillies, seeded and thinly
   sliced
2 red Asian shallots, thinly sliced
2 telegraph (long) cucumbers, sliced into
   thin ribbons
2 large handfuls mint
90 g (3¼ oz/1 cup) bean sprouts, trimmed
40 g (1½ oz/¼ cup) chopped unsalted
   roasted peanuts

1 Thinly slice the beef across the grain. Heat a wok over high heat, then add 1 tablespoon of the oil and swirl to coat the side of the wok. Add half the beef and cook for 1–2 minutes, or until

medium–rare. Remove from the wok and put on a plate. Repeat with remaining oil and beef.

2 Put the garlic, palm sugar, coriander, lime juice, fish sauce, white pepper and ¼ teaspoon salt in a bowl, and stir until the sugar has dissolved. Add the chilli and shallots and mix well.

3 Pour the sauce over the hot beef, mix together well, then allow the beef to cool to room temperature.

4 In a separate bowl, toss together the cucumber and mint, and refrigerate until required.

5 Pile up a bed of the cucumber and mint on a serving platter, then top with the beef and the marinade, then the bean sprouts and peanuts.

thai salads

Most Thai salads are a subtle combination of apparently opposing tastes and textures — crisp raw vegetables and chilli-hot meat or seafood — and are made with a range of ingredients, from rose petals to squid. Raw or rare beef salads are a traditional feature of northeastern Thailand.

laos & cambodia

The cuisine of these two neighbours owes much to the influence of the country that they both border, Thailand, and the abundance of fresh fish caught in the Mekong River in landlocked Laos or the Gulf of Thailand in Cambodia. The fish are cooked simply with aromatic herbs or citrus marinades, while other soups, meat and vegetable dishes may be flavoured with garlic, ginger, chilli, galangal and lime leaves and scattered with fresh basil, coriander and mint.

seafood soup

seafood soup

✴

Preparation time: 30 minutes
Cooking time: 40 minutes
Serves 6

4 tomatoes
500 g (1 lb 2 oz) raw prawns (shrimp)
1 tablespoon oil
5 cm (2 inch) piece fresh ginger, grated
3 tablespoons finely chopped lemongrass,
    white part only
3 small red chillies, finely chopped
2 onions, chopped
750 ml (26 fl oz/3 cups) fish stock
4 kaffir lime (makrut) leaves,
    finely shredded
165 g (5¾ oz/1 cup) chopped pineapple
1 tablespoon tamarind concentrate
1 tablespoon grated palm sugar (jaggery)
    or soft brown sugar
2 tablespoons lime juice
1 tablespoon fish sauce
500 g (1 lb 2 oz) firm white fish fillets, cut
    into 2 cm (¾ inch) cubes)
2 tablespoons chopped coriander
    (cilantro) leaves

1 Score a cross in the base of the tomatoes. Put in a heatproof bowl and cover with boiling water. Leave for 30 seconds, then transfer to cold water and peel the skin away from the cross. Cut the tomatoes in half, scoop out the seeds and chop the flesh.

2 Peel the prawns and gently pull out the dark vein from each prawn back, starting at the head end.

3 Heat the oil in a large saucepan. Add the ginger, lemongrass, chilli and onion and stir over medium heat for 5 minutes or until the onion is golden.

4 Add the tomato to the pan and cook for 3 minutes. Stir in the stock, 750 ml (26 fl oz/3 cups) water, the lime leaves, pineapple, tamarind, palm sugar, lime juice and fish sauce. Cover, bring to the boil, then reduce the heat and simmer for 15 minutes.

5 Add the fish, prawns and coriander to the pan, and simmer for 10 minutes or until the seafood is tender. Serve immediately.

laotian fish balls

✴

Preparation time: 30 minutes
Cooking time: 10 minutes
Makes 24 balls

500 g (1 lb 2 oz) firm white fish fillets
2 tablespoons fish sauce
3 red chillies, seeded and finely chopped
1½ teaspoons finely chopped lemongrass,
    white part only
4 garlic cloves, crushed
3 spring onions (scallions), finely chopped
4 tablespoons chopped coriander
    (cilantro) leaves
1 egg, beaten
2 tablespoons rice flour
oil, for deep-frying
1 lemon, cut into wedges, to serve

1 Finely chop the fish. Alternatively, chop the fish in a food processor but be careful not to overwork it or the fish will be tough. Combine the fish and fish sauce in a bowl. Add the chilli, lemongrass, garlic, spring onion and half the coriander and mix well. Add the egg and rice flour and mix until thoroughly combined.

2 With slightly damp hands, make small balls from the mixture, each with a diameter of approximately 3 cm (1¼ inches).

3 Fill a deep heavy-based saucepan or deep-fryer one-third full of oil and heat to 180°C (350°F), or until a cube of bread dropped into the oil browns in 15 seconds. Add the fish balls in two batches and cook until golden. Drain on paper towels. Sprinkle the remaining coriander over the fish balls and serve immediately with the lemon wedges.

chicken and pumpkin stew

❋ ❋

Preparation time: **20 minutes**
Cooking time: **50 minutes**
Serves 6

110 g (3¾ oz/½ cup) medium-grain rice
2 tablespoons oil
1 kg (2 lb 4 oz) chicken pieces
3 garlic cloves, crushed
3 tablespoons finely chopped lemongrass, white part only
2 teaspoons grated fresh turmeric or 1 teaspoon ground turmeric
2 tablespoons grated fresh galangal
6 kaffir lime (makrut) leaves, finely shredded
6 spring onions (scallions), chopped
1 litre (35 fl oz/4 cups) chicken stock
500 g (1 lb 2 oz) pumpkin (winter squash), cubed
1 small green pawpaw, peeled and chopped
125 g (4½ oz) snake (yard-long) beans, trimmed, cut into short lengths

1 Preheat the oven to 180°C (350°F/ Gas 4). Spread the rice on a baking tray and roast it for 15 minutes or until golden. Remove the rice from the oven,

allow it to cool slightly and then process it in a food processor until finely ground.

2 Heat the oil in a large saucepan; add the chicken pieces in batches and cook for 5 minutes, or until brown. Drain on paper towels.

3 Add the garlic, lemongrass, turmeric, galangal, lime leaves and spring onion to the pan; cook over medium heat for 3 minutes or until spring onion is golden. Return the chicken to the pan; add the stock, cover and simmer for 20 minutes.

4 Add the pumpkin and pawpaw, and simmer, covered, for 10 minutes. Add the beans and simmer, covered, for another 10 minutes, or until the chicken is tender. Stir in the ground rice, bring to the boil, then reduce the heat and simmer, uncovered, for 5 minutes or until the mixture thickens slightly.

NOTE: Green pawpaw is available at Asian food stores. If it is not available, green mango can be substituted.

chicken and pumpkin stew

fish and noodle soup

✵

Preparation time: 15 minutes
Cooking time: 25 minutes
Serves 4

200 g (7 oz) dried rice vermicelli
1 tablespoon oil
2.5 cm (1 inch) piece fresh ginger, grated
3 small red chillies, finely chopped
4 spring onions (scallions), chopped
875 ml (30 fl oz/3½ cups) coconut milk
2 tablespoons fish sauce
2 tablespoons tomato paste
   (concentrated purée)
500 g (1 lb 2 oz) firm white fish fillets,
   cubed
2 ham steaks, diced
150 g (5½ oz) snake (yard-long) beans,
   trimmed, chopped
185 g (6½ oz) bean sprouts, trimmed
1 small handful mint
80 g (2¾ oz/½ cup) unsalted roasted
   peanuts

1   Soak the vermicelli in boiling water
for 6–7 minutes, or until soft, then drain
well. Set aside.
2   Heat the oil in a large, heavy-based
saucepan and cook ginger, chilli and spring
onion for 3 minutes, or until golden. Stir
in the coconut milk, fish sauce and tomato
paste, cover and simmer for 10 minutes.
Add the fish, ham and beans and simmer
for 10 minutes, or until fish is tender.
3   Divide the vermicelli among four
bowls and top with the bean sprouts and
mint. Spoon the soup into the bowls and
sprinkle with peanuts.

steamed spicy chicken

✵ ✵

Preparation time: 40 minutes
Cooking time: 30 minutes
Serves 4

125 ml (4 fl oz/½ cup) coconut cream
2 teaspoons grated palm sugar (jaggery)
   or soft brown sugar

1 tablespoon fish sauce
2 kaffir lime (makrut) leaves,
   shredded
500 g (1 lb 2 oz) boneless, skinless chicken
   breasts, cut into 5 cm (2 inch) strips
180 g (6 oz/4 cups) shredded silverbeet
   (Swiss chard) or spinach

SPICE PASTE
7 dried chillies, seeded
4 lemongrass stems, white part only,
   finely chopped
1 slice fresh galangal, finely chopped
1 slice fresh turmeric, finely chopped

6 cm (2½ inch) strip makrut (kaffir lime)
   zest, chopped
1 teaspoon shrimp paste
4 garlic cloves, chopped
4 red Asian shallots, chopped

1   To make the spice paste, soak the
chillies in hot water for 30 minutes
or until soft; drain. Place the softened
chillies and ½ teaspoon salt in a food
processor and process until a smooth
paste has formed. Add all the other paste
ingredients one at a time while continuing
to run the processor.

steamed spicy chicken

2 Combine the coconut cream, palm sugar, fish sauce and lime leaves in a large bowl. Add the spice paste and stir together until well combined. Stir in the chicken strips.

3 Select a round heatproof serving dish which will fit into a large, deep saucepan. Put the silverbeet onto the serving dish. Spoon the spicy chicken mixture over the silverbeet.

4 Place a saucer or rack on the base of the pan and pour in enough boiling water to cover it. Place the dish on top of the saucer or rack, cover the pan with a tight-fitting lid and steam over medium heat for about 30 minutes or until the chicken is cooked. Check from time to time that there is enough water in the pan. Serve with steamed rice, if desired.

prawns steamed in banana leaves

✳ ✳

Preparation time: 25 minutes + 2 hours
   marinating time
Cooking time: 15 minutes
Serves 4

1 kg (2 lb 4 oz) raw prawns (shrimp)
8 small banana leaves
1 tablespoon sesame seeds
2.5 cm (1 inch) piece fresh ginger, grated
2 small red chillies, finely chopped
4 spring onions (scallions), finely chopped
2 lemongrass stems, white part only,
   finely chopped
2 teaspoons soft brown sugar
1 tablespoon fish sauce
2 tablespoons lime juice
2 tablespoons chopped coriander (cilantro)
   leaves

Cut the banana leaves into 18 cm (7 inch) squares.

Fold the leaf to enclose the filling, then secure the parcel with a wooden skewer.

1 Peel the prawns and gently pull out the dark vein from each prawn back, starting at the head end. Put the banana leaves in a large heatproof bowl, cover with boiling water and leave them to soak for 3 minutes, or until softened. Drain and pat dry. Cut the banana leaves into squares, about 18 cm (7 inches). Toast the sesame seeds in a dry frying pan over medium heat for 3–4 minutes, shaking the pan gently, until the seeds are golden brown. Remove from the pan at once to prevent the seeds burning.

2 Place the ginger, chilli, spring onion and lemongrass in a food processor, and process in short bursts until a paste forms. Transfer the paste to a bowl; stir in the sugar, fish sauce, lime juice, sesame seeds and coriander and mix well. Add the prawns and toss to coat. Cover the bowl and marinate for 2 hours in the refrigerator.

3 Divide the mixture into eight, and place a portion on each banana leaf. Fold the leaf to enclose the mixture, and then secure the parcels with a wooden skewer.

4 Cook the parcels in a bamboo steamer over simmering water for 8–10 minutes or until the prawn filling is cooked.

NOTE: Banana leaves are available from Asian food stores and speciality fruit and vegetable stores or a banana tree!

containers for marinating

As a marinade usually contains an acid, such as vinegar, rice wine, lime juice or lemon juice, always use a non-metallic container to marinate food as acid will react with metal. A dish of glass or glazed china is best. Use a wooden spoon to stir or turn the food.

chicken mince with herbs and spices

chicken mince with herbs and spices

☀

Preparation time: **30 minutes**
Cooking time: **30 minutes**
Serves **4–6**

55 g (2 oz/¼ cup) medium-grain white rice
1 kg (2 lb 4 oz) boneless, skinless chicken thighs
2 tablespoons peanut oil
4 garlic cloves, crushed
2 tablespoons grated fresh galangal
2 small red chillies
4 spring onions (scallions), finely chopped
60 ml (2 fl oz/¼ cup) fish sauce
1 tablespoon shrimp paste
3 tablespoons chopped Vietnamese mint
2 tablespoons chopped basil
4 tablespoons lime juice
lettuce leaves, to serve

1 Preheat the oven to 180°C (350°F/ Gas 4). Spread the rice on a baking tray and roast for 15 minutes or until golden. Cool slightly, then transfer the rice to a food processor and process until finely ground. Set aside.
2 Place the chicken in a food processor and process until finely minced.
3 Heat the oil in a wok or frying pan; add the garlic, galangal, chilli and spring onion and cook over medium heat for 3 minutes. Add the minced (ground) chicken to the wok and stir for 5 minutes, or until the mince is browned, breaking up any large lumps with a wooden spoon. Stir in the fish sauce and shrimp paste and bring to the boil, then reduce the heat and simmer for 5 minutes.
4 Remove the wok from the heat, stir in the rice, mint, basil and lime juice, and mix to combine. Serve with lettuce leaves.

laotian beef salad

☀

Preparation time: **15 minutes + 2 hours marinating time**
Cooking time: **10 minutes**
Serves **4**

500 g (1 lb 2 oz) rump steak
3 tablespoons lemon juice
2 tablespoons finely chopped lemongrass, white part only
1 tablespoon fish sauce
1 onion, thinly sliced
2 tablespoons chopped coriander (cilantro) leaves
1 tablespoon chopped mint, plus mint leaves, extra, to garnish
2 Lebanese (short) cucumbers, chopped
½ small Chinese cabbage (wong bok), shredded

1   Chargrill the beef for 3 minutes on each side or until cooked to medium-rare. Remove, cover and set aside for 5 minutes. Use a sharp knife to cut the beef into 5 mm (¼ inch) thick slices.

2   Heat 4 tablespoons water in a wok, add the sliced beef and cook over medium heat for 2 minutes. Do not overcook. Transfer the beef and liquid to a non-metallic bowl.

3   Add the lemon juice, lemongrass, fish sauce, onion, coriander and mint and mix until well combined. Cover and leave in the refrigerator for 2 hours to marinate.

4   Stir in the chopped cucumber. Serve the salad on a bed of shredded cabbage, garnished with the extra mint leaves.

NOTE: If you prefer your beef more well done, increase the chargrilling time.

laotian dried beef with green pawpaw salad

❋

Preparation time: 30 minutes + 4 hours
    marinating time
Cooking time: 5 hours 5 minutes
Serves 6

1 kg (2 lb 4 oz) piece topside steak,
    partially frozen
2 teaspoons salt
¼ teaspoon chilli powder
1 teaspoon ground black pepper
1 tablespoon soft brown sugar
4 garlic cloves, crushed
2 teaspoons sesame oil
1 tablespoon peanut oil

GREEN PAWPAW SALAD
1 small green pawpaw, peeled
    and seeded
1 carrot
2 garlic cloves, crushed
6 cm (2½ inch) piece fresh ginger,
    finely grated
2 small red chillies
2 tablespoons fish sauce
4 kaffir lime (makrut) leaves, finely shredded

1 tablespoon lime juice
2 teaspoons soft brown sugar
1 teaspoon sesame oil
30 g (1 oz/1 cup) coriander (cilantro) leaves
160 g (5¾ oz/1 cup) unsalted roasted
    peanuts

1   Preheat the oven to 120°C (235°F/ Gas ½).

2   Trim any excess fat from the beef. Cut the beef into 3 mm (⅛ inch) thick slices, then into strips. Mix the salt, chilli powder, pepper, sugar, garlic, sesame oil and peanut oil in a bowl. Add the beef and, using your fingertips, toss it in the oil mixture until coated. Cover and marinate for 4 hours in the refrigerator.

3   Place the beef on a rack in a large baking dish and bake for 5 hours, or until it is dried out.

4   To make the green pawpaw salad, cut the papaya and carrot into shreds, using a citrus zester if you have one. Combine the pawpaw and carrot in a bowl with the remaining ingredients and toss lightly.

5   Cook the beef under a hot grill (broiler) for 3 minutes, then serve with the green pawpaw salad.

NOTE: The dried beef will keep for 3 weeks in an airtight container in the refrigerator or can be frozen for up to 6 months.

laotian dried beef with green pawpaw salad

grilled pork

☀

Preparation time: 10 minutes + 4 hours
   marinating time
Cooking time: 15 minutes
Serves 4

1 kg (2 lb 4 oz) pork chops
8 garlic cloves, crushed
2 tablespoons fish sauce
1 tablespoon soy sauce
2 tablespoons oyster sauce
2 tablespoons finely chopped spring onion
   (scallion)

1   Place the pork in a large glass bowl
and add the garlic, fish sauce, soy sauce,
oyster sauce and ½ teaspoon ground
black pepper. Stir well so that all the meat
is covered with the marinade; cover and
marinate for 4 hours in the refrigerator.

2   Preheat a grill (broiler) to hot; cook
the pork on both sides until browned
and cooked through. If the meat starts to
burn, move it further away from the grill
element. Alternatively, you can cook the
pork on a hot barbecue grill.
3   Arrange the pork on a serving platter
and scatter over the spring onion.

spicy eggplant and fish purée in salad leaves

☀

Preparation time: 45 minutes
Cooking time: 1 hour
Serves 6

1 large eggplant (aubergine), approximately
   800 g (1 lb 12 oz)
12 garlic cloves, unpeeled
4 red Asian shallots, unpeeled
600 g (1 lb 5 oz) white fish fillets
peanut oil, to brush
100 g (3½ oz) dried mung bean vermicelli
2 tablespoons fish sauce
3 red chillies, seeded and finely chopped
2 tablespoons mint, roughly chopped
2 tablespoons coriander (cilantro) leaves,
   roughly chopped
1 mignonette lettuce
1 butter lettuce
50 g (1¾ oz) coriander (cilantro) sprigs

SAUCE
3 tablespoons fish sauce
3 tablespoons lime juice
1 teaspoon caster (superfine) sugar
1 red chilli, seeded and thinly sliced

1   Preheat the oven to 180°C (350°F/
Gas 4). Place the eggplant on a baking
tray and bake for 50 minutes, or until soft
and tender. Add the garlic and shallots
to the baking tray after 15 minutes of
cooking. Allow to cool.
2   Brush the fish with the oil and cook
under a hot grill (broiler) until cooked
through. Allow the fish to cool, then
break into pieces.

3 Place the vermicelli in boiling water and cook for 1–2 minutes or until tender. Drain, cool and chop roughly.

4 Cut the eggplant in half, scoop out the soft flesh and place it in a food processor. Squeeze six of the soft garlic cloves and all the shallots from their skins into the food processor. Add the fish, fish sauce, chilli, mint and coriander, and process until a fine-textured purée forms. Transfer the purée to a bowl, season to taste with salt, and stir in the vermicelli.

5 To make the sauce, place all the ingredients in a food processor. Squeeze the remaining cloves of garlic into the food processor and process until a smooth sauce forms. Heat the sauce in a small saucepan, stirring to dissolve the sugar, and then allow it to cool to room temperature.

6 To serve, place the bowl containing the purée onto a platter and surround it with the lettuce leaves and coriander sprigs. Place the sauce in a separate bowl. The diners help themselves — each takes a lettuce leaf and places a sprig of coriander on top of it. They then place a spoonful of purée and a teaspoon of the sauce on the leaves and roll them up to eat.

lemongrass beef skewers

✻

Preparation time: **15 minutes + 4 hours marinating time**
Cooking time: **5 minutes**
Serves **4**

500 g (1 lb 2 oz) sirloin steak
2 teaspoons chilli flakes
4 lemongrass stems, white part only, chopped
2 slices fresh galangal, chopped
2 slices fresh turmeric, chopped
4 garlic cloves, peeled
1 tablespoon grated palm sugar (jaggery) or soft brown sugar
125 ml (4 fl oz/½ cup) oyster sauce
2 tablespoons oil
lemon basil, to garnish
sliced red chilli, to garnish

1 Soak 10–12 wooden skewers in water for 30 minutes to prevent them burning during cooking.

2 Cut the beef into long, thin strips and put in a non-metallic bowl. Use a mortar and pestle to pound the chilli, lemongrass, galangal, turmeric and garlic to form a paste. Add the palm sugar, oyster sauce, 1 teaspoon salt and the oil and combine well. Spoon the marinade over the beef and mix well. Cover with plastic wrap and refrigerate for 4 hours.

3 Thread the beef onto the skewers. Heat a barbecue grill or hotplate and cook the skewers for 5 minutes, or until browned and cooked through. Serve garnished with the lemon basil and red chilli.

laotian purées

Unique to Laotian cooking are its puréed dishes — raw meat or cooked fish pounded to a smooth, soft consistency, seasoned with chilli and herbs and then served with lettuce and leafy herbs. Another feature of the cuisine is the method of using slow-cooked eggplant as a thickening agent for stewed dishes.

vietnam

The lush greenness of Vietnam produces a wide range of vegetables and herbs that impart a fresh taste and fragrance to its cooking. Bunches of coriander and mint are scattered over steaming bowls of pho, a soupy noodle and meat dish which can be bought on every street corner. The basic flavour of many Vietnamese dishes comes from nuoc mam, a fish sauce that is added to soups and stir-fries, or used in marinades with lemongrass, lemon juice and chillies to give a tangy, pungent flavour to meat and fish.

lemongrass

This long, grass-like herb has a citrus aroma and taste. Trim the base, remove the tough outer layers and thinly slice, finely chop or pound the white interior. For pastes and salads, use the tender, white portion just above the root. The whole stem, trimmed, washed and bruised with the back of a knife, can be added to simmering curries and soups (remove before serving). Dried lemongrass is rather flavourless, so you may prefer to use lemon zest, although either is a poor substitute for the real thing.

stir-fried chicken with lemongrass, ginger and chilli

stir-fried chicken with lemongrass, ginger and chilli

☀

Preparation time: 30 minutes
Cooking time: 15 minutes
Serves 4

2 tablespoons oil
2 brown onions, roughly chopped
4 garlic cloves, finely chopped
5 cm (2 inch) piece fresh ginger, finely grated
3 lemongrass stems, white part only, thinly sliced
2 teaspoons chopped green chilli
500 g (1 lb 2 oz) boneless, skinless chicken thighs, thinly sliced

2 teaspoons sugar
1 tablespoon fish sauce
coriander (cilantro) and Vietnamese mint leaves, finely chopped, to garnish

1 Heat the oil in a heavy-based frying pan or wok over medium heat. Add the onion, garlic, ginger, lemongrass and chilli and stir-fry for 3–5 minutes, or until the mixture is lightly golden. Take care not to burn the mixture or it will become bitter.
2 Increase the heat to high and when the pan is very hot, add the chicken and toss. Sprinkle the sugar over the chicken and cook for about 5 minutes, tossing regularly until the chicken is just cooked. Add the fish sauce, cook for a further 2 minutes, then serve immediately, garnished with the coriander and Vietnamese mint.

crab, prawn and potato fritters

☀

Preparation time: 25 minutes
Cooking time: 20 minutes

[handwritten note: REDUCE or DELETE COCONUT MILK as alternative BIND WITH EGG]

[handwritten note: USE DRY MASHED POTATO IN LIEU OF GRATED RAW]

starting at the head end. Finely chop the prawn meat. Drain the crabmeat. Finely grate the potatoes, squeezing out as much water as possible.
2 Place the prawn meat, crabmeat, potato, flour, coconut milk, fish sauce,

½ teaspoon salt, ½ teaspoon pepper and sugar in a large bowl and combine well.

3 Heat the oil in a frying pan or wok until hot; cook tablespoons of the mixture, about 3 at a time, tossing gently until golden brown. Drain the fritters on paper towels.

4 Arrange the fritters on a bed of lettuce leaves and garnish with the mint leaves. Serve with the Vietnamese dipping sauce.

NOTE: Grate the potatoes just before cooking to keep them from going brown.

caramelised prawns

✳ ✳

Preparation time: **25 minutes**
Cooking time: **15 minutes**
Serves **4**

500 g (1 lb 2 oz) raw prawns (shrimp)
6 spring onions (scallions)
1 tablespoon oil
3 garlic cloves, finely chopped
2 tablespoons caramel sauce
   (see Note)
1 tablespoon fish sauce
1 tablespoon lime juice
1 tablespoon soft brown sugar
¼ red capsicum (pepper), cut into fine
   strips, to garnish

1 Remove the prawn heads and, using a fine needle, devein the prawns, leaving the tails, shells and legs intact. Rinse the prawns under running water and pat dry with paper towels.

2 Finely chop half the spring onions. Cut the rest into 4 cm (1½ inch) long pieces and then finely shred the pieces into thin strips.

3 Heat the oil in a heavy-based frying pan; add the garlic, chopped spring onion and prawns, and cook over medium heat for about 3 minutes, tossing the prawns until they turn pink. Drizzle the caramel sauce and fish sauce over the top and cook for 1 minute. Add the lime juice, sugar, ½ teaspoon salt and remaining spring onion. Toss well and

serve immediately, garnished with the capsicum. If the prawn shells are tender, they can be eaten, but supply finger bowls and napkins at the table so your diners can peel the prawns if they prefer.

NOTE: To make the caramel sauce, combine 4 tablespoons sugar and 60 ml (2 fl oz/¼ cup) water in a small saucepan. Stir over low heat, without boiling, until the sugar has dissolved. Bring the syrup to the boil, reduce the heat and simmer gently for about 5 minutes, until the syrup turns dark golden. Take care not to burn it. Remove the pan from the heat and add 80 ml (2½ fl oz/⅓ cup) water — it will spit and sizzle, and the caramel will form hard lumps. Return the pan to the heat and cook, stirring, until the lumps become liquid again. The sauce can be stored in the refrigerator for up to 1 week.

When water is added to the caramel sauce, hard lumps will form.

Toss the unpeeled prawns in the pan until they turn pink.

Add the lime juice, sugar, salt and remaining spring onion to the pan.

whole barbecued fish

✳

Preparation time: 40 minutes
Cooking time: 20 minutes
Serves 4–6

750 g (1 lb 10 oz) snapper or bream,
    cleaned and scaled
2 teaspoons green peppercorns
2 teaspoons chopped red chilli
3 teaspoons fish sauce
1 tablespoon oil
2 onions, thinly sliced
4 cm (1½ inch) piece fresh ginger,
    thinly sliced
3 garlic cloves, thinly sliced
2 teaspoons sugar
4 spring onions (scallions),
    cut into 4 cm (1½ inch) pieces,
    then finely shredded
lemon and garlic dipping sauce
    (page 148), to serve
lime cheeks, to serve

1 Wash the fish inside and out and pat
dry with paper towels. Cut two diagonal
slashes into the thickest part of the fish
on both sides.
2 Put the peppercorns, chilli and fish
sauce in a food processor and process
until a paste forms. Alternatively, use a
mortar and pestle. Brush the paste lightly
over the fish, cover and refrigerate for
20 minutes.
3 Heat a barbecue hotplate until very hot
and lightly brush it with oil. Cook the fish
for 8 minutes on each side, or until the
flesh flakes easily when tested with a fork.
4 While the fish is cooking, heat the oil
in a frying pan over medium heat. Add
the onion and cook, stirring, for about
5 minutes, or until golden. Add the ginger,
garlic and sugar and cook for a further
3 minutes.
5 Place the fish on a serving plate, top
with the onion mixture, sprinkle over the
spring onion and serve immediately with
the lemon and garlic dipping sauce and
lime wedges.

beef pho (beef soup)

✳ ✳

Preparation time: 15 minutes
Cooking time: 35 minutes
Serves 4

2 litres (70 fl oz/8 cups) beef stock
1 whole star anise
4 cm (1½ inch) piece fresh ginger, sliced
2 pigs' trotters (cut in half)
½ onion, studded with 2 whole cloves
2 lemongrass stems, bruised
2 garlic cloves, crushed
¼ teaspoon ground white pepper
1 tablespoon fish sauce, plus extra,
    to serve
200 g (7 oz) fresh thin rice noodles
300 g (10½ oz) beef fillet, partially frozen,
    thinly sliced
90 g (3¼ oz/1 cup) bean sprouts, trimmed
2 spring onions (scallions), thinly sliced
25 g (1 oz/½ cup) chopped coriander
    (cilantro) leaves, plus extra, to serve

4 tablespoons chopped Vietnamese mint,
    plus extra, to serve
1 red chilli, thinly sliced, plus extra, to serve
2 limes, quartered

1 Put the stock, star anise, ginger, pigs'
trotters, onion, lemongrass, garlic and
white pepper in a wok and bring to the
boil. Reduce the heat to very low and
simmer, covered, for 30 minutes. Strain,
return to the wok and stir in the fish sauce.
2 Meanwhile, put the noodles in a
heatproof bowl, cover with boiling water
and gently separate. Drain well then
refresh under cold running water. Divide
the noodles among four deep soup bowls
then top with beef strips, bean sprouts,
spring onion, coriander, mint and chilli.
Ladle over the broth.
3 Place the extra fish sauce, chilli,
mint and coriander and the lime quarters
in small bowls on a platter, serve with
the soup and allow your guests to
help themselves.

vietnamese chicken salad

❋

Preparation time: 40 minutes
Cooking time: 5 minutes
Serves 4

600 g (1 lb 5 oz) boneless, skinless chicken
    thighs, cooked
125 g (4½ oz/1 cup) thinly sliced celery
2 carrots, cut into 5 cm (2 inch) lengths
75 g (2¾ oz/1 cup) finely shredded cabbage
1 small onion, sliced
3 tablespoons coriander (cilantro) leaves
3 tablespoons finely shredded mint

DRESSING
3 tablespoons caster (superfine) sugar
2 tablespoons water
1 tablespoon fish sauce
1 teaspoon crushed garlic
2 tablespoons white vinegar
1 red chilli, seeded and finely chopped

TOPPING
2 tablespoons peanut oil
1½ teaspoons chopped garlic
50 g (1¾ oz/⅓ cup) unsalted roasted
    peanuts, finely chopped
1 tablespoon soft brown sugar or
    2 teaspoons caster (superfine) sugar

1   Slice the chicken into long, thin strips.
Combine the chicken, celery, carrot,
cabbage, onion, coriander and mint in a
large bowl.
2   To make the dressing, place all the
ingredients in a small bowl. Whisk
until the sugar has dissolved and the
ingredients are well combined.
3   To make the topping, heat the oil
in a wok; add the garlic and cook over
moderate heat, stirring, until pale golden.
Stir in the peanuts and sugar.
4   Pour the dressing over the chicken
mixture and toss to combine. Place
the chicken salad on a serving plate,
and sprinkle over the topping just
before serving.

eggplant slices in black bean sauce

❋

Preparation time: 20 minutes
Cooking time: 35 minutes
Serves 4

500 g (1 lb 2 oz) eggplants (aubergines)
80 ml (2½ fl oz/⅓ cup) oil
4 garlic cloves, finely chopped
4 cm (1½ inch) piece fresh ginger, grated
2 onions, finely chopped
80 ml (2½ fl oz /⅓ cup) chicken stock
2 teaspoons tinned black beans, rinsed well,
    roughly chopped
2 tablespoons oyster sauce
1 tablespoon soy sauce
2 teaspoons fish sauce
4 spring onions (scallions), thinly sliced

1   Slice the eggplants into long slices and
lightly brush each side with oil.
2   Heat a frying pan over moderately
low heat; add the eggplant, four to five
slices at a time, and cook until golden
on both sides; remove from the pan. Do

eggplant slices in black bean sauce

not hurry this process as cooking the eggplant slowly allows the natural sugars to caramelise and produces a wonderful flavour. If the eggplant begins to burn, reduce the heat and sprinkle it with a little water.

3 Increase the heat to moderately high and add any remaining oil, the garlic, ginger, onion and about 1 tablespoon of the stock; cover and cook for 3 minutes. Add the remaining stock, black beans, oyster sauce, soy sauce and fish sauce. Bring to the boil and cook for 2 minutes. Return the eggplant to the pan and simmer for 2 minutes or until it is heated through. Scatter over the spring onion and serve.

NOTE: Always rinse black beans very well before using, as they are extremely salty. They will keep indefinitely if refrigerated after opening.

vermicelli and crabmeat stir-fry

✳

Preparation time: **40 minutes**
Cooking time: **15 minutes**
Serves 4

200 g (7 oz) dried mung bean
    vermicelli
2 tablespoons oil
10 red Asian shallots, very thinly sliced
3 garlic cloves, finely chopped
2 lemongrass stems, white part only,
    very thinly sliced
1 red capsicum (pepper), cut into 4 cm
    (1½ inch) matchsticks
170 g (6 oz) tin crabmeat, well drained
2 tablespoons fish sauce
2 tablespoons lime juice
2 teaspoons sugar
3 spring onions (scallions), thinly sliced

1 Soak the noodles in hot water for 20 minutes or until softened; drain. Use scissors to cut the noodles into short lengths for easy eating.

2 Heat the oil in a wok or heavy-based saucepan; add the shallots, garlic and lemongrass and stir-fry over high heat for 2 minutes. Add the capsicum and cook for 30 seconds, tossing well. Add the vermicelli and toss. Cover and steam for 1 minute, or until the vermicelli is heated through.

3 Add the crabmeat, fish sauce, lime juice and sugar and toss well, using two wooden spoons. Season with salt and pepper to taste, sprinkle with the spring onion and serve.

crabmeat

Fresh crabmeat is always best, but it is expensive and not always easily available. Tinned crabmeat has a slightly different flavour and texture to fresh — salt will have been added. After draining, use a knife or your finger to check for pieces of membrane or shell, and remove. Note that when drained, the crabmeat is only about half the weight shown on the tin.

pork and lettuce parcels

pork and lettuce parcels

✳

Preparation time: 1 hour
Cooking time: 1 hour
Serves 4–6

500 g (1 lb 2 oz) pork loin
5 cm (2 inch) piece fresh ginger, thinly sliced
1 tablespoon fish sauce
20 thin spring onions (scallions)
2 soft-leaf lettuces, such as butter lettuce
1 Lebanese (short) cucumber, thinly sliced
3 tablespoons mint leaves
3 tablespoons coriander (cilantro) leaves
2 green chillies (optional), seeded and
    very thinly sliced
2 teaspoons caster (superfine) sugar
Lemon and garlic dipping sauce (page 148),
    to serve

1 Put the pork, ginger and fish sauce in a large saucepan and cover with cold water. Bring to the boil, then reduce the heat and simmer, covered, for about 45 minutes, or until the pork is tender. Remove the pork and allow to cool. Discard the liquid.
2 Trim both ends from the spring onions so you have long stems of equal length. Bring a large saucepan of water to the boil and blanch the spring onions, two or three at a time, for about 2 minutes, until softened. Remove the spring onions from the hot water with tongs and place in a bowl of iced water. Drain and lay them flat and straight on a tray.
3 Separate the lettuce into leaves. If the leaves have a firm section at the base, trim this away (or making a neat parcel will be difficult).
4 When the pork is cool enough to handle, cut it into thin slices and finely shred each slice. Spread out a lettuce leaf and place about 1 tablespoon of the shredded pork in the centre of the leaf. Top with a few slices of cucumber, a few mint and coriander leaves, a little green chilli, if desired, and a light sprinkling of sugar. Fold a section of the lettuce over the filling,

bring in the sides to meet each other, and carefully roll up the parcel. Tie one of the spring onions around the parcel, trim off the excess or tie it into a bow. Repeat with the remaining ingredients.
5 Arrange the pork and lettuce parcels on a serving platter and serve with the Lemon and garlic dipping sauce.

seared pork skewers

✳

Preparation time: 35 minutes
Cooking time: 15 minutes
Serves 4

500 g (1 lb 2 oz) pork fillet, cut into 2 cm
    (¾ inch) cubes
5 cm (2 inch) piece fresh ginger, finely
    grated
2 garlic cloves, finely chopped
2 tablespoons fish sauce
1 tablespoon dry sherry
2 teaspoons oil
mint, to garnish
Vietnamese dipping sauce (page 148),
    to serve
steamed rice or cooked rice noodles, to serve

1 Soak eight wooden skewers in water for 30 minutes to prevent burning.
2 Place the pork in a bowl with the ginger, garlic, fish sauce, sherry, ½ teaspoon salt and ½ teaspoon pepper and marinate for 20 minutes. Drain the pork and reserve the marinade. Dry the skewers with paper towels and thread the meat onto them.
3 Brush a heavy-based frying pan with oil and heat until extremely hot. Cook the skewers of pork, three at a time, for 3–4 minutes; turn the skewers regularly until the pork becomes a dark golden brown and sprinkle over a little of the marinade. Do not overcook the pork or it will become very dry.
4 Garnish with the mint and serve with the Vietnamese dipping sauce and steamed rice or cooked rice noodles.

warm beef and watercress salad

✳

Preparation time: 25 minutes + 30 minutes
    marinating time
Cooking time: 10 minutes
Serves 4

350 g (12 oz) fillet steak, partially frozen
    (optional) (see Note)
1 tablespoon green peppercorns, roughly
    chopped
4 garlic cloves, crushed
3 lemongrass stems, white part only,
    very thinly sliced
3 tablespoons oil
250 g (9 oz) watercress
125 g (4½ oz) cherry tomatoes, halved
4 spring onions (scallions), chopped
2 tablespoons lime juice

1 Cut the beef into thin slices. Place the beef, peppercorns, garlic, lemongrass, 2 tablespoons of the oil, ¼ teaspoon salt and ¼ teaspoon pepper in a bowl. Mix well, cover and marinate in the refrigerator for 30 minutes.
2 Remove the watercress sprigs from the tough stems, break them into small pieces, and wash and drain them well. Arrange the watercress on a serving platter and place the tomatoes on top, around the outside edge.
3 Heat the remaining oil in a wok or heavy-based frying pan until very hot and lightly smoking. Add the beef mixture and stir-fry it quickly until the beef is just cooked. Add the spring onion and toss through. Remove the beef mixture from the pan, pile it up in the centre of the watercress and sprinkle the lime juice over the top. Serve immediately.

NOTE: Partially freezing the meat for 30 minutes makes it easier to slice thinly.

braised duck with mushrooms

☀ ☀

Preparation time: **20 minutes**
Cooking time: **1 hour 10 minutes**
Serves **6**

15 g (½ oz) dried Chinese mushrooms
1.5 kg (3 lb 5 oz) whole duck
2 teaspoons oil
2 tablespoons soy sauce
2 tablespoons shaoxing rice wine
　(Chinese rice wine)
2 teaspoons sugar
2 wide strips orange zest
125 g (4½ oz) watercress

1 Soak the mushrooms in hot water for 20 minutes. Drain well, discard the stems and thinly slice the caps.

2 Remove the neck and any large pieces of fat from inside the duck carcass. Using a large heavy knife or cleaver, chop the duck into small pieces, cutting through the bone. Arrange the pieces on a rack and pour boiling water over them — the water will plump up the skin and help keep the duck succulent. Drain and pat dry with paper towel.

3 Heat the oil in a wok over medium heat and add the duck. Cook, in batches, for about 8 minutes, turning regularly, until browned. (The darker the browning at this stage, the better the colour when finished.) Between each batch, wipe out

the pan with crumpled paper towels to remove excess oil.

4 Wipe the pan with paper towels again and return all the duck to the pan. Add the mushrooms, soy sauce, rice wine, sugar and orange zest.

5 Bring the mixture to the boil, reduce the heat, cover and simmer gently for 35 minutes or until the duck is tender. Season, to taste, and stand for 10 minutes, covered, before serving.

6 Remove the duck from the sauce and discard the orange zest. Pick off small sprigs of the watercress and arrange them on one side of a large serving platter. Carefully place the duck segments on the other side of the platter — try not to place the duck on the watercress as it will become soggy. Carefully spoon a little of the sauce over the duck and serve.

NOTE: Braising the duck over low heat produces tender, melt-in-the-mouth meat and a delicious sauce. If the heat is too high, the duck will dry out and lose its flavour.

vietnamese coleslaw

☀

Preparation time: **55 minutes**
Cooking time: **10 minutes**
Serves **4**

500 g (1 lb 2 oz) boneless, skinless chicken
　breasts
350 g (12 oz) Chinese cabbage (wong bok),
　finely shredded
3 celery stalks, thinly sliced
1 carrot, cut into fine matchsticks
1½ tablespoons oil
2 tablespoons shredded Vietnamese mint
1 tablespoon chopped garlic chives
1 tablespoon crisp fried onion

DRESSING
4 tablespoons rice vinegar
2 tablespoons caster (superfine) sugar
1 tablespoon fish sauce
1 tablespoon lime juice
1 onion, finely sliced

1 Place the chicken in a frying pan with enough water to just cover it. Poach the chicken over low heat for 8–10 minutes or until it is cooked — do not let the water boil; it should just simmer gently. Drain and cool. When the chicken is cool enough to touch, shred it into fine pieces using your fingertips.

2 To make the dressing, place the vinegar, sugar, fish sauce, lime juice, ½ teaspoon salt, ½ teaspoon pepper and the onion in a small bowl and toss well to combine. Let it stand for at least 20 minutes so that the onion absorbs all the flavours.

3 Place the chicken, cabbage, celery, carrot, oil and dressing in a bowl and toss well. Arrange the salad on a serving plate, scatter over the mint, chives and crisp fried onion, and serve immediately.

vietnamese spring rolls

❋ ❋

Preparation time: 50 minutes
Cooking time: 20 minutes
Makes 20

50 g (1¾ oz) dried mung bean vermicelli
2 tablespoons black fungus
500 g (1 lb 2 oz) raw prawns (shrimp)
20 rice paper wrappers
150 g (5½ oz) minced (ground) pork
4 spring onions (scallions), chopped
45 g (1¾ oz/½ cup) bean sprouts, trimmed, roughly chopped
1 teaspoon sugar
1 egg, beaten
oil, for deep-frying
20 lettuce leaves, to serve
90 g (3¼ oz/1 cup) bean sprouts, extra, trimmed
1 large handful mint
Vietnamese dipping sauce (page 148), to serve

1 Put the vermicelli and fungus in separate heatproof bowls. Cover with hot water and soak for 10 minutes, or until soft. Drain both, and chop the fungus roughly. Peel the prawns and gently pull out the dark vein from each prawn back, starting at the head end. Finely chop the prawn meat.

2 Use a pastry brush to brush both sides of each rice paper wrapper liberally with water. Allow to stand for 2 minutes, or until they become soft and pliable. Stack the wrappers on a plate. Sprinkle over a little extra water and cover the plate with plastic wrap to keep the wrappers moist until needed.

3 Combine vermicelli, fungus, prawn meat, pork, spring onion, bean sprouts, sugar and salt and pepper in a bowl.

4 Put 1 tablespoon of the filling along the base of a wrapper. Fold in the sides, roll the wrapper up tightly, and brush the seam with the egg. Repeat with the remaining wrappers and filling.

5 Press the rolls with paper towels to remove any excess water. Heat 4–5 cm (1½–2 inches) oil in a wok or deep frying pan to 180°C (350°F), or until a cube of bread dropped in the oil browns in 15 seconds. Add the spring rolls in batches and cook for 2–3 minutes, or until dark golden brown. Drain on paper towels.

6 To serve, put a spring roll in each lettuce leaf, top with 1 tablespoon bean sprouts and two mint leaves, and roll up to form a neat parcel. Serve with the Vietnamese dipping sauce.

dipping sauces

A small bowl of one of these delicious sauces will enhance the flavour of dishes ranging from spring rolls, satays and fritters, to noodles and fish dishes.

sweet chilli sauce

Remove the seeds from 6 large red chillies and soak for 15 minutes in hot water. Process with 1 tablespoon chopped red chilli, 60 ml (2 fl oz/¼ cup) white vinegar, 250 g (9 oz/1 cup) caster (superfine) sugar, 1 teaspoon salt and 4 chopped garlic cloves until smooth. Transfer to a saucepan and cook over medium heat for 15 minutes, stirring frequently until thickened. Cool. Stir in 2 teaspoons fish sauce.

sesame seed sauce

Toast 100 g (3½ oz) Japanese white sesame seeds in a dry frying pan over medium heat for 3–4 minutes, shaking the pan gently, until the seeds are golden brown; remove from the pan at once to prevent burning. Grind the seeds using a mortar and pestle until a paste is formed. Add 2 teaspoons oil, if necessary, to assist in forming a paste. Mix the paste with 125 ml (4 fl oz/½ cup) Japanese soy sauce, 2 tablespoons mirin, 3 teaspoons caster (superfine) sugar, ½ teaspoon instant dashi granules and 125 ml (4 fl oz/½ cup) warm water. Store, covered, in the refrigerator and use within 2 days of preparation.

soy and ginger sauce

In a bowl combine 1 tablespoon grated fresh ginger, 2 teaspoons sugar and 250 ml (9 fl oz/1 cup) soy sauce. Mix well and serve immediately.

peanut satay sauce

Place 160 g (5¾ oz/1 cup) unsalted roasted peanuts in a food processor and process until finely chopped. Heat 2 tablespoons oil in a medium saucepan. Add 1 chopped onion and cook over medium heat for 5 minutes or until softened. Add 2 crushed garlic cloves, 2 teaspoons grated fresh ginger, ½ teaspoon chilli powder, 2 teaspoons curry powder and 1 teaspoon ground cumin, and cook, stirring, for 2 minutes. Add 420 ml (14½ fl oz/1⅔ cups) coconut milk, 3 tablespoons soft brown sugar and chopped peanuts. Reduce the heat and cook for 5 minutes or until the sauce thickens. Add 1 tablespoon lemon juice, season and serve. (For a smoother sauce, process in a food processor for 30 seconds.)

lemon and garlic dipping sauce

In a small bowl, stir 60 ml (2 fl oz/¼ cup) lemon juice, 2 tablespoons fish sauce and 1 tablespoon caster (superfine) sugar until the sugar has dissolved. Stir in 2 chopped small red chillies and 3 finely chopped garlic cloves.

vietnamese dipping sauce

In a bowl, mix together 2 tablespoons fish sauce, 2 tablespoons cold water, 2 tablespoons chopped coriander (cilantro) leaves, 1 teaspoon chopped red chilli and 1 teaspoon soft brown sugar.

thai dipping sauce

In a small saucepan, combine 125 g (4½ oz/½ cup) sugar, 125 ml (4 fl oz/½ cup) water, 60 ml (2 fl oz/¼ cup) white vinegar, 1 tablespoon fish sauce and 1 small chopped red chilli. Bring to the boil and simmer, uncovered, for 5 minutes or until slightly thickened. Remove from the heat and cool slightly. Stir in ¼ small, peeled, seeded and finely chopped Lebanese (short) cucumber, ¼ small finely chopped carrot, and 1 tablespoon chopped roasted peanuts.

fried rice noodle pancake with garlic beef

mung bean vermicelli

Mung bean vermicelli, made by extruding a paste of mung bean flour and water, readily absorb the flavours of other foods and are popular throughout China, Southeast Asia and Japan. For vegetarians, the boiled noodles can be mixed with herbs, spices and flavourings to take the place of meat or prawns in stuffings or salads. In Indonesia, Malaysia and Singapore they are used as an ingredient in some sweet drinks and desserts.

fried rice noodle pancake with garlic beef

❋ ❋

Preparation time: 20 minutes + 30 minutes marinating time
Cooking time: 25 minutes
Serves 4–6

350 g (12 oz) fillet steak, thinly sliced
1 red capsicum (pepper), cut into short, thin strips
6 garlic cloves, finely chopped
4 tablespoons oil

400 g (14 oz) thick fresh rice noodles
1 tablespoon sugar
2 tablespoons fish sauce
125 ml (4 fl oz/½ cup) beef stock
2 teaspoons cornflour (cornstarch)
4 spring onions (scallions), thinly sliced

1 Place the beef, capsicum, garlic, ¼ teaspoon pepper and half the oil in a large bowl; mix well to combine and marinate for 30 minutes.
2 Gently separate the noodles. Heat the remaining oil in a heavy-based frying pan over medium heat, swirling the oil to coat the pan well. Add the noodles and press them down firmly with a spatula to form a large flat pancake the size of the pan. Cook the noodles for 10–15 minutes, pressing down occasionally, until the base is very crisp and golden. Do not disturb or lift the noodles as they need to form a solid pancake. Run a spatula underneath to loosen the base then turn it over with 2 spatulas and cook the other side. Be patient because if the pancake is moved before it sets it will break up. Transfer to a plate, cover and keep warm.
3 Heat a heavy-based saucepan or wok. Sprinkle the sugar and fish sauce over the beef mixture. Add the beef mixture to the pan in two batches, and toss it over high heat for 2–3 minutes. Place the stock and cornflour in a bowl and stir until a smooth paste forms. Add the cornflour mixture to the meat and toss for 1 minute. Do not overcook the meat or it will become tough.
4 Place the pancake on a large serving plate, cut it into serving wedges and place the beef mixture on top, piling it up in the centre. Garnish with the spring onion and serve immediately.

green pawpaw, chicken and fresh herb salad

❋

Preparation time: 40 minutes
Cooking time: 10 minutes
Serves 4

350 g (12 oz) boneless, skinless chicken breasts
1 large green pawpaw
20 g (¾ oz/1 cup) Vietnamese mint
15 g (½ oz/½ cup) coriander (cilantro) leaves
2 red chillies, seeded and thinly sliced
2 tablespoons fish sauce
1 tablespoon rice vinegar
1 tablespoon lime juice
2 teaspoons sugar
2 tablespoons finely chopped unsalted roasted peanuts

1 Place the chicken in a frying pan with enough water to just cover it. Simmer gently for 8–10 minutes or until cooked. Remove from the liquid, cool completely, then slice thinly.

2 Peel the pawpaw, then grate the flesh into long shreds. Mix gently with the mint, coriander, chilli, fish sauce, vinegar, lime juice and sugar.

3 Arrange the pawpaw mixture on a serving plate and top with the chicken. Scatter with the peanuts and serve immediately.

NOTE: Green pawpaw is underripe pawpaw, used for tartness and texture.

chicken with pineapple and cashews

☀

Preparation time: **35 minutes**
Cooking time: **30 minutes**
Serves **4**

2 tablespoons shredded coconut
80 g (2¾ oz/½ cup) raw cashews
2 tablespoons oil
1 large onion, cut into large chunks
4 garlic cloves, finely chopped
2 teaspoons chopped red chilli
350 g (12 oz) boneless, skinless chicken thighs, chopped
½ red capsicum (pepper), chopped
½ green capsicum (pepper), chopped

2 tablespoons oyster sauce
1 tablespoon fish sauce
1 teaspoon sugar
320 g (11¼ oz/2 cups) chopped fresh pineapple
3 spring onions (scallions), chopped

1 Preheat the oven to 150°C (300°F/Gas 2). Spread the coconut on a baking tray and toast in the oven for 10 minutes or until dark golden, shaking the tray occasionally. Remove the coconut from the tray immediately, to prevent burning, and set aside.

2 Increase the heat to 180°C (350°F/Gas 4). Roast the cashews on a baking tray in the oven for about 15 minutes, until deep golden. Remove the cashews from the tray and set aside to cool.

3 Heat the oil in a wok or large, deep frying pan; add the onion, garlic and chilli and stir-fry over medium heat for 2 minutes, then remove from the wok. Increase the heat to high; add the chicken and red and green capsicum, in two batches, and stir-fry until the chicken is light brown. Return the onion mixture to the wok; add the oyster sauce, fish sauce, sugar and pineapple and toss for 2 minutes. Toss the cashews through.

4 Arrange the chicken mixture on a serving plate, scatter the toasted coconut and the spring onion over the top, and serve immediately.

chicken with pineapple and cashews

chilli prawn and snake bean stir-fry

✳

Preparation time: 35 minutes
Cooking time: 10 minutes
Serves 4

300 g (10½ oz) raw prawns (shrimp)
250 g (9 oz) snake (yard-long) beans
2 tablespoons oil
2 onions, very thinly sliced
5 garlic cloves, finely chopped
2 lemongrass stems, white part only, very
    thinly sliced
3 red chillies, seeded and very thinly sliced
2 teaspoons sugar
1 tablespoon fish sauce
1 tablespoon rice vinegar
garlic chives, snipped, to garnish

1 Peel the prawns and gently pull out the dark vein from each prawn back, starting at the head end. Top and tail the beans and cut them into 2 cm (¾ inch) pieces.
2 Heat the oil in a large heavy-based wok, add the onion, garlic, lemongrass and chilli and stir-fry over moderately high heat for 4 minutes, or until the onion is soft and golden.
3 Add the beans to the wok and stir-fry for 2–3 minutes or until they become bright green. Add the prawns and sugar and toss gently for 2 minutes. Add the fish sauce and vinegar, toss well and serve immediately, sprinkled with the garlic chives.

NOTE: The equivalent weight of green beans may be used if snake beans are unavailable.

sweet braised pumpkin

✳

Preparation time: 20 minutes
Cooking time: 15 minutes
Serves 4

750 g (1 lb 10 oz) pumpkin (winter
    squash)
1½ tablespoons oil
3 garlic cloves, finely chopped
4 cm (1½ inch) piece fresh ginger,
    finely grated
6 red Asian shallots, chopped
1 tablespoon soft brown sugar
125 ml (4 fl oz/½ cup) chicken stock
2 tablespoons fish sauce
1 tablespoon lime juice

1 Peel the pumpkin and cut it into large chunks.
2 Heat the oil in a heavy-based frying pan; add the garlic, ginger and shallots and cook over medium heat for 3 minutes, stirring regularly.
3 Add the pumpkin and sprinkle with the sugar. Cook for 7–8 minutes, turning the pieces regularly, until the pumpkin is golden and just tender.
4 Add the stock and fish sauce, bring to the boil, then reduce the heat and simmer until all the liquid has evaporated, turning the pumpkin over regularly. Sprinkle with the lime juice, season to taste with salt and pepper, and serve. Delicious as an accompaniment to meat dishes such as curries, or on its own with plenty of steamed rice.

NOTE: The sweeter pumpkins, such as butternut (squash) and jap, will produce a dish with a delicious flavour and a soft texture.

sweet braised pumpkin

vietnamese pancakes in lettuce leaves

❋ ❋ ❋

Preparation time: 20 minutes + 45 minutes
standing time
Cooking time: 30 minutes
Makes 10

175 g (6 oz/1 cup) rice flour
2 teaspoons cornflour (cornstarch)
½ teaspoon curry powder (see Note)
½ teaspoon ground turmeric
250 ml (9 fl oz/1 cup) coconut milk
60 ml (2 fl oz/¼ cup) coconut cream
300 g (10½ oz) raw prawns (shrimp)
2 teaspoons oil
150 g (5½ oz) pork ribs, boned and thinly
sliced
4 spring onions (scallions), chopped
150 g (5½ oz) bean sprouts, trimmed
10 large lettuce leaves
20 g (¾ oz/1 cup) mint

DIPPING SAUCE
2 tablespoons fish sauce
2 tablespoons lime juice
1–2 teaspoons chopped fresh red chilli
½ teaspoon sugar

1 Place the rice flour, cornflour, curry powder, turmeric, coconut milk, 125 ml (4 fl oz/½ cup) water and coconut cream in a food processor, and process for 30 seconds or until smooth. Cover and set aside for 45 minutes so the batter thickens. Peel the prawns and gently pull out the dark vein from each prawn back, starting at the head end. Finely chop the prawn meat.

2 Heat 1 teaspoon of the oil in a heavy-based frying pan; cook the pork in batches over moderately high heat for 1–2 minutes or until browned.

3 Stir the batter well. Heat the remaining oil and add 2 tablespoons of the batter to the pan, swirling it to form a small round pancake. Cook the pancake for 30 seconds or until it begins to crisp on the underside. Place 2 pieces of pork, 1 tablespoon of the prawn meat, 1 tablespoon of the spring onion and 1 tablespoon of the bean sprouts in the centre of the pancake. Cover the pan and cook for 1–2 minutes, or until the prawns are pink and the vegetables soften. (The base of the pancake will be very crisp, the top side will be set but soft.) Place the pancake on a platter and repeat with the remaining ingredients.

4 Place each cooked pancake inside a lettuce leaf and top with 2 mint leaves. Fold the lettuce to form a parcel. Serve with the dipping sauce.

5 To make the dipping sauce, combine all the ingredients in a bowl and whisk until well blended.

NOTE: Use a mild Asian curry powder labelled 'for meat', available from Asian food stores. A standard supermarket curry powder is not suitable for this recipe.

chopping pork mince

For some dishes, such as meatballs, you need a really finely chopped minced (ground) meat, which will hold together well and keep its shape during cooking. If you have bought minced (ground) meat from your butcher, chopping it at home will give it this finer texture.

spicy grilled fish pieces

paste forms, adding the oil to help with the grinding.

2 Cut the fish into large bite-sized pieces. Place the fish in a bowl with the spice paste, toss well and cover and refrigerate for 15 minutes.

3 Place the fish on a foil-lined grill tray and cook under a hot grill (broiler) for 3–4 minutes, turning the pieces over so the fish browns on all sides.

4 Arrange the fish on a serving plate. Sprinkle over the fish sauce and garnish with the watercress or coriander leaves. Serve immediately with steamed rice, if desired.

vermicelli with stir-fried squid and tomatoes

☀

Preparation time: **35 minutes**
Cooking time: **20 minutes**
Serves **4**

100 g (3½ oz) dried mung bean
    vermicelli
350 g (12 oz) squid tubes, cut
    into rings
2 tablespoons fish sauce
2 tablespoons oil
3 garlic cloves, finely chopped
3 lemongrass stems, white part only,
    thinly sliced
2 teaspoons sugar
1 red onion, thinly sliced
2 ripe tomatoes, diced
2 tablespoons lime juice
2 tablespoons snipped garlic chives

1 Soak the vermicelli in hot water for 5 to 10 minutes or until softened; drain.
2 Place the squid in a bowl with 1 tablespoon of the fish sauce, 1 tablespoon of the oil, half the garlic, half the lemongrass, and the sugar, ¼ teaspoon salt and ¼ teaspoon pepper. Mix well to combine and marinate for 15 minutes.
3 Heat a wok until it is extremely hot; add the squid in two batches, stir-fry until

spicy grilled fish pieces

☀

Preparation time: **30 minutes**
Cooking time: **10 minutes**
Serves **4**

3 garlic cloves
4 red Asian shallots
3 lemongrass stems, white part only,
    thinly sliced

1 teaspoon ground turmeric
1 teaspoon galangal powder
2 red chillies
2 tablespoons oil
500 g (1 lb 2 oz) boneless white fish fillets
1 tablespoon fish sauce
watercress or coriander (cilantro) leaves,
    to garnish

1 Place the garlic, shallots, lemon grass, turmeric, galangal powder, chillies, ¼ teaspoon salt and ¼ teaspoon pepper in a food processor and process until a

it just changes colour, and remove it from the wok. Reheat the wok until hot; add the remaining oil, garlic, lemongrass and onion, and stir-fry for 1 minute. Add the tomato and toss well. Add the vermicelli and return the squid (with any juices) to the wok, and toss well. Add the lime juice, chives and remaining fish sauce, and serve immediately.

vietnamese pork and prawn salad

☀

Preparation time: 30 minutes + 1 hour marinating time
Cooking time: 10 minutes
Serves 6–8

250 g (9 oz) pork fillet
300 g (10½ oz) raw prawns (shrimp)
60 ml (2 fl oz/¼ cup) white vinegar
1 tablespoon sugar
1 carrot, cut into matchsticks
1 Lebanese (short) cucumber, cut into matchsticks
1 red capsicum (pepper), cut into matchsticks
1 Chinese cabbage (wong bok), finely shredded
1 tablespoon oil
100 g (3½ oz) unsalted roasted peanuts, roughly chopped

DRESSING
2 red Asian shallots, finely chopped
1 garlic clove, crushed
1 tablespoon fish sauce
1 tablespoon lime juice
1 teaspoon brown sugar
1 teaspoon sesame oil
1 tablespoon chopped Vietnamese mint

1 Cut the pork into thin strips. Peel the prawns, leaving the tails intact. Gently pull out the dark vein from each prawn back, starting at the head end.
2 Place the vinegar, 125 ml (4 fl oz/ ½ cup) water and sugar into a bowl and mix to combine. Add the carrot, cucumber, capsicum and Chinese cabbage and toss to coat in the marinade. Cover and refrigerate for 1 hour.
3 Heat the oil in a wok; stir-fry the pork in two batches over high heat for 3 minutes or until browned. Remove the pork from the wok. Add the prawns and stir-fry over high heat for 3 minutes or until bright pink.
4 Remove the vegetables from the marinade and drain thoroughly. Combine the vegetables with the pork, prawns and peanuts and toss well. Pour the dressing over the salad and toss to coat.
5 To make the dressing, combine the shallots, garlic, fish sauce, lime juice, brown sugar and sesame oil. Add the Vietnamese mint and mix together well.

pork ball soup with noodles

※

Preparation time: 25 minutes
Cooking time: 35 minutes
Serves 4

250 g (9 oz) pork bones
5 cm (2 inch) piece fresh ginger,
    thinly sliced
6 spring onions (scallions), chopped
300 g (10½ oz) shanghai noodles

250 g (9 oz) minced (ground) pork
2 tablespoons fish sauce
150 g (5½ oz) fresh pineapple, cut into
    small chunks
100 g (3½ oz) bean sprouts, trimmed
2 tablespoons shredded mint

1 Place the pork bones, ginger,
1 teaspoon salt, 1 teaspoon pepper
and 1 litre (35 fl oz/4 cups) water in a
saucepan, and bring it to the boil. Skim
off any scum, add the spring onion and
simmer for 20 minutes. Remove and
discard the bones then set the stock aside.

2 Cook the noodles in a saucepan of
boiling water for 5 minutes. Drain and
rinse in cold water.
3 Chop the pork very finely with a
cleaver or large knife for 3 minutes or
until the meat feels very soft and spongy.
Wet your hands and roll 2 teaspoons of
pork at a time into small balls.
4 Return the stock to the heat and bring
it to the boil. Add the pork balls and
cook for 4 minutes. Add the fish sauce
and pineapple.
5 Place the noodles in individual soup
bowls and ladle the hot stock over
them, making sure each bowl has pork
balls and pineapple. Scatter the bean
sprouts and mint over the soup, and
serve immediately.

peppery pork with vegetables

※ ※

Preparation time: 1 hour
Cooking time: 20 minutes
Serves 4

2 teaspoons black peppercorns
350 g (12 oz) pork loin
1 tablespoon fish sauce
4 garlic cloves, very thinly sliced
4 spring onions (scallions), finely chopped
3 tablespoons oil
8 red Asian shallots, thinly sliced
200 g (7 oz) baby corn, cut in half
    lengthways
100 g (3½ oz) green beans, trimmed, cut
    into short lengths
1 teaspoon sugar
150 g (5½ oz) broccoli, cut into small florets
200 g (7 oz) bean sprouts, trimmed
steamed rice, to serve

1 Dry-fry the peppercorns in a hot
frying pan for 2 minutes, shaking the
pan constantly. Place the peppercorns in
a mortar and using a pestle pound until
roughly ground.
2 Cut the pork into thin pieces. Place
the pork, pepper, fish sauce, garlic,

pork ball soup with noodles

¼ teaspoon salt, spring onion and half the oil in a bowl. Mix well to combine and refrigerate, covered, for 20 minutes.

3 Heat a wok to extremely hot and stir-fry the pork in three batches for about 1½ minutes, or until just golden brown, reheating the wok between batches.

4 Heat the remaining oil in the wok; add the shallots, corn and beans and stir-fry over medium heat for 1 minute. Sprinkle over 1 tablespoon water and the sugar; cover and steam for 1 minute. Add the broccoli and steam for 1 minute more. Return the pork and any juices to the wok, add the bean sprouts and stir-fry for 30 seconds. Serve with the steamed rice.

beef fondue with rice paper wrappers and salad

✾ ✾

Preparation time: **20 minutes**
Cooking time: **30 minutes**
Serves **4**

1 red onion, thinly sliced
185 ml (6 fl oz/¾ cup) rice vinegar
3 red chillies, finely chopped
2 tablespoons fish sauce
2 tablespoons lime juice
6 garlic cloves, finely chopped
2 tablespoons sugar
500 g (1 lb 2 oz) beef fillet
410 g (14½ oz) tinned chopped tomatoes
12 rice paper wrappers (plus a few extras to allow for breakages)
75 g (2¾ oz) iceberg lettuce leaves, shredded
10 g (¼ oz/½ cup) mint leaves
1 small Lebanese (short) cucumber, sliced

1 Place the onion and 3 tablespoons of the vinegar in a small bowl; mix to combine and set aside. To make a dipping sauce, place the chilli, fish sauce, lime juice, half the garlic and half the sugar in a small bowl; mix to combine and set aside for the flavours to mingle. Cut the beef into thin slices, season with ½ teaspoon pepper and set aside.

2 Place 1 litre (35 fl oz/4 cups) water in a large saucepan and bring it to the boil. Add the tomatoes and the remaining garlic, sugar and vinegar, and simmer for 20 minutes.

3 Use a pastry brush to brush both sides of each rice paper wrapper liberally with water. Allow to stand for 2 minutes or until they become soft and pliable. Stack the wrappers on a plate. Sprinkle over a little extra water and cover with plastic wrap to keep the wrappers moist until needed.

4 Place the tomato mixture in a food processor and process until smooth.

Return the tomato stock to the pan and reheat to simmering point. Add the beef in batches to the simmering stock, and cook it quickly, just until it changes colour, then place it in a serving bowl.

5 To serve, place the rice paper wrappers, shredded lettuce, mint leaves and sliced cucumber on a serving platter in separate piles. Each diner takes a wrapper, places a few slices of beef on it along with a little of the lettuce, mint, cucumber and the marinated onion, then rolls it up and dips it in the dipping sauce to eat.

korea

Caught between Japan and China, Korean food is a wonderful combination of the two, mixed with its own distinctive elements. The food has a warming robustness that defies the winter ice and snow, most notably in its national dish, kimchi, a spicy pickle served at every meal. Korean meals are made up of many small, tempting dishes, flavoured with soy sauce, ginger, bean paste and toasted sesame seeds, while the centrepiece may be a steaming hotpot or thinly sliced meat, grilled at the table.

egg strip bundles

✹ ✹

Preparation time: 25 minutes
Cooking time: 15 minutes
Serves 4

1 tablespoon white sesame seeds
10 spring onions (scallions)
5 eggs
¼ teaspoon white pepper
3 teaspoons oil
2 tablespoons rice vinegar
2 tablespoons Japanese soy sauce
     (shoshoyu)

1   Toast the sesame seeds in a dry frying
pan over medium heat for 3–4 minutes,
shaking the pan gently, until the seeds are
golden brown; remove from the pan at
once to prevent burning.
2   Trim the white ends from the spring
onions and discard; take off the outside
layer and discard. Make a bunch of the
green stems, then trim them all to the
same size, cutting off the skinny tip.
Plunge 2 spring onions at a time into a
large saucepan of boiling water and cook
for about 30 seconds or until softened;
remove with tongs and place in iced
water. Repeat for all the spring onions.
Drain well and dry lightly on paper
towels. Cut each spring onion in half
lengthways using a small sharp knife.
3   Beat the eggs with ¼ teaspoon salt and
pepper, to taste, until they are foamy.
4   Brush a medium-sized frying pan with
the oil, and place it over medium heat.
Pour in half the eggs, cover and cook for
2 minutes. Run a spatula around the edge
of the omelette to loosen it, then turn the
omelette over and cook it for a further
2 minutes. Remove the omelette from the
pan, and cook the remaining egg mixture.
Trim the curved edges from the omelettes
to make a square shape. Cut thin strips
of omelette about 7 cm (2¾ inches) long
and 5 mm (¼ inch) wide.
5   Gather together eight strips of egg,
carefully wrap one piece of spring onion
four or so times around the middle of the
bundle, tucking in the ends. Repeat with

the remaining egg strips and arrange the
bundles on a serving platter. Combine
the vinegar, soy sauce and sesame seeds,
drizzle over the bundles and serve.

barbecued beef

✹

Preparation time: 15 minutes + 30 minutes
     freezing + 2 hours marinating time
Cooking time: 15 minutes
Serves 4–6

500 g (1 lb 2 oz) scotch fillet or sirloin steak
40 g (1½ oz/¼ cup) sesame seeds
125 ml (4 fl oz/½ cup) soy sauce
2 garlic cloves, finely chopped
3 spring onions (scallions),
     finely chopped
1 tablespoon sesame oil
1 tablespoon vegetable oil
kimchi, to serve (see Note)

1   Freeze the beef for 30 minutes.
Remove from the freezer and slice into
long, thin strips, cutting across the natural
grain of the beef.
2   Toast the sesame seeds in a dry frying
pan over medium heat for 3–4 minutes,
shaking the pan gently, until the seeds are
golden brown. Remove from the pan at

barbecued beef

once to prevent burning. Crush the seeds in a food mill or use a mortar and pestle.

3 Combine the beef, soy sauce, garlic, spring onion and half the sesame seeds in a bowl, mixing well. Cover and refrigerate for 2 hours.

4 Combine the sesame and vegetable oils and brush a little oil onto a chargrill pan, heavy-based frying pan or barbecue hotplate. Heat to very hot and cook the beef in three batches, searing each side for about 1 minute (don't overcook the beef or it will become chewy). Brush the pan with more oil and allow it to reheat to very hot between batches. Sprinkle the remaining crushed sesame seeds over the beef before serving. Serve with ready-made or homemade kimchi, if desired.

NOTE: Pickled vegetables are a popular accompaniment to meals in Korea. Most common is kimchi, made with pickled cabbage leaves and spiced with chilli. Ready-made kimchi is found in the refrigerator in Korean grocery stores and large Asian grocery stores.

kimchi

☀

Preparation time: **9 days**
Cooking time: **nil**
Makes **about 3 cups**

1 large Chinese cabbage (wong bok)
160 g (5¾ oz/½ cup) sea salt
½ teaspoon cayenne pepper
5 spring onions (scallions), finely chopped
2 garlic cloves, finely chopped
5 cm (2 inch) piece fresh ginger, finely grated
3 teaspoons–3 tablespoons chopped fresh chilli (see Note)
1 tablespoon caster (superfine) sugar

1 Cut the cabbage in half, then into large bite-sized pieces. Place a layer of cabbage in a large bowl and sprinkle with a little salt. Continue with layers of cabbage and salt, finishing with a salt layer. Cover with a dinner plate that will fit as snugly

as possible over the top of the cabbage. Weigh down the plate with tins or a small brick and leave the bowl in a cool place for 5 days.

2 Remove the weights and plate, pour off any liquid, then rinse the cabbage well under cold running water. Squeeze out any excess water and combine the cabbage with the cayenne pepper, spring onion, garlic, ginger, chilli and sugar. Mix well to combine before spooning the

cabbage into a large sterilised jar. Pour 625 ml (21½ fl oz/2½ cups) cold water over the top and seal with a tight-fitting lid. Refrigerate for 3–4 days before eating.

NOTE: Kimchi is an accompaniment eaten with Korean main meals and with steamed rice. For an authentic flavour, use 3 tablespoons chilli. Bottled chopped chilli can be used instead of fresh chilli.

pickles & chutneys

Just a spoonful of these spicy relishes will lift an
Indian dish, while the pickled vegetables and ginger
are traditional in Japanese and Korean meals.

lime oil pickle

Cut 12 limes into eight thin wedges each, sprinkle with salt
and set aside. In a medium frying pan, dry roast 3 teaspoons
mustard seeds and 2 teaspoons each ground turmeric, cumin
seeds, fennel seeds and fenugreek seeds for 1–2 minutes.
Remove and grind to a fine powder using a mortar and pestle.
Over low heat, fry 5 chopped green chillies, 4 sliced garlic cloves
and 2 teaspoons grated fresh ginger in 1 tablespoon oil until
golden brown. Add 500 ml (17 fl oz/2 cups) oil, 1 tablespoon
sugar, the lime wedges and spices; simmer over low heat for
10 minutes, stirring occasionally. Spoon into warm sterilised
jars, seal and cool. Store in the refrigerator for up to 3 months.

sweet mango chutney

Peel 3 large green mangoes, remove stones, slice, and sprinkle
with salt. Seed 2 red chillies; chop finely. Blend ½ teaspoon
garam masala with 330 g (11½ oz/1½ cups) raw (demerara)
sugar and place in a large saucepan with 250 ml (9 fl oz/1 cup)
white vinegar; bring to the boil. Reduce the heat and simmer for
5 minutes. Add the mango, chilli, 1 tablespoon finely grated fresh
ginger and 95 g (3¼ oz/½ cup) finely chopped dates. Simmer
for 1 hour or until the mango is tender. Pour into warm sterilised
jars, seal and cool. Store in the refrigerator for up to 3 months.

pickled vegetables

Put 80 ml (2½ fl oz/⅓ cup) rice (or white) vinegar, 2 teaspoons
salt and 1 teaspoon sugar into a large non-metallic bowl. Pour
over 500 ml (17 fl oz/2 cups) boiling water, mix well and allow
to cool until lukewarm. Cut 250 g (9 oz) cabbage into 4 cm
(1½ inch) strips, 1 small Lebanese (short) cucumber and
2 carrots into matchsticks and 1 white onion into thick rings,
and add to the warm pickling mixture. Put a flat plate on top
of the vegetables. Place a small bowl filled with water on top of
the plate to weigh it down and submerge the vegetables. Leave
for 3 days in the refrigerator. Place into sterilised jars, seal and
store in the refrigerator for up to 1 month.

eggplant pickle

Cut 1 kg (2 lb 4 oz) slender eggplants (aubergines) lengthways
and sprinkle lightly with salt. In a food processor, place 6 garlic
cloves, 2.5 cm (1 inch) piece roughly chopped fresh ginger,
4 teaspoons garam masala, 1 teaspoon ground turmeric,
1 teaspoon chilli powder and 1 tablespoon oil; process until a
paste forms. Rinse the salt off the eggplant and pat dry. Heat
80 ml (2½ fl oz/⅓ cup) oil in a large frying pan and fry the
eggplant for 5 minutes or until golden brown. Add the paste and
fry for 2 minutes. Stir in 420 ml (14½ fl oz/1⅔ cups) oil and
cook, uncovered, for 10–15 minutes, stirring occasionally. Spoon
into warm sterilised jars, seal and cool. Store in a cool, dark
place for up to 2 months. Refrigerate after opening.

pickled ginger

Cut 125 g (4½ oz) fresh ginger into 2.5 cm (1 inch) pieces.
Sprinkle with 2 teaspoons salt, cover and refrigerate for 1 week.
With a very sharp knife, cut into paper-thin slices across the
grain. Over low heat dissolve 2 tablespoons sugar in 125 ml
(4 fl oz/½ cup) rice vinegar and 2 tablespoons water. Bring to
the boil and simmer for 1 minute. Place the ginger in sterilised
jars, cover with the marinade, seal and refrigerate for 1 week
before using. The ginger will turn pale pink or it can be
coloured using 1 teaspoon grenadine. Store in the refrigerator
for up to 3 months.

shredded potato pancakes

with the garlic, spring onion, soy sauce, white wine, sesame oil, sugar and chilli. Mix well and then place in a serving bowl.

2 Peel the potatoes and grate them on the coarse side of a grater. Place the potato in a large bowl with the onion, egg and cornflour, and season with salt and pepper to taste. Stir very well, making certain that the cornflour is mixed in thoroughly.

3 Heat the oil in a large heavy-based frying pan (an electric frying pan is good for this). Drop about 1 rounded tablespoon of mixture onto the hot surface and spread it out gently with the back of a spoon so the pancake is about 6 cm (2½ inches) in size. Cook for 2–3 minutes or until golden brown. Turn it over with a spatula and cook another 2 minutes on the other side. Cook four to five pancakes, or as many as you can fit in the pan at one time. Do not have the pan too hot or the pancakes will burn and not cook through. Keep the cooked pancakes warm in a 120°C (235°F/Gas 1–2) oven while cooking the remaining pancakes.

4 Serve with the dipping sauce as a snack or with rice and kimchi (page 161) as part of a meal.

NOTE: Have all the ingredients ready before the potatoes are grated as they discolour quickly.

shredded potato pancakes

✹ ✹

Preparation time: 25 minutes
Cooking time: 30 minutes
Makes about 18

500 g (1 lb 2 oz) potatoes
1 large onion, very finely chopped
2 eggs, beaten
2 tablespoons cornflour
   (cornstarch)
60 ml (2 fl oz/¼ cup) oil

DIPPING SAUCE
2 teaspoons white sesame seeds
2 garlic cloves, finely chopped
2 spring onions (scallions), very thinly sliced
60 ml (2 fl oz/¼ cup) soy sauce
1 tablespoon white wine
1 tablespoon sesame oil
2 teaspoons caster (superfine) sugar
1 teaspoon chopped red chilli

1 To make the dipping sauce, toast the sesame seeds in a dry frying pan over medium heat for 3–4 minutes, shaking the pan gently, until they are golden brown; remove from the pan at once to prevent burning and cool for 5 minutes. Combine

pork with spinach

✹ ✹

Preparation time: 20 minutes
Cooking time: 15 minutes
Serves 4

1 tablespoon white sesame seeds
400 g (14 oz) English spinach
2 garlic cloves, very thinly sliced
3 spring onions (scallions), chopped
½ teaspoon cayenne pepper
300 g (10½ oz) pork loin, cut into thick strips
2 tablespoons oil
2 teaspoons sesame oil
2 tablespoons Japanese soy sauce (shoshoyu)
2 teaspoons sugar

1 Toast the sesame seeds in a dry frying pan over medium heat for 3–4 minutes, shaking the pan gently, until the seeds are golden brown; remove from the pan at once to prevent burning.

2 Trim the ends from the spinach, roughly chop the leaves and wash to remove grit.

3 Combine the garlic, spring onion, cayenne pepper and pork, mixing well. Heat the oils in a heavy-based frying pan and stir-fry the pork quickly in three batches over very high heat until golden. Remove the pork and set aside.

4 Add the soy sauce, sugar and spinach, and toss lightly. Cover and cook for 2 minutes or until the spinach is just soft. Return the pork to the pan, add sesame seeds, toss well and serve immediately.

meat dumpling soup

✤ ✤

Preparation time: 45 minutes
Cooking time: 35 minutes
Serves 4–6

1 tablespoon white sesame seeds
2 tablespoons oil
2 garlic cloves, finely chopped
150 g (5½ oz) lean minced
   (ground) pork
200 g (7 oz) lean minced (ground) beef
200 g (7 oz) Chinese cabbage (wong bok),
   finely shredded
100 g (3½ oz) bean sprouts, trimmed
   and chopped
100 g (3½ oz) mushrooms, finely
   chopped
3 spring onions (scallions), finely chopped
150 g (5½ oz) gow gee dumpling wrappers

SOUP
2.5 litres (87 fl oz/10 cups) beef stock
2 tablespoons soy sauce
3 cm (1¼ inch) piece fresh ginger, very
   thinly shredded
4 spring onions (scallions), chopped

1 To make the filling, toast the sesame seeds in a dry frying pan over medium heat for 3–4 minutes, shaking the pan gently, until the seeds are golden brown. Remove from the pan at once to prevent burning. Crush the seeds in a food mill or use a mortar and pestle.

2 Heat the oil in a saucepan. Cook the garlic and the pork and beef over medium heat until the meat changes colour, breaking up any lumps with a fork. Add the cabbage, bean sprouts, mushrooms and 80 ml (2½ fl oz/⅓ cup) water. Cook, stirring occasionally, for 5–6 minutes, or until the water evaporates and the vegetables soften. Add the spring onion, crushed sesame seeds and season, to taste. Set aside.

3 Work with one gow gee wrapper at a time and keep the extra wrappers covered with a damp tea towel (dish towel). Place 1 teaspoon of filling on a wrapper, just off-centre, and gently smooth out the filling a little. Brush the edges of the wrapper with a little water and fold it over the filling to form a semi-circle. Press the edges together to seal. Repeat with the extra wrappers and filling.

4 To make the soup, combine the stock, soy sauce, ginger and half the spring onion in a large saucepan. Bring to the boil and simmer for 15 minutes.

5 Drop the dumplings into the soup and cook gently for 5 minutes, or until they change colour and look plump. Garnish with the remaining spring onion and serve immediately.

potato noodles
with vegetables

※

Preparation time: 25 minutes
Cooking time: 15 minutes
Serves 4

4 spring onions (scallions)
2 carrots
500 g (1 lb 2 oz) baby bok choy
  (pak choy) or 250 g (9 oz) spinach
300 g (10½ oz) dried potato starch
  noodles (see Note)
10 g (¼ oz/⅓ cup) black fungus
  (see Note)

60 ml (2 fl oz/¼ cup) sesame oil
2 tablespoons vegetable oil
3 garlic cloves, finely chopped
4 cm (1½ inch) piece fresh ginger,
  finely grated
60 ml (2 fl oz/¼ cup) Japanese
  soy sauce (shoshoyu) (see Note)
2 tablespoons mirin
1 teaspoon sugar
2 tablespoons sesame and seaweed
  sprinkle (see Note)

1 Finely chop two of the spring onions. Slice the remaining spring onions into 4 cm (1½ inch) pieces. Cut the carrots into 4 cm (1½ inch) batons. Roughly chop the baby bok choy.

2 Cook the noodles in a large saucepan of boiling water for about 5 minutes, or until they are translucent. Drain and rinse thoroughly under cold running water until the noodles are cold (this will also remove any excess starch). Use scissors to roughly chop the noodles into shorter lengths (this will make them easier to eat with chopsticks).

3 Pour hot water over the black fungus and soak for about 10 minutes.

4 Heat 1 tablespoon of the sesame oil with the vegetable oil in a large heavy-based frying pan or wok. Cook the garlic, ginger and finely chopped spring onion for 3 minutes over medium heat, stirring regularly. Add the carrot and stir-fry for 1 minute. Add the drained cooled noodles, sliced spring onion, baby bok choy, remaining sesame oil, soy sauce, mirin and sugar. Toss well to coat the noodles with the sauce. Cover and cook over low heat for 2 minutes. Add the drained fungus, then cover and cook for 2 minutes. Scatter over the sesame and seaweed sprinkle and serve immediately.

NOTE: Potato starch noodles are also known as Korean pasta and are available from Asian food stores. Dried black fungus, Japanese soy sauce and sesame and seaweed sprinkle are all available from Asian food stores.

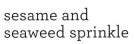

sesame and seaweed sprinkle

Also known as gomashio, this combination of finely chopped nori, black sesame seeds and salt is used in Japanese and Korean cooking sprinkled on noodles, salads and egg dishes. It is available in shaker containers from Japanese food stores.

spare ribs with sesame seeds

✻

Preparation time: **30 minutes**
Cooking time: **1 hour**
Serves 4–6

1 tablespoon white sesame seeds
1 kg (2 lb 4 oz) pork spare ribs, cut into 3 cm (1¼ inch) pieces
2 tablespoons oil
2 spring onions (scallions), finely chopped
4 cm (1½ inch) piece fresh ginger, grated
3 garlic cloves, finely chopped
2 tablespoons caster (superfine) sugar
2 tablespoons sake
1 tablespoon soy sauce
2 teaspoons sesame oil
2 teaspoons cornflour (cornstarch)
steamed rice, to serve
kimchi (optional), to serve

1 Toast the sesame seeds in a dry frying pan over medium heat for 3–4 minutes, shaking the pan gently, until the seeds are golden brown. Remove the seeds from the pan immediately, to prevent them burning. Crush the seeds in a food mill or use a mortar and pestle.
2 Trim the pork of excess fat. Heat the oil in a heavy-based frying pan. Brown the spare ribs over high heat, turning regularly, until dark golden brown. Drain any excess oil from the pan. Add half the sesame seeds, the spring onion, ginger, garlic, sugar, sake, soy sauce, sesame oil and 310 ml (10¾ fl oz/1¼ cup) hot water; stir well to evenly coat the ribs. Bring to the boil over medium heat, then cover and simmer 45–50 minutes, stirring occasionally.
3 Mix the cornflour with a little water and add to the pan, stirring constantly, until it boils and thickens. Sprinkle with remaining sesame seeds. Serve with the steamed rice and kimchi (page 161), if desired.

NOTE: Make sure the rib pieces can be held easily with chopsticks — if necessary, cut them into smaller pieces.

When the peas and rice are cool, purée them in a food processor.

When the base is cooked, gently lift and turn the pancakes and cook them for another 2 minutes.

split pea and rice pancakes with vegetables

split pea and rice pancakes with vegetables

✳ ✳

Preparation time: **30 minutes**
Cooking time: **1 hour**
Makes **about 15**

200 g (7 oz) dried split green peas
100 g (3½ oz) medium-grain rice
60 g (2¼ oz/½ cup) plain (all-purpose) flour
2 eggs, beaten
1 carrot
½ green capsicum (pepper)
½ red capsicum (pepper)
6 spring onions (scallions)
3 cm (1¼ inch) piece fresh ginger
2 garlic cloves
2 teaspoons soy sauce
2 tablespoons oil
1 tablespoon sesame oil
spring onions (scallions), thinly sliced, to garnish
sweet chilli sauce, to serve

1 Wash the peas and rice in a colander under cold running water until the water runs clear. Place in a saucepan, cover with cold water and bring to the boil. Cook for 25 minutes, adding more water if necessary, or until the peas are very soft. Cool, then purée in a food processor. Add the flour, eggs and most of 250 ml (9 fl oz/1 cup) water and pulse until a smooth batter forms, adding more water until it is a thick pouring consistency. (You may need to add a little extra water.)
2 Cut the carrot, capsicums and spring onions into fine matchsticks about 3 cm (1¼ inches) long. Finely grate the ginger and chop the garlic. Pour the batter into a bowl and stir in the vegetables, ginger, garlic and soy sauce.
3 Heat a heavy-based frying pan over medium heat. When hot, brush with a little oil and sesame oil. Pour in 2 tablespoons of batter and cook for 3–5 minutes. When the base is cooked, gently run a spatula around the bottom of the pancake to release it from the pan. Turn the pancake over and cook the other side for 2 minutes. Cover the pan for about 30 seconds to ensure the pancake is cooked, then place it on a plate. Keep it warm in a very slow oven while the other pancakes cook.
4 Scatter the spring onion over the pancakes. Serve with sweet chilli sauce.

vermicelli with stir-fried beef and vegetables

✳ ✳

Preparation time: **40 minutes**
Cooking time: **25 minutes**
Serves **4**

8 dried Chinese mushrooms
150 g (5½ oz) dried mung bean vermicelli
1 tablespoon white sesame seeds
150 g (5½ oz) sirloin steak, partially frozen
4 garlic cloves, finely chopped
2 tablespoons soy sauce
2 teaspoons sesame oil
1–2 teaspoons chopped red chilli

1 large carrot
½ red capsicum (pepper)
75 g (2½ oz) asparagus spears
2 tablespoons oil
6 spring onions (scallions), thinly sliced
soy sauce and sesame oil, extra, to serve

1 Soak the mushrooms in hot water for 20 minutes. Drain, then squeeze to remove any excess liquid. Discard the stems and chop the caps finely, reserving 2 tablespoons of the soaking liquid. Soak the vermicelli for 10 minutes; drain.
2 Toast the sesame seeds in a dry frying pan over medium heat for 3–4 minutes, shaking the pan gently, until the seeds are golden brown; remove from the pan at once to prevent burning.
3 Slice the beef into very thin strips. Combine the beef, garlic, soy sauce, 2 tablespoons water, sesame oil and chilli; marinate for 15 minutes. Cut the carrot, capsicum and asparagus into thin strips about 4 cm (1½ inches) long. Mix the mushrooms with the beef; drain off any liquid and set aside.
4 Heat a wok or large heavy-based frying pan over medium heat until very hot. Add a little oil; stir-fry the beef and mushroom mixture in two batches. Sear the beef quickly, but do not overcook it; remove from the wok. Add a little oil; stir-fry the vegetables for 2 minutes, then cover with a lid and steam for 1 minute, or until just softened. Add vermicelli, reserved liquid and spring onion; toss well. Return beef to the wok, cover and steam for 1 minute.
5 Divide the vermicelli among four bowls, sprinkle with the sesame seeds and serve with the extra soy sauce and sesame oil.

chicken stew

❋

Preparation time: **30 minutes**
Cooking time: **50 minutes**
Serves **4**

1.6 kg (3 lb 8 oz) whole chicken
6 garlic cloves, finely chopped
4 spring onions (scallions), chopped

1 teaspoon Korean chilli powder
2 tablespoons Japanese soy sauce (shoshoyu)
2 tablespoons sesame oil
1 tablespoon rice vinegar
2 zucchini (courgettes), thickly sliced
steamed rice, to serve

1 Using a cleaver or large cook's knife, cut the chicken into quarters, then into small eating pieces, chopping straight through the bone.
2 Combine the chicken, garlic, spring onion, chilli powder, soy sauce, sesame oil, vinegar and zucchini in a heavy-based saucepan or flameproof casserole dish. Toss the chicken well to coat it in the sauce. Cover and cook over a low heat for 45–50 minutes or until the chicken is very tender. The chicken should come off the bone easily, so it can be eaten with chopsticks. Serve with the steamed rice.

NOTE: Korean chilli powder may be replaced with 1 teaspoon of cayenne pepper and sweet paprika for each teaspoon of chilli powder.

japan

Japanese food is a treat for the eye as well as the palate. Meals are beautifully presented and only the freshest of ingredients are used. Japanese food contains few spices; instead chefs concentrate on bringing out the natural taste of the individual ingredients in a dish. The characteristic flavour of Japanese food comes from dashi, a stock made from dried fish and dried kelp; the rice wines mirin and sake; and miso, tofu and Japanese soy sauce (shoshoyu), all products of soy beans.

salmon sushi roll

✳ ✳ ✳

Preparation time: 45 minutes + 1 hour
    draining time
Cooking time: 15 minutes
Makes about 30

220 g (7¾ oz/1 cup) Japanese medium-
    grain rice
1 tablespoon rice vinegar
2 teaspoons caster (superfine) sugar
125 g (4½ oz) sashimi-grade salmon
1 small Lebanese (short) cucumber, peeled
½ small avocado
4 sheets roasted nori (dried seaweed),
    18 x 20 cm (7 x 8 inches)
wasabi paste
3 tablespoons pickled ginger
Japanese soy sauce (shoshoyu), to serve

1 Wash the rice under cold running water
until the water runs clear, then drain
thoroughly. Leave the rice in the strainer to
drain for 1 hour. Put the rice in a saucepan
and cover with 300 ml (10½ fl oz) water.

Cover the pan and bring the water to the
boil, then reduce the heat to very low and
simmer for 10 minutes. Remove the pan
from the heat, remove the lid and put a
clean cloth across the top to absorb excess
moisture. Set aside for 10 minutes.
2 To make the sushi dressing, combine
the vinegar, sugar and ¼ teaspoon salt in a
small bowl.
3 Spread the rice over the base of a
non-metallic dish or bowl, pour the sushi
dressing over the top and use a rice paddle
or spatula to mix the dressing through
the rice. Fan the rice until it cools to room
temperature. Cover with a damp cloth and
set it aside, but do not refrigerate.
4 Using a very sharp knife, cut the
salmon into thin strips. Cut the cucumber
and avocado into matchstick strips about 5
cm (2 inches) in length.
5 Put a nori sheet on a sushi mat, with
the nori shiny side down and with the
longest sides at the top and bottom. Top
with a quarter of the rice, spreading it
over the nori, leaving a 2 cm (¾ inch)
gap at the edge furthest away from you.

Spread a very small amount of wasabi
along the centre of the rice. Arrange a
quarter of the pieces of salmon, cucumber,
avocado and ginger along the top of the
wasabi. Starting with the end nearest
to you, tightly roll up the mat and the
nori, making sure you do not tuck the
edge of the mat under the roll. When
you have finished rolling, press the mat
to make a round roll and press the nori
edges together to seal. Repeat with the
remaining ingredients.
6 Use a sharp knife to trim the ends and
cut the rolls into 2.5 cm (1 inch) rounds.
Serve the sushi with small bowls of soy
sauce and extra wasabi — your guests
can mix them together to their taste for a
dipping sauce.

NOTE: Sushi can be made up to 4 hours
in advance and kept on a plate, covered
with plastic wrap. Keep the large rolls
intact and slice just before serving. Don't
refrigerate or the rice will become hard.

salmon sushi roll

steamed sake chicken

✳

Preparation time: 25 minutes + 30 minutes
    marinating time
Cooking time: 20 minutes
Serves 4

500 g (1 lb 2 oz) boneless chicken breasts,
    with skin on
80 ml (2½ fl oz/⅓ cup) sake
2 tablespoons lemon juice
4 cm (1½ inch) piece fresh ginger, cut into
    very thin matchsticks
steamed rice, optional, to serve

SAUCE
2 tablespoons Japanese soy sauce
    (shoshoyu)
1 tablespoon mirin
1 teaspoon sesame oil
1 spring onion (scallion), sliced

GARNISH
2 spring onions (scallions)
½ small red capsicum (pepper)

mixed sashimi

sashimi and sushi

The fortuitous discovery that fresh fish fillets stored on rice sprinkled with rice vinegar not only remained fresh but took on a pleasing flavour is said to have been made in the huts of humble Japanese fishermen. Today, specialist sushi bars are devoted to the dish; sashimi, accompanied by sake, is traditionally served as first course, and an array of sushi with various toppings follow. The chefs who slice the fish and prepare the delicacies are highly skilled masters of their art.

1 Use a fork to prick the skin on the chicken in several places. Put the chicken, skin side up, in a shallow non-metallic dish and sprinkle with 1 teaspoon salt. Combine the sake, lemon juice and ginger in a bowl. Pour over the chicken, then cover and marinate in the refrigerator for 30–40 minutes.

2 To make the sauce, combine the soy sauce, mirin, sesame oil and spring onion in a small bowl.

3 To make the garnish, peel the outside layer from the spring onions, then cut thinly into diagonal pieces. Lay the capsicum flat on a board, skin side down. Holding a knife in a horizontal position, cut just under the membrane surface to remove the top layer, then discard it. Cut the capsicum into very thin 3 cm (1¼ inch) long strips.

4 Line the base of a bamboo or metal steamer with baking paper. Remove the chicken from the marinade and arrange it, skin side up, in the steamer. Fill a wok or frying pan with 500 ml (17 fl oz/ 2 cups) water and bring to the boil. Sit the steamer in the wok, cover and cook over gently boiling water for 15–20 minutes, or until the chicken is cooked.

5 Cut the chicken into bite-sized pieces (remove the skin if you prefer) and arrange in the centre of a serving plate. Drizzle over the sauce. Arrange the capsicum strips in a bundle on the side of the plate and scatter the spring onion over the chicken. Serve warm or cold, with rice if desired.

mixed sashimi

❋ ❋

Preparation time: 30 minutes
Cooking time: nil
Serves 4

500 g (1 lb 2 oz) sashimi-grade fish (such as tuna, salmon, kingfish, ocean trout, snapper, whiting, bream and/or jewfish)
1 carrot
1 daikon, peeled
Japanese soy sauce (shoshoyu), to serve
wasabi paste, to serve

1 Use a very sharp, flat-bladed knife to remove any skin from the fish. Place the fish in the freezer and chill it until it is just firm enough to be cut thinly and evenly into slices, about 5 mm (¼ inch) in width. Try to make each cut one motion in one direction, taking care not to saw the fish.

2 Use a zester to scrape the carrot and daikon into long fine strips, or cut them into thin matchstick strips. Arrange the sashimi on a platter. Garnish with the carrot and daikon and serve with the soy sauce and wasabi.

tofu miso soup

smoked salmon rice balls

✳ ✳

Preparation time: **20 minutes + 1 hour draining time**
Cooking time: **15 minutes**
Makes **about 20 balls**

275 g (9¾ oz/1¼ cups) Japanese medium-grain rice
55 g (2 oz) smoked salmon, chopped
2 tablespoons finely chopped pickled ginger
2 spring onions (scallions), finely chopped
2 teaspoons black sesame seeds, toasted

1 Wash the rice under cold running water until the water runs clear, then drain thoroughly. Leave the rice in the strainer to drain for 1 hour. Put the rice in a saucepan with 330 ml (11¼ fl oz/ 1⅓ cups) water. Cover the pan and bring to the boil, then reduce the heat to very low and simmer for 10 minutes. Remove the pan from the heat, remove the lid and put a clean cloth across the top to absorb excess moisture. Set aside for 10 minutes.
2 Combine the salmon, ginger and spring onion in a small bowl. Using wet hands, form 1 heaped tablespoon of rice into a ball, push 2 teaspoons of the salmon mixture into the centre of the rice and remould the ball around it. Repeat with the remaining rice and salmon, keeping your hands wet to prevent the rice from sticking. Arrange all the balls on a serving platter and sprinkle with sesame seeds.

tofu miso soup

✳

Preparation time: **10 minutes**
Cooking time: **15 minutes**
Serves **4**

80 g (2¾ oz/½ cup) dashi granules
100 g (3½ oz) miso paste
1 tablespoon mirin
250 g (9 oz) firm tofu, cubed
1 spring onion (scallion), sliced,
   to garnish

1 Use a wooden spoon to combine 1 litre (35 fl oz/4 cups) water and the dashi granules in a small saucepan and bring to the boil.
2 Combine the miso paste and mirin in a small bowl, then add to the pan. Stir the miso over medium heat, taking care not to let the mixture boil once the miso has dissolved, or it will lose flavour. Add the tofu cubes to the hot stock and heat, without boiling, over medium heat for 5 minutes. Serve in individual bowls, garnished with the spring onion.

making dashi stock from granules

Dashi, Japanese soup stock, can be made from granules (dashi-no-moto) which are dissolved in hot water. The strength of the granules varies according to the brand. However, as a general rule use 80 g (2¾ oz/½ cup) of granules to 1 litre (35 fl oz/4 cups) water. This can be strengthened or diluted to taste.

sukiyaki

✳ ✳ ✳

Preparation time: 1 hour
Cooking time: 15 minutes
Serves 6

500 g (1 lb 2 oz) scotch fillet, partially
    frozen
3 small white onions, each cut into 6 wedges
5 spring onions (scallions), white part only,
    cut into 4 cm (1½ inch) lengths
1 large carrot, cut into 4 cm (1½ inch)
    matchsticks
400 g (14 oz) small button mushrooms,
    stalks discarded, caps halved
½ small Chinese cabbage (wong bok), cut
    into bite-sized pieces
180 g (6¼ oz/2 cups) bean sprouts,
    trimmed
225 g (8 oz) tin bamboo shoots, drained,
    trimmed into even-sized pieces
100 g (3½ oz) firm tofu, cut into 2 cm
    (¾ inch) cubes
100 g (3½ oz) fresh shirataki noodles
60 ml (2 fl oz/¼ cup) oil
6 eggs

SAUCE
80 ml (2½ fl oz/⅓ cup) Japanese soy sauce
    (shoshoyu)
60 ml (2 fl oz/¼ cup) beef stock
60 ml (2 fl oz/¼ cup) sake
60 ml (2 fl oz/¼ cup) mirin
2 tablespoons caster (superfine) sugar

1   Use a very sharp knife to slice the partially frozen beef as thinly as possible, then arrange the slices on a large tray or platter, leaving room for the vegetables, tofu and noodles. Cover the beef and refrigerate the platter while preparing the remaining ingredients.

2   Arrange the prepared vegetables and tofu on the platter with the beef.

3   Cook the noodles in a saucepan of boiling water for about 3 minutes, or until just soft; do not overcook them or they will fall apart. Drain thoroughly and, if you like, use scissors to cut the cooked noodles into shorter lengths that can be picked up easily with chopsticks. Arrange the noodles on the platter with the meat and vegetables.

4   To make the sauce, combine the soy sauce, stock, sake, mirin and sugar in a small bowl and stir until the sugar has dissolved.

5   Set the table with individual place settings, each with a serving bowl, a bowl of rice (see Note), a bowl to break an egg into, chopsticks and napkins. Place an electric frying pan on the table so it is within easy reach of each diner.

6   When all the diners are seated, heat the frying pan and brush it lightly with a little of the oil. When the pan is very hot, take about a third of each of the vegetables and cook them quickly for about 2 minutes, tossing constantly. Push the vegetables to the side of the pan. Add about a third of the beef in one layer and sear the slices for 30 seconds on each side, taking care not to overcook them. Drizzle a little of the sauce over the meat. Add some of the noodles and tofu to the pan and gently toss with the other ingredients.

7   Each diner breaks an egg into their bowl and whisks it with chopsticks. Mouthfuls of sukiyaki are then selected from the hot pan, dipped into the egg and eaten. When the diners are ready for more, the pan is reheated and the cooking process repeated.

NOTE: Some people prefer to have sukiyaki on rice but it is not traditionally served with rice.

sukiyaki

Buddhist prohibitions against eating flesh meant that red meat was not part of the Japanese diet until the mid-nineteenth century when, weakened by foreign influence, the taboo was abandoned. The beef dish sukiyaki dates from this time. A feature of the dish is the thin, translucent, jelly-like noodles (called shirataki noodles) which are made from the starchy root of a plant known in Japan as devil's tongue. Shirataki noodles are also available dried.

savoury egg custard

Preparation time: 20 minutes
Cooking time: 30 minutes
Serves 6

200 g (7 oz) boneless, skinless chicken breasts, cut into bite-sized pieces
2 teaspoons sake
2 teaspoons Japanese soy sauce (shoshoyu)
2 leeks, sliced
1 small carrot, sliced
200 g (7 oz) English spinach, chopped

CUSTARD
1 litre (35 fl oz/4 cups) boiling water
80 g (2¾ oz/½ cup) dashi granules
2 tablespoons Japanese soy sauce (shoshoyu)
6 eggs

1 Place the chicken pieces into six heatproof bowls. Combine the sake and soy sauce, and pour the mixture over the chicken.
2 Divide the vegetables between the six bowls.
3 To make the custard, combine the water and dashi granules in a heatproof bowl and stir to dissolve; cool completely. Combine the dashi, soy sauce and eggs, and strain equal amounts into the six bowls.
4 Cover the bowls with foil, place them in a steamer, and cook over high heat for 20–30 minutes. Test the custard by inserting a fine skewer into the centre; it is cooked when the skewer comes out with no moisture clinging to it. Serve immediately.

savoury egg custard

prawn and vegetable tempura

Preparation time: 40 minutes
Cooking time: 15 minutes
Serves 4

20 raw large prawns (shrimp)
plain or tempura flour, for coating
215 g (7½ oz/1¾ cups) tempura flour
435 ml (15¼ fl oz/1¾ cups) iced water
2 egg yolks
oil, for deep frying
1 large zucchini (courgette), cut into strips
1 red capsicum (pepper), cut into strips
1 onion, cut into rings
Japanese soy sauce (shoshoyu), to serve

1 Peel the prawns, leaving the tails intact. Gently pull out the dark vein from each prawn back, starting at the head end. Make a shallow incision in the underside of the prawns and then open up the cut to straighten the prawns out.
2 Coat the prawns lightly with flour, leaving the tail uncoated, and shake off the excess. In a bowl, gently mix the tempura flour, water and egg yolks and use at once (the batter will be lumpy — don't overmix).
3 Heat the oil in a deep saucepan or wok to moderately hot. Working with a few at a time, dip each prawn into the batter, still leaving the tail uncoated. Fry briefly in the hot oil until lightly golden; remove from the pan and drain well on paper towels. Repeat this process with the vegetable pieces, doing about 2–3 pieces at a time. Serve immediately with soy sauce. Add strips of fresh ginger to the soy sauce if you like.

NOTE: Tempura flour is available from Asian food stores, and makes the lightest tempura batter. Plain (all-purpose) flour can be used but the batter will be slightly heavier.

steak in roasted sesame seed marinade

✹✹

Preparation time: 25 minutes + 30 minutes
 marinating time
Cooking time: 15 minutes
Serves 4

2 tablespoons white Japanese sesame seeds
1 garlic clove, crushed
3 cm (1¼ inch) piece fresh ginger, finely grated
2 tablespoons Japanese soy sauce
 (shoshoyu)
1 tablespoon sake
1 teaspoon caster (superfine) sugar
500 g (1 lb 2 oz) scotch fillet, cut into
 4 steaks
3 spring onions (scallions), to garnish
1 tablespoon oil
steamed rice, to serve

DIPPING SAUCE
4 cm (1½ inch) piece fresh ginger
½ teaspoon shichimi togarashi (see far right)
125 ml (4 fl oz/½ cup) Japanese soy sauce
 (shoshoyu)
2 teaspoons dashi granules

tonkatsu

1 Toast the sesame seeds in a dry frying
pan over moderately low heat for
2 minutes, shaking the pan constantly,
until the seeds begin to pop. Crush the
toasted seeds in a mortar and pestle.
2 Place the crushed sesame seeds,
garlic, ginger, soy sauce, sake and sugar
in a bowl and whisk until the sugar has
dissolved. Place the beef in a shallow
dish; spoon the marinade over the top
and marinate for 30 minutes.
3 To make the dipping sauce, cut the
ginger lengthways into very fine strips
about 4 cm (1½ inches) long. Place the
ginger, shichimi togarashi, soy sauce, dashi
and 2 tablespoons water in a small bowl
and whisk lightly until well combined.
4 Cut the spring onions lengthways into
very fine strips about 4 cm (1½ inches)
long. Place the strips in a bowl of iced
water and leave until they are crisp and
curled; drain.

5 Lightly brush the oil over the beef and
then grill (broil) or fry them for
4–6 minutes on each side — don't
overcook or the beef will become very
tough. Set the beef aside for 5 minutes
before cutting into diagonal slices.
Arrange the slices on serving plates and
then drizzle over a little of the dipping
sauce. Garnish with the spring onion
curls and serve with steamed rice and the
remaining dipping sauce.

tonkatsu

✹✹

Preparation time: 35 minutes + 2 hours chilling
 time
Cooking time: 15 minutes
Makes 40–50 slices

500 g (1 lb 2 oz) pork schnitzels, trimmed
 of sinew

60 g (2¼ oz/½ cup) plain (all-purpose)
 flour
5 egg yolks
120 g (4¼ oz/2 cups) Japanese breadcrumbs
 (panko)
1 sheet nori (dried seaweed)
oil, for shallow frying
250 ml (9 fl oz/1 cup) tonkatsu sauce (see
 far right)

1 Sprinkle the pork with a good pinch
each of salt and pepper, and lightly coat
with the flour.
2 Beat the egg yolks with 2 tablespoons
water. Dip each schnitzel in the egg, then
in the breadcrumbs, pressing them on
to ensure an even coating. Refrigerate
the pork in a single layer on a plate,
uncovered, for at least 2 hours.
3 Use a sharp knife to shred the nori
very finely and then break into strips
about 4 cm (1½ inches) long. Set aside
until serving time.

4 Heat 2 cm (¾ inch) oil in a deep, heavy-based saucepan to 180°C (350°F), or until a cube of bread browns in 15 seconds. Cook two or three schnitzels at a time until golden brown on both sides, then drain on crumpled paper towels. Repeat the process with the remaining schnitzels.

5 Slice the schnitzels into 1 cm (½ inch) strips and reassemble into the original shape. Sprinkle with the nori strips and serve with the tonkatsu sauce.

chilled soba noodles

※

Preparation time: **25 minutes**
Cooking time: **15 minutes**
Serves 4

250 g (9 oz) dried soba (buckwheat) noodles
4 cm (1½ inch) piece fresh ginger
1 carrot
4 spring onions (scallions), outside layer removed
1 sheet nori, to garnish
pickled ginger, to garnish
pickled daikon, thinly sliced, to garnish

DIPPING SAUCE
3 tablespoons dashi granules
125 ml (4 fl oz/½ cup) Japanese soy sauce (shoshoyu)
80 ml (2½ fl oz/⅓ cup) mirin

1 Put the noodles in a large saucepan of boiling water. When the water returns to the boil, pour in 250 ml (9 fl oz/1 cup) cold water. Bring the water back to the boil and cook the noodles for 2–3 minutes, or until just tender — take care not to overcook them. Drain the noodles in a colander and then cool under cold running water. Drain thoroughly and set aside.

2 Cut the ginger and carrot into fine matchsticks about 4 cm (1½ inches) long. Slice the spring onions very thinly. Bring a small saucepan of water to the boil, add the ginger, carrot and spring onion and blanch for about 30 seconds. Drain and place in a bowl of iced water to cool. Drain again when the vegetables are cool.

3 To make the dipping sauce, combine 375 ml (13 fl oz/1½ cups) water, the dashi granules, soy sauce, mirin and a good pinch each of salt and pepper in a small saucepan. Bring the sauce to the boil, then cool completely. When ready to serve, pour the sauce into four small dipping bowls.

4 Gently toss the cooled noodles and vegetables to combine. Arrange in four individual serving bowls.

5 Toast the nori by holding it with tongs over low heat and moving it back and forth for about 15 seconds. Cut it into thin strips with scissors, and scatter the strips over the noodles. Place a little pickled ginger and daikon on the side of each plate. Serve the noodles with the dipping sauce. The noodles should be dipped into the sauce before being eaten.

japanese condiments

Shichimi togarashi ('seven spice red pepper') contains a roughly ground mixture of red chilli flakes, Japanese pepper (sansho), white sesame seeds, black sesame seeds (in some mixtures replaced by mustard seeds), the dried seaweed nori, dried tangerine or mandarin peel and white poppy seeds. *Tonkatsu sauce* is a type of barbecue sauce that usually contains tomato sauce (ketchup), dark soy sauce, sake, worcestershire sauce and mustard. Both are available from Asian food stores.

teas

It was China that first introduced tea to the rest of the world. Whether black or green, plain or highly spiced, tea is an important part of the meal in most Asian countries.

black tea

Mainly produced in India, China and Sri Lanka, black tea leaves undergo fermentation which gives them their characteristic full, aromatic flavour and rich colour and strength.

Assam: Grown in north east India, this classic tea has a strong, full-flavoured malty taste and is ideal for drinking with milk.

Darjeeling: Grown in the foothills of the Himalayas, this prized tea has a subtle 'muscatel' flavour and a reddish-brown colour.

Ceylon: Produced in the high-altitude areas of Sri Lanka and known for its excellent quality, this tea has a strong rich flavour.

Lapsang souchong: A famous tea from China and Taiwan, this is rich and full-bodied, with a distinctive smoky, tarry taste due to the unique smoking process it undergoes.

Yunnan: Often used in blended teas, this Chinese tea produces a sweet light golden liquid, considered to have health-giving properties.

oolong tea

Semi-fermented oolong teas are stronger than green teas but milder than black. They are often scented with jasmine, gardenia or rose petals and are then known as pouchong. Oolong tea originated in China, but the highest grade is now produced in Taiwan.

Formosa: These Taiwanese leaves produce a dark tea with a natural fruity flavour.

green tea

A favourite in the East, green tea is served with meals in many Asian restaurants and is believed to aid digestion. It is always made weak: only 1 teaspoon of tea for the whole pot. Sugar and milk are never added.

Gunpowder: A high-quality, small Chinese leaf which yields a very pale green, fruity and slightly bitter tea.

Jasmine: This Chinese green tea is scented with jasmine petals and traditionally served with yum cha.

Sencha: A Japanese tea with a delicate, light flavour and colour.

Genmai-cha: This blend of rolled Japanese green tea leaves and toasted, puffed rice is a nutty-flavoured tea.

blended tea

Blended teas are a combination of 15–20 different tea leaves. They were introduced to avoid by fluctuations in availability.

English breakfast: A mix of a number of strong Indian leaves and Ceylon tea which produces a full-flavoured, fragrant tea.

Irish breakfast: A strong, fragrant tea which is a combination of Assam and Ceylon leaves.

Russian caravan: Originally transported from India to Russia by camels, this is a blend of Keemun, Assam and Chinese green leaves.

Earl Grey: Scented with oil of bergamot, this blend of Keemun and Darjeeling leaves produces a pale tea with a citrus flavour.

brewing the perfect cup of tea

1 Use a china or glazed earthenware teapot that will retain the heat, and warm it by swirling a little hot water around the sides and emptying it out.

2 Measure out the tea carefully: 1 heaped teaspoon leaves for each cup and 1 for the pot.

3 Follow the old adage 'bring your teapot to the kettle, not the kettle to the teapot' to ensure the water is still on the boil when it is poured onto the tea leaves. This will agitate the leaves and release the full flavour of the tea.

4 Put the lid on the pot and leave for 5 minutes to infuse.

5 If using, add milk to the cup before the tea. The scalding tea will slightly cook the milk and blend the flavours.

6 Stir the pot and pour tea through a strainer into each cup. Add sugar to taste and a slice of lemon if desired.

udon noodle soup

udon noodle soup

※

Preparation time: 20 minutes
Cooking time: 15 minutes
Serves 4

400 g (14 oz) dried udon noodles
3 teaspoons dashi granules
2 leeks, white part only, thinly sliced
200 g (7 oz) pork loin, cut into thin strips
125 ml (4 fl oz/½ cup) Japanese soy sauce
    (shoshoyu)
2 tablespoons mirin
4 spring onions (scallions), finely chopped,
    plus extra, to garnish
shichimi togarashi (see Note), to serve

1 Cook the noodles in a large saucepan
of rapidly boiling water for 5 minutes,
or until tender. Drain and cover to keep
warm.
2 Combine 1 litre (35 fl oz/4 cups) water
and the dashi in a large saucepan and
bring to the boil. Add the leek, reduce the
heat and simmer for 5 minutes. Add the
pork, soy sauce, mirin and spring onion
and simmer for 2 minutes, or until the
pork is cooked. Divide the noodles among
four serving bowls and ladle the soup
over the top. Garnish with spring onion
and sprinkle with the shichimi togarashi.

NOTE: Shichimi togarashi is a Japanese
spice mix containing seven flavours.
Ingredients can vary, but it always contains
togarashi, a hot Japanese chilli. It is
available in Asian or Japanese food stores.

eggs scrambled with prawns and peas

※

Preparation time: 25 minutes
Cooking time: 10 minutes
Serves 4

10 g (¼ oz/¼ cup) dried shiitake
    mushrooms
250 g (9 oz) raw prawns (shrimp)

4 eggs
1 teaspoon dashi granules
2 teaspoons Japanese soy sauce (shoshoyu)
2 teaspoons sake
2 teaspoons oil
100 g (3½ oz) frozen peas
3 spring onions (scallions), thinly sliced
steamed rice, to serve

1 Soak the mushrooms in hot water
for 15 minutes; drain and slice. Peel the
prawns and gently pull out the dark vein
from each prawn back, starting at the
head end.
2 Place the eggs, dashi, soy sauce
and sake in a bowl and beat until well
combined.
3 Heat the oil in a frying pan; add the
prawns and stir-fry over medium heat for
2 minutes or until just cooked. Add the
peas, cover and steam for 2 minutes.
4 Pour in the egg mixture; cook over
low heat until lightly set, stirring gently
occasionally so the egg sets in large curds.
Sprinkle over the spring onions and serve
immediately with steamed rice.

chicken domburi

※ ※

Preparation time: 35 minutes
Cooking time: 35 minutes
Serves 4

2 cups (440 g/15½ oz) medium-grain rice
2 tablespoons oil
200 g (7 oz) boneless, skinless chicken
    breast, cut into thin strips
2 onions, thinly sliced
80 ml (2½ fl oz/⅓ cup) Japanese soy sauce
    (shoshoyu)
2 tablespoons mirin
1 teaspoon dashi granules

5 eggs, lightly beaten
2 sheets nori
2 spring onions (scallions), sliced

1 Wash the rice in a colander under
cold running water until the water runs
clear. Place the rice in a medium-sized
heavy-based pan, add 600 ml (21 fl oz)
water and bring to the boil over high
heat. Cover the pan with a tight-fitting
lid, reduce the heat to as low as possible
(otherwise the rice in the bottom of the
pan will burn) and cook for 15 minutes.
Turn the heat to very high for 15–20
seconds then remove the pan from the
heat. Set the pan aside for 12 minutes,
without lifting the lid (don't allow the
steam to escape).
2 Heat the oil in a frying pan over high
heat, and stir-fry the chicken until golden
and tender; set aside. Reheat the pan, add
the onion and cook, stirring occasionally,
for 3 minutes or until beginning to soften.
Add 80 ml (2½ fl oz/⅓ cup) water, soy
sauce, mirin and dashi. Stir to dissolve the
dashi and bring the stock to the boil. Cook
for 3 minutes or until onion is tender.
3 Return the chicken to the pan and pour
in the egg, stirring gently to just break up
the egg. Cover and simmer over very low
heat for 2–3 minutes or until the eggs are
just set. Remove the pan from the heat.
4 Toast the nori by holding it over low
heat and moving it back and forth for
about 15 seconds; crumble it into small
pieces.
5 Transfer the rice to an earthenware
dish, carefully spoon over the chicken and
egg mixture and sprinkle over the nori.
Garnish with the spring onion.

NOTE: Domburi is an earthenware dish,
but the food served in the dish has also
taken on the name.

a noisy affair

While etiquette dictates that Japanese mealtimes
should be silent affairs, an exception is made
for noodles, which may be eaten with gusto
and much lip-smacking. Some say this allows
an intake of air to cool the noodles, but chilled
noodles, a favourite summer dish in Japan, are
eaten with the same enthusiastic slurping.

marinated salmon strips

☀

Preparation time: **15 minutes + 1 hour marinating time**
Cooking time: **nil**
Serves **4**

2 sashimi-grade salmon fillets, each about 400 g (14 oz), skinned
4 cm (1½ inch) piece fresh ginger, finely grated
1 garlic clove, finely chopped
3 spring onions (scallions), finely chopped
1 teaspoon sugar
2 tablespoons Japanese soy sauce (shoshoyu)
125 ml (4 fl oz/½ cup) sake
pickled ginger, to garnish
pickled cucumber, to garnish

1 Cut the salmon into thin strips and arrange them in a single layer in a large deep dish.
2 Put the ginger, garlic, spring onion, sugar, 1 teaspoon salt, soy sauce and sake in a small bowl and stir to combine. Pour the marinade over the salmon, cover and refrigerate for 1 hour.
3 Arrange the salmon, strip by strip, on a serving plate. Garnish with the pickled ginger and cucumber and serve chilled.

inari sushi

☀ ☀

Preparation time: **10 minutes**
Cooking time: **40 minutes + 15 minutes**
Makes **6**

220 g (7¾ oz/1 cup) medium-grain rice
2 tablespoons Japanese white sesame seeds
2 tablespoons rice vinegar
1 tablespoon caster (superfine) sugar
1 teaspoon mirin
6 inari pouches (see Note)

1 Wash the rice under cold running water until the water runs clear; drain thoroughly. Place the rice and 500 ml (17 fl oz/2 cups) water in a medium saucepan, and bring to the boil. Reduce the heat and simmer, uncovered, for 4–5 minutes or until the water is absorbed. Cover, reduce the heat to very low and cook for another 4–5 minutes. Remove the pan from the heat and let stand, covered, for 10 minutes.
2 Toast the sesame seeds in a dry frying pan over medium heat for 3–4 minutes, shaking the pan gently, until the seeds are golden brown; remove the seeds from the pan at once to prevent burning.
3 Add the combined vinegar, sugar, mirin and 1 teaspoon salt to the rice, tossing with a wooden spoon until the rice is cool.

inari sushi

4 Gently separate the inari pouches and open them up. Place a ball of the rice mixture inside. Sprinkle the rice with the toasted sesame seeds and press the inari closed with your fingers. Serve on a plate, cut side down.

NOTE: Inari are small 'pouches' made from bean curd and are available from Japanese food shops.

hand-shaped tuna sushi

☀ ☀

Preparation time: **20 minutes**
Cooking time: **30 minutes + 10 minutes cooling**
Makes **about 30**

220 g (7¾ oz/1 cup) medium-grain rice
2 tablespoons rice vinegar
1 tablespoon caster (superfine) sugar
300 g (10½ oz) very fresh tuna
wasabi, to taste
Japanese soy sauce (shoshoyu), and wasabi, extra, to serve

1 Wash the rice under cold running water until the water runs clear; drain thoroughly. Place the rice and 500 ml (17 fl oz/2 cups) water in a medium saucepan and bring it to the boil. Reduce the heat; simmer, uncovered, for 4–5 minutes or until the water is absorbed. Reduce the heat to very low. Cover and cook for another 4–5 minutes. Remove the pan from the heat and let stand, covered, for 10 minutes.
2 Add the combined vinegar, sugar and 1 teaspoon salt to the rice, tossing with a wooden spoon until the rice is cool.
3 Cut the tuna into strips about 5 cm (2 inches) long. Place a little wasabi on each.
4 Use your hands to roll a tablespoon of rice into a ball. Place the rice ball onto a strip of fish and then gently mould the tuna around the rice. Flatten the ball slightly to elongate. Repeat with the remaining ingredients. Serve with the soy sauce and wasabi.

Grate the piece of fresh ginger.

Use a sharp knife to cut the salmon into thin strips.

Place all the ingredients for the marinade in a small bowl and stir together well.

marinated salmon strips

grilled fish steaks

1 Finely grate the ginger. Squeeze the ginger firmly with your fingertips to remove all the juice; reserve the juice and discard the dry pulp. Place the ginger juice, soy sauce, mirin, spring onion and sugar in a small bowl and stir until the sugar has dissolved.

2 Place the fish in a shallow dish. Pour the marinade over the fish and marinate for 15 minutes. Drain the fish, reserving the marinade, and place it on a foil-lined grill (broiler) tray.

3 Cook the fish under medium heat for about 3 minutes each side, carefully turning the fish over with spatulas.

4 Pour the reserved marinade into a small saucepan and boil it over high heat for 2 minutes until thickened. Drizzle the marinade over the fish, garnish with the cucumber and pickled ginger, and serve with steamed rice if desired.

teriyaki chicken

✹

Preparation time: 15 minutes
Cooking time: 40 minutes
Serves 6

125 ml (4 fl oz/½ cup) Japanese soy sauce (shoshoyu)
2 tablespoons mirin
1 tablespoon sugar
2 tablespoons oil
12 chicken drumsticks
steamed rice, to serve

1 Place the soy sauce, mirin and sugar in a small saucepan and stir over low heat until the sugar has dissolved. Bring to the boil, reduce the heat and simmer, uncovered, for 2 minutes.

2 Heat the oil in a large heavy-based frying pan; add the chicken drumsticks in batches and cook over high heat until browned on both sides.

3 Return all the chicken to the pan, add the sauce, cover and cook for 20 minutes or until the chicken is tender. Serve with the steamed rice.

grilled fish steaks

✹ ✹

Preparation time: 30 minutes
Cooking time: 10 minutes
Serves 4

5 cm (2 inch) piece fresh ginger
3 tablespoons Japanese soy sauce (shoshoyu)
1 tablespoon mirin
3 spring onions (scallions), very finely chopped
3 teaspoons sugar
4 small fish cutlets (such as tuna, blue eye, jewfish), each about 150 g (5½ oz)
cucumber slices, to garnish
pickled ginger (page 162), to garnish
steamed rice (optional), to serve

eggplant kebabs
with miso

☀

Preparation time: **15 minutes**
Cooking time: **15 minutes**
Makes **10**

2 eggplants (aubergines), cut into 2 cm
    (¾ inch) cubes
2 tablespoons Japanese white
    sesame seeds
140 g (5 oz/½ cup) red miso paste
2 tablespoons mirin
2 tablespoons sake
60 ml (2 fl oz/¼ cup) oil
steamed rice, to serve

1 Soak 10 wooden skewers in water
for 30 minutes to ensure they don't
burn during cooking. Put the eggplant
in a colander and sprinkle generously
with salt. Set aside for 15 minutes, or
until the moisture is drawn out of the
eggplant (this removes the bitterness).
Rinse thoroughly and pat dry with
paper towels.
2 Drain the skewers and dry with paper
towels. Thread the eggplant cubes onto
the skewers.
3 Put the sesame seeds in a dry frying
pan over medium heat and toast for
3–4 minutes, shaking the pan gently, until
the seeds are golden brown. Remove the
seeds from the pan at once to prevent
burning.
4 Combine the miso, mirin and sake in
a small saucepan. Bring to the boil, then
reduce the heat and simmer for
5 minutes.
5 Heat the oil on a barbecue
hotplate and cook the eggplant skewers
for 5 minutes, turning frequently until
golden brown. Spread the miso topping
over the eggplant skewers and sprinkle
with the sesame seeds. Serve with
steamed rice.

green beans in sesame seed sauce

✹ ✹

Preparation time: **10** minutes
Cooking time: **10** minutes
Serves **4**

500 g (1 lb 2 oz) green beans, trimmed
2 tablespoons Japanese white sesame
    seeds (see Note)
6 cm (2½ inch) fresh ginger, finely sliced
1 tablespoon Japanese soy sauce (shoshoyu)
1 tablespoon mirin
3 teaspoons sugar
1 teaspoon Japanese white sesame
    seeds, extra

1 Cook the beans in a large saucepan of boiling water for 2 minutes. Drain, then plunge into iced water to stop the cooking process. Drain again and set aside.
2 Toast the sesame seeds in a dry frying pan, over medium heat, for 3–4 minutes, shaking the pan gently, until the seeds are golden brown; remove the seeds from the pan at once to prevent browning. Pound the seeds using a mortar and pestle until a paste forms (the mixture will become damp as oil is released from the seeds).
3 Combine the sesame seed paste with the ginger, soy sauce, mirin and sugar. Pour the sauce over the beans, scatter over the extra sesame seeds and serve.

NOTE: Japanese sesame seeds are plump and large, with a fuller flavour than other sesame seeds. The beans can be marinated in the sauce overnight.

yakitori (skewered chicken)

✹

Preparation time: **20** minutes
Cooking time: **10** minutes
Makes **25** skewers

1 kg (2 lb 4 oz) boneless, skinless chicken
    thighs
6 spring onions (scallions)
125 ml (4 fl oz/½ cup) sake
185 ml (6 fl oz/¾ cup) soy sauce (see Note)
125 ml (4 fl oz/½ cup) mirin
2 tablespoons sugar

1 Soak 25 wooden skewers in water for 30 minutes to ensure they don't burn during cooking. Cut the chicken into bite-sized pieces. Trim the spring onions, then cut diagonally into 2 cm (¾ inch) lengths.
2 Combine the sake, soy sauce, mirin and sugar in a small saucepan. Bring to the boil, then remove from the heat and set aside.
3 Drain the skewers and dry with paper towels. Thread the chicken and spring onion pieces alternately onto the skewers. Place the skewers on a foil-lined tray and

green beans in sesame seed sauce

cook under a preheated moderate grill (broiler), turning and brushing frequently with the sauce, for 7–8 minutes, or until the chicken is cooked through. Yakitori is traditionally served as a snack with beer.

NOTE: For this dish, it is best to use a darker soy sauce rather than the lighter Japanese one.

salmon nabe

Preparation time: **20 minutes**
Cooking time: **40 minutes**
Serves 3–4

12 dried shiitake mushrooms
250 g (9 oz) firm tofu
½ Chinese cabbage (wong bok)
4 salmon cutlets
2 x 5 cm (2 inch) pieces tinned bamboo
  shoots
2 litres (70 fl oz/8 cups) dashi
80 ml (2½ fl oz/⅓ cup) Japanese
  soy sauce
60 ml (2 fl oz/¼ cup) mirin or sake

SESAME SEED SAUCE
100 g (3½ oz) white sesame seeds
2 teaspoons oil
125 ml (4 fl oz/½ cup) Japanese
  soy sauce (shoshoyu)
2 tablespoons mirin
3 teaspoons caster (superfine) sugar
½ teaspoon instant dashi granules

salmon nabe

1 Soak the mushrooms in warm water for 15 minutes, then drain. Remove stems.Cut the tofu into 12 squares. Roughly shred the cabbage into 5 cm (2 inch) wide pieces.
2 Place the mushrooms, tofu, cabbage, salmon, bamboo shoots, dashi, soy sauce, mirin and a pinch of salt in a large saucepan and bring to the boil. Reduce the heat, cover and simmer over medium heat for 15 minutes. Turn the salmon cutlets over and simmer for a further 15 minutes, or until tender.
3 To make the sesame seed sauce, toast the sesame seeds in a frying pan over medium heat for 3–4 minutes, shaking the pan gently, until the seeds are golden brown. Remove from the pan at once to prevent burning. Grind the seeds using a mortar and pestle until a paste is formed. Add the oil, if necessary, to assist in forming a paste. Mix the paste with the soy sauce, mirin, sugar, dashi granules and 125 ml (4 fl oz/½ cup) warm water.

4 Pour the salmon nabe into warmed serving bowls and serve with the sesame seed sauce.

NOTE: This dish is traditionally cooked in a clay pot over a burner and served in the same pot. Diners dip the fish and vegetable pieces into the accompanying sauce and the broth is served in small bowls at the end of the meal.

noodle-coated prawns

1 Peel the prawns, leaving the tails intact. Gently pull out the dark vein from each prawn back, starting at the head end. Make a shallow incision in the underside of the prawns and then open up the cut to straighten the prawns out. Cut the nori into strips about 7 cm (2¾ inches) long and 1.5 cm (⅝ inch) wide. To make the batter, put the flour, egg yolk and water in a bowl and whisk until just combined. To make the sauce, combine all ingredients in a small bowl and mix well.

2 Break the noodles so that they are the same length as the prawns, not including the tails. Place the noodles on a board. Dip a prawn into the batter, then lay it, lengthways, on the noodles and gather up the noodles to cover the prawns all around. Press so they stick to the prawn. Wrap a strip of nori around the centre of the prawn, dampen the ends with a little water and press to seal. Repeat with the rest of the prawns.

3 Fill a deep-fryer or heavy-based saucepan one-third full of oil and heat to 170°C (325°F), or until a cube of bread dropped into the oil browns in 20 seconds. Cook the prawn bundles in two batches, until the noodles are golden brown. Serve immediately with the sauce.

rice with chicken and mushrooms

✳

Preparation time: 30 minutes
Cooking time: 40 minutes
Serves 4–6

500 g (1 lb 2 oz) medium-grain white rice
8 dried shiitake mushrooms
2 tablespoons Japanese soy sauce (shoshoyu)
2 tablespoons sake
2 teaspoons sugar
600 g (1 lb 5 oz) boneless, skinless chicken breasts, cut into strips
200 g (7 oz) frozen peas
2 eggs, lightly beaten

noodle-coated prawns

✳ ✳

Preparation time: 20 minutes
Cooking time: 15 minutes
Serves 2

6 raw large prawns (shrimp)
¼ sheet nori
100 g (3½ oz) somen noodles
oil, for deep-frying

BATTER
125 g (4½ oz/1 cup) plain (all-purpose) flour
1 egg yolk
250 ml (9 fl oz/1 cup) iced water

SOY AND GINGER SAUCE
1 tablespoon finely grated fresh ginger
2 teaspoons sugar
250 ml (9 fl oz/1 cup) soy sauce

1   Wash the rice thoroughly in a sieve under cold running water until the water runs clear. Place the rice in a heavy-based saucepan with 600 ml (21 fl oz) water and bring it to the boil. Reduce the heat to very low, cover and cook for 15 minutes. Remove the pan from the heat and leave, with the lid on, for 20 minutes.

2   Soak mushrooms in hot water for about 15 minutes, until soft. Drain well and slice into thin strips, discarding the hard stem.

3   Combine the soy sauce, sake and sugar in a frying pan. Cook over low heat stirring until the sugar has dissolved. Add the mushrooms, chicken and peas. Cover and cook for 5 minutes until the chicken is cooked. Set aside and cover to keep warm.

4   Heat a non-stick frying pan; pour in the egg and cook over medium heat, swirling the pan gently until the egg sets. Turn the omelette over and cook the other side. Remove the omelette from the pan and cut it into thin strips.

5   Arrange the rice in individual serving bowls, spoon over the chicken mixture with a little of the soy liquid and scatter over the egg strips. Serve immediately.

skewers of beef, capsicum and spring onion

✳ ✳

Preparation time: **25 minutes + 20 minutes marinating time**
Cooking time: **20 minutes**
Makes **12**

60 ml (2 fl oz/¼ cup) Japanese soy sauce (shoshoyu)
2 tablespoons mirin
2 teaspoons sesame oil
1 teaspoon sugar
2 tablespoons Japanese white sesame seeds
350 g (12 oz) scotch fillet, cut into bite-sized cubes
1 green capsicum (pepper), cut into small bite-sized pieces
6 spring onions (scallions), white part only, cut into short lengths

oil, for shallow frying
2 eggs, beaten
60 g (2¼ oz/½ cup) plain (all-purpose) flour

1   Soak 12 small wooden skewers in water for 30 minutes to ensure they don't burn during cooking.

2   Put the soy sauce, mirin, sesame oil, sugar and half the sesame seeds in a large bowl. Add the beef to the marinade, toss to combine, and marinate for 20 minutes.

Drain the beef and gently pat dry with paper towels. Thread a piece of beef, capsicum and spring onion onto each skewer, repeating this pattern once more.

3   Heat 1 cm (½ inch) of oil in a deep heavy-based frying pan until hot. Roll each skewer in the beaten egg, then lightly coat it in the flour. Add the skewers to the pan in two or three batches and fry until golden brown, turning each skewer regularly. Sprinkle over the remaining sesame seeds and serve immediately.

india & pakistan

At the heart of Indian and Pakistani cooking are the spices, which are ground up to produce masalas, aromatic blends created freshly for each different dish. The variety of food reflects the religious, cultural and geographic diversity of the sub-continent itself. In Pakistan and the north of India, the cooking is meat-based: curries, tikkas and koftas mopped up with fresh breads. The dishes of the south are predominantly vegetarian, spicy-hot and bursting with colour. Special dishes are prepared for religious or cultural events, from a festive pan of biryani, flavoured with aromatic saffron, to coconut sweets, served up at weddings and other celebrations.

madras curry

☀

Preparation time: **20 minutes**
Cooking time: **1 hour 30 minutes**
Serves **4**

1 kg (2 lb 4 oz) skirt or
    chuck steak
1 tablespoon ground coriander
1½ tablespoons ground cumin
1 teaspoon brown mustard seeds
½ teaspoon cracked black
    peppercorns
1 teaspoon chilli powder
1 teaspoon ground turmeric
2 teaspoons crushed garlic
2 teaspoons grated fresh ginger
2–3 tablespoons white vinegar
1 tablespoon oil or ghee
1 onion, chopped
60 g (2¼ oz/¼ cup) tomato paste
    (concentrated purée)
250 ml (9 fl oz/1 cup) beef
    stock
steamed rice, to serve

1 Trim the excess fat and sinew
from the beef, and cut it into 2.5 cm
(1 inch) cubes.
2 Put the coriander, cumin, mustard
seeds, peppercorns, chilli powder,
turmeric, garlic, ginger and 1 teaspoon
salt in a small bowl and stir to combine.
Add the vinegar and mix to a smooth
paste.
3 Heat the oil in a large frying pan.
Add the onion and cook over medium
heat until just soft. Add the spice paste
and stir for 1 minute. Add the beef and
cook, stirring, until it is coated with the
spice paste. Add the tomato paste and
stock. Simmer, covered, for about 1 hour
30 minutes, or until the meat is tender.
Serve with steamed rice.

hot lentil soup

✻

Preparation time: **15 minutes**
Cooking time: **45 minutes**
Serves **6**

95 g (3¼ oz/½ cup) brown lentils
    (see Note)
2 tablespoons ghee or oil
1 onion, finely chopped
½ teaspoon finely grated fresh ginger
1 large potato, cut into small cubes
2 large tomatoes, chopped
2 teaspoons ground coriander
1 teaspoon ground cumin
½ teaspoon ground turmeric
½ teaspoon chilli flakes
2 tablespoons desiccated coconut
1–2 teaspoons tamarind concentrate
150 g (5½ oz) finely shredded
    cabbage
1 tablespoon chopped coriander
    (cilantro) or mint leaves (optional),
    to garnish
chapattis, to serve

1 Place the lentils in a medium saucepan, cover with water, bring to the boil and simmer, uncovered, for about 20 minutes or until tender. Drain well.
2 Heat the ghee in a large saucepan; add the onion and ginger and cook over medium heat until deep brown. Add the potato and tomato, and cook for 5 minutes, then add the ground coriander, cumin, turmeric, chilli and coconut and cook for another 2–3 minutes.
3 Add the drained lentils and 1 litre (35 fl oz/4 cups) water and bring to the boil. Simmer until the lentils and potato begin to break up. Add the tamarind and cabbage. Cook until the cabbage is soft. Season with black pepper to taste. Serve with chopped coriander or mint as a garnish, if desired, and chapattis.

NOTE: Red or yellow lentils, which require less cooking time, can be used instead of brown.

dry potato and pea curry

✻

Preparation time: **15 minutes**
Cooking time: **30 minutes**
Serves **4**

2 onions
750 g (1 lb 10 oz) potatoes
2 teaspoons brown mustard seeds
2 tablespoons ghee or oil
2 garlic cloves, crushed
2 teaspoons finely grated fresh ginger
1 teaspoon ground turmeric
½ teaspoon chilli powder
1 teaspoon ground cumin
1 teaspoon garam masala
100 g (3½ oz/⅔ cup) peas
2 tablespoons chopped mint leaves
steamed rice, to serve

1 Slice the onion and cut the potatoes into cubes. Put the mustard seeds in a large dry saucepan and cook over medium heat until the seeds start to pop. Add the ghee, onion, garlic and ginger, and cook, stirring, until the onion is soft.
2 Add the turmeric, chilli powder, cumin, garam masala and potato. Stir until the potato is coated. Add 125 ml (4 fl oz/ ½ cup) water, cover and simmer for 15–20 minutes, or until the potato is just tender, stirring occasionally.
3 Add the peas and stir until combined. Season to taste. Simmer, covered, for 3–5 minutes, or until the potato is cooked through and the liquid is absorbed. Stir in the mint and serve with steamed rice.

dry potato and pea curry

the tandoor oven

Tandoori is the name given to food that is traditionally threaded onto spits and cooked in a tandoor or clay oven. Barrel-shaped and often as high as a man, the ovens are usually set into the ground with a small circular opening at the top. Long spits, laden with meats marinated in an aromatic spice paste, are lowered in to roast over the white-hot coals.

tandoori chicken

☀

Preparation time: 25 minutes + 4 hours
  30 minutes marinating time
Cooking time: 45 minutes
Serves 4–6

6 boneless, skinless chicken thighs
60 ml (2 fl oz/¼ cup) lemon juice
½ small onion, chopped
4 garlic cloves
1 tablespoon finely grated fresh ginger
3 teaspoons coriander seeds
1 tablespoon cumin seeds
1 tablespoon lemon juice, extra
¼ teaspoon paprika
pinch of chilli powder
250 g (9 oz/1 cup) plain yoghurt
red food colouring
steamed rice, to serve
cooked poppadoms, to serve

1 Remove the skin from the chicken pieces and brush the flesh with the lemon juice; cover and marinate in the refrigerator for 30 minutes.
2 Place the onion, garlic, ginger, coriander and cumin seeds, extra lemon juice and 1 teaspoon salt in a food processor and process until a smooth paste forms. Combine the spice paste with the paprika, chilli powder and yoghurt, and mix together until smooth. Add enough drops of food colouring to make the mixture a deep red colour.
3 Place the chicken pieces in a large shallow dish, and spread liberally with the spicy yoghurt mixture. Cover with plastic wrap and refrigerate. Marinate the chicken for at least 4 hours or overnight.
4 Preheat the oven to 180°C (350°F/ Gas 4). Place the chicken pieces on a wire rack over a large baking dish. Bake for 45 minutes, or until the chicken pieces are tender and cooked through. Serve with steamed rice and poppadoms.

Brush the skinned chicken thighs with lemon juice.

Add several drops of red food colouring to the spice and yoghurt mixture.

onion bhaji

✳ ✳

Preparation time: 20 minutes
Cooking time: 15 minutes
Makes 25–30

80 g (2¾ oz/¾ cup) besan (chickpea
    flour)
60 g (2¼ oz/½ cup) plain (all-purpose)
    flour
1½ teaspoons bicarbonate of soda
    (baking soda)
1 teaspoon chilli powder
1 egg, lightly beaten
4 large onions, halved and thinly sliced
4 garlic cloves, chopped
oil, for shallow frying
chilli sauce or mango chutney, to serve

1   Sift the flours, bicarbonate of soda and
chilli powder into a bowl. Make a well in
the centre, add the combined egg and
310 ml (10¾ fl oz/1¼ cups) water and
stir to make a smooth creamy batter,
adding a little more water if necessary.
Add the onion and garlic and mix well.
2   Heat the oil, about 1 cm (½ inch)
deep, in a wide flat frying pan. Drop in
tablespoons of the mixture and press into
patties. Fry the bhaji on both sides until
golden brown and cooked through; drain
on paper towels. Serve hot with chilli
sauce or mango chutney.

NOTE: Use sweet paprika instead of chilli
powder for a milder taste.

pork vindaloo

pork vindaloo

✳

Preparation time: 20 minutes
Cooking time: 1 hour 55 minutes
Serves 4

1 kg (2 lb 4 oz) pork fillets
60 ml (2 fl oz/¼ cup) vegetable oil
2 onions, finely chopped
4 garlic cloves, finely chopped
1 tablespoon finely chopped fresh ginger
1 tablespoon garam masala

2 teaspoons brown mustard seeds
4 tablespoons ready-made vindaloo curry
    paste
1 tablespoon white vinegar
steamed rice, to serve
cooked poppadoms, to serve

1   Trim the pork of any excess fat and
sinew and cut into bite-sized pieces.
2   Heat a wok over medium heat, add
the oil and swirl to coat the base and
side. Add the pork in small batches and
cook for 5–7 minutes, or until browned.
Remove from the wok.

3   Add the onion, garlic, ginger, garam
masala and mustard seeds to the wok,
and cook, stirring, for 5 minutes, or until
the onion is soft. Add the vindaloo paste
and cook for 2 minutes.
4   Return all the pork to the wok, add
750 ml (26 fl oz/3 cups) water and
bring to the boil. Reduce the heat and
simmer, covered, for 1½ hours, or until
the pork is tender. Stir in the vinegar
15 minutes before serving and season to
taste with salt. Serve with steamed rice
and poppadoms.

yoghurt

In India, yoghurt is known as dahi and is served with almost every meal, either as raita or lassi (a smooth drink). It is also stirred into sauces to thicken and flavour, or mixed with spices and used as a marinade. The Aryans introduced cattle to India in the second millennium BC and with them came dairy products, namely cream and yoghurt. Today, yoghurt in India and Sri Lanka is produced from buffalo milk, which is far higher in butterfat than Western cow's milk. Coconut milk is still more popular in the south of India, with its largely vegetarian population.

rogan josh

rogan josh

✹

Preparation time: 25 minutes
Cooking time: 1 hour 30 minutes
Serves 4–6

1 kg (2 lb 4 oz) lamb
1 tablespoon ghee or oil
2 onions, chopped
125 g (4½ oz/½ cup) plain yoghurt
1 teaspoon chilli powder
1 tablespoon ground coriander
2 teaspoons ground cumin
1 teaspoon ground cardamom
½ teaspoon ground cloves
1 teaspoon ground turmeric
3 garlic cloves, crushed
1 tablespoon finely grated fresh ginger
400 g (14 oz) tin chopped tomatoes
3 teaspoons garam masala
30 g (1 oz/¼ cup) slivered almonds
coriander (cilantro) leaves, to garnish

1 Cut the lamb into 2.5 cm (1 inch) cubes.
2 Heat the ghee in a large saucepan; add the onion and cook, stirring, until soft. Add the yoghurt, chilli powder, coriander, cumin, cardamom, cloves, turmeric, garlic and ginger. Combine well. Add 1 teaspoon salt and the undrained tomatoes, and simmer, uncovered, for 5 minutes.
3 Add the lamb and stir until coated. Cover and cook over low heat for 1 to 1½ hours, or until the lamb is tender, stirring occasionally. Uncover and simmer until the liquid is thick.
4 Meanwhile toast the almonds in a dry frying pan over medium heat for 3–4 minutes, shaking the pan gently, until the nuts are golden brown; remove from the pan at once to prevent burning.
5 Sprinkle the lamb with the garam masala and mix through. Serve with the almonds sprinkled over and garnished with coriander, on a bed of steamed rice.

chicken tikka

✹

Preparation time: 30 minutes + 4 hours marinating time
Cooking time: 15 minutes
Makes 12

750 g (1 lb 10 oz) boneless, skinless chicken thighs
¼ onion, chopped
2 garlic cloves, crushed
1 tablespoon finely grated fresh ginger
2 tablespoons lemon juice
3 teaspoons ground coriander
3 teaspoons ground cumin
3 teaspoons garam masala
90 g (3¼ oz/⅓ cup) plain yoghurt

1 Cut the chicken into 3 cm (1¼ inch) cubes. Soak 12 wooden skewers in water for 30 minutes to ensure they don't burn during cooking.

2 Place the onion, garlic, ginger, lemon juice and spices in a food processor and process until finely chopped. Add the yoghurt and 1 teaspoon salt and process briefly to combine.

3 Thread the chicken pieces onto the skewers. Place the skewers in a large baking dish; coat the chicken with the spice mixture, and marinate for at least 4 hours or overnight, covered, in the refrigerator.

4 Cook the chicken on a hot barbecue grill or in a large, well-greased frying pan over high heat for about 5 minutes each side, or until golden brown and cooked through.

lentil bhuja casserole

✳ ✳

Preparation time: 40 minutes + overnight soaking + 30 minutes chilling time
Cooking time: 1 hour 10 minutes
Serves 4–6

375 g (13 oz/2 cups) green lentils
2 carrots
1 large onion
1 large potato
1 teaspoon ground cumin
1 teaspoon ground coriander
1 teaspoon ground turmeric
90 g (3¼ oz/¾ cup) plain (all-purpose) flour
oil, for pan-frying
2 tablespoons oil, extra
2 garlic cloves, crushed
1 tablespoon finely grated fresh ginger
250 ml (9 fl oz/1 cup) tomato passata (puréed tomatoes)
500 ml (17 fl oz/2 cups) vegetable stock
250 ml (9 fl oz/1 cup) pouring (whipping) cream
200 g (7 oz) green beans, trimmed
pitta bread, to serve

1 Cover the lentils with cold water and soak overnight. Drain well.

2 Slice the carrots. Grate the onion and potato and drain the excess liquid. Combine the lentils, onion, potato, cumin, coriander, turmeric and flour in a bowl, and mix well. Roll the mixture into walnut-sized balls and place them on a foil-lined tray. Cover and refrigerate for 30 minutes.

3 Heat the oil, about 2 cm (¾ inch) deep, in a frying pan. Add the lentil balls in small batches and fry over high heat for 5 minutes, or until golden brown. Drain on paper towels.

4 Heat the extra oil in a large saucepan. Add the garlic and ginger and cook, stirring, over medium heat for 1 minute. Stir in the tomato passata, stock and cream. Bring to the boil, reduce the heat and simmer, uncovered, for 10 minutes. Add the lentil balls, beans and carrot, cover and simmer for 35 minutes, stirring occasionally. Serve with pitta bread.

NOTE: Make sure your hands are dry when shaping the lentil mixture into balls. The lentil balls can be made a day ahead and stored in an airtight container in the refrigerator.

lentil bhuja casserole

Roll the lentil mixture into walnut-sized balls.

Fry the lentil balls over high heat until they are golden brown.

Add the lentil balls, beans and carrot to the curry sauce.

chickpea curry

☀

Preparation time: 20 minutes
Cooking time: 30 minutes
Serves 4–6

2 x 400 g (14 oz) tins chickpeas
(garbanzo beans)
3 tablespoons ghee, oil or butter
2 onions, finely chopped
1 teaspoon finely grated fresh ginger
½ teaspoon crushed garlic
1–2 green chillies, seeded and finely
chopped
½ teaspoon ground turmeric
2 large, ripe tomatoes, seeded and chopped
1 tablespoon ground coriander
2 teaspoons garam masala
2 tablespoons lemon juice
2–3 tablespoons chopped coriander
(cilantro) leaves

1   Drain the chickpeas, reserving the liquid.

2   Heat the ghee in a large saucepan;
add the onion, ginger, garlic, chilli and
turmeric and cook over medium heat until
the onion is soft and golden.
3   Add the tomato and cook until soft. Add
the coriander and chickpeas, and cook for
10 minutes. Add 250 ml (9 fl oz/1 cup) of
the reserved chickpea liquid and cook for a
further 10 minutes.
4   Add the garam masala, lemon juice
and coriander, and cook gently for
2–3 minutes, adding more liquid, if
needed, to make a sauce. Pour the
chickpeas into a serving dish.

chickpea curry

vegetable korma

☀

Preparation time: 20 minutes
Cooking time: 50 minutes
Serves 4–6

3 tomatoes
1 onion
300 g (10½ oz) cauliflower
300 g (10½ oz) pumpkin (winter squash)
3 slender eggplants (aubergines)
2 carrots
125 g (4½ oz) green beans, trimmed
2 tablespoons oil
2 tablespoons ready-made green masala
paste
1 teaspoon chilli powder
1 tablespoon finely grated fresh ginger
375 ml (13 fl oz/1½ cups) vegetable stock
steamed rice, to serve

1   Score a cross in the base of each
tomato. Put in a heatproof bowl and cover
with boiling water. Leave for 30 seconds,
then transfer to cold water, drain and
peel the skin away from the cross. Cut the
tomatoes in half, scoop out the seeds and
chop the flesh. Chop the onion. Cut the
cauliflower into florets. Cut the pumpkin,
eggplants and carrots into large pieces.
Chop the beans.
2   Heat the oil in a large heavy-based
saucepan. Add the masala paste and cook
over medium heat for 2 minutes, or until
the oil separates from the paste. Add the

garam masala

Although one of the best known Indian spice
mixtures, garam masala does not contain
turmeric, the ingredient that gives many curries
their characteristic yellow colour. Garam masala
was popularised in northern India during the
Moghul reign of the seventeenth and eighteenth
centuries; curries there are usually brown or pale
in colour. (See recipe on page 114.)

chilli powder, ginger and onion, and cook for 3 minutes, or until the onion softens.
3 Add the cauliflower, pumpkin, eggplant and carrot and stir to coat in the paste mixture. Stir in the tomato and stock and bring to the boil, then reduce the heat and simmer, uncovered, for 30 minutes. Add the beans and cook for 10 minutes or until the vegetables are tender. Serve with steamed rice.

lamb kofta

☀

Preparation time: **25 minutes**
Cooking time: **50 minutes**
Serves 4–6

1 kg (2 lb 4 oz) minced (ground) lamb
1 onion, finely chopped
2 green chillies, finely chopped
3 teaspoons finely grated fresh ginger
3 garlic cloves, crushed
1 teaspoon ground cardamom
1 egg
25 g (1 oz/⅓ cup) fresh breadcrumbs
2 tablespoons ghee or oil
steamed rice, to serve

SAUCE
1 tablespoon ghee or oil
1 onion, sliced
1 green chilli, finely chopped
3 teaspoons finely grated fresh ginger
2 garlic cloves, crushed
1 teaspoon ground turmeric
3 teaspoons ground coriander
2 teaspoons ground cumin
1 teaspoon chilli powder
2 tablespoons white vinegar
185 g (6½ oz/¾ cup) plain yoghurt
310 ml (10¾ fl oz/1¼ cups) coconut
    milk

Mix the mince with the other ingredients until well combined.

Cook the meatballs in two batches until browned all over.

Mix together the yoghurt and coconut milk and stir in.

1 Line a baking tray with baking paper. Place the lamb in a large bowl. Add the onion, chilli, ginger, garlic, cardamom, egg and breadcrumbs, and season well. Mix until combined. Roll level tablespoons of the mixture into balls, and place them on the prepared tray.

2 Heat the ghee in a frying pan, add the meatballs in two batches and cook over medium heat for 5 minutes at a time, or until browned all over. Transfer the meatballs to a large bowl.
3 To make the sauce, heat the ghee in the cleaned frying pan, add the onion, chilli, ginger, garlic and turmeric, and cook, stirring, over low heat until the onion is soft. Add the coriander, cumin,

chilli powder, vinegar, meatballs and 350 ml (12 fl oz) water and stir gently. Cover and simmer for 30 minutes. Stir in the combined yoghurt and coconut milk and simmer for another 10 minutes with the pan partially covered. Serve with steamed rice.

raitas & relishes

Add interest to your curries with one of these spicy, fresh relishes, then cool down with a chilled vegetable or herb yoghurt raita. All of these recipes serve four, as an accompaniment.

cucumber raita

Mix 2 peeled, finely chopped Lebanese (short) cucumbers with 250 g (9 oz/1 cup) plain yoghurt. Fry 1 teaspoon each ground cumin and mustard seeds in a dry frying pan for 1 minute until aromatic. Add to the yoghurt mixture with ½ teaspoon grated fresh ginger. Season well with salt and pepper and garnish with paprika. Serve chilled.

carrot raita

Place 35 g (1¼ oz/¼ cup) chopped pistachio nuts, 40 g (1½ oz/ ⅓ cup) sultanas (golden raisins) and 80 ml (2½ fl oz/⅓ cup) boiling water in a small bowl. Soak for 30 minutes, then drain and pat dry with paper towels. In another bowl, place 2 grated carrots, 185 g/6½ oz/¾ cup) plain yoghurt, 1 teaspoon crushed cardamom seeds, 1 teaspoon ground cumin and ¼ teaspoon chilli powder and mix well. Chill for 30 minutes. Stir the pistachio nut mixture into the yoghurt mixture, keeping a couple of tablespoons aside to garnish. Serve chilled.

coriander chutney

Wash, dry and roughly chop 1 bunch (90 g/3¼ oz) coriander (cilantro), including the roots. Place in a food processor with 25 g (1 oz/¼ cup) desiccated coconut, 1 tablespoon soft brown sugar, 1 teaspoon salt, 1 tablespoon grated fresh ginger, 1 small chopped onion, 2 tablespoons lemon juice and 1–2 small green seeded chillies. Process for about 1 minute, or until finely chopped. Serve chilled.

fresh mint relish

Finely chop 50 g (1¾ oz) mint, 2 spring onions (scallions) and 1 green chilli. Mix with 1 crushed garlic clove, 1 teaspoon caster (superfine) sugar, ½ teaspoon salt and 2 tablespoons lemon juice. Cover and chill for at least 1 hour. Garnish with fine slices of lemon and spring onion and serve.

fresh tomato relish

Mix together 2 diced tomatoes, 3 finely sliced spring onions (scallions), 2 tablespoons finely chopped coriander (cilantro) leaves, 1 finely sliced green chilli, 1 tablespoon lemon juice and 1 teaspoon soft brown sugar. Season with salt and pepper. Serve chilled.

coconut bananas

Peel 2 large bananas and cut into thick slices. Dip into 80 ml (2½ fl oz/⅓ cup) lemon juice, then toss in enough desiccated coconut to coat each piece. Serve at room temperature.

yoghurt and mint raita

Combine 250 g (9 oz/1 cup) plain yoghurt, 20 g (¾ oz/⅓ cup) chopped mint and a pinch of cayenne pepper and mix well. Serve chilled.

chicken mulligatawny

✳

Preparation time: 25 minutes + overnight chilling time
Cooking time: 4 hours
Serves 6

2 tomatoes, peeled
20 g (¾ oz) ghee
1 large onion, finely chopped
3 garlic cloves, crushed
8 curry leaves
55 g (2 oz/¼ cup) madras curry paste
250 g (9 oz/1 cup) red lentils, washed and drained
70 g (2½ oz/⅓ cup) short-grain rice
250 ml (9 fl oz/1 cup) coconut cream
2 tablespoons coriander (cilantro) leaves
mango chutney, to serve

STOCK
1.5 kg (3 lb 5 oz) whole chicken
1 carrot, chopped
2 celery stalks, chopped
4 spring onions (scallions), chopped
2 cm (¾ inch) piece of fresh ginger, sliced

1 To make the stock, put all the ingredients and 4 litres (140 fl oz/ 16 cups) cold water in a large stockpot or saucepan. Bring to the boil, removing any scum that rises to the surface. Reduce the heat to low and simmer, partly covered, for 3 hours. Continue to remove any scum from the surface. Carefully remove the chicken and cool. Strain the stock into a bowl and cool. Cover and refrigerate overnight. Discard the skin and bones from the chicken and shred the flesh into small pieces. Cover and refrigerate overnight.
2 Score a cross in the base of the tomatoes. Put in a heatproof bowl and cover with boiling water. Leave for 30 seconds then transfer to a bowl of cold water and peel the skin away from the cross. Cut the tomatoes in half, scoop out the seeds and chop the flesh.
3 Melt the ghee in a large saucepan over medium heat. Cook the onion for 5 minutes, or until softened but not browned. Add the garlic and curry leaves and cook for 1 minute. Add the curry paste, cook for 1 minute, then stir in the

lentils. Pour in the stock and bring to the boil over high heat, removing any scum from the surface. Reduce the heat, add the tomato and simmer for 30 minutes, or until the lentils are soft.
4 Meanwhile, bring a large saucepan of water to the boil. Add the rice and cook for 12 minutes, stirring once or twice. Drain. Stir the rice into the soup with the chicken and coconut cream until warmed through — don't allow it to boil or it will curdle. Season. Sprinkle with the coriander and serve with the mango chutney.

balti lamb

✳ ✳

Preparation time: 15 minutes
Cooking time: 1 hour 30 minutes
Serves 4

1 kg (2 lb 4 oz) lamb leg steaks
375ml (13 fl oz/1½ cups) boiling water
1 tablespoon balti masala paste (page 114)
2 tablespoons ghee or oil
3 garlic cloves, crushed
1 tablespoon garam masala
1 large onion, finely chopped
4 tablespoons balti masala paste (page 114), extra
2 tablespoons chopped coriander (cilantro) leaves
coriander (cilantro) leaves, extra, to garnish
roti or naan bread, to serve

1 Preheat the oven to 190°C (375°F/ Gas 5).
2 Cut the lamb into 3 cm (1¼ inch) cubes.
3 Place the meat, boiling water and masala paste in a large casserole dish. Cover and cook for 30–40 minutes, or until slightly undercooked. Drain and reserve the stock.
4 Heat the ghee in a balti pan or wok; stir-fry the garlic and garam masala for 1 minute. Add the onion and cook over medium heat until the onion is soft and golden brown. Increase the heat, add the extra masala paste and the lamb. Stir-fry for 5 minutes to brown the meat.

chicken mulligatawny

pea, egg and ricotta curry

balti dishes

Balti is a type of curry originating in a region of northeastern Pakistan formerly known as Baltistan, and cooked in a traditional two-handled, cast-iron balti pan, karahi, which is similar to a wok. (Any lidded, heavy-based saucepan is a suitable replacement.) Traditional balti recipes are based on meat with subtle aromatic spices and only a small amount of chilli. The curry is slightly oily, contains fresh garlic, ginger and coriander, and is spiced with fennel, black mustard seeds, cloves, cardamom, coriander seeds, cumin, cassia bark and garam masala.

5 Slowly add the reserved stock and simmer over low heat, stirring for 15 minutes.

6 Add the coriander leaves and 250 ml (9 fl oz/1 cup) water. Simmer for 15 minutes or until the lamb is tender and the sauce is thickened slightly. Season to taste. Garnish with coriander leaves and serve with roti or naan bread.

pea, egg and ricotta curry

※

Preparation time: **15 minutes**
Cooking time: **30 minutes**
Serves **4**

4 hard-boiled eggs
½ teaspoon ground turmeric
2 small onions
125 g (4½ oz) baked ricotta cheese (see Note)

45 ml (1½ fl oz) melted ghee or oil
1 bay leaf
1 teaspoon finely chopped garlic
1½ teaspoons ground coriander
1½ teaspoons garam masala
½ teaspoon chilli powder (optional)
125 g (4½ oz/½ cup) tinned peeled, chopped tomatoes
1 tablespoon tomato paste (concentrated purée)
1 tablespoon plain yoghurt
80 g (2¾ oz/½ cup) frozen peas
2 tablespoons finely chopped coriander (cilantro) leaves

1 Peel the eggs and coat them with the turmeric. Finely chop the onion and cut the ricotta into 1 cm (½ inch) cubes.

2 Melt the ghee in a large saucepan and cook the eggs over moderate heat for 2 minutes until they are light brown, stirring constantly. Set aside.

3 Add the bay leaf, onion and garlic to the pan and cook over moderately high heat, stirring frequently, until the mixture is well-reduced and pale gold. Lower the heat if the mixture is browning too quickly. Add the ground coriander, garam masala and chilli powder, if using, and cook until aromatic.

4 Add the tomatoes, tomato paste and 125 ml (4 fl oz/½ cup) water. Cover and simmer for 5 minutes. Return the eggs to the pan with the ricotta, yoghurt, peas and ¼ teaspoon salt and cook for 5 minutes. Remove the bay leaf, sprinkle with the coriander and serve immediately.

NOTE: Baked ricotta cheese is available from delicatessens and some supermarkets, but it is easy enough to prepare your own. Preheat the oven to 160°C (315°F/Gas 2–3). Slice the required amount of fresh ricotta cheese (not cottage cheese or blended ricotta) into 3 cm (1¼ inch) thick slices. Place the ricotta on a lightly greased baking tray and bake for 25 minutes.

saffron

Saffron is prized for the fragrance, subtle flavour and the orange colour it imparts to foods. The wiry, vivid red-orange saffron threads are actually tiny stigmas of the saffron crocus flower — each delicate bloom must be plucked by hand and its three thread-like stigmas removed and dried. It takes more than 150 000 fresh flowers to produce 1 kg (2 lb 4 oz) saffron, which explains why it is the world's most expensive spice. Fortunately, only scant amounts are needed — ¼ teaspoon of loosely packed threads is sufficient to flavour and colour a dish to serve six people.

saffron yoghurt chicken

☀

Preparation time: 30 minutes
Cooking time: 1 hour 15 minutes
Serves 4–6

1.5 kg (3 lb 5 oz) whole chicken
½ teaspoon saffron threads
2 tablespoons hot milk
3 garlic cloves, crushed
3 cm (1¼ inch) piece fresh ginger, finely grated
½ teaspoon ground turmeric
½ teaspoon ground cumin
¼ teaspoon ground cardamom
¼ teaspoon ground cloves
¼ teaspoon ground cinnamon
¼ teaspoon ground mace
90 g (3¼ oz/⅓ cup) plain yoghurt
1 tablespoon ghee or oil

1 Preheat the oven to 180°C (350°F/ Gas 4).
2 Wash the chicken and pat dry. Remove any excess fat from inside the cavity.
3 Soak the saffron threads in the hot milk for 10 minutes, then squeeze the saffron to release the flavour and colour into the milk.
4 Transfer the saffron milk to a larger bowl; add the remaining ingredients and mix to combine.
5 Carefully lift the skin on the breast side of the chicken by working your fingers between the skin and the flesh. Pat half the spice mixture over the flesh. Rub the remaining spice mixture over the skin.
6 Place the chicken on a wire rack in a baking dish. Pour 250 ml (9 fl oz/1 cup) water into the dish; this will keep the chicken moist while it cooks. Roast the chicken for 1¼ hours or until browned and tender. Transfer the chicken to a serving dish, cover loosely with foil and allow to stand for 5 minutes before carving.

NOTE: Mace is a spice ground from the membrane which covers the nutmeg seed. It has a more subtle flavour than nutmeg.

samosas and cucumber raita

☀

Preparation time: 30 minutes
Cooking time: 25 minutes
Makes 24

1 tablespoon vegetable oil
1 onion, chopped
1 teaspoon finely grated fresh ginger
1 garlic clove, crushed
2 teaspoons ground coriander
2 teaspoons ground cumin
2 teaspoons garam masala
1½ teaspoons chilli powder
¼ teaspoon ground turmeric
300 g (10½ oz) potatoes, cut into 1 cm
    (½ inch) cubes and boiled
40 g (1½ oz/⅓ cup) frozen peas
2 tablespoons chopped coriander
    (cilantro) leaves
1 teaspoon lemon juice
6 sheets ready-rolled puff pastry
oil, for deep-frying

CUCUMBER RAITA
2 Lebanese (short) cucumbers, peeled,
    seeded and finely chopped
250 g (9 oz/1 cup) plain yoghurt
1 teaspoon cumin seeds
1 teaspoon mustard seeds
½ teaspoon finely grated fresh ginger

1   To make the raita, put the cucumber and yoghurt in a bowl and mix together well.

2   Dry-fry the cumin and mustard seeds in a small frying pan over medium heat for 1 minute, or until aromatic and lightly browned, then add to the yoghurt mixture. Stir in the ginger, season to taste with salt and pepper, and mix together well. Refrigerate until needed.

3   Heat a wok over medium heat, add the oil and swirl to coat the base and side. Add the onion, ginger and garlic and cook for 2 minutes, or until softened. Add the spices, boiled potato, peas and 2 teaspoons water. Cook for 1 minute, or until all the moisture evaporates. Remove from the heat and stir in the coriander leaves and lemon juice.

4   Cut out 12 rounds from the pastry sheets using a 12.5 cm (4¾ inch) cutter, then cut each round in half. Shape 1 semi-circle into a cone, wet the edges and seal the side seam, leaving an opening large enough for the filling. Spoon 3 teaspoons of the filling into the cone, then seal. Repeat to make 23 more samosas.

5   Fill a wok or deep heavy-based saucepan one-third full of oil and heat to 180°C (350°F), or until a cube of bread dropped into the oil browns in 15 seconds. Cook the samosas in batches for 1–2 minutes, or until golden. Drain on crumpled paper towels and season. Serve with the chilled cucumber raita.

NOTE: Raita can be made ahead of time and stored in the refrigerator in an airtight container for up to 3 days.

Mix together the vegetables, currants, spices, lemon juice and soy sauce.

Fold the pastry over the filling to make a semicircle and press the edges together with a fork.

Cook the samosas two at a time until golden brown and puffed.

saag paneer

garlic, ginger, chilli and onion in a food
processor and process to form a paste.
4 Heat the ghee in a wok, add the
paste and cook over medium heat for
5 minutes, or until the ghee begins to
separate from the paste. Add the cumin,
nutmeg, remaining yoghurt, 1 teaspoon
salt and 250 ml (9 fl oz/1 cup) water
and simmer for 5 minutes. Transfer
the mixture to a food processor, add
the steamed spinach and process until
smooth. Return the mixture to the wok,
add the chopped cheese and cream, and
cook for 10 minutes or until the sauce is
heated through.

saag paneer

✹ ✹

Preparation time: **20 minutes + 3 hours
standing time**
Cooking time: **30 minutes**
Serves **4**

2 litres (70 fl oz/8 cups) milk
80 ml (2½ fl oz/⅓ cup) lemon juice
100 g (3½ oz/⅓ cup) plain yoghurt
500 g (1 lb 2 oz) spinach
2 garlic cloves
2 cm (¾ inch) piece fresh ginger, finely grated
2 green chillies, chopped
1 onion, chopped
2 tablespoons ghee or oil
1 teaspoon ground cumin
½ teaspoon freshly grated nutmeg
125 ml (4 fl oz/½ cup) pouring (whipping)
   cream

1 Heat the milk in a large saucepan until
just boiling. Reduce the heat, add the
lemon juice and 2 tablespoons yoghurt,
and stir until the mixture begins to curdle.
Remove the pan from the heat and allow
the milk mixture to stand for 5 minutes or
until curds start to form.
2 Line a colander with muslin
(cheesecloth). Pour the curd mixture into
the colander and leave until most of the
liquid drains away. Gather up the corners
of the muslin, hold them together and
squeeze as much moisture as possible
from the curd. Return the muslin-wrapped
curd to the colander and leave in a cool
place for 3 hours until the curd is very
firm and all the whey has drained away.
Cut the cheese into 4 cm (1½ inch) cubes.
3 Steam the spinach over simmering
water until tender. Squeeze out any
excess moisture and chop finely. Place the

lamb dopiaza

✹ ✹

Preparation time: **20 minutes**
Cooking time: **2 hours**
Serves **4–6**

1 kg (2 lb 4 oz) onions
5 garlic cloves
5 cm (2 inch) piece fresh ginger, finely grated
2 red chillies
1 teaspoon paprika
4 tablespoons chopped coriander (cilantro)
   leaves
2 tablespoons ground coriander
2 teaspoons black cumin seeds
4 tablespoons plain yoghurt
4 tablespoons ghee or oil
1 kg (2 lb 4 oz) diced lamb
6 cardamom pods, lightly crushed
1 teaspoon garam masala
steamed rice and naan bread, to serve

1 Slice half the onions and set aside;
roughly chop the remaining onions.
2 Place the chopped onion, garlic,
ginger, chilli, paprika, fresh and ground
coriander, cumin seeds and yoghurt in a
food processor and process until a smooth
paste has formed.
3 Heat the ghee in a large saucepan; add
the sliced onion and cook over medium
heat for 10 minutes or until golden brown.
Remove the onion from the pan using a
slotted spoon and drain on paper towels.

4 Add the lamb to the pan in batches and cook over high heat until browned. Remove from the pan and cover loosely with foil.

5 Add the onion paste to the pan; cook for 5 minutes, or until the ghee starts to separate from the paste. Reduce the heat to low, return the meat to the pan with the cardamom pods, cover and cook for 1 hour or until the meat is tender.

6 Add the fried onion and sprinkle the garam masala over the lamb; cover and continue cooking for 15 minutes. Serve with steamed rice and naan bread.

butter chicken

✳ ✳

Preparation time: 30 minutes + 4 hours
  marinating time
Cooking time: 30 minutes
Serves 4

1 kg (2 lb 4 oz) boneless, skinless chicken
  thighs
60 ml (2 fl oz/¼ cup) lemon juice
250g (9 oz/1 cup) plain yoghurt
1 onion, chopped
2 garlic cloves, crushed
3 cm (1¼ inch) piece fresh ginger,
  finely grated
1 green chilli, chopped
2 teaspoons garam masala
2 teaspoons yellow food colouring
1 teaspoon red food colouring
125 g (4½ oz/½ cup) tomato paste
  (concentrated purée)
2 cm (¾ inch) piece fresh ginger, extra,
  finely grated
250 ml (9 fl oz/1 cup) pouring (whipping)
  cream
1 teaspoon garam masala, extra
2 teaspoons sugar
¼ teaspoon chilli powder
1 tablespoon lemon juice
1 teaspoon ground cumin
100 g (3½ oz) butter
steamed rice, to serve
kaffir lime (makrut) leaves, shredded, to serve

1 Cut the chicken into strips 2 cm (¾ inch) thick. Sprinkle with 1 teaspoon salt and the lemon juice.

2 Place the yoghurt, onion, garlic, ginger, chilli and garam masala in a food processor and process until smooth.

3 Combine the food colourings in a small bowl, brush over the chicken and turn to coat. Add the yoghurt mixture and toss to combine. Cover and refrigerate for 4 hours. Remove the chicken from the marinade and allow to drain for 5 minutes.

4 Preheat the oven to 220°C (425°F/ Gas 7). Bake the chicken in a shallow baking dish for 15 minutes, or until tender. Drain off any excess juice, cover loosely with foil and keep warm.

5 Combine the tomato paste and 125 ml (4 fl oz/½ cup) water in a large bowl. Add the ginger, cream, extra garam masala, sugar, chilli powder, lemon juice and cumin and stir to combine.

6 Melt the butter in a large saucepan over medium heat. Stir in the tomato mixture and bring to the boil. Cook for 2 minutes, then reduce the heat and add the chicken strips. Stir to coat the chicken in the sauce and simmer for 2 minutes longer or until heated through. Serve with steamed rice and shredded lime leaves.

ghee

Ghee is clarified butter or pure butter fat. It gives a rich buttery taste to food and, because it has no milk solids, won't burn at high temperatures. Butter or a flavourless oil can be substituted for ghee. Alternatively, a mixture of half ghee and half extra light olive oil (which has little taste) has both the rich flavour of ghee and the health benefits of olive oil.

breads

One of the surprises of northern Indian cuisine is the beautiful breads. From paper-thin parathas to puffed-up naan, they are traditionally cooked in a clay oven and torn apart to mop up curries.

parathas

Place 280 g (10 oz/2¼ cups) atta flour and a pinch of salt in a large bowl. Rub in 40 g (1½ oz) ghee with your fingertips until fine and crumbly. Make a well in the centre and gradually add 185 ml (6 fl oz/¾ cup) cold water to form a firm dough. Turn onto a well-floured surface and knead until smooth. Cover with plastic wrap and set aside for 40 minutes. Divide into 10 portions. Roll each on a floured surface to a 13 cm (5 inch) circle. Brush lightly with melted ghee or oil. Cut through each round to the centre and roll tightly to form a cone shape, then press down on the pointed top. Re-roll into a 13 cm (5 inch) circle again. Cook one at a time in hot oil or ghee in a frying pan until puffed and lightly browned on both sides. Drain on paper towels. Makes 10.

naan

Preheat the oven to 200°C (400°F/Gas 6). Sift together 500 g (1 lb 2 oz) plain (all-purpose) flour, 1 teaspoon baking powder, ½ teaspoon bicarbonate of soda (baking soda) and 1 teaspoon salt. Add 1 beaten egg, 1 tablespoon melted ghee or butter, 125g (4½ oz/½ cup) plain yoghurt and gradually add 250 ml (9 fl oz/1 cup) milk or enough to form a soft dough. Cover with a damp cloth and leave in a warm place for 2 hours. Knead on a well-floured surface for 2–3 minutes, or until smooth. Divide into eight portions and roll each one into an oval 15 cm (6 inches) long. Brush with water and place, wet side down, on greased baking trays. Brush with melted ghee or butter and bake for 8–10 minutes, or until golden brown. Makes 8.

puris

Sift together 375 g (13 oz/2½ cups) wholemeal (wholewheat) flour and a pinch of salt. With your fingertips, rub in 1 tablespoon ghee or oil. Gradually add 250 ml (9 fl oz/1 cup) water to form a firm dough. Knead on a lightly floured surface until smooth. Cover with plastic wrap and set aside for 50 minutes. Divide into 18 portions and roll each into a 14 cm (5½ inch) circle. Heat 3 cm (1¼ inches) oil in a deep frying pan until moderately hot; fry one at a time, spooning oil over until they puff up and swell. Cook on each side until golden brown. Drain on paper towels. Serve immediately. Makes 18.

chapattis

Place 280 g (10 oz/2¼ cups) atta flour and a pinch of salt in a large bowl. Gradually add 250 ml (9 fl oz/1 cup) water, or enough to form a firm dough. Knead on a lightly floured surface until smooth. Cover with plastic wrap and set aside for 50 minutes. Divide into 14 portions and roll into 14 cm (5½ inch) circles. Brush a heated frying pan with a little melted ghee or oil. Cook over medium heat, flattening the surface, until both sides are golden brown and bubbles appear. Makes 14.

poppadoms

Poppadoms are thin wafers made of lentil, rice or potato flour. They can be found at Asian food stores. Use tongs to slide them one at a time into 2 cm (¾ inch) very hot oil — they should puff at once. Turn over, remove quickly and drain on paper towels.

dal

✳

Preparation time: **15 minutes**
Cooking time: **1 hour**
Serves **4–6**

250 g (9 oz/1 cup) red lentils
4 cm (1½ inch) piece fresh ginger, cut into
   3 slices
½ teaspoon ground turmeric
3 tablespoons ghee or oil
2 garlic cloves, crushed
1 onion, finely chopped
pinch of asafoetida (optional, see Note)

1 teaspoon cumin seeds
1 teaspoon ground coriander
¼ teaspoon chilli powder
1 tablespoon chopped coriander (cilantro)

1 Place the lentils and 1 litre (35 fl oz/
4 cups) water in a saucepan over
medium heat and bring to the boil.
Reduce the heat to low, add the ginger
and turmeric, and simmer, covered, for
1 hour or until the lentils are tender.
Stir every 5 minutes during the last
30 minutes to prevent the lentils sticking
to the pan. Remove the ginger and stir
in ½ teaspoon salt.

2 Meanwhile, heat the ghee in a frying
pan. Add the garlic and onion, and cook
over medium heat for 3 minutes, or until
the onion is golden. Add the asafoetida, if
using, cumin seeds, ground coriander and
chilli powder, and cook for 2 minutes.
3 Add the onion mixture and fresh
coriander to the lentils and stir gently to
combine. Serve immediately.

NOTE: Asafoetida is a spice from the gum
of a plant native to Afghanistan and Iran.
When used sparingly, it has a subtle flavour.

indian prawn fritters

✳

Preparation time: **25 minutes + 30 minutes
   chilling time**
Cooking time: **20 minutes**
Makes **15**

350 g (12 oz) raw prawns (shrimp)
1 onion, roughly chopped
2 garlic cloves, chopped
4 cm (1½ inch) piece fresh ginger, finely
   grated
1–2 tablespoons ready-made curry paste
   (see Note)
2 tablespoons lemon juice
15 g (½ oz/½ cup) coriander (cilantro)
   leaves
1 teaspoon ground turmeric
55 g (2 oz/½ cup) besan (chickpea flour)
oil, for shallow frying
plain yoghurt, to serve
lemon wedges, to serve

1 Peel the prawns and gently pull out the
dark vein from each prawn back, starting
at the head. Place the prawns, onion,
garlic, ginger, curry paste, lemon juice,
coriander, turmeric, ½ teaspoon salt and
¼ teaspoon pepper in a food processor
and process for 20–30 seconds or until
well combined. Cover and refrigerate for
30 minutes.
2 Roll tablespoons of the prawn mixture
into round patties and lightly coat in
besan flour. Heat about 2 cm (¾ inch) oil
in a frying pan; add the fritters in batches,

and cook over medium heat for 3 minutes or until golden brown. Drain on paper towels and serve with plain yoghurt and lemon wedges.

NOTE: Curry pastes suitable to use with prawns are rogan josh, balti, tikka masala, vindaloo and tandoori.

indian fried fish

☀

Preparation time: **15 minutes**
Cooking time: **20 minutes**
Serves 4

500 g (1 lb 2 oz) firm white fish fillets
80 g (2¾ oz/¾ cup) besan (chickpea flour)
1 teaspoon garam masala
¼ teaspoon chilli powder
¼ teaspoon ground turmeric
2 tablespoons chopped coriander
  (cilantro) leaves
2 eggs, lightly beaten
oil, for shallow frying
steamed rice, to serve

1 Wash the fish fillets, pat them dry with paper towels, and cut them in half lengthways.
2 Sift the besan, 1 teaspoon salt, garam masala, chilli powder, turmeric and ¼ teaspoon pepper into a bowl. Add the coriander and stir to combine, then spread the mixture out on a plate.
3 Dip each fish fillet into the egg, then into the spiced flour, shaking off any excess.
4 Heat 2 cm (¾ inch) oil in a frying pan; fry the coated fish fillets in batches over high heat for 5 minutes or until crisp and golden. Serve with steamed rice and your choice of raitas (see page 202).

indian fried fish

goan spiced mussels

goan spiced mussels

✳

Preparation time: 20 minutes
Cooking time: 20 minutes
Serves 4

1 kg (2 lb 4 oz) black mussels
3 tablespoons ghee or oil
5 garlic cloves, crushed
5 cm (2 inch) piece fresh ginger, finely
    grated
2 onions, finely chopped
3 red chillies, finely chopped
2 teaspoons ground cumin
2 teaspoons ground coriander
4 tomatoes, peeled, seeded and
    chopped
500 ml (17 fl oz/2 cups) fish stock
50 g (1¾ oz/1 cup) chopped coriander
    (cilantro) leaves
2 tablespoons lemon juice
steamed rice, to serve

1 Remove the beards from the mussels
and scrub them under cold water to
remove any excess grit. Discard any which
are already open.
2 Heat the ghee in a wok, add the garlic,
ginger and onion and cook over medium
heat for 5 minutes, or until the onion is
soft and golden. Add the chilli, cumin,
coriander and tomato, and cook for
5 minutes.
3 Add the mussels and stock and bring to
the boil. Reduce the heat and simmer for
5 minutes. Discard any mussels that have
not opened after this time.
4 Remove the wok from the heat, stir
through the chopped coriander and lemon
juice, and serve with steamed rice.

hyderabadi fish

✳

Preparation time: 20 minutes
Cooking time: 30 minutes
Serves 4

3 tablespoons desiccated coconut
2 tablespoons cumin seeds

india and the british

Colonial rule brought the British into contact with the rich cuisine of the Indian region. Many of the flavours were so much to their liking they became standard fare in Britain. Chutney, for example, now the traditional English accompaniment to cold meats, has its origin in the sweet-sour 'chatni' designed to partner fiery curries. Even Worcestershire sauce was originally an Indian recipe and owes its piquant flavour in large part to tamarind. The British breakfast dish kedgeree — curried rice with flaked smoked fish and garnished with hard-boiled eggs — comes from the Indian kadgeri, which is rice with onions, lentils and eggs.

Mulligatawny soup is another British adaptation, this time of the southern Indian 'pepper water'. And while Indian teas helped establish the 'cuppa' as the British national drink, the returning colonials also brought back an enduring taste for lime with their gin.

3 tablespoons sesame seeds
1 tablespoon fenugreek seeds
2 onions, finely chopped
3 tablespoons oil
500 g (1 lb 2 oz) firm white fish
    fillets, cut into 5 cm (2 inch) pieces
1 tablespoon ground coriander
1 teaspoon ground ginger
1 teaspoon chilli powder
1 teaspoon ground turmeric
1 tomato, chopped
1 tablespoon tamarind
    concentrate
60 ml (2 fl oz/¼ cup) water

1 Dry-fry the coconut, cumin, sesame seeds, fenugreek and onion in a frying pan for 10 minutes or until aromatic.
2 Using a mortar and pestle or food processor, process the mixture until a paste is formed.
3 Heat the oil in a large deep frying pan; add the fish and cook over medium heat for 5 minutes.
4 Add the coconut mixture and the remaining ingredients and stir gently to combine. Cover and simmer for 5–10 minutes or until the fish is tender. Serve with steamed rice.

cauliflower, tomato and green pea curry

✵

Preparation time: **25 minutes**
Cooking time: **20 minutes**
Serves 4–6

1 small cauliflower
1 onion
2 large tomatoes
235 g (8½ oz/1½ cups) peas
60 ml (2 fl oz/¼ cup) ghee or oil
1 teaspoon crushed garlic
1 teaspoon finely grated fresh ginger
¾ teaspoon ground turmeric
1 tablespoon ground coriander
1 tablespoon ready-made vindaloo paste
2 teaspoons sugar
2 cardamom pods, lightly crushed
185 g (6½ oz/¾ cup) plain yoghurt

1 Cut the cauliflower into small florets. Thinly slice the onion and cut the tomatoes into thin wedges. Steam the cauliflower and peas until tender.
2 Heat the ghee in a large saucepan and cook the onion, garlic and ginger over medium heat until soft and golden. Add the turmeric, coriander, vindaloo paste, sugar, cardamom pods and yoghurt and cook for 3–4 minutes. Add the tomato and cook for 3–4 minutes.
3 Add the cauliflower and peas and simmer for 3–4 minutes. Serve with steamed rice.

cauliflower, tomato and green pea curry

vegetable pakoras

✻ ✻

Preparation time: 30 minutes
Cooking time: 20 minutes
Makes about 40

1 large potato
1 small cauliflower
1 small red capsicum (pepper)
1 onion
2 cabbage or 5 English spinach leaves
165 g (5¾ oz/1½ cups) besan (chickpea flour)
3 tablespoons plain (all-purpose) flour
2 teaspoons garam masala
2 teaspoons ground coriander
1 teaspoon bicarbonate of soda (baking soda)
1 teaspoon chilli powder
1 tablespoon lemon juice
½ cup frozen corn kernels, thawed
oil, for shallow frying
sweet mango chutney or tamarind sauce, to serve

1 Boil the potato until just tender, then peel and chop finely.
2 Finely chop the cauliflower, capsicum and onion. Shred the cabbage or spinach leaves.
3 Sift the flours, garam masala, coriander, bicarbonate of soda and chilli powder into a bowl. Make a well in the centre, add 375 ml (13 fl oz/1½ cups) water and the lemon juice, and stir to make a smooth creamy batter, adding a little more water if necessary. Add the vegetables and mix in evenly.
4 Heat about 2 cm (¾ inch) oil in a frying pan; place tablespoons of the mixture in the oil, about eight at a time, and fry over moderately high heat until golden; drain on paper towels. Serve hot with sweet mango chutney or tamarind sauce.

vegetable pakoras

battered chicken

✻ ✻

Preparation time: 30 minutes + 3 hours marinating time
Cooking time: 30 minutes
Serves 6

6 small chicken thighs, about 150 g (5½ oz) each
6 garlic cloves, crushed
5 cm (2 inch) piece fresh ginger, finely grated
3 tablespoons lime juice
125 g (4½ oz/½ cup) plain yoghurt
oil, for deep-frying

BATTER
80 g (2¾ oz/¾ cup) besan (chickpea flour)
1 teaspoon baking powder
1 teaspoon garam masala
¼ teaspoon ground turmeric
2 eggs, lightly beaten
2 tablespoons plain yoghurt

1 Remove the skin from the chicken and cut three deep incisions in each thigh.

2 Combine the garlic, ginger, ½ teaspoon salt, ½ teaspoon pepper, the lime juice and yoghurt in a large bowl. Add the chicken and toss to coat thoroughly. Cover and refrigerate for 3 hours.

3 To make the batter, sift the besan, baking powder, garam masala and turmeric into a bowl. Make a well in the centre, add the combined egg, yoghurt and 60 ml (2 fl oz/¼ cup) water, and stir until smooth.

4 Heat the oil in a wok or large frying pan. Dip each chicken thigh into the batter and deep-fry in batches for 8–10 minutes or until the chicken is crisp and tender. Serve with mango chutney.

spiced roast leg of lamb

✳ ✳

Preparation time: **35 minutes**
Cooking time: **2 hours**
Serves **6**

2 kg (4 lb 8 oz) leg of lamb
1 tablespoon lemon juice
1 garlic bulb, unpeeled
2 tablespoons ghee or oil
1½ tablespoons ground coriander
2 teaspoons ground cumin
2 cinnamon sticks
2 whole cloves
4 bay leaves
1 teaspoon chilli powder
4 cardamom pods, lightly crushed
125 g (4½ oz/½ cup) plain yoghurt
mint leaves, to garnish (optional)

spiced roast leg of lamb

1 Preheat the oven to 180°C (350°F/ Gas 4).

2 Trim the excess fat from the lamb. Rub it all over with lemon juice and pepper, and place it in a roasting tin with the whole garlic and ghee. Bake for about 50 minutes, or until garlic cloves are soft.

3 Squeeze the soft cooked garlic pulp from the skins. Spread the garlic evenly over the lamb and sprinkle over the coriander and cumin. Add the cinnamon sticks, cloves, bay leaves, chilli powder and cardamom pods to the pan.

4 Roast the lamb for a further 50 minutes, or until cooked, basting it occasionally with the pan juices. Remove the lamb and set aside for 10–15 minutes before carving.

5 Add 375 ml (13 fl oz/1½ cups) water to the roasting tin and stir to combine the juices. Place the pan on the stovetop; cook over high heat until the liquid reduces and thickens. Remove the whole spices, and season with salt and pepper to taste. Stir in the yoghurt and heat through. Serve the sauce with the carved roast, garnished with mint leaves, if desired.

burma

The food of Burma reflects the influences of her many neighbours, especially the two largest, China and India. China's influence can be seen in the use of noodles and soy sauce, while Burmese curries are Indian in origin, though not as highly spiced. They are flavoured with lots of garlic, ginger, turmeric, chilli, onion and shrimp paste and served with bowls of home-made chutneys and pickles. Bowls of piping-hot rice are served at every meal; though, unlike in other Asian countries, the rice is boiled until it is soft and moist, not steamed.

mixed vegetable salad

✹

Preparation time: 25 minutes
Cooking time: 15 minutes
Serves 6

200 g (7 oz) green beans, trimmed, cut on
    the diagonal into 3 cm (1¼ inch) lengths
½ small cabbage, finely shredded
2 carrots, sliced
3 tablespoons white sesame seeds
125 ml (4 fl oz/½ cup) oil
2 onions, sliced
3 garlic cloves, thinly sliced
½ teaspoon ground turmeric
½ teaspoon paprika
125 g (4½ oz/1 cup) tinned bamboo
    shoots, sliced
90 g (3¼ oz/1 cup) bean sprouts, trimmed
1 Lebanese (short) cucumber, sliced
2 tablespoons lemon juice

1 Place the beans, cabbage and carrot
in separate heatproof bowls, cover with
boiling water and leave for 1 minute, then
drain. Plunge the vegetables into iced
water, then drain again.
2 Heat a wok; add the sesame seeds and
cook, stirring, over a moderate heat until
they turn golden brown. Set aside.
3 Heat the oil in the wok; add the onion,
and cook over a low heat until soft and
golden. Add the garlic and cook for
2 more minutes. Add the turmeric and
paprika and cook for a further 2 minutes.
Drain on paper towels. Reserve the oil.
4 Place the blanched vegetables and
the bamboo shoots, bean sprouts and
cucumber in a serving dish and drizzle
over 2 tablespoons of the reserved
cooking oil. Add the onion and garlic and
toss through the vegetables along with
½ teaspoon salt and the lemon juice.
Scatter the sesame seeds over the salad
and serve as an accompaniment to a curry.

fish in banana leaves

✹

Preparation time: 30 minutes
Cooking time: 15 minutes
Serves 6

3 large banana leaves (see Note)
1 kg (2 lb 4 oz) firm white fish fillets
125 ml (4 fl oz/½ cup) coconut cream
2 garlic cloves, crushed
1 small onion, finely chopped
1 tablespoon finely chopped fresh ginger
2 teaspoons sesame oil
2 teaspoons salt
1 teaspoon ground turmeric
1 teaspoon paprika
¼ teaspoon chilli powder
2 teaspoons rice flour
2 tablespoons chopped coriander (cilantro)
    leaves
boiled rice, to serve

1 Cut the banana leaves into six squares
of about 25 cm (10 inches). Place the
banana leaf pieces in a heatproof dish
and pour boiling water over them. Leave
for about 30 seconds, by which time the
leaves should be pliable; drain.
2 Cut the fish into 3 cm (1¼ inch) cubes.
Place the fish in a large bowl and add
the coconut cream, garlic, onion, ginger,
sesame oil, salt, turmeric, paprika, chilli
powder, rice flour and coriander. Use your
hands to combine the ingredients well,
making sure the fish is well covered with
the mixture.
3 Divide the fish mixture evenly and
place each portion in the centre of a
banana leaf piece. Fold in the sides of
each piece to form a type of envelope.
Hold the leaf in place with a toothpick or
wooden skewer.
4 Fill a large saucepan or steamer with
5 cm (2 inches) water. Place fish parcels
on a steaming rack and cover and steam
for 10–15 minutes, or until cooked. Open
one parcel to check that the fish is cooked
before serving. Serve with the boiled rice.

NOTE: If banana leaves are not available,
cook the fish mixture in foil parcels.

Soak the banana leaf pieces in
boiling water until they are pliable.

Use your hands to combine the fish
mixture well.

coconut prawn curry

Preparation time: **25 minutes**
Cooking time: **15 minutes**
Serves **4**

750 g (1 lb 10 oz) raw prawns (shrimp)
1 teaspoon ground turmeric
155 g (5½ oz/1 cup) roughly chopped onion
4 garlic cloves, crushed
½ teaspoon paprika
1 teaspoon seeded, finely chopped red chilli
pinch of ground cloves
¼ teaspoon ground cardamom
1 teaspoon finely chopped fresh ginger
3 tablespoons oil
2 tomatoes, diced
250 ml (9 fl oz/1 cup) coconut cream
2 tablespoons coriander (cilantro) leaves
boiled rice, to serve

1 Peel the prawns, leaving the tails intact. Gently pull out the dark vein from each prawn back, starting at the head end. Toss the prawns with the turmeric.
2 Place the onion, garlic, paprika, chilli, cloves, cardamom and ginger in a food processor and process until a paste forms.
3 Heat the oil in a deep-sided frying pan; carefully add the spicy paste (it will splutter at this stage), stir it into the oil and cook over low heat for about 10 minutes. If the mixture starts to burn, add a little water. When the paste is cooked it should be a golden brown colour and will have oil around the edges.
4 Stir in the prawns, tomato and coconut cream, and simmer for about 5 minutes or until the prawns are cooked. Stir in the coriander, season with salt and serve with the boiled rice.

fried pork curry

Preparation time: **30 minutes**
Cooking time: **2 hours**
Serves **6**

310 g (11 oz/2 cups) roughly chopped onion
15 garlic cloves, crushed
4 tablespoons finely chopped fresh ginger
3 tablespoons peanut oil
1 tablespoon sesame oil
1½ teaspoons chilli powder
1 teaspoon ground turmeric
1.5 kg (3 lb 5 oz) boneless pork, cut into
    3 cm (1¼ inch) cubes
1 tablespoon white vinegar
250 ml (9 fl oz/1 cup) water or chicken stock
2 tablespoons coriander (cilantro) leaves
    (optional)

1 Place the onion, garlic and ginger in a food processor and process until a thick rough paste forms.
2 Heat the peanut oil and sesame oil in a large frying pan; add the paste and cook over medium heat for about 15 minutes until it becomes a golden brown colour and has oil around the edges. Add the chilli powder, turmeric and pork, and stir well for a few minutes until the pork is well coated with the mixture.
3 Add the vinegar and water, cover and simmer gently for 1½ hours or until the meat is tender. If necessary reduce the liquid by removing the lid and allowing the sauce to evaporate. Season with salt, to taste (the dish will need more if you use water rather than stock), and scatter over the coriander, if desired. Serve with boiled rice.

fried pork curry

Seafood, the product of the country's extensive coastline, features prominently in Burmese cuisine. The national dish is moh hin gha, a spicy fish soup with noodles. In Burmese cities, a 'take-away' family meal can be bought from street vendors who scoop steaming heaps of noodles into a supplied bowl, then ladle over the soup (which traditionally includes banana heart).

fish soup with noodles

✳ ✳

Preparation time: 40 minutes
Cooking time: 25 minutes
Serves 8

750 g (1 lb 10 oz) firm white fish fillets, cut
    into 3 cm (1¼ inch) pieces
2 teaspoons ground turmeric
3 lemongrass stems
80 ml (2½ fl oz/⅓ cup) peanut oil
2 onions, thinly sliced
6 garlic cloves, crushed
2 teaspoons finely chopped fresh ginger
2 teaspoons paprika
1 tablespoon rice flour
500 ml (17 fl oz/2 cups) coconut milk
125 ml (4 fl oz/½ cup) fish sauce
500 g (1 lb 2 oz) somen noodles

GARNISHES
4 hard-boiled eggs, peeled and quartered
coriander (cilantro) leaves, chopped
spring onion (scallion), thinly sliced
4 limes, quartered
fish sauce, to taste
4 tablespoons chilli flakes
80 g (2¾ oz/½ cup) unsalted roasted
    peanuts, roughly chopped

1 Place the fish pieces on a plate and sprinkle with 1½ teaspoons salt and the turmeric. Set aside for 10 minutes.
2 Trim the lemongrass stems to about 18 cm (7 inches) long. Bruise the white fleshy ends so that the aroma will be released during cooking, and tie the stems into loops.
3 Heat the peanut oil in a large saucepan. Add the onion and cook over medium heat for 10 minutes, or until soft and lightly golden. Add the garlic and ginger and cook for 1 minute. Add the fish, paprika and rice flour and combine well. Pour in 1.5 litres (52 fl oz/6 cups) water, the coconut milk and fish sauce, and stir. Add the loops of lemongrass and simmer for 10 minutes, or until the fish is cooked.
4 Meanwhile, cook the noodles in a large saucepan of boiling water for 8–10 minutes, or until tender. Drain.
5 Place a mound of noodles in eight warm individual serving bowls and ladle over the fish soup. Offer the garnishes in separate small bowls so the diners can add them to their own taste.

mixed noodle and rice salad

☀

Preparation time: 1 hour
Cooking time: 40 minutes
Serves 6

300 g (10½ oz/1½ cups) long-grain rice
120 g (4¼ oz) fine dried egg noodles
60 g (2¼ oz) dried mung bean vermicelli
120 g (4¼ oz) dried rice vermicelli
90 g (3¼ oz/1 cup) bean sprouts, trimmed
2 potatoes, peeled and sliced
3 eggs
1 teaspoon oil
125 ml (4 fl oz/½ cup) peanut oil
4 large onions, quartered and thinly sliced
20 garlic cloves, thinly sliced
2 red chillies, seeded and sliced

25 g (1 oz/¾ cup) dried shrimps,
    ground to a powder
125 ml (4 fl oz/½ cup) fish sauce
185 ml (6 fl oz/¾ cup) tamarind concentrate
2 tablespoons chilli powder

1   Fill two large saucepans with salted water and bring to the boil. To one, add the rice and cook for about 12 minutes or until tender. Drain, rinse and set aside. Add the egg noodles to the other pan and cook them for a couple of minutes until tender. Transfer the egg noodles to a colander, rinse under cold water and set aside. Place the mung bean vermicelli and rice vermicelli in separate heatproof bowls, cover them with boiling water and leave for 1–2 minutes until tender; rinse under cold water and drain. Place the bean sprouts in a heatproof bowl, cover them with boiling water and leave for

mixed noodle and rice salad

30 seconds; rinse under cold water and drain. Cook the potato in a large saucepan of boiling water until tender, drain, then rinse under cold water and set aside.
2   Beat the eggs with ½ teaspoon salt and 1 tablespoon water. Heat the oil in a small frying pan; add the egg and cook over moderately low heat, gently drawing in the edges of the omelette to allow the uncooked egg to run to the outside. When the omelette is cooked through, flip it over and lightly brown the other side. Remove the omelette from the pan and allow it to cool before cutting it into thin strips.
3   Heat the peanut oil in a large frying pan; cook the onion, garlic and chilli separately over a moderately high heat until crispy, adding more oil if necessary.
4   Arrange the assorted noodles, rice, potato and bean sprouts on a large platter; place the omelette strips, chilli, onion, garlic, dried shrimp, fish sauce, tamarind and chilli powder in separate small dishes. The diners then serve themselves the salad ingredients and garnishes.

burmese chicken

☀

Preparation time: 15 minutes
Cooking time: 1 hour
Serves 4–6

1.5 kg (3 lb 5 oz) whole chicken or chicken
    pieces (legs, thighs, wings, breasts)
2 tablespoons ghee or oil
2 onions, chopped
3 bay leaves
2 teaspoons ground turmeric
¼ teaspoon chilli powder
½ teaspoon ground cardamom
½ teaspoon ground cumin
½ teaspoon ground coriander
½ teaspoon ground ginger
1 cinnamon stick
2 lemongrass stems, white part only,
    chopped
6 garlic cloves, crushed
1 tablespoon grated fresh ginger
250 ml (9 fl oz/1 cup) chicken stock

twelve varieties soup

rice burmese-style

In Burma, rice is not cooked by the absorption method. Instead, it is boiled in plenty of water, drained, then returned to the heat and covered to finish cooking.

1 If using a whole chicken, cut into pieces.
2 Heat the ghee in a large saucepan; add the onion and cook, stirring, until the onion is soft. Add the bay leaves, turmeric, chilli powder, cardamom, cumin, coriander, ground ginger, cinnamon stick, lemongrass, garlic and fresh ginger. Cook, stirring, for 1 minute or until aromatic.
3 Add the chicken pieces and stir to coat with the mixture. Stir in the stock and simmer, covered, for 45 minutes to 1 hour or until the chicken is tender.

twelve varieties soup

✳

Preparation time: 45 minutes
Cooking time: 20 minutes
Serves 8

300 g (10½ oz) pork liver or lamb liver
200 g (7 oz) boneless, skinless chicken
  breast

30 g (1 oz) dried Chinese mushrooms
60 ml (2 fl oz/¼ cup) oil
3 onions, thinly sliced
4 garlic cloves, finely chopped
1 teaspoon finely chopped fresh ginger
2 tablespoons fish sauce
40 g (1½ oz/⅓ cup) sliced green beans,
  trimmed
40 g (1½ oz/⅓ cup) small cauliflower florets
30 g (1 oz/⅓ cup) sliced button mushrooms
15 g (½ oz/⅓ cup) shredded Chinese
  cabbage (wong bok)
20 g (¾ oz/⅓ cup) shredded spinach
30 g (1 oz/⅓ cup) bean sprouts, trimmed
3 spring onions (scallions), thinly sliced
1 tablespoon coriander (cilantro) leaves
3 eggs
1 tablespoon soy sauce
lime wedges (optional), to serve

1 Cook the liver in simmering water for 5 minutes. Remove from the heat, allow to cool and slice thinly. Cut the chicken into thin slices. Soak the mushrooms in hot water for 20 minutes. Drain, then squeeze to remove any excess liquid. Discard the stems and chop the caps finely.
2 Heat the oil in a wok, add the onion and cook over medium heat for 5 minutes, or until golden. Add the slices of liver and chicken and stir to combine. Add the garlic and ginger and cook for 1 minute, then pour in the fish sauce and cook for a further 2 minutes.
3 Put the Chinese mushrooms, beans, cauliflower, button mushrooms and onion mixture in a large saucepan. Add 2 litres (70 fl oz/8 cups) water, bring to the boil and cook until the vegetables are just tender. Add the cabbage, spinach and bean sprouts and cook for a further 5 minutes, or until just tender. Stir in the spring onion and coriander.
4 Break the eggs into the boiling soup and stir immediately. (The eggs will break up and cook.) Add the soy sauce and ¼ teaspoon pepper. Serve immediately with the lime wedges to squeeze into the soup, if desired.

dry fish curry

through, turning it so it cooks evenly. Transfer the fish to a warm serving dish. If the remaining sauce is very liquid, reduce it over high heat until it thickens, then spoon it over the fish. Scatter the coriander over the fish and serve with the boiled rice and lemon wedges.

beef, potato and okra curry

※

Preparation time: **35 minutes**
Cooking time: **2 hours 25 minutes**
Serves **4**

800 g (1 lb 12 oz) chuck or
  skirt steak
2 potatoes
200 g (7 oz) okra
155 g (5½ oz/1 cup) roughly
  chopped onion
4 garlic cloves, crushed
3 teaspoons finely chopped
  fresh ginger
1 teaspoon ground turmeric
½ teaspoon paprika
½ teaspoon chilli powder
4 tablespoons oil
1 tablespoon sesame oil
1 teaspoon ground cumin
375 ml (13 fl oz/1½ cups) water
  or beef stock
2 tablespoons garlic chives,
  finely snipped
1 lemon, cut into wedges
boiled rice, to serve

1 Cut the beef into 3 cm (1¼ inch) cubes. Peel and cube the potatoes. Trim the okra; if large, halve them lengthways, otherwise leave whole.
2 Place the onion, garlic, ginger, turmeric, paprika and chilli powder in a food processor and process until a thick paste forms.
3 Heat the oils in a large heavy-based saucepan; add the onion mixture and cook over low heat for about 20 minutes, adding a little water if the mixture

dry fish curry

※ ※

Preparation time: **20 minutes**
Cooking time: **25 minutes**
Serves **6**

1 kg (2 lb 4 oz) firm white fish fillets, such
  as sea perch
2 tablespoons fish sauce
310 g (11 oz/2 cups) roughly chopped onion
4 garlic cloves, crushed
2 teaspoons finely chopped fresh ginger
2 teaspoons turmeric
1 red chilli, seeded and finely chopped
3 tablespoons oil
2 tablespoons chopped coriander (cilantro)
  leaves
boiled rice, to serve
lemon wedges, to serve

1 Cut the fish into 4 cm (1½ inch) cubes. Place the fish pieces in a shallow dish and pour over the fish sauce.
2 Place the onion, garlic, ginger, turmeric, chilli and 1 teaspoon salt into a food processor and process until a paste has formed.
3 Heat the oil in a deep-sided frying pan; carefully add the spicy paste (at this stage it will splutter), stir it into the oil, lower the heat and cook gently for about 10 minutes. If the mixture starts to burn, add a little water. When the paste is cooked it should be a golden brown colour and have oil around the edges.
4 Remove the fish pieces from the fish sauce and add them to the pan, stirring to cover them with the spicy paste. Raise the heat to medium and cook for about 5 minutes or until the fish is cooked

starts to stick or burn. When the paste is cooked, it should be a golden brown colour with oil forming around the edges.

4 Add the beef and cook, stirring, for 5 minutes, until browned. Add the cumin and combine well. Pour in the water and simmer, covered, for about 2 hours or until the meat is tender. Add the potato and okra in the last 45 minutes of cooking; remove the lid for the final 10 minutes until the sauce reduces and thickens. Season with salt, to taste, sprinkle over the garlic chives, and serve with the lemon wedges and boiled rice.

chicken curry

☀

Preparation time: **45 minutes**
Cooking time: **1 hour**
Serves **6**

1 kg (2 lb 4 oz) chicken thigh cutlets
2 large onions, roughly chopped
3 large garlic cloves, roughly chopped
5 cm (2 inch) piece fresh ginger, roughly
   chopped
2 tablespoons peanut oil
½ teaspoon shrimp paste
500 ml (17 fl oz/2 cups) coconut milk
1 teaspoon chilli powder (optional)
200 g (7 oz) dried rice vermicelli

ACCOMPANIMENTS
6 spring onions (scallions), sliced on
   the diagonal
10 g (¼ oz) chopped coriander
   (cilantro) leaves
2 tablespoons garlic flakes,
   lightly fried
2 tablespoons onion flakes, lightly fried
3 lemons, cut into wedges
12 dried chillies, fried in oil until crisp
fish sauce

1 Wash the chicken under cold water and pat dry with paper towels.

2 Place the onion, garlic and ginger in a food processor and process until smooth. Add a little water to help blend the mixture if necessary.

3 Heat the oil in a large saucepan; add the onion mixture and shrimp paste and cook, stirring, over high heat for 5 minutes. Add the chicken, and cook over medium heat, turning it until it browns. Add 1 teaspoon salt, the coconut milk and chilli powder, if using. Bring to the boil, reduce the heat and simmer, covered, for 30 minutes, stirring the mixture occasionally. Uncover the pan and cook for 15 minutes, or until the chicken is tender.

4 Place the noodles in a heatproof bowl, cover them with boiling water and leave them for 10 minutes. Drain the noodles and place them in a serving bowl.

5 Place the accompaniments in separate small bowls. The diners help themselves to a portion of the noodles, chicken curry and some, or all, of the accompaniments; the result will be as hot and tart as each person prefers.

chicken curry

sri lanka

Despite its size, this tiny, beautiful island has an amazing variety of food and cooking styles. Traders and conquerors have left their gastronomic mark, but there is also a huge range of distinctive indigenous dishes. In most Sri Lankan households the main meal will be rice with one or two curries, soup, vegetables and a selection of sambols. Popular breakfast foods include crispy coconut and rice flour pancakes called 'hoppers'.

lamb with palm sugar

lamb with
palm sugar

☀

Preparation time: 20 minutes
Cooking time: 1 hour 45 minutes
Serves 4

2 tablespoons oil
500 g (1 lb 2 oz) diced lamb
2 teaspoons chilli powder
1 tablespoon chopped lemongrass,
   white part only
1 tablespoon finely grated fresh ginger
300 g (10½ oz) sweet potato,
   peeled and sliced
2 tablespoons grated palm sugar
   (jaggery) or soft brown sugar
2 tablespoons lime juice
250 ml (9 fl oz/1 cup) water

1 Heat the oil in a large heavy-based
saucepan; add the lamb in batches and
cook over high heat until browned. Drain
on paper towels.
2 Add the chilli powder, the lemongrass
and the ginger to the pan, and cook for
1 minute.
3 Return the meat to the pan with the
sweet potato, palm sugar, lime juice and
water; bring to the boil, reduce the heat
and simmer, covered, for 1 hour. Remove
the lid and simmer uncovered for 30
minutes or until the meat is tender.

tamarind fish

☀

Preparation time: 15 minutes + 1 hour
   marinating time
Cooking time: 15 minutes
Serves 6

2 garlic cloves, crushed
2 tablespoons tamarind concentrate
1 tablespoon Ceylon curry powder
   (pages 114–15)
½ teaspoon ground turmeric
1 tablespoon lemon juice
2 red chillies, finely chopped

sri lankan food

Sri Lankan food reflects the cooking methods
and flavours of the many countries which in
the past have traded with or colonised the
island. From the Portuguese, who ruled in the
sixteenth and seventeenth centuries, come

many of the sweetmeats served at festive
occasions; frikkadels, a dish of fried meatballs,
is a legacy of Dutch reign in the seventeenth and
eighteenth centuries.

6 fish steaks (such as swordfish, cod or warehou) about 150 g (5 oz) each
3 tablespoons oil
125 ml (4 fl oz/½ cup) coconut milk

1 Combine the garlic, tamarind, curry powder, turmeric, lemon juice and chilli.
2 Place the fish steaks in a shallow ovenproof dish. Brush the garlic mixture over both sides of the fish; cover and refrigerate for 1 hour.
3 Heat the oil in a large frying pan over medium heat. Add the fish and cook for 2 minutes on each side. Stir in the coconut milk, reduce heat, cover and simmer gently for 10 minutes or until the fish flakes when tested with a fork.

frikkadels

✳

Preparation time: **30 minutes**
Cooking time: **40 minutes**
Makes **about 25**

45 g (1¾ oz/½ cup) desiccated coconut
500 g (1 lb 2 oz) minced (ground) beef
1 garlic clove, crushed
1 onion, finely chopped
1 teaspoon ground cumin
¼ teaspoon ground cinnamon
½ teaspoon finely grated lime zest
1 tablespoon chopped dill
1 egg, lightly beaten
100 g (3½ oz/1 cup) dry breadcrumbs
oil, for deep-frying

YOGHURT DIPPING SAUCE
250 g (9 oz/1 cup) plain yoghurt
1 large handful mint, finely chopped
pinch of cayenne pepper

1 Preheat the oven to 150°C (300°F/ Gas 2). Spread the coconut on a baking tray and toast it in the oven for 10 minutes, or until dark golden, shaking the tray occasionally.
2 Put the toasted coconut, beef, garlic, onion, cumin, cinnamon, lime zest and dill in a large bowl and mix to combine.

Season with salt and pepper. Shape tablespoons of the mixture into balls. Dip the meatballs in the egg and then toss to coat in the breadcrumbs.
3 Fill a deep heavy-based saucepan or deep-fryer one-third full of oil and heat to 180°C (350°F), or until a cube of bread dropped into the oil browns in

15 seconds. Add the meatballs in batches and cook for 5 minutes, or until deep golden brown and cooked through. Drain on paper towels.
4 To make the yoghurt dipping sauce, combine the ingredients in a bowl and stir to combine. Serve the frikkadels with the dipping sauce.

Combine the coconut, beef, garlic, onion, spices, zest and dill.

Use your hands to roll tablespoons of the mixture into balls.

Deep-fry the balls until they are golden brown, then remove and drain on paper towels.

chicken omelette with coconut gravy

chicken omelette with coconut gravy

✳ ✳

Preparation time: 20 minutes
Cooking time: 25 minutes
Serves 4

½ barbecued chicken
1 large tomato, finely chopped
1 tablespoon chopped fresh dill
8 eggs
2 spring onions (scallions), chopped
lemon wedges, to serve

COCONUT GRAVY   ·
410 ml (14¼ fl oz) coconut milk
½ teaspoon ground turmeric
2 cm (¾ inch) piece fresh ginger, finely
   grated
1 cinnamon stick
1 tablespoon lemon juice

1   Remove the bones from the chicken and shred the meat. Combine the chicken meat, tomato and dill in a bowl. Whisk the eggs and spring onion together in a large bowl.
2   Cook a quarter of the egg mixture in a lightly greased 25 cm (10 inch) non-stick frying pan. When the omelette is cooked, place a quarter of the chicken mixture in the centre, and fold in the four edges to form a parcel. Carefully transfer the omelette to a plate and repeat three times with the remaining mixture. Serve with the coconut gravy and lemon wedges.
3   To make the coconut gravy, place all the ingredients in a small saucepan and simmer for 15 minutes, or until the gravy thickens slightly.

white vegetable curry

✳

Preparation time: 40 minutes
Cooking time: 35 minutes
Serves 4 as part of a meal

300 g (10½ oz) pumpkin (winter squash)
200 g (7 oz) potato

250 g (9 oz) okra
2 tablespoons oil
1 garlic clove, crushed
3 green chillies, seeded and very
   finely chopped
½ teaspoon ground turmeric
½ teaspoon fenugreek seeds
1 onion, chopped
8 curry leaves
1 cinnamon stick
500 ml (17 fl oz/2 cups) coconut milk
steamed rice, to serve

1   Peel the pumpkin and cut into 2 cm (¾ inch) cubes. Peel the potato and cut into 2 cm (¾ inch) cubes. Trim the stems from the okra.
2   Heat the oil in a large heavy-based saucepan; add the garlic, chilli, turmeric, fenugreek seeds and onion, and cook over medium heat for 5 minutes or until the onion is soft.
3   Add the pumpkin, potato, okra, curry leaves, cinnamon stick and coconut milk. Bring to the boil, reduce the heat and simmer, uncovered, for 25–30 minutes or until the vegetables are tender. Serve with the steamed rice.

simmered beef in coconut gravy

✳

Preparation time: 30 minutes
Cooking time: 2 hours 20 minutes
Serves 4–6

2 kg (4 lb 8 oz) piece blade steak
2 tablespoons oil
3 tablespoons Ceylon curry powder
   (pages 114–15)
3 garlic cloves, crushed
2 tablespoons finely grated fresh ginger
3 tablespoons chopped lemongrass, white
   part only
2 onions, chopped
3 tablespoons tamarind concentrate
3 tablespoons vinegar
500 ml (17 fl oz/2 cups) beef stock
500 ml (17 fl oz/2 cups) coconut milk

1   Trim the meat of all fat and sinew and tie with kitchen string so that the meat holds its shape.
2   Heat the oil in a large heavy-based saucepan; add the meat and cook over high heat until it browns. Remove the meat from the pan and set aside.
3   Reduce the heat to medium; add the curry powder, garlic, ginger, lemongrass and onion, and cook for 5 minutes or until the oil begins to separate from the spices.
4   Return the meat to the pan; add the tamarind, vinegar, stock and coconut milk, and bring to the boil; reduce the heat, cover and simmer for 1 hour 45 minutes, or until the meat is tender.
5   Remove the meat from the pan and keep it warm. Bring the liquid to the boil and cook it, uncovered, for 10 minutes or until a thick gravy forms. Slice the meat and serve topped with the gravy.

NOTE: If Ceylon curry powder is not available or you do not have time to make your own, ask for a curry powder blend made for meat at an Asian food store.

egghoppers with eggplant (aubergine) sambol

✹ ✹ ✹

Preparation time: 40 minutes +
   1 hour 10 minutes standing time
Cooking time: 2 hours 45 minutes
Makes 12–15

2 teaspoons dried yeast
125 ml (4 fl oz/½ cup) warm water
1 teaspoon caster (superfine) sugar
330 g (11 oz/1½ cups) medium-grain
   white rice
265 g (9 oz/1½ cups) rice flour
2 teaspoons salt
1.125 litres (39 fl oz/4½ cups) coconut
   milk
12–15 eggs

EGGPLANT SAMBOL
2 eggplants (aubergines), cut into 2 cm
   (¾ inch) cubes
60 ml (2 fl oz/¼ cup) oil
2 spring onions (scallions), finely chopped
1 teaspoon soft brown sugar
2 red chillies, finely chopped
2 green chillies, finely chopped
2 tablespoons chopped coriander
   (cilantro) leaves
1 tablespoon lemon juice

1 Preheat the oven to 180°C (350°F/
Gas 4). Place the yeast, warm water and
sugar in a small bowl. Put the bowl in a
warm, draught-free area for 10 minutes,
or until foaming.
2 Spread the rice on a baking tray and
toast in the oven for about 15 minutes,
until golden. Cool slightly, transfer
to a food processor and process until
finely ground.
3 Combine the ground rice, rice flour
and salt in a large bowl. Gradually whisk
in the yeast mixture and coconut milk
and mix to a smooth batter. Cover and set
aside in a warm, draught-free area
for 1 hour.
4 To make the eggplant sambol, sprinkle
the eggplant with salt and leave for
20 minutes; rinse and thoroughly pat dry
with paper towels. Heat the oil in a large
frying pan; add the eggplant, and cook
over high heat for 10 minutes or until
golden brown. Remove from the pan and
toss through the spring onion, sugar, chilli,
coriander and lemon juice. Set aside.
5 Lightly grease a 23 cm (9 inch)
non-stick frying pan. Pour 80 ml
(2½ fl oz/⅓ cup) batter into the pan or
enough to thinly coat the base of the pan;
swirl the pan to cover the base. Crack
1 egg into the centre of the pan, and cook
over low heat for 5–10 minutes — time
will vary depending on the pan you use.
When the edges are crisp and golden and
the egghopper is cooked, gently remove
it from the pan by sliding it out over the
side of the pan. Cover the egghopper
and keep it warm while cooking the
remainder. Serve the egghoppers with
the eggplant sambol.

cashew nut curry

❄

Preparation time: 15 minutes
Cooking time: 55 minutes
Serves 6 as part of a shared meal

1 onion
2 green chillies
1 pandanus leaf (see Note)
750 ml (26 fl oz/3 cups) coconut
    milk
1 tablespoon finely grated fresh ginger
½ teaspoon ground turmeric
3 cm (1¼ inch) piece fresh galangal
8 curry leaves
1 cinnamon stick
250 g (9 oz) cashew nuts
2 tablespoons chopped coriander
    (cilantro) leaves

1 Chop the onion. Cut the chillies in
half, remove the seeds and finely chop.
Shred the pandanus leaf lengthways
into about three sections, and tie into
a large knot.
2 Combine the coconut milk, onion,
ginger, turmeric, galangal, chilli, curry
leaves, cinnamon stick and pandanus
leaf in a saucepan and bring to the
boil. Reduce the heat and simmer for
20 minutes. Add the cashew nuts, and
cook for a further 30 minutes, or until
the nuts are tender.
3 Remove from the heat and discard the
galangal, cinnamon stick and pandanus
leaf. Sprinkle over the coriander and serve
with rice and a couple of other dishes.

NOTE: Popular in Southeast Asian
cooking, pandanus leaves are most often
used to flavour rice dishes. They are
available from Asian food stores.

red pork curry

❄

Preparation time: 20 minutes + 1 hour
    marinating time
Cooking time: 20 minutes
Serves 4

red pork curry

4 dried red chillies
125 ml (4 fl oz/½ cup) boiling water
1 onion, chopped
2 garlic cloves, chopped
2 cm (¾ inch) piece fresh ginger, finely
    grated
1 tablespoon finely chopped lemongrass,
    white part only
500 g (1 lb 2 oz) pork fillet, cut into 2½ cm
    (1 inch) pieces
2 tablespoons tamarind concentrate
2 tablespoons ghee or oil
125 ml (4 fl oz/½ cup) coconut milk
red chillies, sliced, to garnish
coriander (cilantro) sprigs, to garnish

1 Place the chillies in a heatproof bowl,
pour over the boiling water and soak for
10 minutes.
2 Process the chillies and soaking water,
onion, garlic, ginger and lemongrass in a
food processor until a paste has formed.
3 Place the pork in a shallow dish, add
the chilli paste and tamarind, and mix to
combine. Cover and refrigerate for 1 hour.
4 Heat the ghee in a wok, then add the
pork in batches, and cook over high heat
for 5 minutes. Return all meat to the pan
with any leftover marinade, stir in the
coconut milk, and simmer for 5 minutes.
Garnish with chilli and coriander.

spicy seafood

✳

Preparation time: 20 minutes
Cooking time: 15 minutes
Serves 4

500 g (1 lb 2 oz) raw prawns (shrimp)
2 squid tubes
250 g (9 oz) mussels
3 tablespoons oil
2 onions, sliced
2 garlic cloves, crushed
1 tablespoon finely grated fresh ginger
½ teaspoon ground turmeric
1 teaspoon chilli powder
1 teaspoon paprika
60 ml (2 fl oz/¼ cup) tomato passata
    (puréed tomatoes)
1 teaspoon grated palm sugar (jaggery) or
    soft brown sugar
steamed rice, to serve

1   Peel the prawns. Gently pull out the dark vein from each prawn back, starting at the head end. Cut the squid tubes into 6 cm (2½ inch) squares and score a criss-cross pattern lightly into the flesh with a small sharp knife. Scrub the mussels and remove the hairy beards.
2   Heat the oil in a large heavy-based saucepan or wok; add the onion, garlic and ginger, and cook over medium heat for 3–5 minutes or until the onion is soft.
3   Add the turmeric, chilli powder and paprika, and cook for 2 minutes or until the oil begins to separate from the spices.
4   Add the seafood to the pan and cook over high heat for 3–5 minutes or until the prawns are pink. Stir in the tomato passata and sugar and stir-fry for 3 minutes or until the sauce is heated through. Serve with the steamed rice.

sri lankan lentils

✳

Preparation time: 15 minutes
Cooking time: 1 hour
Serves 4

spicy seafood

2 tablespoons oil
2 onions, thinly sliced
2 small red chillies, finely chopped
2 teaspoons dried shrimp
1 teaspoon ground turmeric
500 g (1 lb 2 oz/2 cups) red lentils
4 curry leaves
500 ml (17 fl oz/2 cups) coconut
    milk
250 ml (9 fl oz/1 cup) vegetable
    stock
1 cinnamon stick
10 cm (4 inch) lemongrass stem

1   Heat the oil in a medium saucepan over medium heat. Cook the onion for 10 minutes, or until it is a deep golden brown. Remove half the onion and set aside to use as a garnish.
2   Add the chilli, dried shrimp and turmeric, and cook for 2 minutes. Stir in lentils, curry leaves, coconut milk, stock, cinnamon stick and lemongrass; bring to the boil, reduce heat and simmer, uncovered, for 45 minutes. Remove the cinnamon stick and lemongrass. Garnish with reserved onion.

fish with flaked coconut

✹ ✹

Preparation time: **20 minutes**
Cooking time: **50 minutes**
Serves **4**

45 g (1¾ oz/½ cup) desiccated coconut
110 g (3¾ oz/2 cups) flaked coconut
500 g (1 lb 2 oz) firm white fish fillets
½ teaspoon freshly ground black pepper
1 teaspoon ground turmeric
1 tablespoon lime juice
1 whole star anise
1 cinnamon stick
2 teaspoons cumin seeds
1 dried chilli
2 tablespoons oil
3 garlic cloves, crushed
3 onions, thinly sliced
steamed rice, to serve

1   Spread the desiccated and flaked coconut on a baking tray and toast it in a 150°C (300°F/Gas 2) oven for 10 minutes or until it is dark golden, shaking the tray occasionally.
2   Place the fish, pepper, turmeric and lime juice in a frying pan, cover with water and simmer gently for 15 minutes or until the fish flakes when tested with a fork. Remove the fish fillets from the liquid and allow to cool slightly before flaking it into pieces.
3   Dry-roast the star anise, cinnamon stick, cumin seeds and chilli in a frying pan over medium heat for 5 minutes. Transfer to a food processor or use a mortar and pestle and grind to a fine powder.
4   Heat the oil in a wok; add the garlic, onion and spice powder, and stir-fry over medium–high heat for 10 minutes or until the onion is soft.
5   Add the fish and coconut to the wok. Use two wooden spoons to toss the fish in the pan for 5 minutes or until heated through. Serve with the steamed rice.

sri lankan curries

Unlike the curry powders of India, the spices that go into Ceylon curry powder — used in the black or brown curries that are characteristic of Sri Lanka — are roasted until dark, giving the mixture a completely different flavour and aroma. Dishes made with Ceylon curry powder have a distinctive deep colour. Chillies, ground or powdered, give red curries both colour and heat, which can be scorching! White curries, on the other hand, are based on coconut milk and are usually mild.

desserts

A burst of cooling sweetness is the perfect end to an Asian meal. Most Asian desserts make use of the natural sweetness of tropical fruits — coconuts, bananas and mangoes. Sticky rice, black or white, pancakes and semolina are often included to balance the tartness of the fruit, while ice creams and chilled custards refresh the palate.

coconut
semolina slice

❈

Preparation time: **20 minutes**
Cooking time: **1 hour**
Serves **8–10**

50 g (1¾ oz) sesame seeds
125 g (4½ oz/1 cup) fine semolina
230 g (8 oz/1 cup) caster (superfine) sugar
750 ml (26 fl oz/3 cups) coconut cream
2 tablespoons ghee or oil
2 eggs, separated
¼ teaspoon ground cardamom
fresh fruit, to serve

1 Preheat the oven to 160°C (315°F/
Gas 2–3). Lightly grease an 18 x 28 cm
(7 x 11¼ inch) shallow tin.
2 Toast the sesame seeds in a dry frying
pan over medium heat for 3–4 minutes,
shaking the pan gently, until the seeds are
golden brown; remove from the pan at
once to prevent burning.
3 Put the semolina, sugar and coconut
cream in a large saucepan and stir over
medium heat for 5 minutes, or until
boiling. Add the ghee and continue
stirring until the mixture comes away
from the sides of the pan. Set aside
to cool.
4 Whisk the egg whites until stiff peaks
form. Fold the egg whites, egg yolks
and cardamom into the cooled semolina
mixture. Spoon the mixture into the
prepared tin and sprinkle with the sesame
seeds. Bake for 45 minutes, or until pale
brown. Cut into diamond shapes and
serve with fresh fruit.

sago pudding

✷

Preparation time: 20 minutes + 1 hour soaking
    and 2 hours chilling time
Cooking time: 20 minutes
Serves 6

200 g (7 oz/1 cup) sago
185 g (6½ oz/1 cup) lightly packed soft
    brown sugar
250 ml (9 fl oz/1 cup) coconut cream, well
    chilled

1   Soak the sago in 750 ml
(26 fl oz/3 cups) water for 1 hour. Pour
into a saucepan, add 2 tablespoons of
the sugar and bring to the boil over low
heat, stirring constantly. Reduce the
heat and simmer, stirring occasionally,
for 8 minutes. Cover and cook for
2–3 minutes, until the mixture is thick
and the sago grains are translucent.
2   Half-fill six wet 125 ml (4 fl oz/½ cup)
moulds with the sago mixture. Refrigerate
for 2 hours, or until set.
3   Combine the remaining sugar with
250 ml (9 fl oz/1 cup) water in a small
saucepan and cook over low heat until
the sugar has dissolved. Simmer for 5–7
minutes, or until the syrup thickens.
Remove from the heat and cool.
4   To serve, unmould the sago by wiping
a cloth dipped in hot water over the
mould and turn out onto a plate. Top with
the sugar syrup and coconut cream.

banana and coconut pancakes

✷ ✷

Preparation time: 10 minutes
Cooking time: 30 minutes
Serves 4–6

1 tablespoon shredded coconut
40 g (1½ oz/⅓ cup) plain (all-purpose) flour
2 tablespoons rice flour
55 g (2 oz/¼ cup) caster (superfine) sugar
25 g (1 oz/¼ cup) desiccated coconut

banana and coconut pancakes

250 ml (9 fl oz/1 cup) coconut milk
1 egg, lightly beaten
butter, for frying
60 g (2¼ oz) butter, extra
4 large bananas, cut on the diagonal into
    thick slices
60 g (2¼ oz/⅓ cup) lightly packed soft
    brown sugar
80 ml (2½ fl oz/⅓ cup) lime juice
finely shredded lime zest, to serve

1   Spread the shredded coconut on
a baking tray and toast it in a 150°C
(300°F/Gas 2) oven for 10 minutes, or
until it is dark golden, shaking the tray
occasionally. Remove from the tray and
set aside. Sift the flours into a bowl.
Add the sugar and desiccated coconut
and mix. Make a well in the centre, pour
in the combined coconut milk and egg,
and beat until smooth.

2   Melt a little butter in a non-stick
frying pan. Pour 60 ml (2 fl oz/¼ cup)
of the pancake mixture into the pan
and cook over medium heat until the
underside is golden. Turn the pancake
over and cook the other side. Transfer
to a plate and cover with a tea towel
(dish towel) to keep warm. Repeat
with the remaining pancake batter,
buttering the pan when necessary.
3   Heat the extra butter in the pan, add
the banana, toss until coated, and cook
over medium heat until the banana
starts to soften and brown. Sprinkle
with the brown sugar and shake the pan
gently until the sugar melts. Stir in the
lime juice. Divide the banana among
the pancakes and fold over to enclose.
Sprinkle with the toasted coconut and
shredded lime zest.

sticky rice

Sticky rice is also known as glutinous rice, though it does not contain gluten but a large amount of starch. It needs to be soaked before steaming. It is usually served as a dessert, but some Asian countries (for example, Laos) use it as an accompaniment to savoury dishes instead of white long grain.

sticky rice with mangoes

❋ ❋

Preparation time: 40 minutes + overnight soaking time
Cooking time: 1 hour
Serves 4

400 g (14 oz/2 cups) glutinous white rice
1 tablespoon white sesame seeds
250 ml (9 fl oz/1 cup) coconut milk
70 g (2½ oz/½ cup) grated palm sugar (jaggery) or soft brown sugar
2–3 mangoes, peeled, stoned and sliced
60 ml (2 fl oz/¼ cup) coconut cream
mint leaves, to garnish

1 Put the rice in a sieve and wash it under cold running water until the water runs clear. Put the rice in a glass or ceramic bowl, cover it with water and leave it to soak overnight, or for a minimum of 12 hours. Drain the rice.

2 Line a metal or bamboo steamer with muslin (cheesecloth). Place the rice on top of the muslin and cover the steamer with a tight-fitting lid. Place the steamer over a saucepan of boiling water and steam over low–medium heat for 50 minutes, or until the rice is cooked. Transfer the rice to a large bowl and fluff it up with a fork.

3 Toast the sesame seeds in a dry frying pan over medium heat for 3–4 minutes, shaking the pan gently, until the seeds are golden brown. Remove from the pan at once to prevent burning.

4 Pour the coconut milk into a small saucepan, then add the palm sugar and ¼ teaspoon salt. Slowly bring the mixture to the boil, stirring constantly until the sugar has dissolved. Reduce the heat and simmer for 5 minutes, or until the mixture thickens slightly. Stir the mixture often while it is simmering, and take care that it does not stick to the bottom of the pan.

5 Slowly pour the coconut milk mixture over the top of the rice. Use a fork to lift and fluff the rice. Do not stir the liquid through, otherwise the rice will become too gluggy. Let the rice mixture rest for 20 minutes before carefully spooning it into the centre of four warmed serving plates. Arrange the mango slices around the rice mounds. Spoon a little coconut cream over the rice, sprinkle with the sesame seeds, and garnish with the mint.

chinese fortune cookies

✳ ✳

Preparation time: 55 minutes
Cooking time: 50 minutes
Makes about 30

3 egg whites
60 g (2¼ oz/½ cup) icing (confectioners')
  sugar, sifted
45 g (1¾ oz) unsalted butter, melted
60 g (2¼ oz/½ cup) plain (all-purpose) flour

1 Preheat the oven to 180ºC (350ºF/
Gas 4). Line a baking tray with baking
paper. Draw three circles with 8 cm
(3¼ inch) diameters on the paper.
2 Put the egg whites in a bowl and whisk
until just frothy. Add the icing sugar and
butter and stir until smooth. Add the flour
and mix until smooth. Allow to stand for
15 minutes.
3 Use a flat-bladed knife to spread
1½ level teaspoons of the mixture over
each circle. Bake for 5 minutes, or until
slightly brown around the edges. Working
quickly, remove the cookies from the tray
by sliding a flat-bladed knife under each.
Place a written fortune message on each
cookie. Fold the cookie in half to form a
semi-circle, then fold again over a blunt-
edged object like the rim of a glass. Allow
to cool on a wire rack. Repeat with the
remaining mixture.

NOTE: Cook no more than two or three
cookies at a time, otherwise they will
harden too quickly and break when folding.

spicy coconut custard

✳ ✳

Preparation time: 20 minutes
Cooking time: 1 hour
Makes 8

2 cinnamon sticks
1 teaspoon freshly grated nutmeg
2 teaspoons whole cloves
310 ml (10¾ fl oz/1¼ cups) pouring
  (whipping) cream
90 g (3¼ oz) chopped palm sugar
  (jaggery) or soft brown sugar
270 ml (9½ fl oz) tin coconut milk
3 eggs, lightly beaten
2 egg yolks, lightly beaten
whipped cream, to serve
toasted shredded coconut, to serve

1 Preheat the oven to 160ºC (315ºF/
Gas 2–3). Combine the cinnamon, nutmeg,
cloves, cream and 250 ml (9 fl oz/1 cup)
water in a saucepan. Bring to simmering
point, reduce the heat to very low and
leave for 5 minutes to allow the spices to
infuse the liquid. Add the palm sugar and
coconut milk, return to low heat and stir
until the sugar has dissolved.
2 Whisk the eggs and egg yolks in a bowl
until combined. Stir in the spiced mixture,
then strain, discarding the whole spices.
Pour into eight 125 ml (4 fl oz/½ cup)
ramekins or dariole moulds. Place in
a baking dish and pour in enough hot
water to come halfway up the sides of the
ramekins. Bake for 40–45 minutes until
set. The custards should wobble slightly
when the dish is shaken lightly. Remove
the custards from the baking dish.
Serve hot or chilled with whipped
cream and the toasted shredded coconut
sprinkled over the top.

spicy coconut custard

mango ice cream

☀

Preparation time: 20 minutes + freezing time
Cooking time: nil
Serves 6

400 g (14 oz) fresh mango flesh (see Note)
125 g (4½ oz/½ cup) caster (superfine)
    sugar
3 tablespoons mango or apricot nectar
250 ml (9 fl oz/1 cup) pouring
    (whipping) cream
extra mango slices

1 Place the mango in a food processor and process until smooth. Transfer the mango purée to a bowl and add the sugar and nectar. Stir until the sugar has dissolved.
2 Whisk the cream in a small bowl until stiff peaks form and then gently fold it through the mango mixture.

3 Spoon the mixture into a shallow cake tin, cover and freeze for 1½ hours or until half-frozen.
4 Quickly spoon the mixture into a food processor and process for 30 seconds, or until smooth. Return the mixture to the tin or a plastic container, cover and freeze completely.
5 Remove the ice cream from the freezer 15 minutes before serving to allow it to soften a little. Serve the ice cream in scoops with some extra mango.

NOTE: Frozen or tinned mango can be used if fresh mango is not available.

sticky black rice

☀ ☀

Preparation time: 10 minutes + 8 hours
    soaking time
Cooking time: 40 minutes
Serves 6–8

400 g (14 oz/2 cups) black rice
500 ml (17 fl oz/2 cups) coconut milk
90 g (3¼ oz/½ cup) grated palm sugar
    (jaggery) or soft brown sugar
3 tablespoons caster (superfine)
    sugar
3 fresh pandanus leaves, shredded
    and knotted
3 tablespoons coconut cream
3 tablespoons creamed corn

1 Place the rice in a large glass or ceramic bowl and add enough water to cover it. Soak the rice for at least 8 hours or overnight. Drain the rice and transfer it to a medium saucepan with 1 litre (35 fl oz/4 cups) water. Slowly bring to the boil, stirring frequently, then simmer for 20 minutes, or until tender. Drain.
2 In a large heavy-based saucepan, heat the coconut milk until almost boiling. Add the palm sugar, caster sugar and pandanus leaves, and stir until the sugars dissolve. Add the rice and stir for 3–4 minutes without boiling.
3 Turn off the heat, cover the pan and let it stand for 15 minutes to allow

mango ice cream

the flavours to be absorbed. Remove the pandanus leaves. Serve the rice warm with the coconut cream and creamed corn.

almond jelly

☀

Preparation time: 5 minutes + 1 hour chilling time
Cooking time: 5 minutes
Serves 4–6

80 g (2¾ oz/⅓ cup) caster (superfine) sugar
2 teaspoons agar-agar (see Note)
170 ml (5½ fl oz/⅔ cup) evaporated milk
½ teaspoon natural almond extract
3 mandarins, peeled and segmented, or 300 g (10½ oz) cherries, pitted and chilled

1 Put 500 ml (17 fl oz/2 cups) cold water and the sugar in a small saucepan. Sprinkle over the agar-agar. Bring the mixture to the boil and simmer for about 1 minute. Remove from the heat and add the evaporated milk and natural almond extract.

2 Pour the mixture into a shallow 18 x 28 cm (7 x 11¼ inch) cake tin to set. Chill for at least 1 hour. Cut the jelly into diamond shapes, and serve with the fruit.

NOTE: Agar-agar is similar to gelatin but does not need refrigeration to help it set. If it is unavailable, use 3 teaspoons of powdered gelatin sprinkled over 125 ml (4 fl oz/½ cup) cold water to soften. Stir the gelatin mixture into the water and sugar mixture, bring to the boil, then remove it from the heat — there is no need to simmer. Proceed with the method as described but refrigerate the jelly for 5 hours instead.

egg tarts

✹ ✹ ✹

Preparation time: 45 minutes + 30 minutes
  chilling time
Cooking time: 15 minutes
Makes 18

OUTER DOUGH
165 g (5¾ oz/1⅓ cups) plain (all-purpose)
  flour
2 tablespoons icing (confectioners') sugar
2 tablespoons oil

INNER DOUGH
125 g (4½ oz/1 cup) plain (all-purpose) flour
100 g (3½ oz) lard, chopped

CUSTARD
55 g (2 oz/¼ cup) caster (superfine) sugar
2 eggs

1 To make the outer dough, sift the flour
and icing sugar into a bowl. Make a well
in the centre. Combine the oil with 80 ml
(2½ fl oz/⅓ cup) water and pour into the
dry ingredients. Mix with a flat-bladed
knife, using a cutting action, to form a
rough dough. (If the flour is very dry, add a
little water.) Turn out onto a lightly floured
surface and gather together in a smooth
ball. Cover and set aside for 15 minutes.
2 To make the inner dough, sift flour into
a bowl. Using your fingertips, rub the lard
into the flour until the mixture resembles
breadcrumbs. Press the dough together into
a ball, cover and set aside for 15 minutes.
3 On a lightly floured surface, roll
the outer dough into a rectangle about
10 x 20 cm (4 x 8 inches). On a lightly
floured surface, roll the inner dough into
a smaller rectangle, one-third the size of
the outer dough. Place the inner dough
in the centre of the outer dough. Fold the
outer dough over the inner dough so the
short edges overlap and the inner dough
is enclosed. Pinch the edges together to
seal. Roll the dough away from you in one
direction into a long rectangle, until it is
about half as thick as it was previously.
Fold the pastry into three layers by taking
the left-hand edge over first, and then
folding the right-hand edge on top. Wrap
the dough in plastic wrap and refrigerate
for 30 minutes. Preheat the oven to 210ºC
(415ºF/Gas 6–7). Brush two 12-hole round-
based patty pans with melted butter or oil.
4 To make the custard, place 80 ml
(2½ fl oz/⅓ cup) water and the sugar in
a saucepan and stir, without boiling, until
sugar has dissolved. Bring to the boil and
simmer, without stirring, for 1 minute.
Cool the mixture for 5 minutes. Put the
eggs in a bowl and whisk lightly with a
fork. Whisk the sugar syrup into the eggs
until just combined. Strain.
5 Place the pastry on a lightly floured
surface. With one open end towards
you, roll out to a rectangle about 3 mm
(⅛ inch) thick. Cut out rounds of pastry
using a 7 cm (2¾ inch) fluted cutter.
Carefully place the pastry rounds into
the prepared patty pans. Fill each pastry
case two-thirds full with the egg custard
mixture. Bake for 15 minutes, or until
just set. Be careful not to overcook. Leave
the egg tarts to cool for 3 minutes before
removing from the tin. Cool the tarts on a
wire rack, and serve warm or cold.

egg tarts

Fold the outer dough over the
inner dough so the short edges
of the outer dough overlap.

Roll the dough in one direction into
a long rectangle until it is about
half as thick as it was before.

Cut out the rounds of pastry using
a fluted cutter and carefully place
the rounds into the patty pans.

sweet won tons

✸ ✸

Preparation time: **15 minutes**
Cooking time: **30 minutes**
Makes **30**

125 g (4½ oz) fresh dates, pitted
    and chopped
2 bananas, finely chopped
45 g (1¾ oz/½ cup) flaked almonds,
    lightly crushed
½ teaspoon ground cinnamon
60 won ton wrappers
oil, for deep-frying
icing (confectioners') sugar, to dust

1 Mix together the dates, banana, almonds and cinnamon. Put 2 teaspoons of the fruit mixture into the centre of a won ton wrapper, and brush the edges lightly with water. Place another won ton wrapper on top at an angle so the wrappers make a star shape. Place the won tons on a baking tray lined with baking paper. Repeat with the remaining ingredients (do not stack the won tons on top of each other).
2 Fill a deep-fryer or large heavy-based saucepan one-third full of oil and heat to 180ºC (350ºF), or until a cube of bread dropped into the oil browns in 15 seconds. Deep-fry the won tons, in small batches for 2 minutes, or until crisp and golden. Drain on paper towels. Dust lightly with the icing sugar before serving.

index

Page numbers in *italics* refer to
photographs. Page numbers in **bold**
refer to margin notes.

A copywriter by trade, Diana Rosie has created award-winning campaigns for a variety of popular brands, and occasionally helps her filmmaker husband with script-writing. After living in Hong Kong, London and Peru, she has finally settled comfortably into a country cottage, where she writes by the range.

Find her on Twitter — @DiWrite

ALBERTO'S LOST BIRTHDAY

Alberto is an old man, who remembers nothing before his arrival at an orphanage during the Spanish Civil War. He rarely thinks about his missing childhood — but when seven-year-old Tino discovers that his grandfather has never had a birthday party, never blown out candles on a birthday cake, never received a single birthday present, he's determined that things should change. And so the two set out to find Alberto's birthday. As their search unfolds, Alberto realises that he has lost more than a birthday. He has lost a part of himself. But, with his grandson's help, he might just find it again.

DIANA ROSIE

ALBERTO'S LOST BIRTHDAY

Complete and Unabridged

ULVERSCROFT
Leicester

First published in Great Britain in 2016 by
Mantle
an imprint of Pan Macmillan
London

First Large Print Edition
published 2017
by arrangement with
Pan Macmillan
London

C463716679

*A catalogue record for this book is available
from the British Library.*

ISBN 978–1–4448–3158–0

Published by
F. A. Thorpe (Publishing)
Anstey, Leicestershire

Set by Words & Graphics Ltd.
Anstey, Leicestershire
Printed and bound in Great Britain by
T. J. International Ltd., Padstow, Cornwall

This book is printed on acid-free paper

For John, who brings me sunshine.

1

Reaching through the dense leaves, Alberto grasped the lemon and twisted it off its stalk. The hefty fruit was as large as his hand, and he inspected its waxy pores before lifting it to his nose and sniffing. Nodding, he placed it in the rope bag alongside the muscat grapes. He knew the boy loved to peel the tough grape skins and suck on the sweet pulp inside.

Before he left for the day, he looked down across the stone terraces of his land. Below the lemon trees ran lines of aged almond trees, their branches heavy with nuts. Further down, rows of gnarled grape vines stood stoutly in the dusty ground.

At the bottom, softly shaded by pine trees, lay Alberto's garden, where herbs and flowers flourished. This small patch took more work than all the rest, and carrying the water from the stone irrigation channel tired him. But whenever he picked a large bunch of scented flowers to leave at his wife's grave, he knew his garden would be the last thing he would give up.

When his wife was alive, the two of them

would walk to their land together. Over the three kilometres he would listen to her good-humoured chatter about the children and the foreigners whose villas she cleaned. These days, however, Alberto's joints ached at the change of the seasons, and often his own weariness surprised him. He had been reluctantly grateful when one of his daughters and her husband had presented him with a second-hand moped a few years ago. 'Apu's put-put' the boy called it, and Alberto used it regularly to come to the land, and on the odd occasion when he had to go to town.

Now, the old man carefully strapped the bag onto the back of the moped, kicked away the stand with the heel of his espadrille and climbed on. Pedalling briefly to start the rat-a-tat engine, he steered slowly out onto the main road.

Put-putting home in the late sun, Alberto planned how his grandson could help him pick lemons and harvest the almonds. Together, they would visit the local cafes and restaurants on the beachfront to sell their wares. He told his daughter the boy was an extra pair of hands to help him during the school holidays, but they both knew it was more than that.

When he got back to the village, he parked the bike down the alley beside his apartment, locking it behind an iron grille. Carrying the rope bag, he climbed the tiled stairs to his front door but was surprised to find it open. He wasn't expecting the boy until the weekend.

Inside the cool, shadowy room, his rheumy eyes took a moment to adjust. His daughter was sitting at the table, tugging at a white handkerchief in her hand. Her son stood at her side, stock-still, staring intently with large brown eyes at his grandfather.

Alberto smiled reassuringly at the boy, who seemed to relax a tiny amount.

The old man's voice was gravelly, but his words were soft. 'Rosa? What's wrong?'

His daughter glanced at him briefly. 'There's been an accident.'

Alberto sat opposite her, the raffia seat creaking under his weight. 'Juan Carlos?'

At the mention of her husband's name, his daughter nodded and began to cry, raising the handkerchief to her face to hide her tears. The child looked at his mother anxiously. Alberto wished his wife were here. She had always known the words to use to ease an emotional situation, how to express sympathy with just the touch of her hand. These small gestures of love and support were a mystery to Alberto, so he waited for his daughter to compose herself.

She wiped her eyes and nose with the handkerchief. 'He's been hurt in an explosion,' she explained. 'A boiler at Señor Medina's house. No one knows what happened. Juan Carlos is always so good with the old plumbing.'

Alberto nodded, waiting for his daughter to continue. The boy stood so still and silent the old man had almost forgotten he was there.

Rosa took a deep breath and said, 'He's in the hospital. He has very bad burns. He's stable at the moment, but it's serious. They will know more in the morning.'

'Juan Carlos is a strong man,' said Alberto as kindly as his gruff voice would allow.

His daughter looked at him and sighed. 'You're right, Papá. But I have to be with him tonight. Juan Carlos's mother is at the hospital now and I need to return — but it's no place for a child.'

Alberto looked at his grandson and smiled at him. The boy stared back. 'Of course he can stay here.'

'I didn't have the chance to pack a bag; you could go round to our apartment — '

Alberto shook his head. 'No need. He'll be fine. Now, go to your husband.'

Rosa looked at her father and smiled weakly. 'Thank you.'

Alberto stood and put a large, leathery

hand on his grandson's small shoulder. The boy looked up at him.

Rosa stood too and turned to hug her son. Alberto watched the child collapse into his mother's arms, sinking his face into her dark curls. She held him for a few moments before straightening up. Blinking away the tears, she stroked the boy's soft brown hair and smiled brightly at him. 'Now, Tino, be a good boy for Apu. And don't worry about your papá — Grandma and I will be with him tonight.'

She turned to her father and gingerly kissed his bristly cheek. 'Thank you, Papá,' she whispered.

As she left the apartment, closing the door behind her, the old man saw the boy stiffen. Quickly he picked up the rope bag, took Tino's hand and led him into the kitchen. He pulled the fruit out of the bag and put the grapes into the sink. Instinctively, the child leant over to turn on the tap and began washing the dust off the grapes.

Alberto took out the bread he'd bought in the village that morning. He tore the end off the long loaf, then reached up into the cupboard overhead and brought out a small bar of chocolate. Breaking off a few squares, he pushed them deep into the middle of the bread. He turned on the grill of his ancient oven, opened the door and put the bread on the shelf.

The boy had finished washing the grapes, so Alberto passed him a tea towel to dry them while he boiled the kettle. When he'd finished, Tino fetched the bowl from the table in the next room and carefully placed the bunches of grapes in it.

Alberto made the boy a cup of weak tea with milk and sugar, and himself a strong cup of black coffee. The child took great care in carrying the glass bowl full of fruit to the table, then sat on a chair while his grandfather placed his tea in front of him. Alberto felt two large brown eyes follow him as he returned to the oven and lifted out the bread.

Insensitive to the heat, he wrapped the toasted loaf in a paper serviette, brought it to the child and sat down opposite him. Tino held it, looking at it as if trying to decide if he was hungry. But as the thin smell of warm, melted chocolate rose from the toasted bread, he began nibbling its crunchy edge.

Alberto sipped his coffee, watching his grandson blowing at and biting past the crust into the chocolate-coated dough. Alberto remembered eating this once as a child and being comforted by the simple treat.

As the boy munched on, Alberto got up

and crossed the tiny apartment to the bathroom, which lay off a corridor. He turned the bath taps on full, and while rusty brown water gushed into the bath, he opened the bathroom cabinet. It was almost bare, housing only his razor and shaving foam; toothbrush and paste; a plastic bottle of aspirin that his daughter insisted he take, though he rarely did; and some bubble bath he kept for the boy's visits.

The water had begun to run clear, so he put in the plug and poured out some bubble bath. Then he returned to the boy, who had finished his bread and was holding his mug of tea with both hands.

Alberto placed a hand on the child's head and gently stroked the soft hair.

Tino twisted his head to look up at his grandfather.

'Are you all right?' asked Alberto huskily.

'Yes, Apu,' he nodded, attempting a smile.

'Good. Now finish your tea. It's time for your bath.'

★　★　★

Clean and sleepy, the boy climbed into bed dressed in his grandfather's stripy pyjama top with the sleeves rolled up. Sitting on the bed, the old man tucked the sheet in and laid a light blanket over him.

'Apu?' whispered the little boy.

'Yes.'

'Is Papá going to die?'

'I don't know,' he replied after a brief pause. While he knew his daughter often sugar-coated difficult news, he had always been completely honest with his own children.

The child's large eyes peered up at him.

'I am not a doctor. The hospital is full of doctors. They will do everything they can to make him better.'

'But will he be all right?' Tino persisted.

'Your father is a good man. And he still has a great many things to do in his life. Like watching you grow up. I know he will fight as hard as he can,' said Alberto.

The boy nodded thoughtfully.

'Apu?'

'Yes.'

'How old were you when your papá died?'

The question took him aback, and for a moment he studied his grandchild, considering his answer.

'I don't know,' he said finally, shaking his head.

'Why not?'

'Well,' began Alberto, 'it was the civil war — '

'Spain was in a war? Who were they fighting?'

'Themselves,' said the old man.

'How can a country fight itself?'

'When people have different views, it can end in a fight. You must have seen that at school.'

Tino nodded.

'Some people take the side of one person in the fight, and some people take the other person's side.'

The boy nodded again.

'Well, in this case, the whole country took one side or another. And the whole country fought each other.'

'Who was on the right side?'

'It wasn't that simple. It was a fight between the rich and the poor. Between people who believed in God and people who didn't. Between people who wanted to do things in the traditional way and those who wanted to be more modern.'

'I would be on the side of the poor people who believed in God,' the child stated.

'Well then, you would have been on both sides,' said the old man.

'What?'

'It's true. In those days, the Church was very rich and powerful. The poor workers and farmers wanted change; they wanted their own land and better working conditions. The Church did not want change. So the two were on opposite sides in the war.'

Tino shook his head, unable to understand.

'At the time, I think it seemed an easy decision. You were either for freedom — freedom from poverty, freedom from greedy bosses, even freedom from the Church — or you wanted things to stay the same, and for the government to be very strict about keeping it that way.'

'And what happened? Who won?'

'The people who wanted to keep things as they were. A man called General Franco won the war.'

'Does he still run Spain?'

'No,' said Alberto. 'Franco died many years ago and Spain has changed a great deal since then.'

'Apu?' said the boy.

'Yes.'

'Which side were you on?'

'I was just a boy. I wasn't on a side.'

'But you must have wanted one side to win more than the other.'

'Well,' said Alberto thoughtfully, 'I lived in an orphanage that was run by the Church, so they taught me that we must believe in God and anyone who didn't was an evil person. But when the war was over, I worked with farmers and workers who had fought on the other side. I knew what it was to be hungry, and can understand why they fought for a better life.'

'But, Apu, you can't be on both sides.'

The old man sighed. 'I do not like violence, but I suppose if I'd had to fight for one side, it would have been the *Rojos*.'

'The *Rojos*? Which side was that?'

'The Republican side. The ones who wanted change.'

'Why the *Rojos*, Apu? Why choose that side?'

'It's just a feeling that it was the right side. When it comes to difficult decisions, you can listen to your head or your heart. I am not an educated man, so I listen to my heart.'

The old man smiled at the boy and kissed the top of his head.

'Now,' he said, 'time for sleep.'

'But, Apu, you didn't tell me about your papá.'

'There's nothing to tell. He probably died in the war. Many people did.'

'Probably?'

'I don't remember.'

'You don't remember when your papá went to heaven?' said the boy.

'I was brought up in an orphanage, but I don't remember anything before I arrived

11

there. It's as if my memory was wiped clean. I've tried to remember, but I can't. Not a face, not a name. I tried to find out, but many records were destroyed during the war.'

'How old were you when you went to live at the orphanage?'

'About your age, maybe? I don't know.'

'I don't understand,' said the boy. He shook his head in puzzlement.

'I know which year I arrived at the orphanage. But I don't know what year I was born.'

Tino thought for a moment, his brow wrinkled. 'So,' he said hesitantly, 'so you don't know how old you are? Even now?'

'No.'

'And you don't know when your birthday is?'

'No,' said Alberto. 'I don't have a birthday.'

2

ISABEL

Afternoon, 7 March 1937

I look at the pitiful box of vegetables and my stomach sinks. How am I going to feed nearly a hundred orphans on such a meagre amount?

'Jorge!' I shout through the open kitchen window.

'Señorita?' comes the reply as Jorge's face appears outside.

'Are there any more vegetables in the garden? Look at this delivery we've just received — I can't feed them all on this.'

'There's not much, señorita, but I'll see what I can do.'

'Thank you, Jorge,' I smile. At least I know I can trust someone to help.

Rummaging around in the pantry, I find some old potatoes. With the eggs, I can make some dumplings. Thank the good Lord for our chickens.

Before she died, my mother had taught me how to make a meal from barely nothing. As the oldest child, it was a skill that helped me feed my father and five siblings. When my sister turned fifteen, I taught her all I could about running the home so that I could leave — our father needed one less mouth to feed.

My sister and I had been in the market one day when I'd overheard two women talking.

'Did you know they've turned the old house on the hill into an orphanage?' one had said to the other.

'Yes,' the second had replied. 'I heard they were bringing children from both sides.'

'Republican children too?'

'That's right. They want to teach them the mistakes of their parents. And the priests will make them accept God into their lives.'

'Well, that's something, isn't it? At least there will be a chance of salvation for the children. Can you imagine? Those poor things having no Communion, growing up without faith? I think it's disgusting. What kind of parent — '

I had interrupted the women to ask if they thought the orphanage would be taking on staff, and they told me where I could go to find out.

I'd been hired by Señora Peña, a large, red-faced woman whose husband was an administrator for the Nationalists. The orphanage had already taken in children from all around the region and she needed a cook to run the kitchen.

As the war has gone on, I've noticed more children arrive, and the food boxes become smaller. Every mealtime is a challenge, but I do my best to see these children have as good a meal as I can serve them.

As I set to preparing the dinner, the señora waddles into the kitchen and places a large silver tray on the table.

'The bishop has finished taking coffee with the father and is doing a tour of the classes. He wishes to visit the dining room when the children are eating their dinner, so make sure the meal is on time and plentiful.'

'Yes, señora,' I reply. There is little point in showing her the half-empty box of vegetables; she would only say there was more than enough for such small stomachs.

'And tidy this mess up in case he wishes to see the kitchen.' She waves her plump hand over the tray before bustling out of the room.

I finish making the dumplings and prepare a stew with the vegetables from the box. Jorge arrives with a handful of carrots, which I gratefully accept and add to the stew.

'Jorge, you deserve a cup of coffee,' I say, picking up the coffee pot.

'There's coffee?' asks Jorge, surprised.

'The bishop is here,' I reply.

'Ah,' says Jorge, nodding as he sits at the long kitchen table.

While the stew and dumplings bubble and the coffee brews, I clear the best china from the tray. As I pick up the plates, a glint of colour catches my eye. There, nestling under a saucer, is a piece of paper I recognize immediately. It is a chocolate-bar wrapper.

Holding my breath, I gently pull the paper, praying it isn't empty. It isn't. Unnoticed, the last few squares of chocolate have been left, hidden and forgotten.

'Look, Jorge,' I whisper, holding up the chocolate.

Jorge's eyes widen. 'What are you going to do with that?' he asks.

I know he is hoping I will share it with him. And for a moment I am tempted. I can't remember the last time I tasted chocolate — probably not since before the war began.

'I'll know when the time is right,' I say. I fold the wrapper carefully round the precious squares and pop it into my apron pocket.

Jorge tries to hide his disappointment as he nods his consent. 'I'll go and set up the chairs for dinner,' he says quietly as he limps out.

Poor Jorge. He told me he was injured in a farming accident as a young boy. He says his limp has never bothered him, but I know it does. He rarely talks about it, but others do,

16

and I know it was his leg that stopped him from fighting for the Nationalist forces. Now he feels he's failed to do his duty.

I know this because every Sunday, Señora Peña allows me to have the morning off to go to church. After the service, sitting in the shade of an old tree, the women sit and gossip. One day, I asked them about my friend at the orphanage and the story came out.

Jorge had a younger brother. An idealistic young man, he had become a local member of the Socialist Party. He had driven Jorge demented with his talk of oppression and rights for workers. Jorge is a religious man, and when his brother had spoken of a godless society, Jorge had not been able to hold his tongue. Their bitter argument turned violent and Jorge had thrown his brother out of the house.

The young man left for the city and became a political activist. Two years ago, Jorge heard that his brother had been arrested. The family have not heard from him since. Jorge still does not know if his brother was executed while a political prisoner, or if he was released when the Coalition of Socialists won the elections last year. Either way, Jorge believes the Republican movement took his brother from him.

When the war began, Jorge tried to join the army to fight for the Nationalists. I think he saw it as his chance to exert revenge on the Republicans — to beat the *Rojos*. He was rejected because of his limp. He tried again in two different towns but was told the pride of the Spanish National Army would not allow it. He argued that his passion for the cause would make him a better soldier than if he had two good legs. He was still refused.

Looking for another way to serve the Nationalists, he found work at the orphanage. He provides as much food as he can from the grounds and helps out as a handyman. I know he smuggles a few of the vegetables home to his wife and children, but he is a good man and cares for the orphans.

And the good Lord knows the poor little things need someone to care for them. They range in age from toddlers barely able to feed themselves to young adults who will soon be sent back out into the world. Many have been taken from their parents; some have seen their parents shot; all have witnessed things a child should not see.

The Church directs a strict programme of re-education at the orphanage, which the priests and Señora Peña follow enthusiastically. So the children are taught, often cruelly, that their parents were evil *Rojos* whose actions have condemned them to an eternity in hell. The father drills the children until their *generalísimo* salute is perfect.

Jorge and I are not allowed to spend time with the orphans. We keep our heads down and provide what we can from the garden and the meagre rations the Church sends. It is our small contribution to the war.

But despite knowing the fight against the anti-religious Republicans is right and just, my heart hurts when I see the little ones. They are constantly hungry, their shoes are worn through, and despite our best efforts, they are crawling with lice. And while the grand old house should be filled with their laughter and play, it is often silent with fear. These children have learnt to accept their lot. While the country fights on, their war is already lost.

★   ★   ★

As some of the older children and I finish serving the measly stew to the orphans, the bishop arrives at the dining room, flanked by the father and Señora Peña. Quickly, I withdraw to the kitchen and start the washing-up.

Jorge's face appears at the window. 'Isabel, another one's just arrived.'

Nodding, I dry my hands on my apron and hurry through the back door. The last thing Señora Peña will want is a scruffy orphan arriving unannounced in the middle of the bishop's visit.

Outside, a truck is parked on the driveway. Jorge is talking to the driver, a tall soldier, smart in his uniform. Beside them is a small boy. He is covered in dust and dirt, his shorts and jacket are torn, and one knee is caked in dried blood. He stands, looking at his boots.

'Good afternoon, señorita,' says the soldier as I approach.

'Good afternoon,' I smile at him. The soldier's eyes are implausibly dark and the sunlight makes them twinkle. He smiles back — so warmly and generously that I stop, realizing how rare such a smile is these days.

'Who is this?' I ask, nodding at the boy.

The soldier ruffles the boy's hair and says, 'My friend here doesn't talk much. He didn't seem keen on telling me his name. Or anything else for that matter. But he needs a new home. This is the only orphanage I could think of, so I brought him here.'

Bending down, I look at the boy. Sun-bleached curls frame his face.

'Hello,' I say cheerfully. 'My name is Isabel. What's yours?'

The boy doesn't even seem to register my

20

existence and continues to look at his boots.

I try again. 'Where are you from, child?'

He continues to ignore me.

After a pause, Jorge asks the soldier where he found the boy.

The soldier glances around, but realizing there's no one to hear, he says quietly, 'I heard the fighting had reached my home town. I was delivering supplies not far away, so I took a detour to check my family were all right. Father Francisco from my family's church was looking after him. He wouldn't tell me how the child had come to him, but he asked that I take him out of danger.'

The soldier looks down at the boy sadly. 'He hasn't spoken a word, and we've been driving most of the day.'

'He's probably seen things he doesn't want to talk about,' says Jorge softly.

'We passed a stretch where there had recently been a battle. There were dead *Rojos* near the road. It seemed to affect him quite badly,' agrees the soldier.

As I reach to stroke the boy's face, he flinches and, in his terror, looks at me for an instant. His eyes are soft brown, flecked with green. I hear a rustle from his pocket and notice a piece of paper flutter to the ground.

Picking it up, I see it is the torn triangle of an envelope. On one side, the name ALBERT

ROMERO is clearly written. There is more writing on the other side. This is a little harder to decipher, but with a gasp I realize that it is an address in England.

Quickly, I squirrel it into the pocket of my apron and look up. The soldier is sharing a cigarette with Jorge and chatting about whether the fighting will reach us. I don't think they've seen the piece of paper.

Grasping the boy's hand, I say loudly, 'Jorge, I'm taking the boy into the kitchen to get him cleaned up. Don't be long — the señora may need you.'

I turn to the soldier. 'Thank you, señor.'

The soldier smiles back as I turn and walk away.

The boy trots along obediently beside me. As I open the back door, I turn and see the soldier is still looking at me. I lift my hand in a small wave before shooing the child inside.

In the kitchen, I motion the boy over to the long oak table, where he sits, still looking at his boots. I open the bread bin and take out the last crust. I was saving it for my supper, but I can do without. With my finger I drill a hole into the middle of the hard bread and then reach into my apron pocket and take out the chocolate. Unwrapping it carefully, I stuff the chocolate into the bread and pop it into the warm oven.

Then I rinse a cloth in water and approach the boy, who eyes me suspiciously.

'I'm just going to wash your face, Alberto,' I say gently.

I lift his chin and start to wipe the grime off his face. He looks around slowly, taking in his new surroundings.

'This is an orphanage, Alberto. There are lots of other boys and girls like you here. You'll soon have friends. How old are you, Alberto? Have you been to school? You will have lessons here. The priests take the classes and will teach you to read and write.'

I continue cleaning the boy and speaking gently to him as I do so, although he does not respond. Eventually, his face and hands are clean and I rinse the filthy cloth in the sink. Then, opening the oven, I take out the toasted bread, wrap it in a little paper and hand it to the boy.

He accepts it sceptically and sits, holding it.

'Alberto,' I say quietly, hunching down to his level. 'Alberto, the orphanage is run by people who do not like the *Rojos*.' I reach into my pocket, bring out the piece of paper and hold it in front of him. 'Who gave you this?' I ask.

The boy looks at me intently but remains silent.

'Alberto, this is an address in England. Did you meet a Republican soldier? Did he give you this?'

The boy just looks at me.

I sigh and brush a dusty curl off his face.

'Alberto,' I say seriously, holding the paper in front of his face, 'this orphanage is run by the Church and supported by the Nationalists. When you do decide to talk again, do not speak of this.'

I stand, open the oven door and throw in the paper. It instantly curls and blackens; then a small orange flame flares, eating the paper until just a grey sliver of dust is left to settle on the floor of the stove.

I shut the door and turn back to the boy, but he is not looking. He has taken a bite out of the chocolate-soaked bread and is chewing it slowly.

He looks up at me, and I think I see the tiniest trace of a smile.

3

Alberto held the little boy's hand tightly as they walked along the corridor. The smell of disinfectant was pervasive and the child wrinkled his nose. Towards the end of the walkway, they reached a long window and Alberto slowed, looking in.

A large metal bed stood in the middle of the room. Lying on top of the white sheets, bound in white bandages, lay a motionless figure. Wires and tubes appeared from under the wrappings and were connected to a machine beside the bed. A woman in blue pyjamas, cap and face mask was adjusting a drip.

Sitting in a chair beside the bed was Juan Carlos's mother. A semi-transparent yellow garment covered her customary black dress, and plastic booties concealed her black slippers. She too wore a blue face mask and cap. Her eyes were shut and Alberto couldn't tell if she was deep in prayer or dozing.

Leaning over the bandaged head, talking gently to the man within was his daughter. She was wearing the same clinical garments as her mother-in-law, her long, dark curls swept up into a cap.

Absorbed in watching his daughter, he didn't notice Tino let go of his hand, stand on his tiptoes and peer into the room — not until he heard a small gasp. Looking down, he saw the boy's mouth open in shock and his wide eyes filling with tears. Juan Carlos's mother's head snapped up in time to see the old man pulling the reluctant child away from the window.

Leading him to some nearby chairs, Alberto helped the boy into the seat and sat next to him.

'Apu, was that really Papá?' he whispered. Large tears ran down his cheeks.

'Yes, it was,' he replied gently.

At that moment, the door opened and Tino's mother walked out of the room. He jumped up and ran to her, and she took off her mask and bent down to hug him.

Alberto stood. After some quiet words, his daughter wiped the tears from her son's eyes and led him back to Alberto.

'Well?' he asked.

Rosa sighed. He could see she was exhausted.

'The doctor was worried Juan Carlos would go into shock last night. But he's done well over the past few hours and they say he is stable now. The pain relief is very strong. He's not conscious, but we speak to him constantly, so he knows he's not alone.'

Alberto nodded.

'I've been talking to the nurses. They say over the next few days it is essential that he avoids any risk of infection.' She stopped speaking and looked down at her son, who held her hand with both of his. 'I cannot leave Juan Carlos. Could Tino stay with you a little longer?'

'You know he can stay as long as is necessary.'

Smiling weakly, Rosa nodded gratefully to her father.

★   ★   ★

Tap, tap, tap — the long stick struck the top branches and a hard brown shower of nuts bounced onto the green netting under the tree. Tino waited until the last almond had fallen, then, picking out the occasional leaf, gathered the nuts and put them into a large plastic bucket. Then he stepped back to the edge of the netting as his grandfather moved over to some other almond-laden branches and began tapping again.

When the tub was full, Alberto carefully put down the stick. Nodding to the boy, he picked up the tub and carried it over to the edge of the terrace, where they sat, in the shade of a lemon tree. The sun was still in full heat, and the pale brown earth on the terrace was cracked like an over-baked cake.

Alberto opened a bottle of water he had brought and handed it to the boy, who took a long drink. The old man took a few gulps and settled the bottle in the shade. Then he and Tino set to peeling the hard, leathery husks from their harvest, throwing the skins on the ground and putting the nuts with their distinctive pitted shells into a canvas bag.

'Apu?' asked the boy as they worked.

'Yes.'

'If you don't know when your birthday is, do you still get birthday presents or have a party?'

'No.'

'But just because you don't remember the date doesn't mean you can't just pick another date.'

'Hmmmm.'

'It's my birthday soon. I'm going to be eight.'

'I know.'

'Apu?'

'Yes.'

'Would you like to share my birthday with me? We could have a party together.'

The old man stopped and looked at the

boy. 'That's very kind of you,' he said.

He remembered the years that his wife had tried to do the same thing. Although the government had given him a date for his papers — 1 January — he had never thought of it as his birthday. Instead, María Luisa had suggested dates, both random and those that were important to them. He had never agreed, saying it was silly and pointless. But when their children had come along, he had enjoyed the presents and parties she'd organized for them, glad when they'd taken it for granted. That was how a childhood should be.

'I'm too old for birthday parties now,' he said, smiling.

'But, Apu,' continued Tino, 'everyone should have a birthday. Even Grandma has a birthday every year — that's how we know she's so old.'

'Do I need a birthday to know that I am old?' asked Alberto.

'No,' agreed the boy. 'But don't you want to have a birthday?'

The old man shrugged. 'I have managed all these years without one.'

'Everyone should have a birthday, Apu.'

'Why is that?'

'Because a birthday is your day. It's the day when everybody comes to visit you. They bring gifts, and food, and you are with the people who love you. It's a special day, Apu.'

Alberto looked at the boy, bemused.

'You don't know, Apu. Because you've never had a birthday. You don't know how it feels. It's a good day. I want you to know how it feels.'

Alberto nodded. 'Well, maybe you're right. But I would need a date for a birthday.'

'You can share mine.'

'No.' The old man shook his head. 'That is your special day, not mine. It's good of you to offer to share it, but that day is just for you.'

Tino frowned, peeling the tough coat off an almond. 'Then we will have to find your birthday,' he said.

* * *

That evening, Alberto sat in his weathered armchair, sipping a glass of brandy. His other daughter, Cristina, had married well and she and her husband lived in Madrid. Each year at Three Kings, they would visit with their family. They would present Alberto with an expensive bottle of brandy, which he accepted uncomfortably and savoured in private.

The television shouted the results of the lottery, but Alberto paid it no attention. The conversation about his birthday tap, tap, tapped at his mind. It had unsettled him, and he could not understand why. He had spent so many years not knowing his birthday. Why should the idea of it start to nag at him now? Was it that he was getting old, that he wanted to know before he died?

Suddenly, a shriek came from the other room.

Running next door and switching on the bedroom light, he saw the boy sitting up in bed, glossy with sweat. They had been to Rosa's apartment earlier and picked up a bag of clothes, so the child was dressed in his own pyjamas. A small, tatty brown bear lay discarded beside him on the bed.

Alberto moved the bear so he could sit down and gathered the boy into his arms, stroking his damp head.

'Was it a dream?' he asked gruffly.

The boy started sobbing, clinging tightly to his grandfather.

Alberto hushed the boy, rocking him gently.

'Tell me,' he urged in a whisper.

Hiccupping air, the boy burrowed his head deeper into his grandfather's chest. 'It was Papá. He was trying to get out of the bandages, but they just kept wrapping more and more round him. I was shouting to let him out, but they didn't hear me. Apu, they wouldn't listen to me.'

'Shhh,' said the old man. He held the child tightly and rocked him. He tried to reassure him with words he believed to be true. 'The doctors and nurses are helping him get better. They're looking after your papá. Soon they'll take the bandages off and you'll see him again.'

Reluctantly, the old man remembered in the years after the war seeing men horribly disfigured by burns. But, these days, the medics could do so much more for the victims. At least, he hoped they could. He felt the child's tears soak into his shirt.

'Now, now, little one. It was just a bad dream. Dreams like that don't come true. Forget about it and think of things that make you happy. Think how when your papá is better, you'll play football with him at the park.'

Tino snuffled noisily.

'Think about your birthday party,' whispered the old man. 'Your cake, covered with cream, and all those presents waiting to be opened. And the party with your friends and the games you'll play.'

'And your party too, Apu,' sniffed the boy sleepily. 'When we find your birthday.'

Alberto smiled, relieved that something had distracted the child from his distress.

'Yes,' said Alberto quietly. 'We'll have a party when we find my birthday.'

He felt the exhausted child relax in his arms and laid him down on the pillow, tucking the bear into the crook of his arm. Then he stayed awhile, making sure the boy was sound asleep, before going back into the living room, leaving the door open.

Sighing, he rubbed his eyes, picked up the glass of brandy and swallowed the remainder, relishing the sensation as the liquid slid down his throat.

★   ★   ★

Over the next few days, Alberto and the boy spent all of their time together. The old man was concerned to see Tino subdued and tense, so spent as much time as possible on his land keeping the child busy.

Together, they visited tree after tree, tapping the almonds to the ground. When all the nuts were harvested and rid of their husks, the old man loaded the last canvas bags onto the moped and walked the heavy bike along the road.

Back at the apartment, Alberto took two chairs downstairs to the street outside his apartment. He and Tino sat on the pavement, the bags of nuts between them. The old man gave the boy a simple nutcracker.

'Mind your fingers,' he told him.

While the boy set to cracking his first nut, Alberto stood a tall log between his legs and took a small hammer out of his pocket. Lifting an almond out of the nearest canvas bag, he placed it on the top of the neatly cut log and brought the hammer down on it with a swift rap. The almond shell split neatly, and he swept the broken bits onto the ground as he dropped the wrinkled nut into a large glass jar next to the boy.

'Apu?' said Tino as he emptied broken shells onto the pavement.

'Yes.'

'Where was the orphanage you lived at?'

'Inland. It was a big hacienda surrounded by farmland. In the summer, it was as hot as here, but in the winter, it was bitterly cold and often snowed.'

'But, Apu, now you live by the sea. Why did you come here?'

'When the war ended, we were moved to a bigger institution in the city. That was a terrible place and I left as soon as I could. But the country was very poor then and there were no jobs. I was young, but I went looking for work and took it where I could find it. At harvest times, I would work on the farms for my food and keep. At other times, I would work in towns to help the builders reconstruct everything that had been destroyed in the war.

'I travelled all over the country, sometimes walking, sometimes catching a lift on the back of a cart. After a while, I came to the coast. I found work at a farm during the olive harvest. It was at that farm I met my wife, your grandmother.'

Alberto remembered the farm and the long, sunny days he'd spent plucking the fat black olives from the trees, chatting easily with the farmer's youngest daughter. She'd had curvy hips, a sassy attitude and a raucous laugh. She'd made him smile, and at lunch when the family and workers had sat at a long trestle table to eat, she'd served him larger portions than anyone else.

Her father had joked that if María Luisa continued to feed him so well, Alberto would become too fat to work and they'd have to let him go. Alberto had blushed, not used to being included in the lively banter of close family and friends. But the family had warmed to the shy boy María Luisa adored, and when the olive harvest had finished, her father had found more work for him on the farm.

'And so you wanted to stay?' asked his grandson.

'And so I wanted to stay.'

'And you never went back to where the orphanage was?'

'No.'

'We should go there.'

'Why?'

'Because that's where we should start looking for your birthday.'

'Why do you think I'll find my birthday there?'

'I don't know. But I think it's the only place to start, Apu. Don't you?'

Alberto smiled and nodded at the boy.

'Well, if I were going to go looking for my birthday, you're right — it's the best place to start,' he said.

Looking up from his nutcracker, the boy smiled at his grandfather. It was only a small smile, but Alberto was relieved to see it.

'Well, you two look very pleased with yourselves,' said a cheery voice.

A wide woman walked up the street towards them. She was dressed in a blue-and-white patterned dress and carpet slippers. Her rosy cheeks glowed, and her broad smile revealed a missing tooth. Her grey hair was set in large curls, the rollers only recently removed.

'Señora Ortiz,' said Alberto. He politely nodded his head and set down the hammer.

'We're going looking for Apu's birthday, señora,' said Tino gleefully.

'Are you? Well, I hope I can come to the party when you find it!' said the señora. She winked at Alberto.

'Oh yes, Apu. We'll have to organize your first ever birthday party! Mamá can make all the food and there will be presents.'

'That's a lovely idea, little one,' said the señora. She reached down and pinched Tino's cheek. 'The whole village will come to Alberto's birthday party.'

Alberto smiled and shook his head at the silliness.

★ ★ ★

'But, Papá, I don't understand,' said Rosa, frowning.

'It's just for a few days. I think it will be good for him.'

The old man had thought long and hard about it. Each evening, they had come to the hospital to look through the window at Juan Carlos, and each night, the nightmares had returned. Despite spending a busy day outdoors in the sunshine, the child had grey shadows under his eyes.

Worried about him, Alberto had let his grandson chatter on about the search for his birthday, happy that it distracted him from the anxiety he felt over his father. Finally, a week after Juan Carlos's accident, he'd decided to ask his daughter if he could take his grandson away. They would travel inland to the orphanage — if it was still there. Most likely, that would be the end of the search, but at least the journey and change of scene would take Tino's mind off his father.

'But a family should be together — especially at a time like this,' said his daughter. 'And what about Tino? Shouldn't he be near his father?'

'He's having nightmares, Rosa. Seeing his father like this upsets him. He doesn't want to say anything to you, but he's afraid to come into the hospital.'

His daughter looked at him, still confused. 'But what about me, Papá? Doesn't he want to be with me?'

The old man looked at his daughter and saw the anxiety in her eyes. Perhaps he shouldn't have suggested it. A nurse had taken Tino off to the canteen to get a drink and Alberto had seen his opportunity to talk privately to Rosa. But it seemed he had made a mistake. The last thing he wanted to do was upset her more. His daughter knew what was best for her son, not him — it should be her decision.

'Let him go,' said Juan Carlos's mother

from across the corridor.

Alberto and his daughter both looked round in surprise. They hadn't realized she had heard their conversation.

'But — ' said Rosa.

'No. It's not good for him to see his father like this. He enjoys being with his grandfather. And a trip will be good for both of them.'

'We'll only be away a few days,' said Alberto gently. 'And Cristina arrives tomorrow afternoon. You'll have your sister with you.'

'Well . . . ' said his daughter.

'By the time they come home, his father will be much better,' said Juan Carlos's mother firmly.

'Ask him, Rosa,' said Alberto. 'Ask the boy what he wants to do.' As his daughter looked up at him, Alberto nodded to her. After what seemed like an age, she slowly nodded back at him.

Alberto looked across at Juan Carlos's mother as she prepared to go back into the hospital room, tying her mask behind the back of her head. He smiled his thanks at her.

'But,' said Rosa, 'where did you say you were going?'

'He wants to find my birthday.'

'And, after all these years, you want to look for it?'

'Rosa, it's caught his imagination. It's all he talks about. And I let him, because while he's thinking about my birthday, he's not thinking about his father in hospital.'

'But what about you, Papá? Do you want to go back?'

'It was sixty-five years ago; we won't find anything. I expect nothing.'

But in truth, he was looking forward to the trip. As a young man, he had spent years on the road, never knowing where the next day would take him. Meeting people and seeing new places had given him an education, and sometimes he wished he'd travelled further to see what the world had to offer. But marrying and settling down had been good for him, and he had cherished the security he had found with his small family.

The thought of the trip filled him with a sense of anticipation he hadn't experienced in many years.

'Well, if you do find your birthday, I hope you're not expecting presents for all those years we missed!'

Alberto smiled warmly — it was the first time since Juan Carlos's accident that he had seen his daughter's face relax and her eyes soften. If Tino was happy to go, perhaps this trip would be good for all of them.

4

CAPTAIN GARCÍA

Morning, 7 March 1937

Smoothing down my hair, I place my hat carefully on my head. Then I run my thumb and forefinger down my moustache, checking every hair is in place. Next I feel my collar, to make sure there are no creases. And lastly, adjusting my gun holster, I look down and inspect my gleaming jackboots for dust.

A man gains respect by maintaining excellence in everything he does. It is important my men look up to me, not just for my intelligence and courage, but also for my pride in the uniform and all that it stands for.

Perhaps it is because I have been in uniform most of my life that I hold the greatest of regard for it. Born into a military family, there was never any question that I would be anything other than an officer. My sisters are married to soldiers of high rank, and their sons will be enrolled into military academies at a young age, as I was. Like me, they will realize the honour of their duty.

They will learn that the military is the guardian of Spain.

Satisfied, I step outside the small house my squadron has commandeered. The village is quiet for the time of morning. A few of my men stroll around the square; they are far too relaxed for my liking. We have been informed the Republican rabble is nearby and we must be ever vigilant.

Two young women scuttle past, their dark shawls pulled around their faces. They avoid looking at me — they are, no doubt, *Rojos*.

I bark at my men, and startled, they turn and salute me. Instantly their backs straighten and they look like professional soldiers. I command them to patrol the outskirts of the village and report back to me in an hour.

I fully intend to be a general before too long. While my family connections stand me in good stead for promotion, I want to prove my merit to my superiors. My whole life has been designed to take me to the highest levels of the army, and this war has propelled me at even greater speed towards this goal. I will become a general and help Franco achieve a glorious victory.

Scanning the square, I decide to visit the church. Usually, there is a decent cup of coffee and helpful information to be garnered when one introduces oneself to the clergy.

They like to show their support in any way they can.

The church sits on one side of the square. I push open the heavy wooden door and stride inside. It is cool and dark and smells of dust and old incense. In the gloom, I see a few elderly women, kneeling, praying and worrying rosaries. To one side of the altar, an ancient man with a crooked back sweeps the floor. He glances at me and brushes his way into a shadowed corner and out of sight.

My heels click on the stone floor as I approach the altar. When I reach the front, I stop, drop to one knee, cross myself and close my eyes. At that moment, I hear murmurings nearby. Rising, I walk quietly towards the noise. By a side door is the priest, dressed in his black robes. He is talking in a low voice to a small, filthy boy.

'Good morning, Father,' I say loudly.

The priest jumps at the sound of my voice and turns to me, pushing the child behind him. Probably in his early forties, he is relatively tall with receding hair and silver spectacles. The other priests I have known have generally been portly, but this man is well built for his age. For an instant, I imagine him in an officer's uniform, and he looks good in it.

'I am Captain García,' I introduce myself.

'My men and I are here to maintain the security of this town.'

The priest nods and smiles stiffly at me. This is not the sort of welcome I am used to from a cleric.

'Good morning, Captain. I am pleased to meet you. My name is Father Francisco. This is my church, and my village.'

I glance around and notice the old women have slipped out and the church is now empty.

'Father Francisco, there are reports of Republicans in the area, and as you are a respected clergyman of the community, I wish to discuss with you how my men can defend this town. Are you free now?' I nod towards the dirty child.

The priest steps behind the boy, putting his hands on his shoulders protectively.

'Yes, of course. Please accept my apologies. Alberto here has recently arrived at the church. It seems he has lost his family and I am looking after him while we arrange where he will go.'

'I'm sure you can find an orphanage near here,' I reply sharply, annoyed that he puts this child before the welfare of my men and our cause.

A look crosses the priest's face and I wonder momentarily if I have angered him before dismissing the thought.

'Yes, Captain,' he replies politely.

With that, he opens the small door beside him and indicates for me to step outside. The door opens onto a walled cemetery in the church grounds, where stone crosses and gravestones stand to attention in the browned grass. A large carob tree casts a little shade on the rear of the churchyard.

The priest follows me and the boy steps out of the church after him. Pulling the door shut, the priest gestures to a bench leaning against the church wall and the boy obediently sits on it.

I notice the priest look at the ground. I follow his gaze and see I am standing within the rectangular outline of a grave. At its head is a simple cross, but there is no name inscribed on it. It is completely blank.

As I step off the grave and onto the gravel path, the priest asks, 'So, Captain, how may I be of service?'

'Father, I have not breakfasted yet,' I reply. 'I was wondering if we might take a cup of coffee together.'

'Captain,' says the priest smoothly, 'I'm embarrassed to say that I have no coffee. The cafe on the plaza is still open — they serve chicory coffee — perhaps you would like to talk there?'

'Do you not receive extra rations, Father?' I ask, puzzled.

'What I receive, I share,' says the priest piously. 'There are others in more need than myself, and I am more than content with chicory.'

'Never mind the chicory,' I snap. I am becoming annoyed at this confounding behaviour. 'What do you know of the *Rojos'* movements in the area? Will they find support in this village?'

'I'm afraid I have no news to tell of Republicans in this area, Captain,' says the priest, tight-lipped.

'Father, I am sure you are aware of your obligation to tell me of any *Rojo* activity here,' I nudge. I sense his reluctance to divulge information.

Taking a deep breath, the priest speaks quietly. 'Captain, as all over Spain, this village is split. Families, friends and neighbours have been divided by allegiances to one side or the other. The young men have all left to fight. The elderly and women who remain do not voice their loyalties, but fear and distrust lie close to the surface. Just yesterday, we had to pull apart two sisters who would have gouged each other's eyes out if left to fight. Their husbands joined opposing armies, and — '

'This country is at war, Father,' I interrupt.

46

I am not interested in tattle tales of his villagers, and I will not be drawn into a discussion about some women. 'Just tell me what you know about the enemy's movements around here.'

The priest looks at me, his face set. 'There have been rumours that the fighting is drawing near, but I know nothing more. In my services, I continue to pray for a conclusion to the war and a lasting peace for the people of this country.'

'I assume that you are praying for a glorious victory for the *generalísimo*.' I scowl at him. I am growing suspicious of this priest. Could it be that he is a collaborator?

'I do not feel it is my place to take sides. I only know that I am a follower of Christ the Lord,' he replies softly.

As the man talks, I feel a rage stir in me.

'Father,' I say, seething, 'must I remind you, of all people, of the attacks on the Church, and the brutality shown to Catholic priests? The Nationalists stand with the Spanish Church. Together, we will repel this evil.'

'Sir,' replies the priest quietly, 'my position in this village is to support my flock through these difficult times. My only weapon is the word of the Lord. In His glory He tells us to strive for peace, He teaches us that wisdom is better than the weapons of war, and — '

As he speaks, the fury in me rises and I shout at him, 'How dare you preach at me! I have personally seen the bodies of men and women who were buried alive — their only crime being their faith in God. I have seen the ruins of churches where Catholics were locked inside, burnt to death as Republican firefighters looked on. Thousands of your brethren have been murdered and you speak the words of a pacifist! Do their deaths mean nothing to you?'

'Captain,' he replies, his voice low, 'I pray for every soul lost in this futile war. But atrocities should not be matched by further atrocities. Where will it end? Our country will be only flooded with blood.'

'Good God, man!' I holler. 'If it were not for the support of the righteous of this country, your Church would have been destroyed. And where would you be then? As poor as the pathetic creatures scraping a living in the fields.'

The priest pulls his shoulders back and looks me straight in the eye. For a moment, we glare directly at each other. Behind his spectacles, his dark green eyes flash with passion, and as I look into them, I see him make a decision.

'I would be honoured to work alongside

the poor,' he says. His voice wavers, but his words are emphatic.

We stare at each other, both aware of what he has done. These are the words of a Republican: he is a traitor.

In that moment, it is my turn to make a decision.

I suck a ball of saliva behind my teeth and spit it at him with all the venom I can muster.

The spit lands on his left cheek, and for an instant, I am as shocked as he is. I know what I have done is a sacrilege, unforgivable. But this is not a man of the Church. He is the enemy.

As he stands, still staring at me, I turn to leave, but suddenly I hear a shrill voice scream, 'No!'

It is the boy. He has been watching everything, and as I look, he runs towards me.

'Alberto, stop!' shouts the priest, but the boy ignores him. As he reaches me, I see his hands are clenched into small fists, and with a speed and strength I did not expect of him, he lands a blow on my thigh.

It hurts more than I let on, but as he lifts his other arm to hit me again, I strike him hard across the face with the back of my hand. The clout sends him crashing to the ground and he skids across the dirt.

I watch the priest dash over to the boy, spittle still hanging from his cheek.

Taking a deep breath, I adjust my jacket and holster, check my hat and run my fingers over my moustache.

'I can see little reason to defend this pitiful place and its inhabitants,' I say with disdain. Looking down at the priest kneeling by the boy, who is nursing a bloodied knee, I conclude with the words, 'It seems the enemy is already here.'

With that, I turn on my heel and stride past them.

* * *

The wind is strong and the eucalyptus trees creak high above us. For the last ten minutes, it has been quiet on both sides. The brown dust loosened by gunshots has been whipped up and swirls round the patch of land between us. It makes it hard to see where the enemy hides, and the wind steals the sounds that would give them away.

'Captain?' queries the soldier crouching beside me by the ditch wall. His build is solid and stocky, but his gun shakes in his hand, betraying his fear.

'We wait,' I say quietly to him. 'We'll let them give themselves away.'

I glance along the ditch, checking my men. They all keep their heads below the top of the dusty line of fire, awaiting my command. Glancing over the top of the earthy ridge, I see the fallen men lying between us and the Republican enemy.

Earlier in the day, my men brought me word that a band of *Rojos* had been spotted a few miles out of the village. We assembled quickly and went out on foot. Surprise has been our greatest weapon and I knew we did not have time to wait for the reinforcements and armoured vehicles we had been expecting.

We came up behind them near a stretch of road about five miles from the village. They were ambling along, relaxed and chatting among themselves. They must have had no communications that we were in the area, but that is no excuse. At the very least, they should have been securing their flanks. The lack of military discipline appalled me. I quietly directed my men into a nearby ditch, where they swiftly set up the machine gun. And on my command, they opened fire.

Of course, many of the Republican soldiers were shot in the back, and those that turned towards us had little time to raise their guns before we scythed them down. The few that survived managed to dive behind a small hillock on the other side of a dusty patch of land from us. They started firing and shots flew in both directions. Then the wind sprang up, swirling dust around us all, and the firing ceased. Now both sides are waiting for the other to make the first move.

Two of my men are dead. Or rather, one is dead. The other continues to moan and plead for help where he lies, but I refuse to let my men rescue him. I can see no point in risking more soldiers for the sake of a man who will most likely die anyway. I saw the hate in my men's eyes when I refused to let them collect him, but I don't care: I know they will channel that hatred into fighting the enemy.

The gunner sits nearby, our only machine gun wedged into the rocks beside him. He is young, probably about nineteen, and keeps his short hair neatly cropped. I know his name is Luis, but I would never call him that. I cannot be seen to be too personal with my men.

As I watch the gunner, he digs in his pocket for a packet of cigarettes and lifts one to his mouth with a shaking hand. Then, after more digging, he pulls out a box of matches. The first breaks as he strikes it. The second lights, but his hand is shaking so violently he can't get it close to the cigarette.

Instinctively, I reach out and grip his wrist.

Luis looks up at me, surprised, but lets me guide his hand to the cigarette hanging from his lips. As he sucks the life into it, I let go and he nods his thanks.

I can remember when fear had gripped me with such intensity too.

Shortly after the war began, I was given my first command and we were sent to a city that was being occupied. Although my training had been extensive, this was to be my first true battle. However, the *Rojos* had been weakened by the fall of a nearby city, and by the time we arrived, our forces were entering the city's outskirts and we'd joined them.

My instructions had been to take prisoners, but as we stepped over enemy soldiers dead on the road, it was clear that they had been executed. The military academy had instilled in me honour above all, and I did my best to hide my shock.

As we carried on, we heard shots from the city centre. Turning a corner, we came to a small plaza, where dozens of *Rojo* soldiers were standing, their hands behind their heads. They were surrounded by our men, guns trained on them from every direction. A general had noticed me and called me over. Leaving my men, I ran over to speak to him. After the initial formalities, he said, 'I'm glad you're here, García. I have been instructed to be at the bullring. These men need despatching; you may now take over.'

'The prisoners, sir?' I replied, confused.

He looked me square in the face, and I lifted my chin in an attempt to show confidence. I failed.

'This is your first time, isn't it?' he asked quietly.

'Sir, I was highly commended at the academy — '

'Yes, yes, I see,' he interrupted, sighing. 'Look, I know it's not what you learn at the academy, but these filthy *Rojos* need be despatched.'

'But, sir — '

'Just do it!' he snapped. Then, his face softening a little, he said, 'By killing these enemy soldiers, you are protecting your mother and your sisters. Do it in the name of the Lord Himself, for we are the protectorate of the Catholic Church.'

'Yes, sir!' I said loudly, saluting him.

He started towards the motorcycle beside him, but turned back briefly to say, 'Oh, and don't waste bullets, García. One each.'

I nodded at him.

It took all my strength to control my voice as I gave my men their orders. We had corralled the prisoners at one end of the square and led a line out into the centre. The prisoners had realized what was happening, but seeing our numbers were so great, understood that any attempt to escape would be futile.

I could see how uncomfortable my men were with their task, so I decided that I should fire the first shot. I ordered the most senior Republican out in front of the rest and took my pistol from its holster. My enemy stood tall in front of me. He looked noble in front of his men. I unclipped the safety catch on my gun, noticing how badly my hands shook, and knew that the only way to mask my fear was to act quickly.

Dispelling all thoughts of morals, I lifted my gun to the back of his head and pulled the trigger. The man crumpled at my feet.

'Fire!' I instructed my men.

The shots rang out and the line of men fell. Shouts and screams came from the remaining prisoners as my soldiers dragged the bodies into the corner of the plaza. As they brought out the next line of men, a lone voice could be heard. One man had begun singing the 'Himno de Riego'. His voice trembled, but his fellow men quickly joined in the Republican anthem.

Soon, the force of the other voices gave them strength and they'd sung over the sounds of the gunshots as more of their men had fallen.

'*Soldiers, the country calls us to the fight. Let us swear for her to conquer or to die.*'

I let them sing. They sang to the very last man. And when the singing of that accursed song had stopped, we piled the final bodies in the corner of the plaza and moved further on into the city. By then, I was a different man.

When we reached the bullring, we discovered killing on a much larger scale. Men and women, soldiers and civilians were mown down in front of my eyes. Not all of them had been killed outright, and the sounds of the dying had turned my stomach.

But I presented myself to the nearest officer and we soon were recruited into the massacre. Since that day, killing has become easier. Now, I have no compunction in bringing death to my enemy. It is my duty: I do it for my country, for Franco and for God.

★　★　★

The gale continues to roar across the dry, barren land and blows grit from the edge of the ditch into my eyes and mouth. Suddenly, I notice the sound has changed. As I close my eyes and listen carefully, I realize it is not the wind making the noise at all.

Opening my eyes, I search the road behind us. And there, behind a whirl of dust, is an enemy armoured car rattling at speed towards us. I shout at my men, who turn and begin firing.

But the machine gun is facing the wrong way. As Luis struggles to move it, I see a man wearing overalls and a beret lean out of the moving vehicle, aim and fire at my gunner. The bullet hits its target, killing Luis instantly, as the two men beside him dive to the bottom of the ditch.

I gasp briefly, but quickly make myself focus on the situation. I shout my orders. Half of the men are to shoot at the truck as it hurtles along the dusty road; the bullets bounce off the armoured car, but my men continue to fire. The others are to get the machine gun cleaned up and ready it to use again. I turn my back to the body slumped in the ditch. I have come to terms with the realities of war, but have no wish to look at Luis's corpse.

We watch as the vehicle drives alongside us on the road, veering off suddenly towards the mound. There it stops, aims its guns towards us and starts firing again. The soldier standing beside me is too slow to duck behind the ditch edge and is hit in the neck. He falls beside me, grasping at his throat as blood bubbles out of the open wound. He turns his head towards me and reaches out to me. For a moment, I want to take his hand, but I stop myself.

I lean instead out of his reach. I glance away to avoid the pitiful look on his face. Thankfully, it is over quickly and his eyes glaze as he drops to the ground.

Through the settling dust, I can see the rescued Republican soldiers running to the rear of the vehicle, where they start to climb in. We carry on shooting, but it's an impossible task, as the truck rains bullets on us.

Then, incredibly, from the dip in the ridge where I am watching, I see one of the fighters run out from beside the truck. I can't believe it — he was safe. What is he doing? His hat is missing and his blond hair is blowing about in the wind. For a moment, it forms a perfect golden halo round his head. He skids to the ground by the edge of the road where one of their men lies. Slinging his gun over his shoulder, he grabs his comrade underneath his arms and starts to drag him towards the truck.

I look along the ditch and see my men are hunched below the ridge, only occasionally firing an aimless shot over their heads. By contrast, the Republicans are now leaning out of their truck firing at us. I watch as the blond soldier reaches the vehicle, and the others grapple the wounded man into it. The blond man then darts out again, weaving across the land back towards the road's edge.

I have had enough. Crouching low, I run along the ditch, instructing my men to cover me. They immediately start firing towards the truck, and I hear the scream of one of the enemy as he is struck. I carry on, scrambling over the body of a soldier I shouted at this morning.

As the ditch becomes more shallow, I sink to my stomach and start crawling. The ditch has curved towards the road, and I am now quite a distance from my men. Peeking above the edge, on my right I can see my men firing at the truck, which is now on my left. The *Rojos* have not seen me, and as I turn towards the road, I see the blond man kneeling by another fallen soldier.

But this time, he is shaking the soldier, shouting at him. It is clear that the man is dead. I lift my pistol. As I watch, the blond repeats the dead man's name: 'Ramón! Ramón!' Distressed, he runs his fingers through his fringe, pulling the hair off his face.

Spotting my moment, I rise to my knees, aim and fire. The bullet hits the blond in the chest and he falls slowly to the road's edge, a surprised look on his face. Diving back behind the ridge, a barrage of bullets hit the ground around me. I crawl as fast as I can back to my men, who have managed to set up the machine gun again and are firing at the vehicle.

As I reach my men, the armoured truck starts up and, with a lurch and a cloud of dust, rattles back to the road and roars away. My men cheer and slap me on the back. I do not approve of this disrespectful behaviour, but they have, in the main, been brave, so I indulge them in their celebration. They know I have made my point about trying to rescue fallen comrades. It may be loyal, it may be seen as courageous, but it is stupid and futile.

The dust of the armoured vehicle can just be seen in the distance as we scout across the land checking bodies. Occasional shots ring out as the wounded are despatched.

I am just walking round the mound the renegades were hiding behind when I see one of our trucks coming towards us, trundling along the road from the town. The lorry slows down as the driver sees me, but I wave him on — we don't need him, and the *Rojos* ahead will be long gone.

As he drives past, I see the boy who struck me at the churchyard sitting in the cab beside the driver. But he does not see me. He is staring, wide-eyed, at the blond fighter lying by the roadside.

The truck rumbles on as I walk over to the fallen soldier. Standing over him, I wonder if he is German or English. His silky hair has fallen back and reveals a young face with freckles scattered over a pointed nose. I look down at his scruffy, mismatched uniform: the half-turned-up shirt collar, missing jacket buttons and torn trousers. Sneering at his lack of pride in his uniform, I lift my pistol, aim at his forehead and fire.

5

The train softly jigged the small boy in his seat as he tried to navigate the orange segment into his mouth. He looked up at Alberto watching him and giggled. Alberto smiled back. When Rosa had asked Tino if he'd like to go away with his apu, he'd been thoughtful for a while, then asked if Papá would know he wasn't there. His mother had said when he asked, she'd tell him Tino was on an adventure with Apu. At that, the boy had thought some more, then suddenly seemed to make a decision. Yes, he'd said, he wanted to go.

They'd organized the trip quickly, and although he was clearly a little anxious, Tino had chattered as he helped Alberto pack a lunch to eat on the train. Early the next morning, after an hour's journey by bus, they had left the coast and reached the city. There, they bought tickets at the bustling station and found their train's platform.

Alberto had travelled a few times by rail, but the sleek white train they boarded was like transportation that had been sent from the future. The seats were comfortable, but the window was one large sealed unit that could not be opened. Alberto disliked the air-conditioning and felt ill at ease in the modern bullet shooting through the countryside. But the boy loved it and dashed from one window to the other, pointing out sights to his grandfather. There — a sunflower field. There — a church tower. There — a wind farm.

Alberto looked at the wind farm. Row upon row of tall white wind turbines slowly rotated against the backdrop of a cyan sky. Alberto remembered the old wooden windmill on a farm where he had worked when he was young. For a while, he trawled through his memories trying to locate where the farm had been, but he couldn't remember. He shook his head — if he couldn't remember facts from when he was a young man, how would he remember anything from his childhood?

★   ★   ★

Some time later, a metallic voice announced a station. Alberto leant over the boy and gently woke him. He had been exhausted by his excitement and had fallen asleep, his head leaning against the large window. Alberto gave him a nod and stood up, swinging his small bag over his shoulder.

As the train silently slowed to a standstill, they waited by the door, which suddenly slid open in front of them. Stepping out into the dry heat, Alberto took a deep breath and looked around. They were in a small town, but judging by the cranes all around, it would quickly become a larger one.

They walked along the platform as the train doors shut with a quiet clunk and the machine moved off with a hiss. They crossed the modern station of glass and brown brick, out onto the street. It was close to siesta time, so the streets were quiet, the shops pulling down their shutters.

Alberto walked over to a bus stop and squinted at the timetable behind the Perspex. When Tino came over to look, his grandfather showed him where they were going, and together they looked up the time. The bus was not regular, but luckily they only had half an hour to wait. They went back into the station, where a small cafe was open, and Alberto had a coffee, while the boy sucked chocolate milk through a straw. Then the boy took himself to the toilet and Alberto lit a cigarette. Watching Tino ambling back from the bathroom, looking in the counter at the ice creams and humming, the old man knew his decision to get away for a few days had been right.

★   ★   ★

The bus chugged wearily up the hill. When it reached the top, Alberto and Tino looked over the rolling countryside, covered with bottle-green trees. In front of them, the road snaked through the hills into the distance. As the bus eased downwards, Alberto saw a break in the trees and a large terracotta roof.

A little further on, a wide turn-off appeared on the side of the road and the bus slowed, then stopped. Alberto saw a small wooden sign that read, HACIENDA LOS ZORROS.

'Señor!' called the bus driver to his only passengers. 'Your stop.'

As Alberto stood and ushered the boy in front of him, the driver turned to them and explained, 'Los Zorros is the name of this mountain. There used to be many foxes in these hills. They say it was all you could hear at night — like an orchestra of screams. But in the war . . . ' He looked at the child and then up to Alberto. 'Well, in the war, it got too busy round here, so the foxes took their orchestra elsewhere,' he smiled, chuckling.

Tino didn't really understand the joke but smiled at the driver as he climbed off the bus.

'Thank you,' said Alberto to the driver, and

they nodded knowingly at each other.

As the bus rattled off, the old man and the boy stood at the end of a long dirt road. It disappeared into the tall trees' dark arches.

'Apu?'

'Yes.'

'Do you remember this?'

'Yes.'

As they walked out of the bright sun and into the mottled light of the pathway, the boy took his grandfather's hand. The old man found the shaded path unnerving — it was as if memories lurked in the shadows. Holding the child's hand reassured them both.

Birds squawked and cawed high above them, and occasionally they heard a small rustle in the bushes nearby. Although Alberto recalled this wood, it was different now. When he was a child, any bird or rabbit was a meal. The hunting had been intense until the woods were eerily silent, bereft of wildlife — even foxes.

The path bent round to the right, and suddenly they came across a large metal gate locked with an enormous padlock. Alberto stopped and looked at the gate, then at the boy.

'I think someone is telling us not to come in,' he said.

Tino scowled. 'We can't give up already,

Apu. We've come such a long way.'

Alberto shrugged and was considering climbing over it when the child suddenly slipped past him to the end of the gate, where he slid easily between the metal post and a gorse bush.

'Come on, Apu — it's easy,' Tino said to him from the other side of the gate.

Alberto sighed and eased himself round the edge of the gate, scratching his trousers on the prickly gorse.

On the other side of the gate, they walked further, and the light grew dimmer as the trees overhead became more dense. But after a while, they saw the path open out ahead, bathed in sunlight. As they walked out, they blinked up at the imposing white building in front of them. The high walls reached up to a roof covered in burnt-orange tiles. Bright red geraniums sat on small windowsills, creating splashes of colour against the clean white walls. A solid-oak door sported iron studs, and a black grille lay open against the wall to the left of the door.

They stepped out onto the driveway, which swept in a circle at the front of the house. In the centre, on a carpet of bright green grass, stood an old stone fountain, water trickling lazily from a nymph's mouth.

On the edge of the drive, and on either side

of the house, lay carefully manicured gardens featuring red and yellow flowers.

As Alberto looked at the healthy plants with approval, a man carrying a hoe appeared from the side of the house. Looking up with surprise, he crossed the gravel drive towards the old man and small boy.

'Good afternoon, señor,' he said respectfully. 'Can I help you?'

Alberto looked up at the imposing house again, staring for some time.

'Sir?' asked the man.

'I'm sorry,' said Alberto. 'I haven't been here for many years. Can I ask about the owner?'

'Yes, yes. Don García still lives here,' replied the man enthusiastically. 'Of course he is very elderly now, but he has so few visitors, I'm sure he will be delighted to see you both.'

* * *

Their footsteps echoed on the terracotta-tiled floor as they followed the housekeeper through the house. The gardener had introduced them to his wife, who looked after the house and the elderly gentleman owner. She did not seem to share her husband's enthusiasm for the don's visitors, but agreed to take them to him.

Her rubber-soled shoes were silent as she led them through high-ceilinged rooms filled with heavy oak furniture and antique rugs.

The señora stopped in front of two large panelled doors and spoke quietly to Alberto. 'Don García does not hear very well these days, so speak loudly and clearly. He is also not comfortable with children, so I'd ask your grandson only to speak when spoken to, which is unlikely. And I suggest you do not detain the señor for too long — for all our sakes.'

Alberto did not understand her last comment, but nodded to the woman, who turned the handle and slowly swung the giant doors open.

The boy grabbed Alberto's hand as they stepped into the dark room. Heavy curtains, which blocked out most of the sunlight, hung partially closed at the long windows. The housekeeper gently pulled the doors shut behind her and they stood still in the musty-smelling room.

Muskets and pistols hung on the walls, and the chimneybreast was decorated with a selection of sabres and swords. On the opposite wall hung an enormous, elaborately framed painting of Christ on the cross, weeping women at his feet, his wounds bleeding profusely and his pain palpable.

Alberto was mesmerized by the painting until he felt a sharp tug at his hand. He glanced down at the boy, who was biting his lip and staring. Alberto followed his gaze. A man so ancient he was barely more than a skeleton sat in a wheelchair in the gloomiest corner of the room. What was left of his white hair was parted sharply, and he had a patchy but precisely trimmed moustache. He was dressed in a dark, tailored suit, too large for his shrunken frame, and his shoes were brightly polished. Medals adorned his jacket, glinting as he reached down and with great effort began to wheel himself towards them.

When he was a few feet from Alberto, he stopped and, breathing deeply, said in a sharp, rasping voice, 'Can I help you?'

'Don García' — Alberto bowed his head slightly — 'my name is Alberto Romero, and this is my grandson.'

The old man nodded graciously at Alberto, ignoring Tino. 'And why are you here?'

'Señor, many years ago, I lived in this house. My grandson and I have come in search of some information about those times.'

'You lived in this house before me?'

'Yes, señor. It was during the time of the war.'

'The war?'

'That's right.'

'Many say that was a bad time for Spain, eh?'

'Yes,' said Alberto.

'And you? What is your opinion of the war?'

Alberto paused for a moment but answered, 'I was just a boy. Those times have passed. I believe it is better to look forward.'

'Hmm. You say you lived here before I moved here?'

'Yes, that's right.'

Don García sucked audibly on his teeth and ran his thumb and forefinger over his moustache before pointing an emaciated finger at Alberto. 'So you were an orphan?'

Alberto nodded slowly.

'A child of *Rojos*, no doubt.'

'I don't know,' said Alberto carefully. 'I don't remember my parents.'

'Mmm,' said the old man, sceptically.

'So, señor, you didn't visit the house during the war years?'

'No. I was too busy ridding the country of red filth,' sneered the man.

Alberto winced.

Pausing for a moment, he persisted, 'Could I ask when you moved here?'

'Franco himself bequeathed me this house. For my services in the war,' said the old man, tapping his medals. 'Those were the days,' he continued. 'The Franco years. Spain was blooming. Since he's been gone, the country has gone to the dogs — don't you agree?'

Alberto stood silent.

'Eh? Don't you agree?'

'I like being able to choose my government,' said Alberto deliberately.

At this, the ancient man started to laugh a wheezing laugh, but quickly began to gasp for breath. His wheezing soon turned to coughing that shook his entire bony body.

Alberto took a step towards him, but the old man lifted his papery face and scorned, 'Socialist rubbish!'

Alberto heard the boy gasp quietly, and squeezed his hand reassuringly.

'The country's run by snivelling, weak populists. And do you know who is to blame for this country's fall? Do you know who is the traitor?' He paused to take a breath, his watery eyes on Alberto. 'The king!'

With this, Don García began to cough again. He pulled a clean white handkerchief from his top pocket and coughed violently into it, crumpling in his chair.

Alberto began walking towards the door, pulling the riveted child with him.

'I think we will leave you now, señor,' he said firmly.

But as he reached for the door handle, the venomous voice rasped, 'He betrayed Franco — the hero who saved this country from godlessness. He prepared the king to take the reins. And how was he repaid? With treachery. The king turned his back on Franco and all that he stood for.'

Alberto turned to look at the ancient man.

'If the king were to walk into this house right now, do you know what I would do?' García paused, gulping small mouthfuls of air. 'I would spit in his face,' he hissed.

Alberto blinked at the wheezing body in the wheelchair, a wisp of a memory flickering in front of him, gone before he could grasp it. Then, turning quickly, he yanked the door open, grabbed Tino's arm and steered him out of the room. Without speaking, he marched through the house, the boy scampering to keep up.

When they reached the main door, Alberto stepped out into the sunshine and took a deep breath. He turned his face up to the sun and, still breathing deeply, rubbed his chest.

Suddenly, he folded over with a soft groan.

'Apu!' cried Tino, grabbing hold of his leg.

'Señor,' shouted the gardener. He dropped his hoe and dashed towards him.

Alberto lifted his hand to calm him and slowly stood up straight. His face was ashen and he let the gardener take his arm and lead him to a garden bench, where he sat down heavily.

The gardener called into an open window. When his wife's face appeared, he asked her to bring some water.

'Thank you,' said Alberto when he had his breath back. Looking into the gardener's worried face, he smiled and said, 'I'm fine. I just had a shock.'

He turned to the boy, who was on the verge of tears. Alberto reached out and touched his cheek. 'Don't worry, Tino. It will take more than a wicked old man to finish me off.'

Not for the first time, Alberto wondered if he'd done the right thing bringing the boy on this journey.

'Ah. Don García is on ferocious form today, is he?' asked the gardener. 'I'm sorry. I should have warned you. My wife calls me a fool, but it is in my blood to respect my elders, no matter how terrible they are.'

'He *is* a fool,' huffed the housekeeper as she approached with a large glass of water. 'He can't see that the old man is a snake, through and through. It's no wonder he's on his own — and has been all these years.'

Alberto thanked her for the water and gulped it down.

'My husband is only grateful to him,'

continued the housekeeper, 'because he kept his father in employment after the war. His father was a cripple and Don García was cruel to him all his life. But in a time when work was scarce, it was a job, and Papá Jorge could feed his children.'

'My father used to bring me here to help him when his walking became very bad,' continued the gardener. 'And when my father passed away, Don García let me carry on his work. I've worked here all my life. The old man is very particular about the garden, but I think his attention to detail shows.'

Alberto nodded. 'I admired your work when we arrived. The flowers are beautiful.'

'This was all vegetable gardens when my father was here. He had to feed over a hundred orphans during the war. He worked very hard in those years.'

'Yes, I remember,' said Alberto quietly.

'Oh!' cried the gardener. 'You were an orphan here?'

Alberto nodded.

'Do you remember my father?'

'A little,' replied Alberto, squinting. 'We weren't allowed to spend time with anyone like that, but I remember a man with a limp working outside. And a kind woman who prepared our meals — I can't recall her name.'

'Isabel!' stated the gardener proudly.

'Yes,' said Alberto, pleased. 'Señorita Isabel.'

'She left here at the end of the war. She married and went to live in her husband's town. I believe she still runs the restaurant there.'

'Oh,' gasped the boy. 'Apu, maybe Señora Isabel will remember you.'

Alberto looked at Tino, then back to the gardener. 'Is it far from here?'

'It's a few hours' drive. It used to take most of a day to get there, but the new *autopista* makes it a much faster journey. There's a bus that leaves in the morning.'

'In the morning?' repeated Alberto.

'Yes. And if you have nowhere to stay tonight, we would be honoured if you would stay with us.'

'Oh no,' said Alberto quickly, 'we could not impose. If you could direct us to a *hostería* — '

'Nonsense,' replied the gardener's wife sternly. 'You have both had a shock, thanks to that nasty old man. This boy looks quite exhausted. My husband will take you home with him now, while I see to Don García. He has a nurse here during the night, but I'll give him something to make him sleep before I go. He's upset enough people today.'

Taking the glass from Alberto, she patted the boy's head before returning into the house.

'Right,' said the gardener, 'I'll just tidy up my tools.'

As the gardener walked away, Tino turned to his grandfather.

Alberto smiled at him. 'Perhaps Isabel will know something, eh?'

His grandson grinned as he threw his arms around his apu and hugged him tightly.

6

MICHAEL

6 March 1937

I carefully fold the thin pages and slide them into the envelope. Sniffing the envelope, I remember how it smelt of June's perfume when it first arrived. Now, it smells of dirt. I tuck it into my top pocket and lean back against the ditch, looking up at the inky twilight sky. A short distance away, some of the men are singing softly.

What will she be doing now? Helping her mum wash up after tea, perhaps. Listening to the wireless with her brother. Maybe she's sitting at her father's desk, pushing that glorious auburn hair off her face as she writes me another letter.

I have no idea how many letters have gone astray, but each one that makes it to me is precious. I've read all of them so many times I know every word, every scratch of her pen, every smile or tear that accompanies the words. Half of the Spaniards I'm fighting with are illiterate, but they understand love, and they wink at me when they see me with June's letters.

'*And I say thank you to the Señor for the women. Yes, the women and the wine . . .*' sings a smooth, heavily accented Spanish voice, and I see Ramón stroll towards me in the gloom.

'*Amigo*,' I say, 'what's happening?'

'Nothing yet,' replies Ramón as he eases himself down beside me. 'We'll leave once it's dark.'

'Righto,' I say in English.

'Rrrighto,' mimics Ramón with his rolling tongue.

'Shut up,' I tell him in Spanish as he chuckles deeply.

'Rubio,' says Ramón, 'life does not always need to be so serious.'

'Ramón,' I reply sternly, 'there are many serious issues I am concerned about.'

At this, Ramón sighs deeply, waiting for me to begin one of our long political and ideological discussions.

'Serious issues,' I continue, 'such as how much you need a bath.'

'Ha!' roars Ramón, throwing an arm around me. 'This is the serious issue: where will I find the next bottle of wine and beautiful pair of eyes?'

Laughing, we both look up and observe the

blanket of stars that has appeared above us. I imagine that Ramón is thinking of the dark-haired señoritas he will woo with tales of fighting the Fascists and life on the road.

Not for the first time, I am struck by how different we are and how even so we are such good friends. Ramón is from the Basque Country. His family have been farmers there for as long as anyone can remember. Ramón has a wife, four children and a farm full of pigs, which I truly believe he adores more than the children. He is a devout, if selective, Catholic. A naturally happy man, he finds the good in every situation.

When the Fascists launched their revolt across Spain last summer, Ramón joined a peasants' militia to defend the government. He tells me the fighting had been hard around his homeland for many months, but the Republicans had held the enemy at bay. Word of his courage and inspirational leadership had quickly spread, and he had been called to Madrid by central command. At first, he refused, stating that he fought for the autonomous Basque government. But when Franco proclaimed himself *generalísimo* at the end of September, Ramón had realized he was fighting for freedom from fascism. We met in Madrid last November, when I'd first arrived.

'Miguel,' says Ramón softly. I turn to look at him. He rarely calls me by my name. Instead, he and the men call me 'El Rubio', the Blond, because they're not used to seeing such fair colouring.

Still watching the darkening sky, he continues, 'Miguel, I have a bad feeling. Deep in my stomach. I have a very bad feeling.'

I study his face.

His beret pulls back his black hair, exposing strong, rounded features despite a scruffy beard. His mouth, always so quick to smile and laugh, is set in a serious line. I've never heard him speak like this.

I mull over his comment. Ramón is deeply superstitious, and I know there is little I can do to persuade him his feeling is most likely a simple psychological reaction to our situation.

Eventually, I reply, 'It's probably José's cooking.'

Ramón snorts with laughter and turns to me. He knows we can't let his feeling affect us or infect the other men. He reaches into his pocket and pulls out a pack of cigarettes. When he offers, I take one — I'm getting used to the coarse flavour. We smoke in silence as the light fades and the singing becomes quieter.

Stubbing out the cigarette, Ramón puffs

one last cloud of smoke. Rising to his feet, he looks over to the men, who are starting to gather their packs.

'It's time,' he says, and reaching a hand down to me, he smiles, '*Vamanos, muchacho.*'

Smiling, I let him pull me up.

★ ★ ★

The quiet tramping of boots on the dusty road is suddenly interrupted by an almighty fart.

As we all groan, Felipe whispers loudly, 'Hellfire, José! It is not the Nationalists that will be the end of me — it is your beans, goddamit!'

'The noise alone will lead them to us,' comes Ramón's voice from the dark. The moon is slim tonight and there's little light on the road.

'*Hombres*,' replies José, 'you're missing the point. I have given you a secret weapon. With just one bowl of my beans, you could blow up an enemy truck.'

As we snigger, Martín sighs. 'Oh, what I would give for a plate of lamb chops and a cup of cider.'

'Beef stew for me,' says Víctor. 'With my Patricia's bread to mop up the sauce.'

'Men, men,' states Ramón, 'you have not eaten great food until you have tasted my sausages. I know about pigs and I can tell you that a happy pig makes a tasty sausage — '

'Fish and chips,' I interrupt, before Ramón gets carried away talking about his pigs.

'Ha,' scoffs Martín, 'the English are not famous for their food.'

'Ah, Martín, you would love it. Imagine the very best calamari batter — thick and crunchy. Bite through that and inside is soft, steaming fish. And served with it, deep-fried potatoes, with vinegar splashed over them.'

'Vinegar?' I hear Ramón sneer.

'One day, Ramón, I'll take you to the finest fish and chip shop in Liverpool. Then you'll see,' I reply, smiling to myself. For a moment, I can smell the vinegar and hear the bubbling of the fat, and it makes me think of time spent with June.

I first met her when she came into the bookshop, looking for Orwell's *Burmese Days*. As I searched for it, I'd made a comment about British imperialism. In a flash, she had disputed my opinion and accused me of utopianism. Before I knew it, we'd been talking politics for half an hour and she'd had to dash back to the solicitor's office where she worked.

She had left so quickly she had forgotten to

take the book. So when she came back the next day, I'd wrapped her book in brown paper and mentally prepared a speech to ask her out. She'd smiled a slightly crooked smile that I had already come to adore and agreed. That Saturday, we went for a long walk in the damp cold and ended up at the steamy fish and chip shop, where we drank endless cups of tea and talked. As I watched her blow on her vinegar-drenched chips, I knew I had fallen for her.

'I think it sounds delicious,' says a young voice.

'Emilio, is that you?' I gasp. I turn to the indistinguishable figure that spoke.

'Yes, it's me,' replies the youngster.

'Emilio, you're supposed to be securing the flanks.'

'Pah!' he retorts. 'There's no one else on this road — we'd all see a vehicle approaching. All I'm doing is walking into farts.'

Sighing, I reach for Emilio's shadowy arm and pull him to one side.

'Ramón,' I say quietly, 'we'll see you at the next break.'

'Rrrighto, Rubio,' comes the reply.

I know that Emilio is young: he claims to be eighteen, although I think he's closer to sixteen. But the teaching of modern warfare skills is one of the reasons I'm with this group. However, it seems no matter how I try to instil a sense of professionalism in them, the Spanish sense of relaxed optimism always triumphs.

As we fall back from the rest of the group, I gently explain again how important it is to protect the rear. I remind him to use all of his senses, and how to hold his gun ready. I can sense Emilio's sulkiness as I also instruct him not to smoke when he's marking the rear. He sucks on his cigarette and the glowing end casts an orange glimmer across his sullen face.

Walking quietly, I listen to the cicadas, and in the far distance, a dog barks. The air smells faintly of mimosa. The night has a chill to it and I pull up my collar. Emilio finishes his cigarette and I hear him flick the butt towards the bushes on the roadside.

Suddenly, I hear a rustle. Emilio hears it too and we both stop, holding our breath and looking into the darkness. The noise came from where Emilio's cigarette must have landed. It's probably just an animal, but I lift my gun.

When no further noise comes, we edge slowly towards the bushes. Although I can see nothing, I can sense something. An animal would have scampered off as soon as it heard anything large approach. Gently pushing Emilio to the left, I step towards the right of the bushes.

'Show yourself,' I state loudly.

We stand, waiting and alert, but nothing happens.

I'm just about to repeat myself when leaves suddenly rustle and twigs crack. I can just make out the small figure that emerges from behind the outline of the bush.

'Come here!' I say forcefully, trying to hide my confusion.

I hear Emilio shift his gun as the figure wrestles its way out of the bushes. As the black shape makes its way towards me, I reach into my pocket and pull out my lighter.

'Stop there!' I snap when the figure is a few feet from me.

I flick the flint and a fat flame bursts from the lighter. I lower it towards the shadowy form and Emilio and I find ourselves staring at a small boy. He is filthy and dishevelled, with bits of twig and leaves sticking out of his hair.

I drop to my haunches.

'Be careful — it may be some kind of decoy,' whispers Emilio earnestly.

'What's your name?' I ask the child, ignoring Emilio.

'Alberto,' comes the whispered reply.

'How did you get here?'

'I walked.'

'Where from?'

At this, I see the child's chin tremble; then his face crumples and tears start to roll down his cheeks. I drop my gun, pull the boy into my body and hug him hard. Feeling the child sob into my chest, I try to decide the best course of action.

By the time the crying has subsided to muffled snuffling, I've made up my mind.

'Emilio, take the boy ahead to the unit. Tell them to break early. We'll get the boy a cup of tea and look at the map — let's see if we can drop him off somewhere safe.'

'Yes, sir,' says Emilio. At last, he is responding to an order. I hope it's not too dark for the child to see me smile at him. Then I stand and let Emilio take Alberto's hand to lead him off.

★　★　★

By the time I reach the unit, they have built a small fire and are heating some water. Ramón is doing piglet impressions for the child, who giggles at the silliness. The other men look on, smiling.

For an instant, it strikes me that it is this compassion that we are fighting for. The

87

Fascists have no time for kindness, only power and discipline. We believe in supporting the poorest and a fairer life for all. And yet, it is this compassion that could be our downfall.

Dispelling such an unsettling thought, I sit on a rock by the fire. Ramón sees me and, placing his beret on the boy's head, passes him to Emilio.

'So, Rubio,' he says, crossing to me, 'I see you are still recruiting fighters. Don't you think this one is a little young?'

I smile and accept a cup of weak tea from José.

'Did you find out where he came from?' I ask.

'Emilio asked. He can't remember anything. He doesn't know the name of his village or what family he has. The only thing he remembers is his name — Alberto Romero. And a car. He says he remembers a car. He says he's been walking and walking but has no idea for how long.'

'Poor kid. Any idea what we can do with him?'

Felipe hands Ramón the map and he points a dirty finger to a small town.

'This is the nearest place that we know has plenty of Republican support. There are no reports of Nationalists there yet. The best thing to do is take him to the Church — they will look after him.'

I give Ramón a steady stare.

'The Church?' I ask, incredulous.

'Rubio,' replies Ramón curtly, 'this is not the time to have a discussion about religion. No matter what the Church is doing politically, when it comes to situations like this, they will show mercy to a lost child.'

'Suffer the little children, Ramón?' I spit. 'If we leave him in a *Rojo* village, they will assume he is a *Rojo* child. I know you don't want to believe the Church could hurt a child, but there is no guarantee he will be safe. I think we should try to get him to the Red Cross. They may even evacuate him. At least there won't be any fat, barbaric bishops on a religious crusade against — '

'Enough!' hollers Ramón, raising his hand. 'He will be safe with the Church.' Then he drops his hand and speaks softly. 'Do not forget our mission. We have a long way to travel and we cannot make a detour to find the Red Cross. At least if he is taken into an organization like the Church, they may be able to find his family.'

I know Ramón struggles with an inner conflict — his genuine faith versus a greedy, self-serving Church — and perhaps I am pushing him too far. I take a moment; then, reluctantly, I nod. 'You're right.'

I know he will not be swayed in this matter, and despite our friendship, he is the leader of this unit and I must respect his orders.

We return to the map and plan what to do. It is agreed I will take the boy to the village. It's still early, so I should be able to leave him at the church and then get back to the unit before daybreak.

As I gulp down the last of my tea, I turn to José. 'Is there any food for the boy? He needs something to eat. Anything but your beans.'

★   ★   ★

'Alberto, are you sure you can't remember anything about your home?' I press as we walk along the edge of a field. We split from the other men an hour ago, and they followed the road, while the boy and I cut across the fields to get to the town.

'No, nothing,' says the boy.

'Not even your mamá?'

'No,' says Alberto a little hesitantly.

'What?' I urge gently. 'Is there something you remember? Anything at all?'

'Yes, but it's not Mamá,' he replies thoughtfully. 'It's Mimi.'

'Well, that's a start. Maybe she's an aunt or a friend. What do you think?'

90

Alberto is quiet as we step through the grass.

'I don't know. I just remembered the name,' he eventually admits.

'Never mind,' I say encouragingly. 'I'm sure it will come back soon, and then someone will be able to take you home.'

We walk in silence for a while, before Alberto starts hesitantly, 'Why — ' then stops.

'Why what?' I say. 'Come on.'

'Why do they call you 'El Rubio'?' he asks shyly.

'Aha!' I say cheerfully. 'Look at this!' At that, I whip off my black hat and my fair hair flops out. The night's clouds have cleared and I know in the moonlight the blond can be seen — like a golden halo, Ramón often remarks sarcastically. If I'd been at home, June would have trimmed it for me, but I haven't given haircuts much thought lately.

The boy gasps.

'Have you ever seen hair this yellow before?' I ask.

'No, never.'

'Where I live, it's not unusual. In fact, it's really very ordinary.'

'Don't you live in Spain?' asks the boy.

'Well, I do now, but only because of the war. I'm from another country, called England. Have you heard of it?' I put my hat back on, tucking in as much hair as I can.

'Yes, I think so.'

'Well, maybe you learnt about it at school,' I suggest. I hope it will jog a memory.

'I don't know,' says the boy quietly. 'Is that why you talk funny?'

I laugh. 'Yes. It's because usually I talk English. I'm from a city called Liverpool. It's near the ocean and is a famous port. My uncle was a sailor. He married a Spanish lady and brought her back home with him. My aunt María taught me Spanish, and whenever I was at her house, playing with my cousins, we would speak Spanish. And now I speak it every day, but I'll always sound a bit different because it's not my native language.'

'Are you a sailor too?'

'No!' I laugh at the thought. And yet, here I am, a soldier. 'My father has a bookshop. I worked there before I came to Spain. I used to live above the shop with my parents.'

For a moment, I wonder how the bookshop is doing. While I was working with my father, I persuaded him to build up a section of political books. I had been keen because I was so interested in current affairs and politics myself. I had also known it would bring in the union and party leaders, and the sales would be good for business. Dad had been reluctant at first, but soon we had stocked everything from Marx and Lenin to Mussolini's autobiography, and had become well known for our range.

One of the regulars at the bookshop was John, a unionist down at the docks. He had invited me to meetings, where we had listened to speakers talk of the rise of the Fascists and the danger it posed to the Labour movement. It was with John that I had gone to London and volunteered last year.

'Why did you come to my country?' asks Alberto.

'Well, it's complicated,' I say cautiously. Perhaps the boy's family are Nationalists. It's not my place to confuse the child. How do I explain my reasons for coming to fight?

I hear my father's words ringing in my ears. 'Don't go,' he'd said. 'It's not your fight.' But I'd always known I'd fight fascism, ever since I had sat in the cinema and watched the newsreel showing them burning books in Germany, works of literature, philosophy and science all going up in flames. It had sent chills down my spine. I had known that at some point I would have to stand up to the indoctrination, the persecution, the ignorance.

'Alberto,' I begin tentatively, 'there are times when you see someone doing something bad and it makes you so angry that you have to do something about it. I think that the Nationalists are doing something terribly wrong. And even though this is not my country, or my people, I want to try and make things better, fairer. I've come to help the Spanish people fight against what I consider to be unjust and immoral.'

The boy is silent.

'Does that make any sense?' I ask doubtfully, but looking down, I see that the dark shadow of the child is not by my side. Glancing back, I see he is standing still a few feet behind.

'Alberto?'

'I just had a memory,' says the boy softly.

'What was it?'

'I hit another boy.'

'Why?'

'I don't know.'

'Well, that's great! Not great that you're hitting other children, but great that you remember something. Perhaps that's the beginning of your memory coming back.'

The boy is quiet; he seems to be lost in thought.

'Maybe Ramón was right, Alberto,' I say, trying to lift the mood a little. 'Maybe we should take you with us to fight. I bet you've got quite a punch, eh?' I give his shoulder a light tap.

After a pause, he throws a semi-serious punch at my leg.

'Hmm — your technique needs a little work. Look, if you hold your hand like this, you won't hurt your thumb.' I lean down and carefully fold his little hand into a fist. 'And if you're going to hit someone, bring your arm up like this — in a jab. See?'

Alberto jabs his arm quickly and lands a punch on the side of my head. Losing my balance, I fall to the ground heavily.

'Hey,' I say, 'watch what you're doing!' With that, I pull him down and pummel him. He rolls on the ground laughing.

'Who's the champion now, eh?' I ask, tickling the squirming boy. When he's giggling so much he can barely breathe, I stop, worried I might make him sick. As we lie on the grass panting, he rolls towards me and embraces me. I give him a bear hug.

* * *

I squeeze Alberto's hand and he turns his face up to me. I lift my finger to my lips and he nods seriously. Although we believe the village to be on the Republican side, our information is often unreliable. And when there's support for both sides, as there is in this region, we cannot rely on anyone for our security.

I bend down so that the boy and I are on the same level; then, as quietly as we can, we start to run. We pass shops and houses, dark and shut up for the night.

A short distance from the main square, I steer Alberto into a doorway, and we stop to catch our breath.

Suddenly, a dog starts barking ferociously on the other side of the door. Instinctively, I put my hand over Alberto's open mouth, but he stops himself from crying out in fear. I drop again and we make a dash to the shadows in the square.

When we reach the outer walls of the church, we edge around it, making our way down a walkway until we come across a gate. In the dim light, I can see a small graveyard inside. Very slowly I turn the handle, and with a small squeak it opens. I usher Alberto in and he stands against the wall, while I quietly shut the gate behind us.

Across the dusty courtyard is a side door into the church itself, with a small bench beside it. We walk across to the bench and I indicate Alberto should sit down. My plan is to leave the child there for the remaining hours of night. The church will open early and they'll discover him. With the Church supporting the Fascists, I can't risk being found by a priest.

Kneeling beside him, I take out one of June's letters. Carefully, I rip the triangle off the back of the envelope. Tucking the envelope back in my pocket, I fish out a pencil and, leaning on my knee, carefully write ALBERTO ROMERO on the white paper.

I tuck the paper into Alberto's jacket pocket and stand up. I've been dreading this moment, and as the small boy looks up at me with his large, round eyes, I have no idea what to say. After a moment, I punch him softly on the shoulder.

'Good luck, mate,' I whisper in English.

Then, with a crack of metal against wood, the door beside us opens, causing light to flood out of the church. Like startled rabbits, Alberto and I stare at a priest in long black robes, framed by the open door. He is tall and spectacled, and looks me straight in the eye. After what seems an age, he turns to Alberto, then back to me.

It seems as if he understands what is happening. He steps out of the church towards Alberto and places a protective hand on his head, then nods firmly at me. This priest is not what I was expecting — I sense he is a man of integrity.

Alberto is watching me nervously. I flash him a wink. He gives me a tiny smile in return. By the time I pull the gate to behind me, the wooden door is shut, with the priest and Alberto inside. The romantic in me notices a small star directly above the church glow a little more brightly.

The pragmatist in me hopes my instincts are right about the priest.

7

'Papá? Is that you?' Alberto's daughter's voice crackled at him down the phone line.

'Yes, it's me. I didn't know if you'd be at the hospital.'

'No, they sent me home. I'm here and Cristina is too. She arrived this morning. Her mother-in-law is looking after her husband and the children.'

'Good. I'm glad your sister is with you. How is Juan Carlos?'

'He's doing much better. In fact, he was speaking a little today. The doctors are very pleased with his progress.'

'That's good news, Rosa,' the old man sighed, relieved. He nodded at the boy, who was looking up expectantly.

'Papá?'

'He's here,' he said, passing the phone to his grandson.

'Mamá?'

As Alberto walked away, he heard the child chattering excitedly to his mother about where they'd been and who they'd met.

He knew how much the boy's mother would be missing her cherished child. Rosa and Juan Carlos had been through many years of heartbreak trying to have a baby. When first her older sister and then her brother's wife had delivered one baby after another, Rosa had been delighted for them. But María Luisa would tell Alberto of the pain their daughter had silently suffered.

Alberto knew María Luisa blamed herself. She had suffered numerous miscarriages, both before the birth of their first child and in between the others. Rosa herself had been born almost eight years after her elder sister. Superstitious, María Luisa thought she had passed this terrible affliction on to her youngest daughter.

Then, when it seemed Rosa and Juan Carlos had given up, Rosa had fallen pregnant. As she blossomed and grew, she remained cautious, reluctant to express her joy. At the birth, there were complications, and María Luisa told Alberto afterwards that for a short time both Rosa and the baby had been in danger. The child was immediately whisked away for special care.

A few days later, Alberto had gone to visit at the hospital. He watched his pale, exhausted daughter sleeping, and then he and his wife went to see the baby. They joined a worried Juan Carlos peering into an incubator.

As Alberto had looked at the pink, wrinkled baby, it squirmed and raised a tiny clenched fist into the air.

'Look at that,' he said to Juan Carlos. 'You have a little fighter there.'

Juan Carlos turned to Alberto and gave him a weary smile.

'He must take after his grandfather,' he replied.

★　★　★

Alberto walked into the kitchen, where the gardener and his wife were sitting drinking coffee and chatting comfortably.

'Thank you for the use of your phone,' said Alberto. 'You must let me give you some money towards the bill.'

'Nonsense,' they said in unison.

'How is your son-in-law?' asked the gardener.

'My daughter says he's doing much better.'

'Oh good,' said the gardener's wife. She poured Alberto a cup of coffee.

Nodding his thanks, Alberto said, 'So, Isabel is running a restaurant now? I'm not surprised. She always fed us as well as she could at the orphanage. I know there was little food in those days.'

'Yes,' replied the gardener. 'My father used

to say she could turn an old onion and a bit of sawdust into a hearty meal! That's quite a skill, eh?'

'Yes,' nodded Alberto, smiling.

'We went to visit her when I was very young. As I remember, she married after the war. She went to live in her husband's family's town, and he set up a restaurant in the square. I was little, but I remember her.

'My sister was travelling that way last year and went to see if the restaurant was still there. She said that although her husband had died some years ago, Isabel was healthy and well, and the restaurant was doing better than ever.'

'I'm looking forward to seeing her,' said Alberto. 'I doubt she'll remember me — there were so many of us.'

'It's surprising what people remember,' said the gardener's wife.

Just then the boy walked into the kitchen, beaming.

'I told Mamá we were going to find Apu's birthday tomorrow and she said Papá was getting better.'

Alberto got the feeling there was something Tino hadn't mentioned, but the boy seemed happy.

'Excellent,' said the gardener's wife. 'Now, sit down while I make you some warm milk.

Then off to bed — it's late, and tomorrow is another adventure.'

★ ★ ★

Fields of sunflowers lay like yellow eiderdowns as far as Alberto could see. They had left the pine-tree hills some time ago, and now the bus was travelling down a long, straight, empty road.

Tino was chattering as usual, and Alberto was only half listening, nodding occasionally. He felt an uneasy mixture of feelings. There was the anticipation that Isabel would be able to tell him something of his past. But he also knew it was probable she wouldn't remember him, and this would be the end of the journey. The thought of it being over made him sad.

Nevertheless, it was good to see the countryside again. After the dry coast, filled with foreigners and tall buildings, it was pleasing to see how familiar the landscape was inland. The crops had changed over the years, and solar panels and wind farms were peppered across the horizon, but this was the Spain he remembered from his youth. Still and unhurried, colourful and fertile. He hoped his grandson would remember this trip when he was older.

An hour later, the bus pulled into a bus

stop on the outer road of a small town. Alberto helped the boy off the bus and they strolled through the streets. A tiny supermarket bustled with women. Old men sat outside a coffee shop smoking, chatting and enjoying the sun. A lone dog trotted down the pavement, confident in his destination.

At the end of the road, they found themselves in a small square framed by a scattering of shops.

'Apu, look,' said the boy, pointing across the square.

Alberto looked and saw an unfussy restaurant with white walls and a few metal chairs on the pavement outside. Above the open door, a sign read RESTAURANTE LOS NIÑOS.

'That must be it,' said Alberto. He took the boy's hand.

As they walked across the road towards the restaurant, Alberto glanced at the far end of the square. There stood an old stone church. Its large wooden doors were open, and in the tower above hung a bell.

A car tooted, breaking Alberto's reverie, and he realized he was standing in the middle of the road. He hurried Tino across to the other side, but when they reached the pavement outside the restaurant, he turned once again to look at the church.

'Apu? What is it?'

'Nothing,' said Alberto distractedly. 'It's just . . . that church seems familiar. I don't know this town, but I feel I've seen that church before.'

'Maybe Señora Isabel brought you here,' suggested the boy.

Alberto shook his head, confused. 'I don't think so.'

At length he broke his gaze from the church, shrugged and smiled at the boy. Together, they walked into the restaurant.

A long bar stretched the length of the room, with three large barrels sitting on one end. Smoked ham and bunches of garlic hung from the ceiling, and the walls were covered with paintings of food.

With it being so early, the restaurant was empty. Behind the bar was an open door covered by a beaded curtain. Alberto called a hello towards it.

A tall, greying man stepped through the door, the beads creating the sound of running water as he did so.

'Yes?'

'Excuse me,' said Alberto politely, 'I am looking for Doña Isabel.'

The man looked at them with dark eyes that twinkled as a smile broke over his face.

'Mamá! You have a suitor!' he called over his shoulder.

Tino giggled behind his hand.

'What?' came a shout through the beaded curtain as they heard footsteps on the tiled floor. 'Andrés, what is your silliness this time?' The bead curtain separated and a small, wiry woman with short silver hair stepped out. She used a stick to walk, leaning on it with her right hand.

'Mamá, you have a visitor,' explained Andrés.

Isabel looked at Alberto, her pale eyes almost obscured by large glasses.

'Can I help you?' she asked curiously.

Alberto cleared his throat. He had been planning what he would say on the journey to the town, but now his mouth was dry and his mind a blank.

'Doña Isabel, we have met before. That is to say, a long time ago,' Alberto stammered.

Isabel looked at Alberto patiently. Then she looked at the boy. 'Señor, please sit down. Andrés, bring us some sherry. And something for our young friend here.'

Isabel pointed to a table and the boy dutifully climbed onto a seat. Alberto held a chair out as the elderly woman walked slowly to the table. As she sat down, she sighed, 'I am not as quick as I once was. Old age is a terrible thing.'

As Alberto sat, Isabel turned to the boy

and, smiling warmly at him, said, 'Welcome to Los Niños, child. A very long time ago, it was my job to feed lots of children. So when my husband took over this restaurant, he named it Los Niños because he said anyone who walked through the door would be fed as well as possible. Just like the children.'

'My grandpapá was one of the children,' said Tino excitedly.

'What?' Isabel turned from the boy and looked into Alberto's face.

He nodded simply.

At that moment, Andrés arrived at the table carrying a tray. He placed a small glass of chilled sherry in front of his mother, then another in front of Alberto. For the boy, he opened a bottle of lemonade and poured it into a glass. Then he placed a basket of bread and a plate of thinly sliced ham in the middle of the table.

'Is there anything else, Mamá?' he asked kindly.

His mother shook her head.

'I'll take care of the kitchen. Let me know if you need me,' said Andrés. He put a hand softly on his mother's shoulder.

Isabel placed her hand over his, smiling warmly up at him. Alberto noticed some of her fingers were gnarled. While she was probably at least ten years older than him, he had seen his own knuckles and joints swell and knew the ache of arthritis.

As Andrés strolled to the bead curtain, Isabel turned to Alberto.

'Were you at the orphanage?' she asked quietly.

'Yes.'

Slowly, a smile spread across her lips, and behind the glasses, her eyes seemed to flicker with light.

'I always wondered if I would see any of you again.'

'My grandson suggested I make this journey.' Alberto looked at the boy, who grinned widely.

'Eat, child,' said Isabel. She pushed the plate of ham towards him. Still grinning, Tino picked up a sliver of ham and started to gnaw at it as he reached across for a piece of bread.

Isabel turned back to Alberto.

'I apologize for arriving unannounced,' he said. 'This trip was unplanned, and I only heard that you were here yesterday.'

'I am delighted you have come.'

'So am I. Forgive me, but it has been many years and I was unsure if I would recognize you. Now I see you, I know without a doubt it is you.'

'Well, you are at the advantage, señor. I'm afraid I don't remember you.'

Alberto chuckled loudly. 'Of course you don't remember me. I've lost a little hair since the last time you saw me,' he said. He ran a hand over his balding head.

Isabel smiled back at him. 'Perhaps I will remember your name.'

'Alberto. Alberto Romero.'

Isabel gave a small gasp and lifted her hand to her mouth. 'Alberto?'

'Yes. You remember me?'

Isabel took a moment. She carefully smoothed her apron over her black skirt. With a hand that shook slightly, she removed her glasses and laid them in her lap. Alberto could see her eyes were watery.

'I hope I haven't upset you,' he said uncomfortably.

Isabel reached out and patted his hand. 'Alberto,' she answered quietly. 'If it had not been for you, I would not have met my husband.'

Confused, Alberto looked at Isabel, unsure what to say. The boy, sitting on the edge of his seat and watching them intently, sipped his drink and reached for another piece of bread.

'How . . . ?' started Alberto.

'My husband was in the army. For most of the war, he drove lorries, moving supplies. One day, he and his lorry brought you to the orphanage. That was the first time we met.

After that, he found ways to visit whenever he could. Sometimes he brought extra supplies to help me feed you all. Sometimes he only brought his smiling eyes. But that was enough.

'He wanted to marry me long before the end of the war, but I didn't want to leave the children. By the time the war finished, there were so many orphans that the Church arranged for the orphanage to be closed, and the children to be moved to an institution in the city.'

Alberto nodded.

'I stayed to help clean the house for the next owner; then my husband and I married and moved here. He left the army and we took over the restaurant. I did all the cooking, and my husband looked after the customers. It was difficult — there was so little food, and soon I had Andrés — but we managed. And every year on our anniversary, my husband and I would raise a glass in thanks to the small boy who rarely spoke, but who brought us together.'

Isabel smiled, and patted Alberto's hand again.

'I'm pleased to have been of service,' Alberto said, a little embarrassed. 'And I'm sorry your husband is not here. I would have liked to have met him — again.'

'And he would have been pleased to meet you too. How did you find me?'

'We went to the old orphanage. The gardener there is the son of the gardener during the war.'

'Of course, Jorge's family. Are they well?'

'Very well. And now my grandson and I are hoping to continue on to discover more of my childhood. I'm afraid I have no memories of the time before my arrival at the orphanage. Did your husband ever tell you where he brought me from?'

'Here!' said Isabel, tapping the table. 'This village.'

'Apu, that's why you remember the church,' interrupted Tino excitedly.

'Yes,' agreed Isabel. 'You were at the church. My husband came to visit his family, and when the priest saw his lorry, he asked him to take you somewhere safe. The fighting was getting closer and the priest was worried that the church would be in danger.'

'I remember,' said Alberto quietly. He looked into the distance. 'Yes, I remember a priest.'

'By the time I came to live in the town, he was gone. Some said he was taken away by soldiers, but there were many rumours and recriminations at that time. I would have liked to have thanked him.'

111

Alberto nodded thoughtfully.

'I'm afraid I don't know any more,' said Isabel apologetically.

'No, you have been very helpful. You see, I have only tiny flashes of memory — like the church and the priest — but nothing of my family.'

Isabel shook her head sadly. 'You barely spoke when you arrived. So many children had seen such terrible things — it's hardly surprising they didn't want to talk about it.'

Alberto sipped his sherry thoughtfully.

'Why don't you visit the church?' suggested Isabel. 'They may have records of your arrival. And maybe they know what happened to the priest. I'm afraid I can't remember his name.'

'Yes, Apu — let's go and visit the church,' the boy chimed in.

'Tell me, child, why do you call your grandfather 'Apu'?'

'My mamá says when I was little, I couldn't say 'Abuelo'.'

The old man nodded. 'It's true,' he said. 'It was as close as he could get, and it has stuck. My other grandchildren all managed to call their grandparents Abuelo and Abuela, but not this one. I have always been Apu, and his grandmother was Apa.'

'And your wife?'

'I lost her four years ago.' Alberto sighed, surprised the pain still stabbed when he had to admit she was gone.

'I'm sorry. But at least you have this little one with you.'

The old man looked at the boy and smiled at him.

'Oh, Alberto,' said Isabel, 'it broke my heart to see you poor little things. I wasn't allowed to spend time with any of you; Señora Peña saw to that. But I always kept an eye on you in particular — just to make sure you didn't get ill, or in fights.'

Isabel turned to Tino. 'Your grandfather was a very good little boy. He never complained; he worked hard and rarely got into trouble.'

Tino smiled proudly at his apu.

'Señora Peña — I remember her!' chuckled Alberto. 'It always seemed that the thinner we became, the fatter she got!'

'Oh, that woman!' said Isabel, shaking her head. 'And those priests. Always so cruel. I often chastise myself that I didn't stand up for you children. As if you hadn't been through enough.'

This time it was Alberto who laid his hand on hers. 'It was your cooking that kept us all going,' he said.

Isabel smiled, wiped her eyes with the back

of her hand and put her glasses on again.

'Alberto, I'm so glad you visited.'

'So am I.'

For a while, they chatted easily. Isabel spoke of other children she recalled with fondness. Alberto explained they had met the man who had taken over the orphanage and Isabel said she recollected an unpleasant general had once visited the building as they were cleaning it for his arrival.

Eventually, Andrés appeared and asked if they'd like anything else. A coffee perhaps?

'Thank you, but no,' said Alberto.

Andrés nodded and smiled at his mother.

'I think it's time to continue our search,' said Alberto to Isabel. Then, turning to the boy, he said, 'Would you like to visit the church?'

His grandson nodded excitedly.

Alberto reached into his pocket.

'Oh no,' said Isabel, raising her hand. 'Los Niños couldn't accept your money, Alberto. And if you will come back later, I'd be delighted to cook for you once more.'

8

MIMI

5 March 1937

As I press myself behind the back of a giant barrel, I can smell the delicious old oak. Wedging my body between the cask and the stone wall, I smile. The boys will never think of looking for me here.

I fold my skirt into my lap so they won't see it as they pass. Néstor is useless at most games, including hide-and-seek, but Alberto might just spot me if I don't hide well.

I try to hold my breath, but I'm still panting from running through the cellars, so I concentrate on breathing as quietly as I can.

Papá would probably be annoyed if he knew I was hiding here. He doesn't like us playing in the cellars. He likes the stone caverns to be quiet and serene. 'Let the wine age in peace,' he tells us. But I like being down here in the cool. And I like being around the wine.

Papá often explains to us how the wine is made. He makes a story out of it. My favourite bit is the journey of a little grape.

Papá talks about how it needs to be nurtured while it grows on the vine. He tells us how only the best care will make sure the grape has the right flavours to make a fine vintage. When the grape is fully grown, then it allows itself to be picked and turned into wine.

Néstor is always bored by Papá's stories, but I love them. Papá tells Néstor to pay attention because one day the vineyard will be his, but Néstor isn't interested. Last week, Alberto's papá told my papá that he should pass the vineyard on to me because I have a natural feel for it. But Papá just laughed. Later, he told Mamá, and she laughed too as if it were the funniest joke they'd ever heard.

Mamá said that for such a clever man, Alberto's papá has some crazy ideas. I felt bad for Alberto's papá. I know he was doing a nice thing for me. And I know Alberto tells his papá how mean Néstor is to me. Mamá and Papá don't believe me when I tell them he punches and pinches me. They say not to tell tales, and my brother and I should play nicely.

They would be pleased with me now. The three of us have been playing together all afternoon. We know that soon we'll be back at school, so we're playing while we can.

I shift my position a tiny bit. It's uncomfortable behind this barrel, but I know the moment I move, one of the boys will appear and find me.

In the gloomy light, I look at my fingers. My nails are dirty again. Mamá despairs of me ever becoming a lady. I stick a finger in my mouth and work the grime out with my tooth. Then I suck the ball of dirt onto my tongue and stick it out, picking the grit up with my fingertip. I wipe my hand on the back of the barrel and move on to the next finger.

By the time I've finished all ten nails, I have a metallic taste in my mouth, and I'm very bored. Where are the boys?

Stiff and achy, I shift again, but this time I lose my balance. To steady myself, I plant my foot heavily on the floor under the edge of the barrel. I hear a splash and look down with dismay.

There is a puddle of red wine under the cask. One of my white socks is soaked with wine, and as I step into the light, I see red splatters all over the yellow skirt of my dress. Mamá is going to be furious.

Just then, I hear steps running towards me. For a moment, I consider squirming back into my hiding place, but dismiss the thought. I have bigger worries now.

'Ha! I found you!' screeches Néstor as he runs up to me.

I ignore him and try to wipe the wine off my skirt. After all the wine I've got on my clothes over the years, I know it is useless, but I have to try.

'Ha, ha, ha, ha!' my brother screams. He points a fat finger at my skirt.

'Mamá's going to be so angry with you!' he shouts, glorying in his victory.

I will him to shut up. The last thing I want is a fight with him. But Néstor just sneers at me, his chubby face glowing with delight.

Another set of footsteps run towards us. Alberto has heard Néstor's shouting. As I look up, he stops beside my brother. He stares at my dress.

'Oh, Mimi,' he says in a quiet voice.

I know he understands how I am feeling. I am always spilling things and have ruined so many of my clothes. Mamá despairs of me and now I've done it again.

Néstor is sniggering at me and pointing.

'Let's go to Chita,' says Alberto.

Yes, of course. Chita will help. She'll be busy preparing the evening meal right now, but I'm sure she'll do what she can.

As I walk past my brother, he snorts, 'I'm going to tell Mamá.'

'Don't be mean, Néstor,' says Alberto.

'You can't tell me what to do,' says my brother angrily.

Ignoring him, Alberto turns and walks along the length of the cellar with me.

I know Néstor well enough to know he feels humiliated and is fuming. Alberto is only a little older than him, but Néstor is such a baby it's as if the age difference is huge. I've heard Chita say Néstor is spoilt and our parents indulge him too much. If it were up to her, she says, she'd give him a good spanking.

Wishing it were up to Chita, I reach the cellar entrance, Alberto by my side. The wine has seeped into my shoe now and the leather squelches as I walk.

Together, we climb the stone stairs and out into the shady courtyard. The sun is shining through the flowering jacaranda trees above, and the ground is covered in spots of light and purple petals.

Crossing the courtyard, we watch out for any of the workers, but they're all in the fields tending the vines. Papá will probably be out with them, and Mamá will be working at her desk. Since Papá's accountant had to join the army, Mamá has been doing the paperwork. Papá says she's very good with figures, and he hopes I've inherited her mental agility.

Mamá sometimes complains about how things have changed since the war began. Chita can no longer make many of the family's favourite dishes, and Mamá says she feels ill with worry that the *Rojos* will make the vineyard into a *collectivo*. Papá tells her it won't happen and our area is safe from the Republicans.

Alberto's papá sometimes says perhaps it would be a good thing to let the workers have some of the profit from the wine they help make. But Papá says there's not much profit these days, and anyway, he didn't put his whole life into this vineyard just to hand it over to a bunch of scallywags in berets.

Papá always finishes the discussion by telling Alberto's papá he respects their friendship too much to discuss politics. I think it's Papá's way of telling Alberto's papá to keep his opinions to himself.

Alberto's papá works for my papá, but they are also very good friends. He and Alberto eat with us, and they live in an annexe attached to the house. Alberto's papá is a chemist. He measures the levels in the wine, right from when it's just grape juice to when it's very old. He makes sure the wine isn't too high in alcohol or tannins. I don't really understand what he does, but Papá says he's lucky to have such a clever scientist working with his grapes.

These days, Alberto's papá helps in the fields, too. So many men have left to fight that most of the workers in the fields are women. At harvest time, we all go to pick grapes. The neighbours come round too, and Mamá and Chita make as much food as they can for everyone to say thank you.

As we walk across the courtyard to the kitchen, I can smell something frying. For an instant, I forget about my dress and imagine what might be for dinner. Perhaps padrón peppers, or butterbean stew.

Suddenly, there's a shout. 'Hey!'

Alberto and I turn to see Néstor standing at the top of the cellar stairs. He has an ugly sneer on his face.

'You can't tell me what to do!' he shouts at Alberto.

'Be quiet, Néstor,' I hiss at him.

Néstor ignores me and stares at Alberto.

'I'm not. I just think you should be nicer to your sister,' says Alberto.

Although we are the best of friends, I know that Alberto wishes he has brothers and sisters. His mother died when he was a baby, and his papá has never remarried.

'She's just a stupid girl,' Néstor scoffs, walking towards us.

I think my brother wishes Alberto was his friend, and he's jealous of my friendship with him.

'Don't call her stupid,' says Alberto. He

sounds a bit angry now.

'I can call her what I want,' he says. 'It's you that should be careful. You're not a member of this family. You shouldn't even be playing with us. You should be playing with the workers' children.'

'Néstor!' I shout. 'How dare you speak to Alberto like that? You know that Papá and Alberto's papá are friends. Now just stop all this and grow up.'

I am a year and a half older than Néstor, and I know the one way to drive him crazy is to tell him to grow up.

He turns to me, and his small eyes flash with anger. All of a sudden, he steps towards me and, with his sizeable weight behind him, shoves me hard.

My foot turns and I fall. As I hit the ground, I hear the sound of my sleeve ripping. This is becoming the most awful day I can remember.

Néstor hears the noise too and he begins to laugh.

Then, suddenly, Alberto rushes towards my brother and throws a punch at him. It hits him in the face and Néstor falls heavily backwards, holding his nose.

Alberto turns to me. 'Are you all right?' he asks.

I nod, but I'm worried. Papá will not be

happy about Alberto hitting Néstor, no matter how good friends he is with Alberto's papá.

He realizes what I'm thinking and says, 'I'll talk to my papá.'

'He's not your papá!' screams Néstor.

Alberto and I both turn to him. Like me, Néstor's still sitting on the courtyard ground. His nose is bleeding and blood drips onto his shirt.

'Just ignore him,' I tell Alberto. I have a horrible feeling in my stomach — as if something is about to happen that will change everything.

'What are you talking about?' asks Alberto. He obviously does not share my fear.

'I heard Mamá and Papá talking one night,' says Néstor quietly.

'Néstor, I'm going to tell Papá you've been eaves-dropping again.'

He ignores me and carries on. 'They were talking about how when your papá married your mamá, she was already expecting you.'

'That's not true,' says Alberto, but there's a tiny note of uncertainty in his voice.

'Your mamá was expecting you, but the man she married wasn't your real father.'

'Shut up, Néstor!' I shout as loud as I can, hoping to drown out what I know is coming.

'You're a bastard,' says my brother. A nasty

smile breaks out on his face.

Alberto stands looking at him. He shakes his head. 'You're a liar,' he says.

Néstor starts to laugh a screeching, spiteful laugh.

'Take it back,' says Alberto loudly, but Néstor is still laughing.

I hear footsteps coming towards us, but I can't break my stare from what's happening in front of me.

'Take it back!' yells Alberto. He runs towards Néstor and throws himself on top of him, punching and kicking him with all the strength he can muster.

At that moment, Mamá appears from the entrance to the house and Alberto's papá appears at the courtyard's exit. They arrive in time to see Alberto viciously hitting Néstor, and they both run over.

'Alberto!' shouts Alberto's papá. He pulls Alberto away, and he clearly can't quite believe what he just saw. 'What were you doing?' he asks crossly. Then he sees that Alberto has tears running down his face. He can't look at his papá, staring instead at his boots.

Mamá kneels next to Néstor, fussing over him. She wipes the blood from his face with her handkerchief, asking why Alberto was hitting him. But, for once, my brother remains silent, his mouth tightly set.

By now, Chita has heard the commotion and runs into the courtyard. Seeing the boys are being attended to, she heads over to me and helps me to my feet.

'What happened, *chica*?' she asks, beginning to brush the dust off me. She hasn't noticed the wine stains. I follow the boys' lead and do not say anything. I don't think I could say it out loud — not when Alberto's papá is so close.

Alberto's papá is bending over Alberto with his hands gripping the tops of Alberto's arms. He's looking directly into Alberto's face, but Alberto doesn't even glance up.

Then Alberto's papá turns and walks towards the house. I don't know what this means. Is he now refusing to talk to Alberto? What's going to happen next?

He disappears into the dark of the house, but when he returns, he is rolling down his shirtsleeves and putting on his jacket. He carries Alberto's jacket and hands it to him.

Alberto takes the coat without saying anything. Alberto's papá turns to Mamá and says, 'Please accept my apologies for Alberto's behaviour. He and I are going to take a little drive to discuss what's just happened.'

Mamá nods and looks at Alberto. I thought

she would be angry with him, but she doesn't seem to be. Instead, she appears concerned.

With his hands on Alberto's shoulders, Alberto's papá leads him past Chita and me. I stare at Alberto's face, but he doesn't look up — not even for a moment.

Their steps become quieter; then I hear the car doors slam and the engine roars to life. I watch as the old black car chugs past the courtyard, leaving a small cloud of dust behind it.

★　★　★

Waking up, I squint at the light shining through a crack in the shutters. I am mid-stretch when I remember what happened yesterday. I throw back the bedclothes and leap out of bed. In my nightdress and barefoot, I run down the stairs and through the house to the kitchen.

There, sitting at the table, are Mamá and Papá. Chita is at the stove, cooking eggs. No one is speaking as I burst into the warm room.

'Well?' I plead.

Mamá shakes her head.

Alberto and his papá are still not back. When they left last night, we thought they would go for a short drive. Maybe to the river, where Alberto's papá sometimes takes us all fishing.

Chita had postponed dinner, but it became so late Mamá said we would eat and Chita could put theirs aside. After grace, I could only manage a few mouthfuls, and Néstor just pushed his food around his plate. Even Mamá seemed to struggle. Only Papá had eaten well, complimenting Chita on her excellent stew.

After dinner, Mamá had suggested Néstor and I go to bed early, and for the first time ever, we agreed. I had gone to sleep straining to hear the sound of the old engine complaining as Alberto's papá drove it up the drive.

Papá looks at me and sees the tears starting to well in my eyes. He pushes his chair back and nods to me. I climb onto his lap and push my face into his chest, feeling the bristly hair through his white shirt.

'Don't worry, Mimi,' he says softly. 'I'm sure it's just that that old car has broken down. I don't know how Raúl has kept it going so long, but it can't go on forever.'

I look at Mamá and she nods reassuringly at me.

Only Chita does not seem to agree, as she bangs and clatters far more than is necessary to cook eggs.

Mamá asks very softly, 'Mimi, sweetheart, can you tell us what happened yesterday? Why were Alberto and Néstor fighting?'

I don't know what to say, so I burrow my face into Papá's chest.

Mamá perseveres. 'Your brother won't get out of bed today. He says he's not well, but apart from a black eye, I can't see anything wrong with him. Won't you tell us what happened, Mimi?'

I think about the question, but I don't know what to say. I'm too confused. And right now, I'm too worried about where my friend is.

Papá says to Mamá, 'I'm sure it was nothing.' Then he kisses the top of my head and says, 'How about some of Chita's delicious eggs?'

★　★　★

I drag the long stick along the dusty earth, leaving a lined furrow. Leaning over, I take a close look at the vine I'm standing beside. Gnarled and cracked and charcoal grey, it looks ancient. Papá says Noah planted the first vine when he got off the ark. Looking at this vine, I can believe it.

The workers are all having a siesta. It's a hot, dry day and usually I would be in the cool of the house. But I want to be out in the vineyard, waiting for Alberto to come back.

In the distance, I hear a buzzing, like a loud mosquito. Lifting my hand to my eyes, I turn towards the noise. There, at the end of the drive, is a motorcycle.

I drop the stick and start running towards the house. As I run, I keep glancing over to the motorcycle, which is now near the house entrance. There is no question in my mind that it brings news of Alberto.

As I get closer to the house, I see a soldier climb off the bike and walk towards the courtyard. I can just hear him calling for Papá.

Suddenly, I don't want to run anymore. I slow to a walk, putting my hands on my hips and puffing loudly. By the time I reach the entrance to the courtyard, I am dragging my heels. I realize I don't want to know the news.

I stop by the arch, leaning in to see. Mamá and Papá are standing together at the door to the house. The soldier has his back to me, speaking to them. I can't hear what he is saying, but as I watch, Mamá puts her hand over her mouth, and Papá puts his arm around her.

They both look shocked, but Papá seems to be asking the soldier questions. The soldier shakes his head. Papá speaks again, this time more insistent. The soldier reaches into his uniform and pulls out some papers. He hands them to Papá, who looks at them carefully. He shows them to Mamá, and I see her start to cry.

Papá puts the papers into the top pocket of his shirt. He seems to be thanking the soldier, who nods to him and turns on his heel. He walks out of the courtyard, passing me without a glance. I hear him kick-start his motorbike. It takes a few attempts before he gets it going, but then I hear it driving away, its engine sounding like a mosquito again, buzzing into the distance.

Mamá and Papá have seen me. Papá beckons me to come to him. Reluctantly I walk towards them, kicking the jacaranda petals with my shoe. As I reach them, Papá hunches down to look me in the eyes.

'Darling Mimi. It's very bad news.'

I nod to let him know I want him to continue, despite the fact that my stomach is lurching.

'Alberto and his papá were in a motor accident.'

'Is Alberto all right?' I ask, my voice sounding very far away.

'No, Mimi. He isn't.' Papá takes a deep breath. 'Alberto and his papá have both passed away.'

I hear the sound of my own breathing in my ears and it sounds incredibly loud.

Mamá leans down to me and takes my hands in hers so I look at her. There are tears running down her face, but she tries to smile at me.

'They're with Alberto's mamá now, sweetheart.'

I nod but feel as if my body is not my own. My mind seems blank and I can think of nothing — not even my best friend.

I glance up. There at the window, pale and pinched, with a dark shadow under one eye, is Néstor.

9

As they stepped into the church's cool interior, Alberto immediately felt a sense of calm. There was no one around, so he took off his hat and steered the boy down the aisle, pausing only to cross himself before taking a seat on a creaking pew.

'Let's say a prayer for your papá,' said the old man in a low voice.

The little boy nodded, squeezed his eyes shut and clasped his hands together. Alberto smiled at the child's prayer. Taking a deep breath, he looked up at the altar and Christ on the cross. When María Luisa was alive, they had attended church regularly. These days, he only went when obliged by a funeral or Communion. But in the peaceful silence of this small church, he remembered how he could clear his mind and pray.

Closing his eyes, he prayed for Juan Carlos. He thought of his daughter, and her husband's mother sitting beside him in the hospital. He asked God to protect and heal them all. Then Alberto remembered Rosa had her sister with her, and Cristina was away from her husband and children.

Slowly, his joints objecting, Alberto lowered himself onto the leather stool. Dropping his head, he whispered prayers for all of his family. Inevitably, his mind wandered to María Luisa, and he prayed she was at peace. He pictured her as a young woman, her head thrown back with laughter, her arms reaching out towards him. The image gave him an ache to hold her and laugh with her again. She had always breathed such life into him, her energy infectious and indefatigable.

She had hidden her illness from him for as long as she could. When, at last, she could no longer fool him she was losing weight because of a diet, or her fatigue was due to playing with her little grandson, she had admitted she had felt unwell for over a year.

She told Alberto she knew it was serious, and when the doctor confirmed the cancer was fast-moving, and there was little that could be done, she simply nodded in agreement. Alberto had been dumbfounded, unable to comprehend what was happening to his wife and best friend.

As always, María Luisa had organized everything. She'd gathered the children to tell them, and she'd given Alberto clear instructions about her funeral and burial. He had silently accepted her directions and watched like a bystander as the children fussed over her. María Luisa had insisted she would make this as easy for everyone as she could. The whole village had remarked how courageous she was, and Alberto had agreed, but cautiously waited.

Then suddenly her energy vanished, only to be replaced by pain. María Luisa had been bewildered, not comprehending why death was reluctant to follow her plan. It was then Alberto held her hand and told her he would be strong enough for both of them. Looking deep into his eyes, her fear had slowly subsided and eventually she nodded.

From then on, Alberto took control. He announced that with the help of Rosa, he would nurse María Luisa at home. Friends in the village insisted that hospital was best, that caring for a sick woman was no job for a man, but Alberto brushed the comments aside, not interested in anyone else's opinion.

Doctor Herrera had known the family for most of his life and had even delivered Rosa. He supported Alberto in his decision and helped when he could, administering pain relief and sending a nurse to show them how to care for María Luisa as her health deteriorated.

Juan Carlos coordinated the rest of the family — who would visit and when. Cristina came as often as she could, sleeping on a camp bed at Rosa's house.

Soon María Luisa became bedbound, and while her daughters bathed her and changed the bedding in the mornings, Alberto would leave María Luisa and walk out to the land. There, he would tend his small vegetable patch, bringing back what he could for the girls to add to their mother's broth.

In the afternoons, Alberto would sit on María Luisa's bed and talk to her. Holding her hand and speaking softly, he told her who he'd seen in the village and who had sent their best wishes. He talked to her about how the plants and trees were doing on the land, and how large the lemons were growing. He described the colour of the sky and the heat in the sun, how noisy the road was and how fresh the mimosa smelt. María Luisa would listen and occasionally nod, whisper a question or smile.

His daughters were bemused. Their father had always been a man of few words, and yet now, when words were needed, he found them.

Sometimes Alberto picked wild flowers and put them in a small vase by the open bedroom window. María Luisa would look at the flowers, the delicate petals fluttering gently in the breeze.

Once, he watched her gaze rise above the

flowers and up to the sky. The two of them had spent so much of their lives outdoors, he instantly understood her desire to feel the sun on her face again. With the doctor's approval, Rosa carefully wrapped María Luisa in her bedjacket and a soft blanket. Alberto and Juan Carlos then gently carried her down the stairs to where Rosa's brother, Jaime, was waiting in his car. They sat her on the back seat, padded with extra cushions.

Alberto climbed in with her, and with one arm around her bony frame, he asked his son to drive. Slowly, the car crept out of the village and onto the main road. It travelled through the countryside at a snail's pace. María Luisa saw the rows of orange trees and the old white finca, with shocking-pink bougainvillea draped over its front arches. She saw the water gushing down the irrigation channel by the side of the road and spotted a tabby lazing on a stone wall, its tail twitching. Alberto had watched her gaunt face relax as she shut her eyes. Her mouth hadn't moved, but Alberto had seen the smile in her eyes before she closed them.

When they reached Alberto's plot of land, Jaime had parked the car so that his mother could see out towards the terraces. On the nearest edge of the terrace, Cristina, her husband and Jaime's wife stood by a folding table covered with food. Five of María Luisa's grandchildren had been playing chase on the terraces, clambering up the stone walls and racing round the almond trees.

Alberto climbed out of Jaime's car, opened the door by his wife and made her comfortable with the cushions. Juan Carlos's battered old car pulled up, Tino flinging open the door to run to the game. Rosa joined the women, carrying folding chairs, which they set up so they could sit by María Luisa.

With a roar, Juan Carlos rushed towards the children, chasing the little ones, who ran away squealing with laughter. The other two fathers had quickly been dragged into the game too, and as they poured the wine, the wives laughed at their husbands getting dirty and breathless.

Alberto sat by María Luisa, holding her hand and talking quietly to her all afternoon. At times she slept, but mostly she sat, listening to Alberto and watching her family with shining eyes as they chattered and ate, played and laughed.

María Luisa had died three days later.

Rubbing his eyes with his thumb and forefinger, Alberto eased himself back onto the pew. It was only then he noticed the boy wasn't there. Glancing around the church, he couldn't see him anywhere. Panic rising in his chest, he stepped out into the aisle and started walking towards the altar.

It was then that he saw Tino standing in the gloom by a side door. The child was reaching up for the old metal handle when the door swung open with a clang. The boy jumped back and Alberto stepped quickly over to him.

Strong sunlight flooded into the church, making the child and his grandfather squint at the figure at the door.

'Hello!' said a cheery voice.

As his eyes adjusted to the light, Alberto saw a young priest dressed in a black shirt and trousers, his clerical collar pristine white.

'Good afternoon,' he replied gruffly.

'Hello,' said Tino.

The priest smiled at them both, leaving the door open and letting in the warm air.

'Were you looking for me?'

'Yes, we were,' said Alberto.

'Well, why don't we step outside? It's such a lovely day,' the young priest said.

Alberto nodded and led the boy out through the door and into a small cemetery surrounded by a stone wall. At the back of the church stood a large carob tree, pods hanging from its wide branches. Alberto looked around.

The priest indicated an iron bench leaning

on the side of the church, half shaded by the roof. As Alberto sat down heavily, the boy said, 'Apu, can I play?'

When his grandfather nodded at him, Tino immediately ran to the carob tree, searching for the best branches to climb.

The young man sat next to Alberto and smiled brightly at him. 'How can I help you, señor?'

'Romero. Please call me Alberto, Father.'

'Welcome. My name is Father Samuel.'

'Thank you.' Alberto looked again around the small cemetery. The young man waited patiently.

'Many years ago,' started Alberto cautiously, 'when I was just a child, a priest at this church looked after me.'

'Oh, how interesting. When was that?'

'During the war.'

'Aha. Very difficult times,' replied the priest carefully.

'Yes. The priest was a good man and I wonder if you know his name.'

Father Samuel's smile faded. He glanced towards the boy, who was busy climbing the tree. He seemed deep in thought, so Alberto remained quiet.

Eventually, the priest looked at the old man seriously. When he spoke, he lowered his voice. 'I've lived here for four years, and I don't believe I've seen you here before. Can I ask how you came to meet this priest?'

Alberto nodded slowly, understanding Father Samuel's reticence.

'I was lost in the war. I don't remember how I got here, but a tall priest with spectacles took care of me for a short time. He put me on a lorry that took me to an orphanage.' Alberto hesitated, wondering whether to reveal his other memory.

'Is there something else?' asked Father Samuel.

Alberto took a breath. It was all so long ago; surely it meant nothing now. 'I have a memory of an argument, between the priest and a soldier. An officer in Franco's army.'

At this, Father Samuel nodded and took a deep breath. 'Yes, that sounds like Father Francisco.'

Alberto sighed. 'Yes. That was his name — Father Francisco. Do you know what happened to him?'

Samuel looked at Alberto seriously. 'I'm afraid it is not good news. Father Francisco was removed by the army. He was accused of being a traitor and sent to a concentration camp. The records are inconclusive, but I believe he died there.'

Alberto breathed out heavily. 'That seems hard to believe. The Church supported

Franco. I was taught by priests when I was in the orphanage — they often spoke of the Catholic martyrs murdered by the Republicans.'

'Yes, that's right. The Red Terror, they called it. Even before the war, thousands of Catholic clerics were killed. There were horrific reports of atrocities — executions, castrations — I even read that a priest was thrown to the bulls in a bullring.'

Alberto sucked his teeth and shook his head.

'It was understandable that the Church aligned itself with the Nationalists during the war. Your Father Francisco was a rarity: he had a strong social conscience. He refused to take sides, and instead supported those who needed help the most — the poor. But that meant that he was accused of supporting the enemy.

'These days, of course, we consider ourselves a rather more charitable institution, but back then Francisco was sadly ahead of his time.'

'How do you know this about him?' asked Alberto.

Father Samuel smiled softly. He pointed towards the rows of old stone and marble stones marking graves. 'Do you see that grave there? The one with a wooden cross?'

141

Alberto squinted and saw the outline of a grave. At one end stood a small, weathered cross. He couldn't see clearly, but it didn't look as if there was a name on the cross. Nodding, he turned back to the priest.

'Ever since I arrived, I've always spent time out here. I know it's a little unorthodox, but I feel close to God in the sunshine. And it's always so peaceful — I get a great deal of thinking and prayer done here.

'As I walk the cemetery, I look at the names, trying to match them with the families I see every Sunday. When I came across that grave, it had no cross. It looked as if there had been one, but it had been destroyed. I looked in the church records, such as they were, but could find no reference to it. I asked some of the people I met here. The younger ones knew nothing, but a few of the elders gave me the impression they knew something but did not like to speak of it.'

Alberto nodded. 'It's understandable that people are reticent to speak of the war. So many atrocities, so many families destroyed.'

'Yes,' agreed the priest. 'And you know how everyone fell into the Pact of Forgetting — both sides agreeing it was better to look forward than risk looking back to the divides that tore this country apart.'

'What's done is done. There's no point in picking at a sore.'

'Exactly. I didn't want to push anyone, so I left it and, truth be told, I forgot. Life in a small town is busier than you might think, Alberto.

'Then, one day, I was called to administer the last rites to an elderly gentleman. He was very ill and I sat with him for a long time. When he passed, his wife — a woman of great strength — asked me to pray with her for the soul of her husband.

'When we finished, she brought a wooden box to me. She explained that for many years her husband had been a custodian to a few churches in the area. He held the keys and looked after the maintenance of the buildings. She said that when I'd asked about the unnamed grave in the churchyard, her husband told me he knew nothing about it. But in fact he did.

'He had found a body hanging from a tree — a suicide. Together, he and Francisco buried the poor soul in the unmarked grave. She said her husband always had the greatest respect for Father Francisco and his compassion. And when the army took him away, her husband was asked to collect the father's possessions and deliver them to the bishop. He did as he was asked — but didn't hand over everything: he'd come across the small wooden box and realized it contained Father Francisco's diaries. Somehow, he didn't want them falling into the bishop's hands, so hid them in his home. Later, when I asked about the grave, he instructed his wife to give me the box on his death.'

Alberto raised an eyebrow.

'In them,' continued the priest, 'he described his life here and his thoughts and beliefs. Of course, the first diary I searched for was the one explaining the occupant of the unmarked grave. It was written before the war and documented Father Francisco's arrival here at the church.

'He wrote about the death of a friend of his, explaining that his friend had killed himself here in the churchyard — he hanged himself from that tree.'

Father Samuel pointed to the carob tree that the boy was climbing. Alberto felt a slight shiver run through him.

'Because it was a suicide, a mortal sin, he buried the body at night, in an unmarked grave. That in itself was shocking — and I understand why no one had been willing to tell me about the grave when I asked. But as I read on, I discovered something even more dreadful. Father Francisco's friend had also been a priest.'

'A priest?' gasped Alberto.

The father nodded. 'Father Francisco inherited his friend's position here in the church. In his diary, he wrote of wanting to be near the spirit of his friend. But then, reading between the lines, he became comfortable here. He supported the poor and often helped farmers with the harvest. I can imagine he was not popular with the more wealthy members of the community, but the majority of the congregation seemed to warm to him quickly.'

'Father, did you read anything about his time during the war?'

The priest shook his head.

'Do you still have the diaries?' asked Alberto.

'I'm afraid not,' said the father, taking a deep breath. 'When I mentioned the diaries to my bishop, he showed great interest in them. When he asked me for them to read, how could I refuse? I believed them to be — how would one put it? — on loan. But when I mentioned them again to the bishop, he said he had sent them to the Church archivists. Although I have asked for them to be returned, I'm afraid my requests have been refused.' Father Samuel shrugged. 'Such is the Church's will.'

'That's a shame,' said Alberto quietly.

'Yes,' nodded the priest. 'But, from the little I read, it seems Francisco was a good man and a priest who was loyal to his community. I'm sure you'll understand, Alberto, that when the war came and his principles were revealed, the institution of the Church did not see him as the compassionate priest he clearly was. It's very sad.'

Alberto nodded slowly, absorbing the information. Taking a deep breath, he looked up and saw the unmarked grave.

Father Samuel followed Alberto's gaze and said, 'I believe it was Father Francisco's intention to add his friend's name to the cross. It was perhaps indelicate to do so when the village was still in shock over their priest's suicide. Many would probably consider the ignobility of an unmarked grave a fitting end for such a sinner. He was probably waiting for tempers to cool. But then the war came and the strength of feeling about the Church was such that any act like that would only fuel emotions.'

Alberto nodded. 'Poor man,' he said softly, looking towards the grave. 'Do you think he'll ever have his name on his grave?'

'It is my hope. I have submitted a letter to my bishop, asking both for the man's date of birth and any necessary details, and for permission to place a headstone on the grave.'

'Good,' said Alberto.

'Unfortunately,' sighed Father Samuel, his smile slipping again, 'the wheels of the Church roll rather slowly. The bishop referred my request to a higher level. I have been waiting over a year for a reply.'

Shaking his head, Alberto looked back at the grave. 'All this time and they still can't find a way to forgive him.'

'Perhaps,' said Father Samuel quietly, 'they know what drove him to take his life.'

Alberto paused thoughtfully, then shook his head. 'If he was a friend of Father Francisco, he must have been a good man. It is God's decision to forgive, not the Church's.'

Father Samuel nodded. 'I understand, Alberto. But protocol dictates a process must be followed. I shall write to my bishop again.'

Alberto continued to look at the grave. 'Do you know the priest's name?'

'Father Antonio,' said Father Samuel softly.

As the two men regarded the grave, Tino trotted up beside them.

'What are you looking at?' he asked.

'Nothing,' said Alberto. He turned to the child. The boy was filthy. He was grey with dust, and his legs were covered in small scratches.

'Oh dear,' said Father Samuel cheerily.

'Looks like someone could do with a wash. Why don't we let your grandfather have a moment here, and I'll show you where you can get clean?'

They both looked at Alberto, who nodded at them.

Chattering to the boy, the priest led him back into the church. For a moment, Alberto closed his eyes, letting the sun warm his face, and listened to the low buzz of the town on the other side of the wall. Then, opening his eyes, he reached into his trouser pocket and brought out his old penknife.

★ ★ ★

Alberto and the boy walked into Los Niños and looked around. The restaurant was now half full, mostly with men in their work clothes drinking beer and picking at plates of tapas. Andrés, dressed in a white shirt and black trousers, bustled around the customers, filling glasses and collecting plates.

They walked to the bar and Alberto helped the boy onto one of the high stools. The child kicked his feet side to side as Alberto wearily perched on the edge of his.

'Señores,' said Andrés, slipping behind the bar. 'Welcome back. What can I bring you?'

Alberto asked for a beer for himself and a

lemon drink for the boy. When Andrés brought them, Alberto took mouthfuls of the cold beer, reflecting on what he'd heard at the church. The boy crunched his way through a plateful of crisps Andrés had placed in front of him and watched a television that hung from the ceiling at the end of the bar.

Just as Alberto was finishing his beer, the bead curtain rustled and Isabel stepped out of the kitchen.

'Doña Isabel!' said the boy brightly.

'Hello, child,' smiled Isabel. 'Hello, Alberto.'

'Hello,' replied the old man warmly. 'It's good to see you again.'

'So,' said Isabel to Tino as she leant against the side of the bar. 'What have you learnt? Are you any closer to knowing more about your grandpapá's history?'

The child suddenly looked at his grandfather. He had been distracted by the tree and had forgotten the reason for visiting the church.

Alberto nodded at the boy. He was pleased that the child had been able to play for a while.

'I found out the name of the priest who looked after me,' he said as cheerfully as he could.

'What was it, Apu?'

'Father Francisco.'

'Did you find out what happened to him?' asked Isabel.

'He was considered a traitor by the Nationalists,' said Alberto. 'It seems he died during the war.'

'Oh,' said the boy.

Isabel shook her head sadly.

'So we have reached the end of our search,' said Alberto.

'What?' said the boy anxiously.

Alberto frowned. He had expected Tino to be disappointed, but the fretful reaction surprised him.

'Well, there's no more information to be gained from the orphanage, and Doña Isabel has very kindly helped us with everything she could. Now we know about my time here in this village, before the orphanage. But there's nothing else. I don't remember anything before Father Francisco, and we've run out of clues.'

'But can't we ask someone else?' The child seemed agitated.

'Who?'

'Other old people in the town?'

Alberto and Isabel chuckled.

'What will we ask them?' said Alberto gently. ''Excuse me. Do you remember a boy who was in this village for a short time in the 1930s?''

The boy shook his head in alarm. 'But, Apu, it can't be over already.'

'I know — it's sad we didn't get more answers. But we tried, didn't we?'

'But we didn't find your birthday, Apu!' the little boy whined, almost in tears.

Alberto glanced up at Isabel. She looked at him quizzically.

'That's what we are looking for — my birthday.'

'Ah,' said Isabel, looking at Tino. 'I understand. Birthdays are so important to a child.'

'For some reason, it has become important to me too,' said Alberto quietly.

Isabel nodded kindly.

Suddenly, the little boy burst into tears.

10

DANTE

24 May 1934

It's a mistake to come into the kitchen, but the smell is too tempting to resist — a wonderful mixture of frying onions and roasting meat. But one look at my wife directing the dozen or so women and girls, and the military-style manoeuvres involved in the preparation of so many dishes, and I know this is no place for a man.

The large oak table is the centre of activity, with herbs being chopped, fruit being peeled and sausages being sliced. At the far end, away from the oven, Néstor sits in a chair propped up by cushions. With chubby fingers he reaches into a bowl of shelled peas and does his best to put them in his mouth. Beside him stands Mimi, peering over the edge of the table watching Chita gutting fish. The poor girl looks too terrified to move as women work around her, brushing her with their skirts.

'Don Dante!' calls Chita with a smile.

'Have you come to help us?'

My wife turns to me, her face flushed and her usually perfect hair tousled. She tries to smile at me, but I can see she doesn't have the time for unexpected visitors.

'Chita, my wife obviously has everything under control.' I smile at the working women and add, 'The cooking smells magnificent, ladies.' Then, turning to my wife, I say, 'Perhaps I should liberate these two?' and point to the children. With relief she smiles at me and nods.

As I pick Néstor up out of his chair and take Mimi's little hand, my wife steps over to me, wiping her hands on her apron. 'Thank you, dear husband,' she says. She gives me a kiss on the cheek.

'Don't overtire yourself,' I say quietly to her. 'It's a party. I want you to enjoy it too.'

'I'll enjoy it when all the work is done,' she says. She picks up a couple of slices of chorizo from the table beside her. Popping them in my mouth, she smiles and turns back to the stove to stir a bubbling pot.

Chewing the rich, spicy sausage, I lead Mimi out of the kitchen and into the courtyard. There, some of the men are setting up tables and bringing chairs out of the house.

Raúl is kneeling on the floor, attaching

lanterns to a wire for hanging. Alberto is sitting beside him watching. As we approach, I look at Mimi and see her face light up at the sight of her friend. Néstor seems unaffected and sucks on his fingers.

'Can we help?' I ask.

'Dante! Excellent timing. I'm ready to hang these lanterns. Could you take the other end?'

I set Néstor down on the floor beside Alberto, and Mimi flops down alongside them both. They watch as Raúl and I fetch chairs and climb them to carefully attach the wire onto hooks so the lanterns swing over the long tables.

When we've finished, we step back and take a look.

'It's going to be a great party, Dante,' says Raúl. He smiles sadly at me.

I put my hand on his shoulder. 'It's a celebration,' I say softly.

He nods.

I know he must feel strange about today. After many years of hard work on both our parts, Quintero's Winery has produced its first brandy. But the brandy is a memorial to the wife that he has lost.

When Angelita died all those years ago, I wanted to do something that would express the grief we each felt. I had been thinking about expanding my vintage into brandy, and it had seemed a fitting memorial. A beautiful woman of such charm and spirit deserved to be remembered forever, and the first bottle of our new brandy would do so.

The financial outlay to start producing a brandy has cost me a great deal, but now that my wine is the preferred choice of some of the most influential families in the region, the investment seems a good one.

Over the years, Raúl and I have visited other brandy-and sherry-makers around the country. In learning the process, we've inspected the barrels where the wine is aged and followed the ancient instructions for blending.

As a scientist, Raúl has enjoyed the study of the production process. And importantly, I think the project has served him well in overcoming his grief at the death of his wife. For me, it's the history. The process that has been used in Spain for centuries has a slow, methodical procedure that will continue into the future. It appeals to my sense of heritage.

Since I commissioned the building of a series of ageing barrels four years ago, we've been following the process of tapping the oldest barrel and refilling it with wine from the next oldest. As we repeat and repeat, the blending of wines over the years gives the brandy its character.

I am proud I have begun something that Néstor will carry on, and as long as the wine is good and the barrels are cared for, the brandy will only improve over the years. Even the label has been designed in the classical style with a flourish of script and the vine-yard's crest.

Although our first bottle is still very young, we decided this was the perfect excuse for a celebration. It has been a difficult few years. The economic problems of the country have affected us, as they have many others, but we have done what we could for our workers and they seem content, despite the unrest around us. They also know the government is swift in arresting anyone who speaks out against land and business owners.

As my father always said, support your workers and in difficult times they will support you. So, like my father, I treat the workers as extended family. When times are difficult, I gather them and explain how we will be affected. I know many of them supported the Second Republic, with its promise of land to the workers. When nothing happened, the workers were disappointed, but they know that I am modern in my approach to their rights and their pay.

I hope the party tonight will bring us together. It's an opportunity for us to say thank you to the workers for their loyalty. They'll bring their wives and children; they'll eat well, drink too much and taste our first brandy. As Raúl says, it's going to be a great party.

'Let's take a walk,' I suggest to Raúl.

He nods to me and we turn to the children. Mimi is trying to pick up her baby brother, but he's too heavy for her, and as she half lifts, half drags him towards me, his face scrunches up and he starts to cry.

When Mimi was a baby, she rarely cried, but when she did, it was a heartbreaking sound. Maybe it's because she was our first, but often my wife and I, and even Chita, would rush to see what we could do to ease her distress.

Néstor, however, cries often and the sound is shrill and screeching. It's not an endearing noise and, I'm ashamed to say, all too often we placate him with food. He's a portly baby, which is perhaps why he is late to start walking. But my wife insists once he's on his feet and running around, the weight will drop off him.

I lift the boy from Mimi's arms and bounce him up and down until his crying eases. He grabs my ear and pulls hard, grinning a toothy smile. His grip is strong and I have to gently prise his fingers open to release my sore ear.

'Right,' I say loudly, 'who wants to go and inspect the grapes?'

'Me!' shouts Mimi loudly and happily.

Alberto nods enthusiastically.

'Me too!' says Raúl cheerfully.

Together, the four of us stroll out of the courtyard and down to the land. The new season's growth looks good. Lines of vines with large, veined leaves stand healthy and strong. As we walk down the dusty, dry path between the crop, I stop at one vine and fold back a few of the leaves. There, hanging like a bunch of green bullets, are the grapes.

I pick one from its stalk and wipe the dust from it. Bending down, I hold it in front of Mimi and Alberto. Néstor, resting on my hip, looks over my shoulder back towards the house.

'Look, children,' I say to them both. 'What do you think this is?'

'It's a grape,' says Alberto confidently.

Grinning, Mimi shakes her head.

'It's much more than a grape, Alberto,' I say.

The young boy looks confused.

'It is the blood of Christ.'

Poor Alberto looks even more confused.

'It's the toast at a wedding,' I continue. 'It's the completion of a business deal. It's the heart that beats between family and friends. This tiny grape, children, is going to be wine. Wine that may be savoured with a loved one, or shared among many. It may be drunk as soon as it's bought, or hidden away in a cellar. But however and whenever it is drunk, in that moment, it will be a part of people's lives.

'As a family of winemakers,' I continue, 'it is our past and our future. And this grape will take a little piece of us to people we'll never meet, all over Spain. Isn't that incredible?'

Mimi nods enthusiastically. She loves to hear about the wine.

Alberto nods a little more hesitantly. Looking up at his father, he says, 'But I am not a Quintero. Papá and I are Romeros.'

Raúl gives me a worried look, but with a nod I indicate that I will explain.

'Alberto, family is not always about a name. In our case, family is more than birth. It's about an unbreakable bond of love. You and your papá have been a part of my family since before you were born, and that bond is very strong.

'And if ever you wanted proof of your role in this family, you need only look at the bottle of brandy that we will open tonight. You'll see

159

on the label how it celebrates you and your beloved mamá.'

The boy looks a little unsure still. I wonder how much Raúl has spoken to him about his mother. Shifting Néstor on my hip, I hunch down to Alberto's level.

'You are an important member of this family, Alberto. You hold a special place in our hearts. And I hope that in the future you will help Néstor run the Quintero vineyard as your father has helped me. The wine we produce today is the best we've ever made, and that's thanks to your father. It is my ancestor's name on the bottle, but there's as much of your father's soul in every sip as mine.'

I look at Raúl. He seems uncomfortable but bends his head to me in thanks. He is a good man, and I hope I tell him often enough how much I value him.

Alberto smiles at me and his soft brown eyes melt my heart — they are just like his mother's.

Ruffling his curls, I stand straight. 'Right, who can run to the fence and back the fastest?'

Before I've finished speaking, Mimi is off, running as fast as she can, kicking up tiny dust clouds behind her. Alberto gives me one last look before dashing after her.

'Thank you, Dante,' says Raúl quietly as we slowly start to walk in the direction the children are running.

'I mean every word I say.'

Raúl shakes his head and says, 'I mean thank you for taking us into your family. You knew nothing about us when we arrived and yet you took in an inexperienced chemist and his pregnant wife as if it were nothing. And now you talk about Alberto being part of Quintero's future, well, it's incredible.'

'You, Angelita and Alberto have made our lives richer,' I say gently.

'That's kind of you. But you don't know anything about us — our family, our past — '

I raise my hand to stop him. 'When you arrived, it was clear you were keen to start a new life for you and your new family. Who am I to judge your people or where you have come from? That's why I've never asked about your background . . . despite my wife's curiosity. I could see straight away that you would be good for the business and that we would get on.' I smile at him. 'And I was right, so let that be an end to it.'

After a pause, he nods.

'What do you think the brandy will taste like?' I ask him.

Raúl sighs and says, 'After four years of

161

hard work, I just hope to God it tastes like brandy.'

* * *

There's a slight breeze and the lanterns gently sway over the bowed heads at the table. Father Sebastián is saying grace and I take a sneaky glance at my family, friends and workers.

Mimi, sitting beside me, opens one eye and squints at me. I wink at her and she shuts both eyes tight again. I, too, drop my head and listen to the father. He gives thanks to God for the strength to work the fields, for the sunshine that the grapes thrive on, for the love of the people around the table that has helped create wine to be proud of. Finally — as the youngsters start to fidget — he blesses the feast that's laid before us.

Everyone mumbles, '*Amén*'; the sound is quickly replaced by spoons in dishes and cheery talk. A few of the women stand and bring large plates of the roasted baby lamb to serve the men.

I pick up a dish of chorizo and potato, and spoon some onto Mimi's plate, then some onto mine.

Reaching across for some bread, the little girl looks around her, at the people talking

162

and laughing. Some of the men have had a few beers before coming to dinner, so the conversation is flowing easily. There's plenty of wine, so it won't be long before the talk becomes bawdy and I'll suggest my wife takes Mimi up to bed.

But for now, she's enjoying watching and listening, and every now and again she smiles at me or Alberto, who sits opposite her. She hasn't noticed she's spilt tomato sauce down the front of her best dress. Her mother will not be pleased, but I'm sure Chita will be able to remove the stain.

My wife approaches, holding a large plate. 'I've brought you your favourite,' she says. She tilts the dish for me to see. On the plate are partridges, cut in half, surrounded by onions and covered in a sauce of cider, herbs and nutmeg. The smell is wonderful and I shut my eyes and breathe in deeply as she serves me.

As she leans over me to spoon a little more sauce on my plate, I open my eyes and plant a huge kiss on her cheek.

'Dante!' she says loudly, half embarrassed, half amused. The men on the table near us cheer.

'Gentlemen, can there be anything better than fine wine, delicious food and beautiful women?' I say loudly.

'Add family and friends to that list, Dante,' replies Raúl, raising his glass.

'To Don Dante!' shouts one of the men, his cheeks flushed.

'Don Dante!' reply the rest of the table, raising their glasses.

I nod appreciatively at them and smile at my wife as she carries on serving the partridge.

We all eat heartily, and as the table rocks with laughter at a coarse joke, I catch myself chuckling along with them. Glancing towards Raúl, I notice he has slipped out of his seat. His plate is half finished, and as I glance around the courtyard, I see him disappear into the dark of the cellar.

Just then, my wife appears beside me with a plate of food in her hand. At last, she is able to sit and enjoy the meal she has prepared. I quickly stand and offer her my chair. As she sits, I pour her a large glass of wine — she deserves it. She thanks me and turns to Mimi, tutting at the sight of the stained dress. She cuts the child's food up for her and then turns her attention to Alberto, who has a large piece of lamb on the end of his fork, which he's biting into with great enthusiasm.

Picking up my almost empty wine glass, I take this opportunity to leave, and as I walk past the tables of people, some shout my name and raise their drinks. I salute them as I pass. Reaching the cellar entrance, I turn back and see everyone is talking loudly and laughing even more loudly. This fiesta is all I hoped it would be — and we haven't even brought out the brandy yet.

I descend into the gloomy cellar. As my eyes adjust to the light, I walk down the steps to where the large oak barrels line the walls. My shoes tapping on the stone floor, I walk past the rows of barrels looking for Raúl. I find him at the far end of the cellar.

'Raúl,' I say softly.

He turns to me and I see he has tears in his eyes.

I wait as he composes himself. I sense he wants to talk, so I let him take his time.

Eventually, he says, 'I wish she was here, Dante.'

'We all do. Tonight is a celebration of her.'

He nods. I wait for him to go on.

'She wouldn't want me to tell you, but the more you talk about how Alberto and I are part of your family, the more I feel I have to tell you the truth. The truth about why we came here. About why we had to get away.'

I wait.

Eventually, he whispers, 'Alberto . . . is not my son.'

As he looks me in the eye, I try to hide my shock. I step towards him and put a steady hand on his shoulder. 'Wait,' I say firmly.

With that, I turn to the shelves of wine. Down near the bottom is a bottle I placed there just a few days ago. I pick it up and show Raúl the label. It is one of our first bottles of brandy. He looks surprised as I hand it to him to open.

I empty the last wine from my glass and, taking out my handkerchief, wipe it clean.

Raúl eases the cork stopper out and smells the top of the bottle. I hold the glass towards him, and we both watch as the golden liquid fills it.

Swirling the brandy as I would a wine, I look at the small crown it leaves round the glass. I inhale, deeply: I can pick up woody and floral flavours. Then, pushing my nose closer to the liquid, I inhale deeply again. It is fragrant with a fruity aroma. I look at Raúl and raise my eyebrows.

Slowly, I tilt the glass and draw the brandy into my mouth. I let it open up and sense its velvety texture. Then the magic happens. Warm and smooth, the liquid flows down my throat, leaving a full bouquet in the finish. The aftertaste is short, proving the youth of the brandy, but the flavour is good. I am pleased.

Handing the glass to Raúl, I nod with approval.

He does the same as I did, savouring the smell first, then sipping the brandy. He closes his eyes and I see his face relax.

When he opens his eyes, he smiles at me. I smile back. We've done it.

'Now,' I say gently, 'tell me.'

Raúl takes another deep breath and hands me back the glass.

'I had known Angelita most of my life. We met when we were a little older than Alberto and Mimi. I adored her. If it is possible to fall in love as a child, I did. Even as a little girl she was beautiful. That long hair and those soft brown eyes — she just grew more incredible as she got older.

We went to separate schools, but we spent our evenings and weekends together. We would talk of everything — and I thought we would be together forever.

'On the day that I left home to go to university, she went to the station with me. It was there that I kissed her for the first time. I told her that I loved her.

'As I began my studies at university, I planned our life together — how I would become a renowned research scientist, and we would marry and have at least four children.' Smiling, Raúl sadly shakes his head. I hand him the brandy and he takes a deep drink.

'I wrote every week and at first she replied regularly. Then less so. Then barely at all.

'The next time I returned home, I visited her. I was surprised at how much she had changed. She was thin and serious — it was as though her youth and sparkle had disappeared. She was courteous but kept me at a distance.

'I spoke to her sister, Mercedes, about her. She said that Angelita had started disappearing, sometimes late at nights and she refused to speak of where she'd been.

'At first, Mercedes said Angelita had been happier than she'd ever seen her. But over a few months, the happiness had become something darker. During this time, Angelita turned to God. She started to visit church whenever she could. She barely ate, she left school and the life seemed to be seeping out of her.

'Mercedes confided in me that she believed Angelita was having an affair with a married man. She thought her sister was visiting church to repent her sins but the guilt was making her ill.

'I was shocked, appalled and distraught in equal measure. How could she change from being the innocent girl I had given my heart to, to another man's mistress?'

I shake my head and refill the glass. Raúl takes another drink.

'Eventually, I confronted her,' he continues. 'At first, she looked horrified at my accusation. I suppose she was so entrenched in it that she couldn't see what others could. Then she told me that yes, she was having an affair with a man who could never be hers. I begged her to leave him, but she said she loved him with all her heart.

'I became emotional and I'm ashamed to say I wept in front of her. She looked at me with such pity that I had to leave. I returned to university. I threw myself into my work and did well at my exams. The next time I came home, I avoided Angelita's family and her friends. But the day before my return to college, Angelita appeared at our door.

'She looked terrible, dark circles under her beautiful eyes, and her long hair was lank. She asked if I could forgive her and allow her to talk to me. Of course, I said yes to both.

'We went for a walk in the park. There, she told me that the affair was over. He had finished it a few months earlier. I expressed my relief, but she broke down in tears. She told me that she was pregnant. The father had no idea and she couldn't tell him now that they were no longer together.

'We both knew her family would disown her. She told me that no one else knew, not even Mercedes, and she had turned to me, her only true friend, to help. She said she would understand if I wanted nothing to do with her. But I took her to me and held her in my arms.

'The solution seemed obvious to me. She would marry me and we would leave the area. I would raise the child as mine, and she would never have to see the father again. She couldn't believe it — that I would be prepared to take care of her and another man's child without a second thought.

'I told her that I loved her, that the past didn't matter. If she'd have me, we would start a fresh life together.'

I smile at my friend. 'You are a good man, Raúl. A romantic fool, but a good man.'

Taking another sip of brandy, he continues, 'The rest you know. We married quickly and I began looking for work. We chose this area as neither of us had family or friends near here. Meeting you was the best thing that could have happened to us: learning about the wine business alongside having the opportunity to apply my scientific knowledge to winemaking.

'We were happy. As her pregnancy developed, Angelita grew healthy; being so far from that other man seemed to help. Very occasionally I would catch her looking out of the window and I knew she was thinking of him. But she said she loved me and that she was looking forward to the arrival of this baby and many others.'

Raúl takes a deep breath and pauses. Then he carries on. 'You saw what her death did to me. I wasn't sure that I would recover. But the support I found here and the unconditional love of that little baby kept me going.

'I've never said anything to Alberto about his father. I think it's enough that he has no mother. Perhaps when he's older, I'll tell him, or perhaps there will never be a need to tell him.

'Whatever happens, I see him as my son. He is his mother's son in his looks, but he has picked up certain habits and characteristics from me, too. I adore him as I adored her. I'm very lucky, Dante. When I look into his eyes, I have the chance to see my adorable Angelita every day.'

Raúl stops talking and drains the glass.

'Well, your secret is safe with me, Raúl. If you decide to tell Alberto about his father, I will be here to support you. My wife and I are proud to be the family he doesn't have.'

'Thank you, Dante,' says Raúl. 'I've kept this secret for so many years. It is a relief to finally talk to someone about it.'

'I'm proud that you decided to confide in me, my friend,' I say, gripping his arm. 'Now, what do you say — shall we let the rabble outside try our fantastic brandy, or shall we stay down here and keep it to ourselves?'

11

The boy sucked noisily on the ice lolly, occasionally licking orange drips off its end. His grandfather pulled gently on a cigarette — a rare treat he sometimes allowed himself. They sat on a cold stone bench set back from a quiet road. The leaves of a line of palm trees rustled quietly above them, and cast a little shade from the sun.

'Are you all right?' asked Alberto. When the boy had calmed down, he'd taken him out for this small treat.

The boy stopped licking the ice lolly and looked seriously at his grandfather. We have to find your birthday, Apu,' he said.

'It might not be possible,' replied the old man. 'Look how difficult it has become already.'

Tears welled up in the little boy's eyes again.

'Don't be upset. Even if we don't find it, I have found Isabel. I never thought I'd see her again in my lifetime. So something good has — '

'But we have to find your birthday, Apu,' interrupted the child.

'Why? Why is it so important to you?'

Tino looked down, crunching the last mouthful of his lolly and swinging his legs. Alberto waited patiently for him to speak.

'Just because,' Tino eventually said, his bottom lip protruding.

'Because what?' the old man pressed gently.

'Because of God.'

'God?'

'Mmm.'

'What does God have to do with my birthday?'

'Nothing.'

The old man waited again, confused.

After a short wait, the boy sighed loudly.

'It's just fairer, that's all. If you get your birthday back, Papá will get better.'

'What do you mean?'

'I prayed. I said to God, if I help you look for your birthday and we find it, then he'll make Papá better.'

Alberto stared at the child, bemused and touched. 'So you suggested a deal to God? If you do something nice for me, then he'll do something for you?'

The child nodded, still looking at his swinging feet.

'Well, I don't know for sure, but I don't think God does deals. If he makes your papá better, it's because he loves you, and Mamá and Papá.'

'But what if Papá doesn't get better? Does that mean God doesn't love me?'

The old man could see the tears welling up again and heard a wobble in the boy's voice. He pulled the child towards him and held him. 'God will always love you. Just like Mamá and Papá and me.'

The little boy let out a sob, and the old man held him tighter.

'Your papá is getting better — remember what Mamá said? But we must both keep praying, and telling God how much we love Papá.'

The old man sat holding the small boy for quite some time.

★   ★   ★

It was mid-afternoon, and the restaurant was emptying when they sat down to eat their meal. Alberto had accepted Isabel's invitation but told the boy they would start their journey home afterwards.

The old man was more disappointed than he had ever imagined he would be when they'd started this journey. Having had a few of his memories jogged back to life, he wanted to know more. Where had he come from? How had he arrived at this village? What of his family? There was so much to learn, but they had reached the end of their search.

Isabel sat beside him, watching in delight as Tino wolfed down the food she'd put before him. She turned to look at Alberto, who gave her a sad smile.

'I'm sorry,' she said.

'Don't be. This search has brought me to you. I'm glad to have seen you again.'

Isabel smiled back. 'I'm very glad you found me. In fact,' she said, easing herself up from the table, 'I know the perfect thing to mark the occasion.' Isabel turned and walked slowly to the bar, leaning heavily on her stick. Andrés appeared as if from nowhere to help her, but she waved him away.

Leaning behind the bar, she opened a dark wood cabinet and reached towards the back of the shelf. When she stood straight again, Alberto saw she was holding a dark green bottle. 'I save this for very special occasions,' Isabel said. She walked back towards them.

By the time she reached the table, Andrés was placing two brandy glasses beside them.

'And one for yourself, Andrés,' said Isabel.

Andrés raised an eyebrow to her, but Isabel nodded. 'If it weren't for this man, you would never have been born,' she said.

Andrés silently placed another glass on the table.

With her gnarled fingers, Isabel twisted the cork stopper out of the bottle and poured a little into each of the glasses.

'This brandy was my husband's favourite. It's changed now — it's not as good — but luckily my husband bought a case many years ago. This is the last bottle of that case. I can't think of a better person to enjoy it with, Alberto.'

As Tino looked on, Alberto nodded graciously to Isabel.

'What are we toasting, Mamá?' asked Andrés, raising his glass.

'Alberto?' asked Isabel.

The old man paused a moment, swirling the glass and watching the rich umber liquid slide round inside. Finally, he raised his glass and waited while the others raised theirs. The boy raised his glass of pop.

'To friends. Friends we've lost and friends we've found,' said Alberto. He tilted his glass towards Isabel.

'To friends,' they all chorused.

Alberto took a large sip and let the brandy sit in his mouth, savouring its smooth flavour. Swallowing slowly, he turned the bottle to see the label.

'Apu,' said Tino excitedly, 'can I try some?'

'I don't think you'll like it, young man,' said Isabel, laughing.

'But it's a special bottle. I'd like to just try it. Can I, Apu?'

But Alberto wasn't listening. He was staring intently at the brandy bottle. As Isabel and the boy looked at him, he picked up the bottle and looked closely at the label on the front.

'Alberto?' said Isabel.

'Apu?'

Slowly, a smile spread across Alberto's face.

★   ★   ★

'Apu?' came the whisper in the dark.

'Yes,' came the gruff reply.

Alberto shifted in the bed. Andrés had insisted the pair of them should stay the night in his apartment, and his wife had made a fresh bed for Alberto and the boy.

'I told you we were going to find your birthday — and I was right!'

'We haven't found it yet. And I told you that I don't think that God does deals. You have to believe that Papá will get better. Believe it in your heart.'

'I do, Apu,' said the small voice. Then, 'When Papá is better . . . '

'Mmm?'

'Will he be . . . ?'

'What?'

'Will he be the same?'

'You heard your mamá say they were starting to remove the bandages. He is getting better.'

'No. I mean will he be the same as before?'

Alberto sighed. 'I don't know. I hope so.'

'But he was in a big explosion, Apu,' said the boy, becoming distressed.

Closing his eyes, the old man saw a blast — a burst of light and heat. But it wasn't a boiler he saw; it was a car. He frowned and the image began to fade.

'What if he can't do things anymore?' carried on the boy. 'What if he can't play football with me, or take me swimming?'

Alberto shook his head, still trying to dispel the image of a burning car and an unsettling feeling in the pit of his stomach.

'He will always be your father,' he said gently. 'Whatever happens, he will love you and care for you.'

'But he won't be the way he used to be. And the kids at school will laugh at me because there's something wrong with my papá.'

'Stop it,' said Alberto fiercely. 'I will not let you speak like that. If other children laugh, then they are not worth knowing. You will find your true friends. But this is not a time to worry about yourself. Now is the time to be brave — for your father and, more importantly, your mamá.'

In the dark, he heard the boy snuffle. He reached over and patted the boy's head.

'The doctors are very clever these days. They will do everything they can for your papá. It's not like when I was young. When I was at the orphanage, there were children who had been hurt terribly in the war.'

'Really?' came the small voice.

'Yes. Children who had been scarred or lost limbs. Many of them were younger than you and had survived all sorts of dreadful things. One boy I knew had been in a house that was hit by a shell. The house was reduced to rubble. He wasn't dug out by rescuers until the next day. All of his family were dead. They took him to hospital, and he saw injuries there that you couldn't begin to imagine.

'He was nearly completely deaf, after the noise of the explosion. He was confused and scared, so when he could, he ran away from the hospital.'

'Where did he go?'

'He found his way back to his street and some neighbours took him in. He lived with them until hunger and fear drove them to escape the city.'

'So he got away?'

'No. The Nationalists caught them. The older boys and men were shot.'

The boy gasped.

'The women were taken to prison, and the younger children were split up and taken to different orphanages. They were lucky not to have been killed too.'

'And you met him at the orphanage?'

'Yes. His hearing came back slowly, but he couldn't bear loud noises. I was quiet and he felt comfortable with me.'

'It sounds awful, Apu.'

'It was. That's why people never talk about it these days. But when you think things are difficult for you, think of what others have been through. Your troubles will seem easier then.'

There was silence while the boy seemed to contemplate his grandfather's words.

'Now,' said the old man, 'it's late. Time to sleep.'

'First, tell me again what you remembered, please, Apu.'

Alberto yawned, tired. 'It was the label on the brandy bottle. I recalled seeing it before. And when Doña Isabel showed me the wine as well, I remembered a vineyard.'

'Do you remember any people, Apu?'

'No. Just a big house with a courtyard and rows and rows of vines.'

'And the name on the bottle?'

'Quintero? I recognized that too.'

'Is it the name of the people who make the wine?'

'I suppose so.'

'Maybe they know your family, Apu!'

'Maybe. We'll find out tomorrow.'

'Apu?'

'Yes.'

'I think we're going to find your birthday tomorrow.'

Alberto was silent. It had surprised him how much his mood had changed this afternoon: from the disappointment of reaching a dead end to the excitement of finding a new clue. In the bar just before they went to bed, they made plans to visit Quintero's Winery the next day. The address was on the label, and although Alberto had never been to that area as an adult, everything about it seemed familiar.

And yet in the pit of his stomach lay an unsettling feeling — a very mild fear. Perhaps he would not like what he found. Perhaps questions would be answered only with questions. And now all these memories from his time at the orphanage were flooding back too, the war seemed closer. He couldn't remember a time since he'd lost María Luisa that he'd felt such extreme emotions.

But the boy was right. It felt as if answers were within his reach. His family, his birthplace, his birthday: it seemed likely that if they discovered one, the others would follow.

He wondered if his father had been a worker at the vineyard. He knew many vineyards had become collectives during the war. Many wine producers had gone out of business, but as the bottles in Isabel's cabinet proved, Quintero's had not.

He heard the child's breathing become deeper and knew that he was asleep.

Quintero. He had always been sure his name was Romero. Isabel had reminded him of the paper in his pocket that spelt out his name. She had said there was writing on the other side. It was in another language she recalled — German or English, she thought.

He had a vague recollection of a soldier writing the name down, but it was muddled. Soldiers and Father Francisco; the faces and uniforms were unclear to him. But the name — Alberto Romero — had always seemed right.

Yet now he wasn't quite sure. There was something about the name Quintero that gave him a sense of belonging.

Alberto lay in the dark trying to grasp the memory, but it was nothing more than a wisp.

★　★　★

The rhythm of the clapping and the strumming of the guitar reminded Alberto of evenings on the farms he'd worked on as a young man. As the taxi roared down the empty road, the driver tapped his thumbs on the steering wheel in time to the traditional music that echoed around the car.

On the horizon, blue mountains merged into the distant grey clouds. All around them, the undulating land bore line after line of dark green vines. There were no people in the fields, although, far in the distance, Alberto could see a bright red tractor lumbering slowly along.

Alberto looked at the sleeping boy, whose chin was wedged firmly into his chest. It had been a late night, and the whole family had been up early. Andrés had apologized for not being able to drive them to Quintero's, but he had to receive deliveries at the restaurant and he didn't want to leave all the work to his mother. Thanking him, Alberto had told him that he and his mother had done more than enough.

Isabel had come to wish them goodbye and good luck. She had given the boy a parcel of food for the journey, and the family had waved them off as they walked to the bus stop.

The bus had dropped them at the nearest village and they had found a taxi to take them out to the vineyard. They were now only a few minutes away. For the first time, Alberto had a tingle of anticipation in the pit of his stomach.

'Are you taking a tour of the vineyard, señor?' asked the driver.

'Maybe,' said Alberto. He wanted to be left alone to his thoughts.

The driver took the hint and went back to tapping along to the music. As the road gradually began to rise, Alberto saw a building in the distance. Leaning forward, he squinted at it. The driver noticed.

'Señor, that's the old hacienda. That's Quintero's.'

Alberto nodded, staring at it, realizing it meant something to him. He heard the boy stirring and turned to him.

'Apu?' said the sleepy child. He yawned and rubbed his eyes.

'We're nearly there.'

The boy joined his grandfather, looking blearily in the direction he pointed.

'Is that your old house?' he asked, wide-eyed.

'I don't know,' said Alberto quietly. He shook his head.

As they drew level with the stone building, the driver turned off the main road. A large sign proclaimed, QUINTERO'S WINERY — TOURS AND WINE TASTING AVAILABLE. The car rumbled up a wide, dusty drive, and Alberto could see a series of new low-rise buildings behind the large old house.

The taxi pulled up outside the building. Alberto paid with some coins from his small purse. The driver thanked him and gave him his number for when he was ready to be picked up.

The taxi drove off, leaving Alberto and the boy standing outside the building. A sign directed them through a large arch to the reception. Following the arrow, they entered a cool courtyard shaded by jacaranda trees.

Alberto stopped and looked around. It was so familiar to him it was as if he'd only been here last week. The sensation unnerved him, but a bubble of excitement rose in his chest.

Tino looked up at him and smiled. Alberto squeezed his hand. He owed the child a great deal.

They entered the hacienda through a large doorway. Inside, a young woman sat at a reception desk, talking rapidly on the phone. She was discussing the delivery of an order to Sweden. She saw Alberto and raised a finger at him — she would just be a minute.

Alberto gazed around. The room did not seem familiar. Modern furniture created a waiting room, with leaflets, brochures and wine magazines on every table. He had the sense that the building should smell of food, but it did not. It smelt of furniture polish.

He walked back to the open door and looked across the courtyard. On the opposite side, a large sign that said, CELLAR, hung over a wooden door.

Tino came up beside him and leant against his hip.

Finally, the woman finished her conversation and turned to Alberto.

'How may I assist you, señor?' she asked.

'Good morning, señorita,' he said politely. 'Could you tell me, are the owners here today?'

'Do you have a meeting booked?' she asked.

'No,' said Alberto. 'This is not business; it's personal.'

The woman looked at the boy, who smiled at her. She smiled back and her face softened.

'I'll see what I can do, señor. Could I have your name, please?'

187

'Romero.'

'Thank you, Señor Romero. Please take a seat while I call through for you.'

Alberto nodded his thanks and turned to sit in a large leather armchair. He was not used to such expensive furnishings and felt uncomfortable, but the boy followed him and clambered onto his knee.

'Apu?' he whispered.

'Yes.'

'We're nearly there.'

'Let's see.'

Alberto heard the woman talking quietly on the phone, but couldn't make out what she was saying. She seemed to be cajoling the person on the other end. Eventually, she put the phone down and smiled at Alberto.

'The owner will be down shortly. Can I get you anything? Coffee, water?'

'Thank you. No.'

The girl nodded and went back to her work behind the desk.

After a few minutes, Alberto heard steps coming down the stairs, and when a door opened, he saw a middle-aged man approaching. The man was well dressed and clean-shaven, and his shoes clicked on the polished floor as he walked towards them.

The boy jumped off his grandfather's knee and Alberto stood.

'Señor Romero,' said the man smoothly. He offered his hand. 'My name is Javier. I am the owner.'

Alberto shook the man's hand.

'Please, señor, come up to my office,' said Javier. He directed them towards the door from which he had just come.

The old man and small boy climbed the stairs to a large office on the first floor. Windows on both sides of the room gave views over the extensive vineyard. Air-conditioning hummed quietly, and Alberto thought it sad the windows weren't open to allow a cool breeze and the scent of the plants to enter.

The man sat behind a large desk covered in computers and gadgets Alberto did not recognize. On the wall behind the desk was a selection of framed certificates. Alberto sat on an upright chair and Tino stood beside him.

'How may I be of service, Señor Romero?' asked the man when he was settled.

'Could you tell me,' began Alberto awkwardly, 'did your family run this vineyard during the time of the war?'

'My family? The war?' asked Javier, surprised. 'No, no, not at all. My family were not in the wine business at all.'

Alberto remained still.

'My father was a businessman. I took over

his business and now have a number of successful businesses of my own. Three years ago, I decided to branch out into wine. I bought this winery then, and have since bought two more small ones. I'm modernizing and consolidating them.'

'Oh,' said Alberto.

'Yes,' said Javier. 'This winery was not doing well. The processes used were old-fashioned and inefficient. There was no room for growth, and they had no international connections. In just a few years, I've invested a great deal to modernize the production and now our export capacity is as good as any major wine brand you can name.'

Alberto looked out of the window. Disappointment overwhelmed him again. Tino looked at him sadly.

Javier saw their reaction and continued, 'Señor, I believe the family I bought the business from were here during the war.'

Alberto turned to him, his eyes sharp.

'In fact, I know they were. In our literature, we mention that the winery was owned by one family for nearly two centuries. That's where the name came from — the Quintero family. We considered changing it, but it's a solid name that our marketing department believed we could build on.'

Javier stood up and walked to a bureau at

the back of the room.

'If it's the Quinteros you're looking for, this may be of help,' he said, opening a drawer.

Alberto stood and he and the boy crossed the room to join Javier.

Javier pulled a plastic file out of the drawer. He opened it and took out some old black-and-white photos.

'I believe this is the family,' he said. He held up one of the pictures.

Alberto and the boy looked closely. The photo was taken at the front of the house and showed a group of four people. Their clothes suggested it was the 1950s. In the centre was a large, balding man in a white shirt. He was trying to look serious, but Alberto could see his smiling eyes. Next to the man was a smart woman, and beside her, a fat teenage boy and a pretty young woman.

'This,' said Javier, pointing at the boy, 'must be Néstor. It was Néstor Quintero that I bought the winery from.'

Alberto nodded.

Javier gave Alberto the photo and shuffled through the rest of the pictures. 'That one was obviously taken after the war, and others seem to be a bit later. I'm not sure if they help you at all?'

Alberto was peering closely at the girl. The whole family seemed familiar, but the girl was particularly memorable. Turning the photo over, he was disappointed to see there were no names.

'Señor?' said Javier.

'I'm sorry. This is what we are looking for, thank you. I don't suppose you know where Don Quintero lives now?'

Javier paused for a moment.

'I'm sorry to say, señor, that Néstor Quintero died shortly after the sale was completed.'

Alberto's shoulders slumped.

'With the money from the sale, he bought a large house near the city. I remember him saying he never wanted to live on a farm again. Sadly, he had a heart attack not long after he moved to his new home.'

'That's very sad,' agreed Alberto.

'I know he had a wife and children. You could perhaps find them in the phone book?' suggested Javier.

Alberto looked at the photo again in his hand. 'Do you know anything about the girl in the photo?'

'The young woman? Yes, of course, I forgot. She is Néstor's sister. Her name is Miriam.'

'Miriam,' said Alberto, sounding the name. It didn't sound quite right.

'Now, her address we do have,' said Javier.

You do?' asked Alberto, brightening.

'Yes. She became involved in the negotiations for the business. Everything was in Néstor's name, and he was focused on getting the best price he could. To be honest, I would have paid more for it, but he got a fair amount of money.

'Anyway, at first Néstor said he wanted nothing — the business, the house, even the furniture would be included in the price. He said he wanted a fresh start, with nothing of his old life here.

'But, one day, Miriam contacted me direct. She said she had spoken to Néstor and had persuaded him that some items were family heirlooms. Though he wanted nothing, she wished to have something to pass on to her children.

'She mentioned a few pieces of furniture, which was fine as we were planning to modernize the rooms to create offices anyway. But then she said she wanted the collection.'

'The collection?' asked Alberto.

'The collection of wine, señor,' said Javier seriously.

'Ah.'

'Well, you can imagine my disappointment. It was a collection of all the best vintages the vineyard had ever produced. Just a few bottles from selected years. It was an incredible wall of wine down in the cellar. I had planned to make it a feature of the tours.

'In the end, the lawyers got involved. While I think Néstor was angry and just wanted to complete the sale, Miriam persuaded him not to move forward until I agreed to this condition. Through the lawyers we renegotiated the price down.

'I respect Miriam for her decision — after so many years, it's only right that a family's history is maintained. I don't know if it's true, but I did hear that Néstor asked Miriam to pay him for what he had lost in the renegotiations. His own sister. He was not a generous man.'

Alberto nodded.

'But,' said Javier cheerfully, 'after the sale, we organized delivery of the collection to Miriam's house. And as a personal gift, for the past few years we have sent her a bottle of our best wine and brandy to add to the collection. So we have her address in our files. Would you like it?'

Alberto looked down at the photo again. The young woman was smiling and squinting in the sunshine. Her dark hair was swept up in the style of the time, but she looked natural and at home out of doors. Her dark eyes shone and Alberto knew he had to see her again.

'I would very much like to have her address, thank you.'

'No problem,' said Javier. He crossed back to his desk and picked up the phone, then spoke to the receptionist and asked her to find Miriam's address for Señor Romero.

Alberto looked down at the boy and nodded. The child grinned back at him.

'Oh, and, Señor Romero,' said Javier, putting down the receiver, 'if you wouldn't mind, perhaps you would take those photos with you? We found them when we were having some decorating done and have never got round to sending them on.'

'Of course,' said Alberto. He slid the photos into the folder and passed it to the boy. Tino slipped the folder under his arm and held it tightly.

Javier then led them down the stairs and back to reception, where the girl was picking a piece of paper up from the printer.

'Señor Romero, it was good to meet you,' said Javier. He offered a hand. It was clear he was keen to get back to his work.

'Thank you for your time,' said Alberto. He shook Javier's hand.

'I'll leave you in my receptionist's capable hands,' said Javier. He turned and disappeared through the door.

'Here you are, Señor Romero,' said the girl, offering him the piece of paper.

'Thank you,' said Alberto. He looked at the printed details. 'Do you know if this is far from here?'

'No, it's not too far. Maybe twenty minutes on the *autopista*. Would you like me to call a taxi for you?'

Alberto nodded. He was unused to taking taxis — it was an extravagance he couldn't usually justify. But this journey was special and all too soon he would be back at home. Why not enjoy the treat?

'Apu?' said the boy excitedly as the girl called the taxi company.

'Yes.'

'Do you remember Señora Miriam?'

'I believe I do.'

'Do you remember the family?'

'They seem very familiar, yes.'

'But they're not your family?'

'No. They are not my parents.'

'I wonder how you knew them.'

'Miriam will know.'

Tino jiggled with excitement.

'Señor,' said the receptionist, putting down the phone, 'the taxi will be about half an hour.'

'Thank you,' said Alberto.

'Can I offer you anything while you wait? Some coffee?'

'No, thank you,' said Alberto. 'But . . . '

'Yes?'

'No, I don't want to inconvenience you further.'

'Please, señor, I'd be happy to help.'

'I was wondering if it would be possible to see the cellar. Just for a moment?'

The receptionist smiled. 'Señor, it would give me great pleasure to give you a tour of the cellar. To be honest, I've spent all morning talking to businessmen about shipments and payments. It would be nice to smell the oak barrels and talk about the wine for a change.'

Smiling, she opened a drawer and pulled out a large bunch of keys.

'Thank you very much,' said Alberto.

'So,' said the receptionist to the little boy as she led them out into the courtyard and towards the cellar door, 'let's see what you know about how wine is made.'

12

RAÚL

7 November 1932

Her long dark hair is wound in a knot at the top of her head. Her soft brown eyes look to the right, and the tiniest hint of a smile flitters around the edge of her full lips. I know that smile — she is smiling to herself at what she considers a ridiculous situation.

And sitting for a photo would have seemed ridiculous to her. She was young and full of energy and wanted to be out living life — not creating a moment for history. But I, for one, am glad that someone — probably her father — insisted that she sit for that moment.

Holding the picture up to the light, I take a sip of my wine. Again I taste the mustiness and remind myself that I must mention my concerns about the oxidization to Dante. Shaking my head, I recall the days when I could enjoy a glass of wine without performing a chemical analysis.

I turn my attention back to my little Angel. What would she want me to do? For nearly two years, I've avoided this question. There has always been a reason not to think of it.

I was barely able to function those first few months after she died. Dante and his wife had given me all the support they could, and Chita had taken the babe into her care. In fact, it was Chita, rocking baby Alberto and humming him a lullaby one evening, who had commented on his eyes — that they were just like Angelita's. Standing over her, I had looked into the baby's eyes. And I had seen my Angelita looking back at me.

That was the beginning of my recovery. With Chita's help, I learnt how to care for a baby. In the night, I was the one to go to him. It was I who made him weak camomile tea when he was teething. When he started eating, it was I who chopped long slices of pear for him to gnaw on.

Of course, I had also resumed my work for Dante and the vineyard, so my days were occupied. Dante had insisted Alberto and I join the family at mealtimes. Mimi was just a baby too, then, and Chita clucked and cooed over the two of them as Dante, his wife and I ate and talked into the evening.

Alberto was nearly nine months old when Dante had broached the subject. Mimi had been baptized as an infant. Would Alberto be baptized soon? I realized I had been deliberately pushing the thought out of my mind. I explained it was complicated; Angelita's headstrong opinions about religion meant I would need to think about it. Dante nodded and left it at that.

Shortly after, the harvest started. One of our busiest times of the year had given me an excuse to ignore the situation for a while longer. By the time things began to ease, Alberto had begun walking. The joy I took from leading him around the room gave me such delight it was all I could think about.

And so it continued: looking for and finding a reason not to think about baptizing the child. But today, after Mass, Father Sebastián sought me out and asked me directly if I would like him to prepare for Alberto's baptism.

So now there's no more procrastinating. It is time to make a decision. Taking a deep breath, I look at Angelita again. This photo, taken years before we were married, shows a young girl before the complications of life and love. If I had asked that girl if she wanted her child to be baptized, she would have laughed at me and asked why in heaven not.

But the woman I married was scarred by a broken heart and a confused relationship with religion. We were married in a small chapel with only our immediate family present. Even then, she had seemed uncomfortable and agitated during the service and, at one point, had nearly fainted. Everyone assumed it was the importance of the occasion, but I knew it was probably the pregnancy, which we hid from our families. The young priest who performed the rites was patient and caring with her and completed his duties as speedily as he could.

When we arrived at Quintero's, we were asked to join the family at church on our first Sunday. I, of course, agreed, but on the morning, Angelita said she felt ill and asked me to go without her. The following Sunday, she again refused to go. By then, I knew it was not illness that was keeping her away.

One evening as we lay in bed together, my hand resting on her growing belly, I asked her why she refused to go to church. In the darkness, she tried to explain. Once, she had believed unconditionally, she said. Truth be told, at that time she didn't think about it — she recited the words and prayed for childish things. Then she had found herself in a situation where she had needed God. Only He had the answers she was searching for. But God, who had it within His capacity to help her and make her joyous, had taken away her dreams of happiness. In her mind,

He was a spiteful and vengeful God and she would not turn for help from Him again.

Since our engagement, we had never spoken about her affair, but I could see that was where God had disappointed her. She must have asked for God to find a way for this married man and her to be together. But instead her lover had broken off the affair. Unable to blame the man she loved, she blamed God instead.

I had gently suggested that over time she might see that perhaps the Lord really did have her best interests in mind. After all, He had brought us together. At this, she had remained silent but pulled my arm around her. I held her tightly and silently thanked God for bringing her back to me.

Over the months, however, she continued to stay away from church. I worried it might affect our relationship with the Quintero family, but Dante and his wife had fallen in love with my Angelita too, and it seemed we would all forgive her anything.

We never spoke of religion again. I never asked her if she wanted her baby baptized. But in my heart, I knew what her answer would have been.

★ ★ ★

The hypnotic sound of the cicadas reverberates along the river's edge. The afternoon sun is warm, and the air is still. I can smell the faint fragrance of oleander, and, high above, the ash trees gently rustle their leaves.

I check my rod again, but there's no interest from the fish. They're having a lazy Sunday afternoon too. This is my favourite spot for fishing. At least, I make a show of fishing. In fact, I rarely catch anything, much to Chita's amusement.

The truth is, this is my favourite spot for thinking. I found it not long after Angelita's death. Even after two years, I find anywhere near the vineyard has some memory of her. In our home, the small annexe on the edge of the hacienda, I relish the sense of her in every room. Out in the vineyard, I can see her strolling easily down the dusty lines between the vines. On visits to the town, I catch a glimpse of her laughing with the old men sitting on the fountain's edge, or in the market pressing a melon to test its ripeness.

Most of the time, I enjoy the reassurance that she once existed in this place and in all our lives. But early on, there were times when the grief was so intense I wanted to be somewhere she had never been. One day, a few months after her death, I climbed into the car and drove, somehow stumbling across an old track that brought me down to the river. At once, I'd felt at peace. The pain seemed less raw as I listened to the water and felt its fresh air on my face.

When I mentioned the river to Dante, he told me he and his friends had spent many happy afternoons fishing further upstream — it seems the river is full of catfish, and in his day they had caught some big ones. When I saw his enthusiasm, I'd been worried he would want to join me. But he'd found his old fishing rod and given it to me with a smile and some handy tips.

As I sit, my arms resting on my raised knees, I look to the other side of the river. An ancient wall runs along the water's edge, and partway up the hill behind it stands the remains of an old house. The wooden roof has long since collapsed and now the walls of yellow stone are surrounded by weeds and bushes, inside and out. I wonder why the owner abandoned such a picturesque spot.

Beside me, Alberto snuffles in his sleep. He is lying on a blanket in the shade of a tree. Leaning down towards him, I look at his peaceful face. Not for the first time, I wonder what he will look like as an adult. Although he has his mother's eyes, his hair is fairer and curlier than hers, and his chin is stronger.

I always worried about the fact that the

child would not look like me. Angelita soothed my fears, saying that the baby would have dark hair and dark eyes like all Spanish children. I'd laughed at her silliness, and hoped she was in part right.

Lying beside the sleeping child, I watch his small chest rise and fall rhythmically. I wonder what kind of man he will be. His mother was clever and funny and capable of enormous emotion. I am calm and steady, a man who likes routine and order. I have no idea what Alberto's real father was like. It will be interesting to see if he develops any characteristics that are neither his mother's nor mine. A blank slate or his personality already etched into his being: the classic debate will be played out in this little child — but I will be unable to discuss it with anyone.

Dispelling my scientific deliberation, I place a small kiss on the child's forehead and lay my head beside his. I need to think about the baptism. The water gurgles and bubbles nearby, and I feel the sun warm my legs.

★ ★ ★

Opening my eyes, I realize I must have dozed off. The blanket lies empty in front of me. Alberto is no longer on it. Panic rises from my stomach as I sit up quickly and call his name. Since he started walking, he has used his new skill at every opportunity. He's probably very close, I try to persuade myself as I get to my feet.

'Alberto!' I shout, and hear the fear in my voice.

I dash behind the nearby bushes. The little boy loves to play hide-and-seek, so perhaps he's playing now. But he's not. Running back to the blanket, I stand and look around. It's only now that I look towards the river.

A clamp grips my heart as I see a flash of white bobbing up and down on the dark water. For a moment, I cannot move; I cannot breathe. Then I force myself into action and run into the water, knocking the fishing rod over in my haste. The river quickly becomes deep, and as I wade out, the water comes up to my stomach.

As I get closer, I see Alberto is lying face down with his arms floating by his head. I pull his small body to me. He feels heavy and hangs limp in my arms as I drag myself back to the river's edge. Climbing out onto the sandy bank, I shake him and shout his name. His hair sticks to his head, and his sodden clothes cling to him. I don't know what to do. I shake him again, harder this time and his head wobbles.

Stop, I say to myself, taking a shaky breath. Think. Remember your anatomy. Water has filled the lungs. To expel it, apply pressure.

Carefully I place the child down on the blanket, lying him on his stomach, his head turned to the side. I kneel and place my hand on his back and gently push. Nothing happens. I lift my hand and apply pressure again onto the middle of his back. Still nothing. I feel the moment of calm reason start to lift from me and the panic slip back. I know I'm running out of time. Placing both hands on his back, I give the child's body a short, hard push.

Water gushes from Alberto's mouth, and I see his nose wrinkle as he gasps loudly. I gasp too and grapple him into my arms, turning him to look into his face. He coughs violently as yet more water dribbles from his nose and mouth, and his wide eyes look confused and frightened.

'Alberto,' I say quietly. 'Are you all right?'

He answers with a huge howl. I hold him tight and feel his deep sobs. As I rock and shush my crying child, I realize that even in my kneeling position, my legs are shaking so much that I have to sit down. We sit for a long time, and I continue to rock him long after his crying has stopped. The sun is starting to drop and the first of the midges are buzzing around us. The child looks up at me with tired eyes and I share his exhaustion.

'Alberto,' I whisper to him, 'I'm so sorry. I promise I'll never put you in danger again.' I turn my face to the pale blue sky.

'Angelita,' I say out loud, 'I'm sorry, my love, but you can't have him. He is not yours to take. He's mine now. And I will love him better than any father could.'

I look down at Alberto's face. He gazes up at me curiously.

'Let's go home,' I say gently to him. 'I have to speak to Father Sebastián.'

13

The boy whipped the air with a wild fennel stalk. Beside him, Alberto walked steadily along the rocky path. The unlaid road sloped gently upwards, and the old man looked at the green and grey hillside above them. If he were a younger man, he would have happily lived somewhere like this.

The taxi had taken them to a town, where they'd caught a bus to a nearby village. There, they had asked for directions. They'd walked along a quiet road for about a mile; then, when they'd seen the top of a house nestled in the lowlands of a hill, they'd turned up the dirt track towards it. After sitting on the bus, it was good to be stretching their legs.

Soon they reached the house. All that was visible of it was the roof, as a tall white wall surrounded the building. The wall itself could barely be seen under a spread of mature clematis and a thick undergrowth of bright yellow broom and wild onion. The branches of a kumquat tree swung lazily over the wall, its trunk hidden on the other side. Heavy fruit hung from the branches. Alberto lifted the boy up so he could pick the shiny, olive-sized fruit. The boy took two, and when Alberto lowered him to the ground, he handed one to his grandfather.

Nodding to him, Alberto popped the whole fruit into his mouth, biting through the sweet skin to the tart pulp. Tino gnawed at the outside until only the bitter centre was left, which he threw into the bushes.

Alberto rang the bell beside a wooden door almost completely hidden behind a cluster of clematis flowers. Far away, a bell tinkled and instantly a dog started barking. Moving a woody vine, he saw an old sign, with the words PAN Y VINO burnt into the strip of hardwood.

''Bread and Wine,'' read Tino.

Alberto looked down at him and shrugged. The boy shrugged back, smiling.

At that moment, the door swung open. Alberto turned and saw a plump woman with white, curly hair smiling at him. She was wearing trousers and a straw hat, and held a pair of gardening gloves in one hand. A wiry, honey-coloured dog squirmed past her legs and, wagging its tail, tentatively sniffed at Alberto.

'Hello?' said the woman, looking first at Alberto and then at the boy.

'Hello!' said Tino, eyeing the dog with delight.

The old man nodded, suddenly bashful. He took his hat off and held it in front of his chest. 'Forgive the intrusion at your home,' he began quietly.

The woman smiled at him and brushed a curl from her face. The dog moved closer to the little boy, sniffing at his feet. Tino grinned and patted the dog's slim head.

'Are you Miriam Quintero?' Alberto asked quietly. He looked at her intently.

'Goodness,' she replied, chuckling, 'it's been a long time since anyone called me that. Yes, that was my name before I was married.'

Alberto nodded, uncomfortable. He looked down at the boy, who seemed to be holding his breath with excitement.

Turning back to Miriam, he said, 'I think we may have known each other when we were very young.'

'Yes?' replied Miriam curiously.

Alberto nodded again, turning his hat in his hands.

'My name is Alberto. Alberto Romero.'

Miriam stared at Alberto for a moment, the words sinking in. Then dropping the gloves, she slowly raised her hands to her mouth. Her eyes shone with confusion, and she blinked a number of times. She peered at the old man. Her eyes began to well with tears.

'Alberto?' she whispered through her fingers.

Alberto nodded. He could see she had recognized him despite the years. But when he looked at her face, he couldn't see the girl in the photo. He didn't know this woman.

Tentatively, Miriam stepped towards Alberto. She placed a hand on either side of his leathery face and gently kissed him on both cheeks. The tears were pouring down her face as she stepped back. The dog wound his way round her legs, eager for attention.

'We thought you were dead,' she said, her voice quivering.

Alberto looked at her, wishing he could remember.

Miriam wiped her eyes. 'And who is this?' she asked, looking at the boy.

'This is my grandson, Tino.'

Miriam smiled at the boy, then turned back to Alberto, looking into his face again.

'Well, you must both come in.'

'Thank you,' said Alberto.

With a click of her tongue, she nudged the dog towards the door and he bounded through.

The boy bent down, picked up Miriam's gloves and handed them to her. She smiled her thanks, then stepped to one side and, once the old man and the boy had crossed into the garden, shut the door behind them.

Alberto looked around. The garden was stunning. Along the house and exterior wall climbed jasmine and passion flower. The trunk of the kumquat tree was sturdy and leant heavily against the wall. Hibiscus, bandera with its Spanish-flag flowers, angel's trumpet and lilies covered the ground with small stone pathways running through them. Over the entrance to the house hung a spectacular mix of pink and red bougainvillea, and pots of fuchsia lined the steps leading up to the door. The mixture of scents was heady, and Alberto breathed them in deeply.

Miriam led them into the cool house, putting her gloves on a small table by the door. The dog's claws clicked on the tiled floor as he followed her.

'Please,' she said, indicating a large sofa, 'take a seat while I get us some drinks.'

Alberto and the boy sank into the soft cushions. Looking around, they saw a mix of old and new furniture set around the spacious room. Family photographs hung over the fireplace, and a pair of knitting needles stuck out of a bag by a comfy chair.

'Apu?'

'Yes.'

'Do you remember Señora Miriam?'

Alberto turned to the boy, who looked expectantly up at him. Sadly, he shook his head.

'Oh,' said Tino quietly.

Alberto rubbed the line of his jaw, his hard fingers rasping against the bristles. 'I wish I did,' he said.

When Miriam came through from the kitchen carrying a tray, Alberto stood and helped her put it on the table. She set a glass of sweet fizzy water in front of each of them and placed a bowl of olives in the centre of the table. Then she settled herself in the comfy chair opposite them and picked up her drink.

'Thank you,' said Alberto, lifting his glass.

The dog trotted up to the boy and flopped down beside him. Grinning, the child stroked its ears and the dog's eyes closed with pleasure.

'I think he likes you,' said Miriam.

'What's his name?' asked the boy.

'Vito. Because he's always been so full of life.'

They all looked down at the dog, who leant against the boy's leg.

'I still can't believe it's you,' said Miriam, turning to Alberto. 'But it seems you don't remember me.'

Alberto slowly shook his head. 'I feel that I

should, but I can't. I have lost my memory from those days.'

Miriam frowned. 'What do you remember?'

'I was taken to an orphanage, where I spent most of the war. There's very little before that. This one' — Alberto nodded and gestured towards his grandson — 'persuaded me to go looking for my history.'

Miriam smiled kindly at Tino.

'We went to where the orphanage was, but there was a mean old man there,' said the boy. 'Then we met Doña Isabel, and we went to the church. Then Apu saw a bottle of brandy and we went to the vineyard and saw the cellar. Then they said to come here.'

'Well,' said Miriam, 'it sounds like you've had quite an adventure!'

The little boy grinned and nodded before gulping down more of his drink.

'The new owners of Quintero's gave us your address,' explained Alberto.

'Ah,' said Miriam.

'Apu,' said the boy excitedly, 'don't forget the photos!'

Alberto opened his bag, which lay by his feet. He took out the photos and handed them to Miriam.

'Oh!' she said. 'Look at these — so long ago.' She leafed through them until she got to the one Javier had shown them. Smiling, she turned it to show Alberto.

'This is when we were very young. This is my brother, Néstor,' she said, pointing to the teenage boy. 'And of course this is me, and our mother and father. Do you remember any of us?'

'No. There's something there, a glimmer, but it's not clear.' He looked at the photo again. 'Your father looks like a good man.'

Miriam smiled and nodded. 'He was. A very good man. That vineyard was everything to him. He'd be so sad to know that it had been sold. But he left it to Néstor and my brother was never interested. He'd rather have a beer than a glass of wine.

'My father's name was Dante,' Miriam continued. 'He passed away not long after this photo was taken. He and your father were very good friends.'

'My father?' said Alberto quietly.

'Yes. You don't remember him either?'

Alberto shook his head.

'Oh, Alberto, that's sad. I remember him a little. He was very kind and clever — a real gentleman.'

'A gentleman?'

'Yes. He was quietly spoken and polite. And he smiled a great deal. He always had time for us children. I'm sorry, it's not much — but I was very young.'

Alberto shrugged. It didn't matter. It seemed there were no memories to trigger.

'Did he work for your father?'

'Yes, that's right.'

'In the fields?'

'Oh no! He was a chemist. He helped develop the wines. My father was quite advanced in employing a scientist, and your father introduced some new ways of testing and processing the wine. It was the two of them that started the brandy production.'

'And did we live at Quintero's?' asked Alberto.

'Yes, that's right,' said Miriam enthusiastically. 'You and your father lived in a casita out the back of the main building. You used to come into the house and have meals with us.'

'And my mother?' asked Alberto.

'Oh, Alberto,' said Miriam gently. 'I'm afraid I never knew her. Neither did you — she died at your birth.'

Alberto looked down at his clasped hands and sat very still.

Tino regarded his grandfather sadly.

The old man took a deep breath. It seemed there were nuggets of information, important things that he should recall. His father's character, his mother's death — these things should be scorched on his memory. Yet here he was, his family and his past within his grasp, and he still couldn't remember the woman sitting in front of him.

'I'm sorry,' said Alberto. 'It's difficult learning it all as if for the first time.'

'I'm sure,' said Miriam sympathetically. She picked up the bowl of olives and held them out to the small boy. He chose the largest one he could see and quickly popped it into his mouth.

Miriam set the bowl back on the table, putting an olive into her own mouth as she leant back in her chair. As he looked up, Alberto saw the olive dribble a fat dollop of oil onto Miriam's ample chest. Miriam followed Alberto's gaze and glanced down. A large stain marked her white top. Her face fell.

'Oh,' she said in exasperation, 'can you believe it? This was clean this morning. I'm always doing this.'

Alberto's eyes darted between the stain and Miriam's perturbed face. As she pulled out a handkerchief and dabbed at the oil, he watched her face. Then he looked at the stain again.

'Mimi?' he said quietly.

Miriam stopped dabbing and turned to him.

'Mimi,' said Alberto with more conviction.

Miriam nodded slowly at him.

Alberto stood up and stepped round the table towards her. Miriam stood to face him.

'Mimi,' said Alberto hoarsely, 'my friend.'

Smiling through her tears, Mimi nodded again at Alberto. The old man stood uncomfortably in front of her, before Mimi pulled him to her and they hugged.

The little boy grinned and gave Vito a hug.

* * *

Mimi watched the boy climbing up the stone terrace to where Vito waited for him. She tutted and shook her head. 'Poor child,' she said.

Alberto had just told her about Juan Carlos's accident and the boy's reaction to his father's situation. The child had slept well and without nightmares both nights they had been away.

'You must phone your daughter as soon as we get home,' said Mimi firmly.

Together, Alberto and Mimi strolled along the terraces that led from the back of her house. Gnarled olive trees were spaced evenly along the wide terrace, and their feet sank gently into the soft crust of brown earth.

Tino and the dog scampered up and down the ancient walls. Above them, the hill rose, the terraces petering out to bushes and craggy boulders. The sun was starting to lose its strength, and a gentle breeze swept over them.

Mimi had suggested a walk before dinner. At her insistence, Alberto had agreed they would stay the night. She had a big house, and now that her husband was no longer alive and the children had left, she had more than enough space for them both.

As they walked, they talked of their lives since the war. Alberto avoided talk of their childhood. It felt as if the recognition of Mimi, the little girl who was his best friend as a child, had opened the door a crack. He worried that with a push, the door would fly open and the torrent of memories that flooded out would sink him. For now, he wanted to keep the surge at bay.

Instead, he learnt that Mimi had been lucky enough to go to college and study business. She had hoped Néstor would let her help run Quintero's after their father died. She had ideas to grow and modernize the business. But her brother had refused, saying there was no need for change — they would carry on as always. He agreed with Franco that a woman's place was in the home, not at work. Mimi had argued that their father had always been progressive, but Néstor had left all the business affairs to his foreman. Mimi had known the foreman and considered him lazy with little passion for the business.

It was with great difficulty, Mimi told Alberto, that she had walked away from Quintero's. She took a job in a leather shoe company that made workmen's boots. It was hard and she'd had to fight for her independence at a time when the government had been against women in the workplace. But she gained the respect of the bosses and they had given her greater responsibility. After years of persuasion, she eventually convinced them to develop fashion shoes. She found a young designer, and thanks to her shrewd business instinct and Franco's plan to make Spain a modern economy, the shoe company had grown to become the best known in the area.

It was during this time she met her husband. He was an accountant: safe and reliable but with a sharp wit and a big laugh. After the marriage, she continued to work at the shoe company but just one or two days a week. However, when she had her third child, she decided that running the family kept her busy enough.

She had brought up three boys, all of whom had gone to university, and one, she proudly admitted, had become a politician. Her husband had died young, in his fifties. She had never considered remarrying; instead, she put her energy into her garden and her family.

'I am content, Alberto,' she said. 'I have had a wonderful life — and I'm enjoying my older years. And now your arrival — well, I couldn't have asked for a more wonderful surprise.'

'And I am glad to have found you,' replied Alberto.

★ ★ ★

As Mimi fried green peppers in the kitchen, Alberto and his grandson called Rosa. She said that Juan Carlos's recovery had been remarkable.

The doctors had warned both Juan Carlos and Rosa that the healing process would be long and painful, but the prognosis was excellent.

Alberto could hear the relief in his daughter's voice. She said her sister, Cristina, would be leaving the next day, and her mother-in-law was spending less time at the hospital. She joked that Juan Carlos had pleaded for his mother to watch her beloved soap operas at home rather than in his hospital room.

The boy was excited to hear about his father's progress and asked several questions.

Then he filled her in on everything he and his grandfather had learnt and talked to his mother at length about Vito and asked if they could get a dog. His mother replied that when things calmed down, they would talk about it. The boy raced off to tell Mimi, Vito bouncing after him, barking.

'Do you know what you have done?' asked the old man, smiling down the phone.

'Oh, Papá, all this has made me realize there's more to life than worrying about dog hairs. Of course, we'll have to wait until Juan Carlos is well enough.'

'Boys and dogs are a good match,' said Alberto.

'And how about you? It sounds as if you are having quite an adventure! How does it feel to uncover your history?'

'It's unsettling,' he admitted.

He was going to go on, but Rosa interrupted, 'Papá?'

'Yes?'

'When will you be coming home?'

Alberto could hear Rosa's ache for her son in her voice. Alberto sighed silently. Mimi had invited them to stay for a few days. She and Alberto could catch up properly, and the boy and Vito would enjoy each other's company. He had said it would depend on his daughter. Now, listening to her voice, he knew they had to go back.

'Tomorrow, Rosa. We'll come home tomorrow.'

'Oh, Papá, don't come if you're still searching. I wouldn't want you to cut your trip short.'

'No, no. I've found everything here at Mimi's,' said Alberto softly.

★　★　★

Mimi placed the steaming tortilla on the kitchen table. It was thick and golden with flecks of green pepper running through it. Tino took a deep breath, taking in the rich smell of the eggy potato pie.

She handed Alberto a bottle of wine, which he opened, the cork releasing from the neck with a satisfying sound.

While he poured the wine, Mimi served the boy, who sat, distracted by Vito.

'Vito,' said Mimi in a reproving tone.

The dog turned his large dark eyes to his mistress, but after one look at her determined face, got up and trotted, defeated, to his bed in the corner of the room.

'Eat your dinner,' said the old man to the boy.

'One moment, Alberto,' said Mimi firmly. She finished serving herself and sat down.

Closing her eyes and clasping her hands together, she dropped her head. The boy squeezed his eyes tight shut, and Alberto lowered his head.

As Mimi said a short grace, even Vito stopped noisily licking himself and lay still. When she had finished, she nodded at the boy, who hungrily tucked into his meal.

Alberto and Mimi sipped the wine. 'It's a Quintero,' said Mimi.

'I saw,' said Alberto.

'It's from one of our best years, not long before my father died. I have a collection of wines that the vineyard gave me.'

'Yes, the new owner told me. That was how we found you.'

'My father always talked so passionately about the wine. He loved every part of the process, and I believe his heart is in every glass.'

Alberto took another sip and nodded. It was very good.

'So your son-in-law is improving?' asked Mimi.

'Yes. He's doing very well.'

'Do you think you may stay a few more days?'

Alberto paused a moment, before sadly shaking his head. 'Thank you for your kind offer, but my daughter is missing Tino. He's her only child . . . '

Mimi raised her hand. 'There's no need to explain, Alberto. The wonderful thing is that now you've found me, you can visit again. Or I could come to visit you.'

'Will you bring Vito?' asked the boy quickly. The dog lifted his head at the sound of his name.

'Of course,' said Mimi. 'I think Vito would like to see the sea.'

The boy nodded happily as he took another mouthful of tortilla.

'So, Alberto, have you been a gardener all your life?' Mimi asked.

Alberto nodded. 'My education wasn't good, so I took work where I could find it after the war — labouring on building sites, working on farms at harvest time. I was always happier outside. When I met María Luisa on her family's olive farm, I learnt a great deal about agriculture. For our wedding, her father bought us a small plot of land. I grew crops to sell, and for our table.

'Then the tourists began to arrive in the area. They bought and built villas with gardens and plenty of land, but they only stayed in them for a few months a year. María Luisa knew a woman who sold properties to the British and Dutch. Through her, my wife began work as a cleaner — looking after the empty houses and preparing them for their owners' return.

'And I was hired to look after the gardens and the land. Often, the villas came with many terraces of almonds and olive trees. They paid me to maintain them, and often allowed me to take the harvest.

'Some of the families returned over many years, and María Luisa became friends with a few of them. She would show the wives the best places to shop and would learn a few words of their language. If they were interested, I would show the men how to clear the irrigation channels and check for termites in their villas' woodwork.

'María Luisa became good friends with one English family. They spoke a little Spanish and liked to learn the Spanish way of life. One day every summer, María Luisa would make a large paella, and we would carry it up to their house on a hill. Our two families would eat together and the children played, despite none of them speaking the same language. I made their youngest child — a little *rubia* — her own garden. It had a lemon tree and flowers that would be in bloom when the family arrived.'

Alberto smiled at the memories.

'It's interesting you've always worked with plants, Alberto. Have you ever worked with grapes?' asked Mimi.

'Only picking them at harvest time. I did make my own wine once, but even I could barely drink it,' he chuckled.

'I wonder what would have happened if you had stayed at Quintero's. Papá always wanted you to help Néstor run the vineyard — just as your father helped him. But while your father was a scientist, it sounds as if you could have appreciated my father's love of the vine. You would have been a better foreman than the lazy waster my brother hired.'

Alberto shrugged. 'What if the war had not come? What if Néstor had given you Quintero's? What if? We have lived the lives we have lived.'

Mimi nodded. 'Of course you're right. But part of me wonders if, when you lost your memory, some of my father's words remained. He was always talking to us about plants — perhaps somehow a little of his knowledge settled in your memory. It's a nice thought to have. It would have made him happy.'

They all sat in silence for a moment.

'Aunt Mimi?' said the boy earnestly.

'Yes, dear,' Mimi smiled at him.

'Do you know when Apu's birthday is?'

Mimi looked at Alberto. 'You don't remember your birthday?'

He shook his head.

'Oh dear. Let me think. My father liked any excuse for a fiesta, so we would have celebrated your birthday. We were similar in age, you and I, but while my birthday is in June, I'm afraid I can't remember yours.'

The little boy's face fell.

'I'm sorry — both of you.'

Alberto gave Mimi a small smile. 'Don't worry, Mimi. The reason we came on this journey was to find my birthday. But' — he turned to his grandson — 'because of this journey I have found my oldest friend. And I have found some of my memories. I remember playing in the cellars at Quintero's. I remember the warm kitchen that always smelt of food. They're not crystal clear; they're a bit blurry — but they're my memories.' Reaching out, Alberto stroked the boy's head. 'And I have you to thank for that.'

Tino looked at his grandfather and smiled.

'Wait,' said Mimi suddenly.

As they both turned, she stood up and left the room. Vito lifted his head and watched her go, then laid his head back down, his eyebrows twitching.

The boy turned to Alberto with a questioning look and the old man shrugged.

When Mimi returned, she held an old leather-bound book in her hand. She stood in front of Alberto and held it out to him.

Before he could take it, a thin piece of card fell from the book and fluttered onto the floor, landing in front of Vito, who quickly sniffed it with his wet nose.

The boy leant down from his chair and picked up the card. Turning it in his fingers, he revealed a photo of a woman. She was young and attractive with warm, dark eyes, and although the picture was serious, a smile danced around her lips.

'Who's that, Apu?'

Alberto carefully took the old photo, shaking his head. 'I don't know,' he said.

'Alberto,' said Mimi quietly. 'That's your mother.'

The old man caught his breath. He stared at the photo, bringing it closer to his eyes. Immediately, he could see similarities — the shape of her face, her nose, but, most strikingly, her eyes were just like his.

Alberto let out a short breath. The more he looked at the photo, the more familiar it seemed. As if he had seen it many times before.

Turning the photo over, Alberto looked for writing on the smudged paper. There was nothing.

Reading his mind, Mimi said, 'Her name was Angelita.'

'Angelita,' repeated the old man softly.

'Little Angel,' said the boy.

'I kept this to remind me of you,' said Mimi, giving Alberto the book in her hands. 'At first, I kept everything I could — your toys, your schoolbooks, all sorts of things. But over the years, I let them go. When I left home, this was the only thing of yours that I kept. And I have kept it all these years.'

Carefully, the old man turned the book in his hands. Its dark red cover was faded, and the gold edging of the paper only shone in patches. A tatty red ribbon hung from the middle pages. The words HOLY BIBLE were embossed simply on the front cover.

Very slowly, Alberto opened it, releasing a musty smell. An inscription was written in tidy letters on the first page.

To Alberto,
With blessings for a happy and healthy life.
From your father

14

FATHER FRANCISCO

21 July 1931

The mule's ears twitch as it pulls the cart. The peasant beside me seems to have dozed off, but the animal plods on regardless. I'm glad for the peace to gather my thoughts.

It's been three months since the king's abdication and the repercussions are now becoming obvious. A Republic will soon be announced, and the country will be governed by a doctrine that separates State and Church. I, like many of my brethren, am concerned.

But for now, I can put my worries to one side, as I am on my way to visit my old friend Father Sebastián. We worked together in the city many years ago, and have been in touch from time to time, but this will be the first time we've seen each other in many years.

I assume he has heard of my new posting, and the recent tragic events, through the bishop. I'm unsure I can talk about it yet, but I am looking forward to seeing him again.

Without instruction, the mule veers off the road and onto a small path. The man beside me snores gently. I consider waking him, but the animal seems to know where it's going.

It is late morning and the sun is at full strength. My black robes and hat are devilishly hot and not for the first time I wonder who decided on black for our uniform. After all, I don't believe our Lord Jesus wore black — he lived in a hot country too.

All around us, the land is dry and dusty. The summer has been harsh so far, and, as in my village, the people here will be wishing for some unseasonable but welcome rain. There is not a breath of wind. Apart from the regular clomp of the mule's hoofs and the occasional bird, it is deathly quiet.

In the distance, I see a small cluster of houses and buildings. That must be Father Sebastián's town. I realize I am looking forward to being somewhere other than my own home. I have lived in the village for only a few months, but it has been an extremely difficult time. I am pleased to be away from there for a few days.

As we approach the town, I see a few women walking towards us. I nudge the driver awake and instruct him to stop, and they come close enough for me to touch their scarfed heads. I ask them where they are going and they reply shyly that they are going home after market. They point to their meagre bundles wrapped on their backs — the week's simple purchases. They smile at me, revealing missing teeth, and continue on their way. It seems impossible to think that the Church is so threatened by the poor.

We head into the centre of the town and past the small market, now packing up. The driver directs the docile mule up a small street behind the back of the church. We stop outside a large house and my companion points to the door. Thanking him, I let him hand me my bag as I climb down.

I pull the chain and deep inside the house I hear a bell ring. The mule clip-clops up the cobbled street. The driver looks ready for another siesta, and I imagine that he will be happy to go wherever the mule decides to take him.

The door opens and an elderly woman stands in the doorway. 'Father Francisco,' she says politely. 'Welcome.'

She opens the door and lets me into the dark reception room. 'Father Sebastián is expecting you,' she says, leading me down the corridor. The house may be large, but it is simply furnished. Father Sebastián, like me, abhors the ostentatious homes some priests have. For Sebastián, I believe it is a question of style — his being modest and unassuming. For me, I would prefer church funds were used to help the poor than dress a house unnecessarily.

The woman knocks on the door at the end of the corridor and waits for a response. I recognize Sebastián's deep voice instantly and I feel myself relax. The woman opens the door and there, walking towards me, is my old friend.

Portly and red-cheeked, he has put on some weight, but it is so good to see him I decide not to remark on it. He seems pleased to see me as we shake hands.

'Welcome, Francisco,' he says warmly. Then, 'Señora,' he says over my shoulder, 'please bring lunch at your convenience.'

The woman nods and closes the door behind her. It is only one o'clock, so I am surprised to hear of eating already, but the journey has been long and I realize I am hungry.

'How was the trip?' asks Sebastián. He points me towards a comfortable chair.

'Good, thank you,' I reply. 'But extremely hot.'

There's a knock on the door and the señora enters with a small tray. She places a glass of water beside me and gives us each a crystal glass of light sherry before putting the bottle on the table beside Sebastián. He thanks her and she quietly leaves the room.

'So good to see you, friend,' says Sebastián. He smiles and raises his glass. We drink the cool, sharp sherry and pass pleasantries, until there's a second knock on the door and the señora enters again. She carries another tray to the large oak table and starts laying out food. When she has finished, Sebastián and I rise from our chairs and cross to the table. After a brief blessing, Sebastián pours wine from a decanter, while I look at the spread before us.

'What a generous table of food, Sebastián,' I say.

'I am grateful for all I receive,' he replies, smiling.

'And what will you do if the rumours are true and the government stops paying our salaries?' I ask.

'Oh, dear friend, I had to buy very little of this food. Most of it is gifted to me by my loyal congregation.'

I nod, watching him take a large mouthful of asparagus and roasted red pepper. He certainly has won the support of the area's richest families.

Teasing him a little, I say, 'Perhaps the Church should stand alongside the poor

— make a difference where we can.'

'Perhaps, Francisco,' says Sebastián, easing back in his seat and smiling at me. 'And perhaps you should have followed your namesake and become a Franciscan monk.'

'I'm not about to give up my boots, Sebastián,' I reply. 'But you know this new Republic poses a very great threat to us — whatever your political point of view. It plans to stop all religious education and ban all religious processions — even the ringing of church bells.'

He looks at me, appalled. 'No church bells in Spain, Francisco?'

'They want change. And change is not convincing unless everyone can see and hear it. They call the new Republic 'the Beautiful Child'. They've given birth to something they believe is a force for good. I think the only way to survive is to join them in raising their beautiful child.'

He refills his glass and swirls the wine thoughtfully. 'How did it come to this, Francisco?'

'We've been too comfortable for too long, friend,' I reply gently. 'We've become complacent and forgotten our vows. These days, the Spanish Church would most likely consider Christ a Marxist.'

'Hush,' says Sebastián with a laugh. 'You

will land yourself in trouble if you're not careful.'

I smile at him. He is a good man. Mild-mannered and easy-going, he joined the Church for an easy life — as a great many men do. I do not think he is prepared for what may be coming.

'Here, comrade,' says Sebastián. He refills my glass. 'Have another glass of wine with me before you join the revolution.'

★　★　★

It is still humid and warm despite the late hour. A fat, red ball of sun is just about to set behind the far, hazy mountains. I hear Sebastián huffing behind me and slow my pace.

'I don't know why you wouldn't let us take the cart,' says Sebastián. He pats his forehead with a handkerchief.

'I think we both needed some fresh air, friend,' I reply. After an afternoon of eating, drinking and conversing, we had both dozed off in our chairs. Unlike Sebastián, I am unaccustomed to drinking so heartily and awoke feeling thick-headed and slow; when he asked me to help him talk to one of his parishioners, I agreed, pleased to stretch my legs.

Up ahead is a large hacienda. It's an attractive building, and the lines of vines alongside us are well kept.

'What did you say the owner's name was?' I ask.

This gives Sebastián a moment to pause and get his breath. 'Don Dante,' he replies. 'His family have had this vineyard for over one hundred and fifty years. He's very popular in the area. He looks after his workers and is well respected by both them and his customers. I'm sure you'll approve of him.'

I smile at Sebastián. He must think I am far too opinionated for a cleric.

'But it is Raúl I have come to see,' says Sebastián.

'His son?'

'No, his chemist.'

I turn to Sebastián with a quizzical look.

'It's a sad story. Raúl and his wife arrived about a year ago. Dante was looking for someone to help him improve his wine and was open to a little experimentation. Raúl was looking for a job away from the city and they became friends instantly. Dante swears he saw the value of the scientist's contribution very quickly.

'I believe the wife was pregnant when they arrived — a beautiful young woman. I rarely saw her, though. She never came to Mass in all those months. Raúl made excuses for her, but I spoke to Dante about it once. He said she had fallen out of love with religion. It was his opinion that with a little time, she would grow to love it again. She never got the chance. She died in childbirth a few months ago.'

I tut sadly, and for a while we walk in silence.

'And the baby?' I ask eventually.

'Healthy and well,' says Sebastián.

'Excellent.'

'But I am concerned that the father hasn't spoken to me about the baptism yet,' he says.

'Do you think it has something to do with the mother's opinion of religion?' I ask.

'It shouldn't matter,' he says flatly. 'It's his decision now.'

'Perhaps he just needs a little time,' I say.

'After all you've said about the decline of Catholicism in the masses,' says Sebastián seriously, 'surely you think we should make every effort to bring all the children we can into the arms of the Church? That baby should be baptized — the sooner the better.'

'*And now why tarriest thou? Arise, and be baptized, and wash away thy sins, calling on the name of the Lord,*' I quote, quietly.

'Exactly! Don't you remember when we all

worked at the children's hospital in the city? Antonio would baptize newborns in case they didn't survive. Most of their parents would have objected given the chance, but he thought saving their souls was more important.'

At the mention of Antonio's name, I fall silent. This visit has, in part, helped me escape what has been a difficult time.

Sebastián notices and puts a hand on my shoulder. 'What happened?' he asks. I realize he has probably been wanting to ask about our mutual friend since my arrival.

I take a deep breath. 'I truly don't know why he did it. I don't believe I'll ever understand, despite knowing him so well.'

Antonio and I had become friends at the seminary when we began our training. I had chosen the Church; Antonio's family expected it of him. It was me he turned to when, as happened from time to time, he questioned his faith. He worried that he would not live up to what was expected of him. We talked about ideology a great deal, but he rarely seemed to find the answers he was looking for.

After college, we had been sent to work in a hospital in the city, where we met Sebastián. We were shocked to find just how extreme the poverty was — and the poorer the area, the smaller the church attendance. It was hard work, but at last, Antonio had found some contentment in his situation.

He had moved some years later. A priest had passed away and Antonio was asked to take over a church situated in quite a wealthy part of town. We met occasionally after that, but I had to admit I noticed a change in him. He became distant and uncommunicative, and I sensed his demons had returned. At times, he was angry, furious with himself and with God. At other times, he was overwhelmed by remorse, pleading for forgiveness from his sins.

The last time I'd seen him, he'd told me he was leaving the parish. He said he had requested a new post. He said his current position had made him question his faith again — in fact, it had pushed what faith he had to its limit. He thought if he could go somewhere different, somewhere that he was really needed again, it would help him find a way back to God.

He'd been granted a position in the rural village where I now live. I promised to visit as soon as I could, but I never had the chance.

A few months ago, I had been summoned in the middle of the night. The bishop had sent his car and I was driven to the village. The bishop himself met me there. He told me that the church custodian had found Antonio that evening. He had hanged himself.

I sigh at the memory and say, 'You know almost as much as I do, Sebastián.'

'I only know that he took his own life, and that you have now taken over his parish.'

'When the bishop arrived, he discovered that Antonio had left a letter. It was addressed to me, so the bishop had me brought to the village.

'But when I read the suicide note, it revealed little. It thanked me for being such a good friend and begged my forgiveness. He gave no explanation as to why he had been driven to this terrible deed. It had simply said that he was not worthy of being a priest.'

'Where was he laid to rest?' asks Sebastián.

'In the churchyard.'

Sebastián gasps. 'But, Francisco, it's a mortal sin.'

'The bishop wanted his body to be returned to his family. But they are wealthy with strong connections to the Church. It would have ruined them to bury their shamed son. The bishop wanted the problem to go away and I suggested that we bury him in the churchyard in an unmarked grave.'

'Well, I still don't know,' says Sebastián.

'He was our friend,' I say gently.

Sebastián wipes his head with his handkerchief and nods, then gestures for me to continue.

'I then asked the bishop if I could stay on. I felt I owed it to Antonio. I wanted to be where he had suffered so much. And if his spirit remained in some state of purgatory, I could maybe help him.'

'The devil must have been whispering in his ear to commit such a sin,' says Sebastián.

'I don't know,' I reply. 'I don't think we'll ever know. Perhaps it pays to remember that we are only men. Weak and sinful men.'

'If Antonio's spirit remains in the church, I can't feel it,' I continue. 'But every day I pray for him.'

'May God bless him,' says Sebastián.

★　★　★

We approach the front of the house, and Sebastián leads me through an arch into a courtyard. There, a man with a round, kindly face is bouncing a baby on his knee. He beams when he sees us and stands, shifting the baby onto his side. 'Welcome, welcome,' he says cheerily.

Sebastián introduces me and the man — Dante — shakes my hand warmly. 'You are welcome. This is little Mimi,' he says, proudly

244

holding up the child. Sebastián chucks her under the chin.

'Come inside and have a drink,' says Dante.

We step into the warm house, and Dante leads me through to the kitchen. There, sitting at a large table, is a middle-aged woman, her hair wrapped in a scarf. She is holding another baby.

Dipping her head to us, she stands and carries the baby to a Moses basket, where she settles him.

'Father Francisco, have you had far to come?' Dante asks.

I explain where my village is, and we discuss the journey for a while. Sipping the wine, I compliment Dante on its flavour.

'Thank you,' he says. 'I put it down to a satisfying blend of generations of experience and a modern approach to winemaking.'

The door clicks open and I turn to see a young man enter the room. His face looks aged beyond its years, and dark circles lie under his eyes. He is unshaven, and his shirt is crumpled. I can only assume this is Raúl.

'Aha,' cries Dante, 'Raúl, you know Father Sebastián, and this is Father Francisco, who is currently visiting.'

Raúl hides his initial look of surprise with a tired smile.

'How are you, Raúl?' asks Sebastián.

'Fine, thank you, Father,' he replies. It is clear he is not.

'Chita?' he says to the woman as he walks towards the baby in the basket.

'Alberto's fine. I'm just preparing his milk now.'

The young man picks the baby up and, holding him gently, stares into his eyes. Then he pulls the child tightly to him, his own eyes closed firmly.

'Raúl?' says Sebastián gently.

After a moment, the man opens his eyes and looks at the priest.

'When would you like me to perform his baptism?'

A dark look passes over Raúl's face, but he is silent.

'I said, when would you like — ' repeats my friend.

'I heard you, Father,' says the man.

'Well?'

After some thought, Raúl says, 'When I am ready to organize Alberto's christening, I would be honoured if you would perform the ceremony.'

There is a silence; we are all aware that Raúl is procrastinating.

'Raúl, I know you've been through a great trauma . . . ' urges Sebastián.

The young man shakes his head, as if to dispel an annoying voice inside it.

'But,' continues Sebastián, 'this child is ready to be released from original sin.'

'No,' says Raúl weakly.

'It is for Alberto's salvation,' says Sebastián with force.

'No!' shouts Raúl.

The room is still, stunned at this outburst. Raúl buries his head into his son's neck, clearly overcome with grief. As we watch, he takes a deep breath, smelling the baby's sweet scent. For this moment, his world is his son.

Awkwardly, Sebastián reaches out to stroke the child's hair but stops himself. Instead, his gaze directed firmly at the heartbroken young man in front of him, he says softly, 'Forgive me, Raúl.'

Raúl looks up bleary-eyed at the priest and slowly nods.

All of us stand uncomfortably until Dante says, 'Father Sebastián, would you care to see our new casks?'

Sebastián gratefully accepts the invitation, and handing his daughter to Chita, Dante gently leads him out of the kitchen.

'You've done the right thing,' says Chita to Raúl.

I pour him a glass of wine from the bottle on the table and pass it to him. He takes it with a suspicious glance towards me.

'There is no rush,' I say. He is clearly surprised by my words and he nods gratefully at me, but just as he is about to respond, Mimi hiccups and vomits milk over herself and Chita.

'I'll have to change her again.' The woman sighs, walking towards the door.

As she leaves, Raúl smiles. 'She's always doing that.'

I smile back at him, glad that the mood has relaxed.

'Are you all right?' I ask.

'Fine,' he replies.

'I imagine you've said you're fine a great deal over the past few months, when you really aren't.'

Raúl looks me in the eye before returning his attention to baby Alberto.

'Sebastián has told me of your situation and I am sorry for your loss,' I say to him. After years of being a priest, these are words that come easily. But I feel for this man. He looks as if the life has been sucked out of him.

He shrugs and I can see he believes that my words are well meant but insincere.

'I recently lost a very close friend,' I say. 'I have never been married, but I understand the pain of loss.'

Raúl looks at me.

Reaching for my satchel, I pull out a book. It is a Bible. In fact, it is Antonio's Bible. I have been carrying it with me since I found it among his possessions. It is beautiful in its simplicity — a dark red cover and gold-edged pages.

'Raúl, this has been a comfort to me in dark times. Now I hope it helps you as it has me.' I hand the Bible to Raúl, who takes it cautiously.

'And I believe that one day you will be ready to have Alberto baptized. Please accept this gift for him on that day. If you decide not to have him baptized, please give the Bible to him when he's old enough to read it and understand it. That way, you place the decision in his own hands.'

Raúl turns the book, thoughtfully, before looking at me. 'Thank you,' he says.

'Would you like me to bless Alberto before we leave?' I ask.

Raúl smiles down at the baby. The child responds with a gurgle that makes Raúl grin. 'I think a blessing would be fine,' he says.

15

'Alberto,' said Mimi gently, 'do you remember anything about the day you went missing?'

The old man shook his head. He wasn't entirely sure he wanted to remember. That day had changed the course of his life. He could have been part of that comfortable family in the photo. Instead, he had been on his own, all through the years at the orphanage and then his young adult life. Until María Luisa.

Taking a deep breath, Alberto looked at Mimi. This was why he had come on this journey. This was the memory that had been missing for most of his life. Mimi was the only person who could tell him. It had been sixty-five years. It was time.

'Please,' Alberto said hoarsely, 'can you tell me?'

Mimi nodded at Alberto, then topped up his glass of wine. The boy had gone to bed, and Vito was curled up outside his bedroom door. The house was quiet and calm.

Mimi chewed her lip absent-mindedly, as if trying to decide where to begin. Alberto waited.

'Well,' she started carefully, 'you and your father went for a drive. He had a big, old car that he adored. It was late afternoon, and you both left in the car. But you never came back.'

'Where were we going?'

'I don't know,' said Mimi. She stumbled a little over the words.

Alberto looked at Mimi. She shook her head and sighed.

'We were playing. You, me and Néstor. There was an argument and you and Néstor had a fight. Your father came and took you off for a drive — to ease the situation.'

'What was the argument about?'

'Oh, nothing. Childish things,' said Mimi. She looked into her glass.

Alberto looked at Mimi and recalled that his friend had always been a terrible liar. 'Mimi, I've come so far for this. Please tell me the truth.'

Mimi looked at him and gave a deep sigh. Reluctantly, she began to speak again. 'Néstor was not a nice child. He was jealous of our friendship — you and me. Being a little bit younger, he was always trying to keep up with us. My parents, too, must take some of the blame. My father always wanted a boy, and he and my mother spoilt Néstor.' Mimi took a sip of her wine, then continued, 'He was mean to me that day. And you defended me.'

As Alberto listened to Mimi talk, he saw images in his mind's eye to match the words. He saw the courtyard dappled in light. He saw Néstor push Mimi to the ground. He saw his own reaction.

'I hit him,' said Alberto softly.

'You remember?' asked Mimi quickly.

Alberto nodded. He saw Néstor sitting on the ground, blood dripping from his nose onto his white shirt. He saw Néstor say something, saw his mouth move, but he couldn't hear the words. He sensed a rage; then he was standing over Néstor, punching and kicking him with all his strength. Then large hands grasped him and pulled him away from the boy.

'What did he say' — Alberto looked at Mimi — 'to make me so angry?'

She paused, unsure whether to speak.

'Mimi, he said something to me. What was it?'

Mimi breathed in deeply. 'He said that your father was not your real father.'

Alberto saw the scene again, and this time he could hear Néstor's words as they came from his mouth.

You're a bastard.

The old man caught his breath. He winced and closed his eyes. As Mimi watched him,

Alberto rubbed his chest distractedly.

'Are you all right?' said Mimi, concerned.

Alberto opened his eyes and looked at her. 'I'm fine,' he whispered. He leant back in his chair.

'After you left, we never spoke of it again. Néstor hid in his room for days. And although my parents asked repeatedly, neither of us said a word.'

Mimi continued, 'A soldier came the next day to say your father's car had been found. It had crashed and then caught fire. They gave my father your father's papers. They were half burnt, but they were definitely his. The soldier said your father had been thrown from the vehicle and had died in the blaze. When my father asked about you, the soldier said you must have perished too.

'My father wanted to go and look for himself — just in case. But the soldier said the area was very dangerous — the fighting was spreading. And he said no one inside the car could have possibly survived. My mother pleaded with Papá not to go, and in the end he agreed.

'I'm so sorry, Alberto. They truly thought you had died in the car. If I'd known, I would have begged my father to go and search for you. And he would have. He adored you.

'Instead, we learnt to live with the fact that

you and your father were dead. Even Néstor was upset — he blamed himself. He was only a boy. Who could have known a moment of childish spitefulness would have such repercussions?'

Alberto frowned. Memories suddenly overwhelmed him — not just the argument, but the drive with his father and more.

Mimi reached across the table and put her hand on top of his.

Alberto looked up at her and said, 'You wouldn't have found me anyway.'

'What?' said Mimi.

'If you and your father had come to the car to look for me, I wouldn't have been there.'

Now he could see it. All of it. The memories were crystal clear, as if they'd been sealed in a vacuum and now released.

Alberto took a deep breath and started to speak.

'After the fight with Néstor, my father took me to his car. We drove in silence. We were heading in the direction of the river, where he used to take us fishing.

'But then we started talking. He asked why I hit your brother. For a long time I was silent, but he kept asking. I think he knew the answer, but he wanted me to say it. In the end, I did. I said that Néstor had called me a bastard.

'It was then that we missed the turning for the river. I don't think my father noticed until we were quite a long way past it. And then he just carried on, whichever way the road took us. He just drove. And we talked.

'He said that it was true. That he wasn't my real father. But that he was proud to be the man I called 'Papá'. He said he had treated me as his own son, and intended to as long as God gave him breath in his body.

'Of course, I asked him who my father was. He said he didn't know. My mother had had an affair, and it was a man she loved deeply, but he had left her. She had turned to my father then, and was only a few months pregnant when he married her. He told me my mother never spoke of the man again. She had never spoken to anyone of him.

'He said he was sorry. He was sorry about the way I had found out. He was sorry I had never been able to meet my mother or talk to her about it. He said he hoped it would not tarnish my thoughts of my mother. He told me what a wonderful woman she was: clever and beautiful and capable of huge love.

'I told him he was my papá. That I could never consider anyone else my father. He looked at me. He had tears in his eyes. He couldn't speak, he was so overwhelmed with emotion.

'That's when it happened. A tyre burst. You remember how old that car was? We weren't travelling very fast, but when the tyre blew, my father wasn't looking at the road. He was looking at me. It all happened so fast. The car swerved, and although he tried, my father couldn't regain control. We veered into the ditch, then bounced out and spun. That's when we hit the tree.

'When we stopped, Papá was lying across the wheel, and his head was bleeding. I could smell petrol. I couldn't open the door, so I climbed out of the window. I ran to my father's door and started pulling at it, but it was stuck. The smell of petrol was strong, and I remembered Papá had been to the village when the last fuel delivery had been made. The car had nearly a full tank. Under the battered bonnet, I could see a flicker. I knew it was a flame.

'I realized I had to get my father out of the car. I was screaming and shouting at him to wake up. After what seemed like an eternity, he lifted his head and turned to me. I shouted at him to open the door. He moved so slowly I was frantic. But he reached down to the handle on the inside, and as I pulled on the door, it flew open.

'Right at that moment, the front of the car burst into flames. Papá was too groggy to move, so I pulled him from the front seat and onto the road. I was still dragging him when the car exploded. The force blew both of us backwards. I hit my head and must have been unconscious for a while. I don't know how long it was, but when I woke up, Papá was on top of me.

'I wriggled out from under him, calling his name. But the moment I saw him, I knew he was dead. He had taken the brunt of the blast, and his body had shielded me. He was horribly burnt. I could barely look at him.

'I think I screamed. I remember calling for help — I don't know how long for. But the road was completely empty. We had been driving for hours, and I had no idea where we were or how I could get help.

'Then I realized no one could help my father now anyway. I sat down beside him and lifted his bloody head onto my lap. I put my arms around him and held his burnt body. I cried. I sobbed and I rocked his poor, broken body. I grieved for everything I had lost — all the family I would never know, and the one man who was truly my father.'

Alberto can see his father lying in his arms. He can feel his arms, stiff and sore. His father has been dead for some time. It's late and the sun is sinking in the sky. With one last kiss on his father's head, he stands and turns. He walks away from the road and into the bushes. He doesn't know where he's going, but he has to get away from this terrible scene.

Through the bushes and across the fields the child Alberto walks. He doesn't stop. The gorse scratches his legs, and he stumbles many times, but he keeps walking. The night becomes black and he can barely see his feet, but he keeps going.

His mind is a whirl. His father is dead. But he wasn't his father. Who is his father? Should he go home? It isn't his home anymore. Not now his father is dead. He has no mother and no father. He is an orphan.

He shakes his head as he walks, but the thoughts refuse to go away; instead, they shout at him, and the longer he walks, the more confused the thoughts become.

He finally stops for a moment and shuts his eyes. He takes himself inside his head. He sees his thoughts. They clatter and crash into each other. He realizes he doesn't want to think these thoughts anymore. He doesn't want to think about anything anymore. He screws his eyes very tight and looks at the thoughts. As he concentrates, the thoughts soften and swirl around his head. And then, quite purposefully, he sends them away. One by one, they disappear into a mist. His mind becomes blank. Now he doesn't know what to think, what to feel.

Suddenly, he hears talking. He realizes he is near a road and he creeps behind a bush and kneels down. He keeps very still. It is a group of men, soldiers, passing by. They are talking about food. He wonders if he is hungry but can't feel anything.

Waiting for the men to pass by, he is aware of leaves and twigs rubbing against his bare legs. He is just about to stand after the men have passed by when he hears more footsteps. He puts his head down and remains as still as he can.

Suddenly, something lands on his head. He senses more than feels his hair singeing and realizes it is a cigarette. Instinctively, he flicks it off his head. Then he holds his breath, staying as still as he can. He knows his life depends on it.

'Show yourself,' instructs a man's voice. He doesn't move. What should he do? His mind is blank. He does what he is told.

He clambers out of the bushes. He follows the orders and stands where he is instructed. With a sharp click, a flame lights up all their faces. He sees a pale man with freckles and a young man pointing a gun at him. They both wear black hats and dark uniforms.

'What's your name?' demands the pale

man. The way he talks is strange. He doesn't sound the same as people Alberto knows.

'Alberto.'

'How did you get here?'

'I walked.'

'Where from?'

Thoughts try to return. They force against the thin wall he has formed to keep them out. They push and push trying to get back in. *Where from?* they insist. *Where are you from? Who are you, and where are you from?*

With all the effort he can muster, Alberto pushes them out of his mind. He will not think of those things again. He will never let those thoughts back.

And suddenly the soldier is holding him. He realizes he is crying, and with a sense of relief, he collapses into the man's body.

When he has cried his fill, the pale man gives the young soldier an instruction. The young soldier takes his hand, and as he looks up, he sees the pale soldier smile, even in the dark. Obediently, he is led away.

After a short time walking, the young man says to him, 'Alberto, eh? What's your second name?'

'Romero.' He can say that without letting the thoughts back in, but he knows he can't say — can't remember — anything more or else the thoughts will return.

Then more questions. Where does he live? Where was he going? Where are his family? What was he doing walking in the dark?

He has a dim memory of a car, but he says nothing.

★   ★   ★

The memory skips and he is walking again. This time he is with the one they call El Rubio. They are walking in comfortable silence.

He listens to the quiet stamp of their footsteps and the swishing of the grass as it flicks past their legs. He is enjoying each moment, concentrating on all of his senses and filling his mind with this peaceful moment.

'Alberto, are you sure you can't remember anything about your home?' the soldier asks.

He finds he cannot. He tries gently to see if there are any memories, but with relief, he realizes they have gone. Completely gone.

'No, nothing,' he says.

'Not even your mamá?'

Suddenly, he hears his own voice shout, *Mimi!* The memories bubble up again, but he stamps down on them, before they can grow.

The soldier pushes him with more questions. But he finds the more he is prodded for information, the more doors close in his mind. Everything is carefully locked away.

The soldier gives up and for a while they talk easily about his home in England, his strange accent and his sunshine-yellow hair. The Englishman tries to explain why he is fighting in the war. As he listens to talk of a battle for fairness against cruelty, he sees a boy push a girl over. He flies at the boy and hits him in the face.

He realizes he is standing still, and the soldier is talking to him. With reluctance he explains, 'I just had a memory.'

'What was it?'

'I hit another boy,' he replies.

'Why?'

He sees the boy push the girl again, but this time she falls and falls and disappears into black. There's nothing there. The memory has gone.

'I don't know,' he says honestly.

The soldier is talking, but he isn't listening. For the first time, he is trying to remember. He tries to see the scene where he hit another boy. But it's not there. He tries to find something else in his memory — names, places, a home. But there's nothing there. He has dispelled them all. It's not quite as comforting as it should be.

Now the Englishman is talking about fighting and throws an easy punch at his shoulder. He punches the man half-heartedly in the leg. The soldier then shows him how to hit properly, how to hold his hand in a fist.

Remember this, he thinks then. Remember this moment with the Englishman — this is something to remember. This is a new memory.

★ ★ ★

Time skips by again. He is standing in a churchyard. A door is open, flooding light onto him and the soldier. They both stand in front of a priest. He is tall and bespectacled. The priest gives the Englishman a long look, turns to him, then back to the soldier.

In his long robes, the cleric steps forward and puts a hand on his head. He in turn looks to Rubio. After a moment, the man with the yellow hair smiles and winks at him. He relaxes. He is leaving one man he trusts and is in the care of another. He smiles at the Englishman before the priest leads him into the church.

The church feels safe and warm. The priest introduces himself as Father Francisco. Then, without speaking, the priest takes him to a tiny bedroom. There, he pulls back the covers on the bed, takes off the boy's jacket and boots, and helps him climb in. Then all is black.

★   ★   ★

When the sunlight reappears, he sees another soldier. This soldier is wearing an officer's khaki uniform. The officer and Father Francisco are having a discussion — it's very heated; they both seem angry. As he watches, the officer spits in the priest's face.

Fury rises in him and he sees himself running towards the soldier. He remembers Rubio's lesson in how to hit and curls his hand into a fist. With all his might, he punches the officer's leg. He is just about to hit him again when a hand flies towards him and strikes him across the face. He hurtles back and falls to the ground.

Father Francisco rushes to him and kneels down beside him. The officer storms away.

'Alberto,' says the priest, looking into his face, 'you shouldn't have done that. I understand why you did, but these are dangerous times. Take great care of becoming involved in other people's arguments. Captain García could have killed you — and just for the sake of a priest's pride.

'When you are older,' Francisco continues,

'you will understand that there are times when you should get involved, and times when it is better to stand back.'

He watches the priest wipe the spit from his cheek with his sleeve.

'Why did he spit on you, Father?'

The priest looks at him and smiles. 'Because I am still learning when to stand back.'

★ ★ ★

The memory flitters and stutters forward in a staccato fashion, revealing emotions and images. He feels fear as he says goodbye to Father Francisco and climbs into a soldier's truck. He experiences an intense stab of grief as the truck passes fallen fighters and he sees the blond mop of El Rubio. He feels himself sink into a dark, deep hole and sees nothing. Then far away, he hears his name.

'Alberto,' says a woman's voice.

★ ★ ★

'Alberto.'

He blinks. He is holding a chunk of bread. The warm, sweet smell of chocolate wafts from it, and he is just about to take a bite when he hears his name again.

'Alberto.'

He looks up and sees a young woman. She is wearing an apron, and her dark hair is tied up — she has a serious look on her face. She holds a piece of paper in her hand. It is the piece of paper on which El Rubio wrote his name.

He smells the chocolate and feels the warm bread in his hand.

★   ★   ★

'Alberto.'

The old man looked up. Mimi sat in front of him. She held his hand tightly in hers.

'Alberto,' she said again softly.

Gruffly, he said, 'I saw it, Mimi. I saw it. Everything that happened. The memories are coming back.'

'It looks as if they are difficult memories,' said Mimi gently.

Alberto nodded.

Mimi put her hand on his arm. 'I'm so sorry,' she said quietly.

The old man looked at her and gave a sad smile. He lifted his glass of water to take a drink, but the glass shook with the trembling of his hand. Embarrassed, Alberto set the glass back down.

'Brandy?' asked Mimi.

Alberto smiled and nodded.

'Come with me,' said Mimi. 'I'll show you the collection and you can choose a brandy.'

Alberto raised his eyebrows at his friend.

'There is no one else I would rather share these wines with,' said Mimi.

Alberto smiled at her appreciatively.

Mimi led him out the back of the house to some stairs. At the bottom was a large oak door, which Mimi opened with a key.

'We had this cellar built for the collection,' she explained as she pushed the heavy door open, found a light switch and flicked it on.

The cool, stone room was lined with shelves, each filled with dusty bottles. Alberto breathed in the dry, musty air as he followed Mimi inside.

'The ones by the door are the more recent wines, including those sent by Javier. You see this marker here? This signifies the death of my father. To be honest, I'm not very interested in the wines after that. But here' — she waved her hand at the shelves of bottles — 'is the wine that my father and our ancestors before him made.'

Alberto peered at the bottles but was frightened to touch them, conscious of their value.

'There are more than five generations of our family's wines here. Some are better than others; some have not aged well. But there are some outstanding wines. My father was always very careful to maintain the collection, and I still have the log of all the wines stored here.'

'It must make you proud of your family,' said Alberto, taking in the scene.

'Yes,' said Mimi softly. 'Yes, it does. I'm still trying to decide what to do with the collection when I'm gone. My children don't want it — they don't have the historical links. And Néstor's children are even less interested than my brother.

'Of course, it's worth quite a lot of money. Maybe I should just sell the collection, even though the thought pains me, and split the profit in my inheritance. I know I have to make a decision soon, but I keep putting it off,' Mimi sighed.

Alberto nodded uncomfortably. He had barely anything to leave his children and grandchildren.

'Now,' said Mimi, brightening up and rubbing her hands together. 'The brandy collection is down here at the end.'

They crossed to the deepest part of the room, where the single bulb threw only a little light, and the shelves here were densely filled with the stout bottles.

'Our brandy became very popular locally,'

explained Mimi. 'My father was always very proud of it, and the fact that he had expanded the business.' She reached up and brought down a bottle. She wiped the dust off the label and showed it to Alberto.

'This was a good year,' she said. 'My father really had a chance to develop the flavours. He and your father learnt a great deal from those first few years.'

'Did you say he and my father began the brandy production together?' asked Alberto thoughtfully. There was a memory fluttering around his mind.

'Yes,' said Mimi. She paused. She was remembering too: there was something significant about the beginning of the brandy production.

'Could we see an early bottle?' asked Alberto.

Mimi nodded and stepped to the corner of the room. There, she knelt down and wiped the tiny brass labels attached to the bottom shelf.

As she did, Alberto gasped. 'The first brandy,' he said. 'I remember our fathers talking about it. It was a celebration.'

'Yes,' said Mimi, turning to him. 'I remember too. The first bottle — it was dedicated to your mother!'

'And the label on the bottle . . . ' said Alberto.

' . . . shows the years of her birth and her death. Oh, Alberto, she died on your birthday.'

Alberto nodded, suddenly unable to speak. He reached for the wall and placed his hand on the cool stones to steady himself. After all these years of not knowing, he was about to find his birthday.

Mimi reached for one of the bottles and slid it out of its shelf, then handed it to Alberto. Holding it carefully, he stepped towards the light. Mimi joined him, standing close beside him.

Alberto blew hard and a cloud of dust surrounded them. Then he wiped his hand over the label, revealing the Quintero family crest and, in heavy red letters beneath, the words QUINTERO BRANDY. As Alberto squinted at the faded ink, he saw words appear out of what he had first thought was a decorative flourish. It formed two dates.

At the sight of them, the old man smiled at the familiarity of his birthday.

Alberto turned to Mimi. 'Just wait until we tell the boy,' he said.

16

ANGELITA

16 April 1931

A sharp pain jabs me, making me gasp. But almost as soon as it comes, it is gone. I rub my back gently. Through the night, I had noticed aches, but I didn't wake Raúl. Instead, I had watched him sleep, his kind face relaxed. He is a fine man. Often I think he is too good for me. He has integrity and honour, characteristics I fear I lack.

I pour the warmed milk into the bowl of coffee and set it on the table. I pick at a sweet roll and lean against the table — the wood feeling cool on my legs through my smock.

'Good morning, my Angel,' says Raúl, walking into the small kitchen. He reaches out for my hand and kisses its palm.

I smile at him. I'm lucky. He treats me like a princess, not a fallen woman.

He sits down to his breakfast of sweet rolls with honey. Slurping his coffee, he indicates for me to sit with him. I ease my enormous body into the seat next to him.

'How are my wife and child today?' he asks warmly.

'We're fine. I felt a little pain earlier.' I see his eyebrows rise with a mixture of excitement and concern. 'I'm sure it's nothing,' I carry on hurriedly. 'The women say sometimes the body practises for what's to come. It doesn't mean the baby's coming yet.'

'But it's due soon, Angel. Should I call for the midwife?'

'No, Raúl. Not until we're sure. When you've gone to work, I'll go and see Chita.'

'All right. But you must send for me the moment anything happens.'

'Raúl,' I laugh, 'you know there's no point. What can you do except pace and fret? Better that you get on with your work and leave it to the women.'

'I can't bear the thought of you being in pain,' he says sadly.

'But think what the result will be,' I say, rubbing my huge stomach. As if to agree, the baby kicks.

Smiling, I reach for Raúl's hand and place it so he can feel the baby kicking. It's a sensation that Raúl never seems to tire of and he grins widely.

'It is a wonder,' he says, shaking his head.

'What?'

'The miracle of childbirth. The fact that any day a baby will arrive. A baby with ten perfect fingers and ten perfect toes. And, I'm sure, with your perfect beauty.'

There is a moment of discomfort as I wish I could return the compliment — tell him that I want the baby to have his calm and generous temperament. But I cannot.

Raúl sees my unease and, pushing his chair back, pulls me to him. Awkwardly, I sit on his lap, aware of my weight.

'Angelita, I know what you're thinking. Don't worry. This baby will be mine too. I will be there with you, bringing it up. It will be me teaching it to speak and count and read. It will learn my way of doing things. It may not have my nose, but it will have my sense of right and wrong. And I shall be proud of my achievements if it does.'

He rubs my back as I smile weakly at him. Usually it is me reassuring him, telling him that it is of little importance that he is not the baby's blood father. In the last few weeks, however, my mood has changed and I find myself full of doubts and fears.

'Don't be late for work,' I say, standing up and walking to the sink.

Raúl drains the last of his coffee and crosses over to me. He puts his arms around me and nuzzles into my neck.

'I love you, Angel,' he whispers.

I smile and, turning to him, kiss his lips, breathing in his soapy smell.

'I'll have lunch with Dante today,' he says as he heads for the door. 'Put your feet up and have some rest.'

I smile again at him as he leaves.

Washing the dishes, I look out of the window and think about that kiss. Every time I kiss Raúl, I wait for that feeling. That tiny sparkle inside me. The sensation of fairy dust sprinkled on my heart. I wait for it, but it never comes.

If I had not been in love before, I believe I would be happy with Raúl. He is warm and thoughtful, and he adores me. But I have been in love and I know what is missing.

I shake my head, trying to get rid of the thought. I do love Raúl. And he knows I do. But it is not a love that lights up like a fire inside and ignites a glow that cannot be extinguished.

Looking out of the window, my hands resting in the warm water, I think of that searing love. The sensation of pure happiness that surges through you every time you see the man you love. The knowledge that you must be together, that to be apart feels wrong and throws the world out of kilter. And when you are together, it is impossible not to touch him, to kiss him, to hold him. And to know absolutely that he feels the same way.

I shut my eyes and see his face. His eyes flecked with green. His soft brown curls. His strong chin. As I look at him, he says my name. *Angelita*. And he reaches both hands to cup my face and pulls me towards him to kiss him.

'Angelita?'

I turn quickly, flushed, to see Chita peeping in through the door.

'Come in, Chita,' I reply, wiping my hands on a cloth.

'Señor Raúl asked me to visit you,' says Chita, a smile on her face.

I am embarrassed. 'I'm sorry, Chita. You know how he worries. I'm sure it's nothing, just a little pain this morning.'

'You look well — you have a good colour. A little pain is to be expected at this time in your pregnancy. It may mean that the baby will come soon. Or it may not. It's up to the baby when it decides to come. Is it still moving?'

'Oh yes,' I say, laughing. 'It's been very active this morning.'

'Then everything is going well,' says Chita.

'Do you have time for some coffee?' I ask.

'Of course,' she says.

I know Chita works hard and I feel bad

taking her from her chores, but I have few friends here. Everyone has been friendly and welcoming, but I know that some women feel uncomfortable with me. Sometimes they catch their men looking at me and become a little cold towards me.

Luckily, Dante and his wife both treat me as a long-lost sister. I feel at ease with Dante because, for all his cheeky comments, I know that he has no room in his heart for anyone other than his wife. Perhaps that's why he and Raúl get on so well — they are both content.

Chita has been important during my time here. She has helped me learn to be a wife, to look after our home and my new husband. We have never spoken of it, but it's clear she knows that I never had to work in the home before. She is patient and kind to me, and I appreciate her friendship.

She tidies up a little while I make the coffee; then we sit at the table. It's an indulgent feeling. Usually at this time in the morning, we would be working through the day's chores.

'So,' says Chita, 'have you been thinking of names?'

'If it's a girl,' I reply, 'we will call her after my sister.'

'I didn't know you had a sister,' says Chita with interest.

'And if it's a boy,' I carry on quickly, 'we are still having discussions.'

Raúl and I have promised we won't speak of our family here. We agreed that we have started our lives anew. Our old lives are behind us.

But I miss my sister, Mercedes. She and I used to be so close. I know I am the one to have created a distance between us, but I wish we could return to the way things were. Maybe one day we'll go back and I can make amends.

'Discussions?' says Chita. 'It sounds as if you don't agree.'

'Raúl thinks a boy should be named after him — Raulito. If not, he likes Jesus.'

'Well, what's wrong with those names? It is tradition for your firstborn to take his father's name.'

'I think it's confusing to have two people in the same house with the same name. I know everyone does it, but I've always thought it was strange. But also, what if we have another boy? Won't he feel bad that he hasn't got his papá's name?'

Chita smiles. She clearly thinks I'm being ridiculous. 'And what is the reason for rejecting our good Lord's name?' she asks.

I sigh. I can't tell Chita that I have rejected not just his name, but the good Lord himself.

'There are just other names that I prefer.'

'Such as?'

'For most of my pregnancy, I've liked the name Eduardo,' I say. Chita nods approvingly. 'But,' I continue, 'lately I've been thinking about another name. I don't know where it came from — it just popped into my head one day.'

'What is it?'

'Alberto.'

'Alberto,' says Chita, trying it out. 'Yes, it's a good name. What does Raúl think?'

'He says when the baby comes, we'll know which name is right.'

'Well, he's correct,' says Chita.

Suddenly, the pain stabs again and I grasp the table. Chita reaches out and takes my hand.

'How long since the last pain?' she asks when I get my breath back.

'About twenty minutes.'

'And was this pain stronger than the last?'

'Yes, a bit. Has it started?' I ask nervously.

'Maybe,' she says, smiling and sitting back. 'I'll stay a while longer and we'll see what happens.'

I nod, feeling a little fluttering of fear in my stomach.

'Chita, will you do me a favour? Raúl is so anxious; I don't want him to be worried unnecessarily. Please don't tell him until the baby has arrived.'

Chita nods seriously. 'Unless,' she says, raising her finger at me, 'unless it is necessary to tell him.'

I realize she is suggesting that something may go wrong, and if my life is in danger, she will call him.

'Of course,' I agree cautiously.

'Perhaps,' says Chita, her face softening, 'you should have something else to eat. You need to keep your strength up.'

'I have some *magdalenas* in the pantry,' I smile, rising to fetch the plate of fluffy sponge cakes.

'I have noticed,' laughs Chita, 'that you only eat for two when it comes to cakes!'

★ ★ ★

I lean back into the pillow, panting hard. The last contraction was stronger than the others. Since my waters broke an hour ago, everything has changed.

Chita had immediately sent a boy to the town to fetch the midwife. Then she called for a girl to prepare lunch for the Quinteros and Raúl. When she had organized everything, she helped me into my nightdress and busied herself preparing the bed and collecting linen.

279

And now here I am, lying in the bed. I have been watching the clock to count the time between the pains. It is now only five minutes between each one.

There is a knock on the door and Chita opens it. A tiny lady dressed in black, her face creased with smile lines, enters the room.

'Hello, beautiful girl,' she greets me. 'Are you ready for the arrival of your precious little one?'

I nod, unable not to smile at this woman despite the pain.

'My name is María Teresa,' she says, handing a wicker basket to Chita.

'Señora?' I ask, confused. I cannot call someone so elderly whom I have never met before by their given name.

'Dear,' she says patiently, 'we are going to be intimately acquainted by the end of this. Let us be less formal from the beginning.'

'Oh,' I say uneasily.

Chita takes her to the kitchen, where I hear them murmuring quietly.

When they return, María Teresa is wearing an apron and has her sleeves rolled up. 'Shall we see where we are, dear?' she asks.

I nod and let her examine me.

'Ooh,' she says with delight. 'All's going well. It shouldn't be too much longer now, and then you'll have your special little gift.'

I feel myself relax a tiny amount. But the moment is brief and I feel another wave of pain coming fast.

'Now, dear,' says the old woman, grasping my hand, 'breathe. That's it. Breathe. And think of something lovely.'

I squint at her in disbelief.

'Yes, yes,' she nods gleefully. 'Close your eyes and think of something, or someone, that makes you happy.'

I try, but all I can think of is the pain. When it is over, María Teresa pushes my hair away from my damp face and says, 'I know it's difficult, dear, but it will help. Think of a place where you feel relaxed. Or perhaps being with your husband. Or a food that you adore. If you can think of that, and not the pain, it will bring you some relief.'

'I'll try,' I say.

'Very good,' says María Teresa brightly as she bustles into the kitchen.

Chita returns with a bowl of water. Sitting beside me, she sets the bowl on the side table and dips a cloth in it. After wringing it out, she lays the cool cloth on my forehead.

'Thank you, Chita,' I smile at her.

Chita looks sadly at me and says, 'I'm sorry that your mother cannot be here with you. This is a time to be with your daughter.'

I haven't thought of my mother in weeks.

We were never close, but it has been easier than I expected to dispel her from my thoughts. I know Raúl misses his family a great deal, but apart from Mercedes, I do not.

The thought of my mother in this room fills me with horror. Oh no, the last thing I would want right now is my mother by my bedside. Warmth and support do not come naturally to her. She would certainly not approve of the cheery midwife — serious things must be conducted seriously in her opinion.

If my mother knew of my affair, and of this baby, I truly don't know what she would do. Perhaps she would shun me instantly. Turn her back on me and refuse to let any member of my family ever speak to me again. Or she might insist that we tell everyone that the baby was born early, yet remind me regularly that my child is a bastard. And she would insist a child born of sin was instantly baptized to save it from the flames of hell.

It will be difficult enough for me to dissuade Raúl from baptizing the baby. In the past few months, I have been considering this. While I have my opinion about the Church and religion, is it my place to impose it on a baby? My resolution has been that when it is old enough, we must let the child decide independently. I shall have problems explaining this to Raúl, though, I know, as he is more religious than even he realizes.

It is most likely that the child will be influenced by the Catholic society all around us, and want to be a part of it as opposed to excluded from it. And if that's enough, to feel part of something, then so be it. I'll be happy to support that decision. But I shall never return to the Church. It has caused me too much pain, and shown me it is an institution of suffering, not love. It repels me with its oppression and cruelty. As I think of what the Church has done to me, I feel a rage stir within me.

'Another one?' asks Chita, gently patting my head with the cloth.

I realize that the pain is returning and I nod.

María Teresa told me to think of something that makes me happy. I close my eyes tight and think of Raúl. I see his smiling face. I feel nothing but the pain. I try again and remember a day a few months ago when Raúl and I went out in the car. We took a picnic to a field full of wild lavender and we lay in the sun and the scent-filled air.

But still the pain is unbearable. In desperation, I think of the face that I only rarely allow myself to see. He appears in front of me. His earnest look breaks into an easy smile and I see him chuckle. There is a light in his eyes that makes his face glow and I feel myself smile back at him.

'Well,' exclaims María Teresa, 'whatever you're thinking of is working, isn't it?'

Puffing through the fading pain, I nod at the old woman and hope that she doesn't ask me what I'm thinking of.

And so it continues. The pain comes and I think of my lover and the thought of him eases the pain.

Over the hours, I think of the time we spent together. I remember when we first met. The fragrance of incense, the murmuring of the congregation and that handsome face as he leant towards me. It was clear we both felt something when we looked on one another for the first time. He stumbled over his blessing and I nearly choked on the host. Then our new priest smiled the tiniest of smiles at me and I knew I had to see that smile again.

As the pain rushes in again, I recall our first kiss. I had asked him to hear my confession, and confessed my feelings for him. He told me to pray for the Almighty's forgiveness. Then, because it was late, he offered to walk me home. As we crossed the dark, empty park, I stopped and tried to kiss him. At first, he pushed me away, but then, as we looked into each other's eyes, he pulled me to him and kissed me passionately.

The next time the pain comes, I remember our first night together. In his small, musty-smelling room, we hid under the covers. He held me tight and we whispered our love. We were so comfortable with one another, it was as if we had known each other all our lives. Without his robes, he was a man like any other. And yet a man unlike any other I had met.

And then, when there seems to be no respite from the pain, María Teresa tells me to push. As I do, I imagine it is not Chita holding my hand, but Antonio. It is Antonio who whispers in my ear that the baby's head is appearing. His warm voice telling me that I must keep bearing down. I squeeze his hand tightly and scream while he tells me I'm doing well and our baby is nearly with us. When I think I can bear it no longer, I hear Antonio say that our boy has arrived, and it is over.

Chita wraps the bloody bundle in soft cloths, then lifts it towards me. I see the tiny baby screw up his face and release a cry that to me sounds like music. I feel such an incredible surge of love for this tiny being that I can barely breathe. I hold him gently and his warm head falls on my chest.

'It's a boy,' says Chita, wiping my forehead. 'I know,' I say, gazing into my child's face. 'His name is Alberto.'

Chita smiles at me kindly until María Teresa nudges her and whispers urgently.

Ignoring them, I continue to look at my baby, drinking in his face, his tiny tuft of sticky hair, his wrinkled fingers.

I am vaguely aware of Chita quickly leaving the room and returning with fresh towels and sheets. I see her gather bloodstained sheets and rush out of the room with them. I hear the door open and Chita calls for a boy. I hear her speak quickly and quietly to whoever comes before closing the door again.

For a tiny moment, I break my gaze from my beautiful baby to look at María Teresa. Her face is worried and stern. She sees me looking at her and instantly a smile lights her face.

'Nothing to worry about, lovely. There's just a bit too much blood. Chita has sent for the doctor, but I'm sure everything will be fine. You enjoy your gorgeous boy.'

My gorgeous boy squeezes his eyes shut and shakes his head. I sense the figure of Antonio by my side, and the faint scent of incense.

'Welcome, Alberto,' I say quietly to him. 'Your father and I are so pleased you're here.'

Chita comes back to me, a worried look on her face. It snaps me back to reality. Of course I know that Antonio is not here. And the expression on Chita's face makes me say to her, 'Please tell Raúl.'

She nods and dashes out of the room. I hear the door slam and turn back to Alberto, who squirms in his swaddling cloths. 'Albertino,' I whisper to him, 'you must know that you were born out of the truest of loves. Whatever happens, I will always be with you.'

I realize that tears are streaming down my face. The pain is returning, but this time it is too much and I cannot divert my mind from it.

Chita returns to my side, and she speaks. But it's as if she is speaking from a very long distance and I have to strain to hear her. She says that Raúl is outside and the doctor is on his way. I suddenly feel very drowsy and struggle to keep my eyes open. As I strain to look at Alberto, he is gently taken from my arms. I want to object. I want to cry, *No — don't take my baby!* but the desire to sleep is too strong and I succumb.

As I drift away, I see Antonio. I reach out to touch him, but then I see an anxious look on his gaunt face. Looking around, I see Raúl is beside me, smiling. My mother and father stand just behind me. With a sinking feeling I realize what I see is my wedding day.

The man I am in love with, the love of my life, stands before me, reading the scripture. The man that I love, who told me that our love could not be, that it was impossible for us to be together, that what had happened between us was a mortal sin. The man that I love, who chose God above me.

I remember him telling me it was over. All of my pleading and wailing had come to nothing. He had stood firm, pale and miserable, and insisted that God was his one true love.

A short time later, when I discovered I was expecting Antonio's child, I considered telling him. But his words had been so final, I didn't dare try even to speak to him again. In my distress and loneliness, I had turned to an old friend. Raúl had suggested what seemed to be the answer to all our problems. Fear drove me to agree and feign delight when we announced our engagement to our parents.

Just a few short weeks later, I entered the chapel on my wedding day, dressed in my mother's white dress, the long veil hiding my wretchedness. And as I turned from a grinning Raúl to the priest, I saw Antonio. It had never crossed my mind to ask who my father would appoint to conduct the ceremony. The horror of the situation overwhelmed me and I fainted. Raúl caught me, while Antonio looked on, his pain obvious.

My mother's smelling salts and stern words made me compose myself and the marriage continued. I could barely look at either Antonio or Raúl. And when the ceremony was over, I swore I would never step foot in another church. A God that creates such intense love, then forbids it, then throws it back in your face, is not a God that I want to worship.

For a moment, I see Antonio's face again. My heavy veil masks his features, but I see his warm eyes swimming with tears. The sight makes me sigh with sorrow and weariness.

'Angelita,' says an insistent voice.

Stirring, I try to open my eyes, but I am too tired.

'Angelita,' says the voice, louder this time.

I force my eyes open and see the doctor. He is holding my wrist and looking at his watch. I notice María Teresa standing over me, rubbing my stomach. There are no smiles now; her face is stern and set. Behind her, I see Chita standing in the doorway holding a small bundle. I relax, knowing my baby is nearby.

I want to speak to the doctor, ask what is happening, but I don't have the strength. Far away, I hear a splashing sound and see María

Teresa look down with a horrified expression on her face. The doctor drops my arm and steps towards my legs. As I look up, I see Chita disappear out of the door.

Everything is swimming now. I see Raúl, his worried face looking down at me, speaking words I cannot hear. I see Mercedes as a child, laughing as we chase each other across the garden, our white Communion dresses fluttering in the wind. I see Antonio, his handsome face breaking into a large smile as he says my name over and over. And then I see a small boy, with soft brown curls and eyes flecked with green. He looks at me seriously, but as I smile at him, I see the tiniest of smiles turn the corners of his lips.

I think he is the most beautiful child I have ever seen.

17

16 April 2006

Albertino stood on his tiptoes and reached up to the fattest lemon he could see. The leaves rustled as he twisted and broke the stalk. Carefully, he lifted the lemon to his nose and breathed in, as he had seen his grandfather do so many times.

The lemon smelt fresh and sweet and clean, and he nodded to himself before turning and bounding off to the table with it. There, Señora Ortiz was making up jugs of sangria. The boy handed the large lemon to her and she smiled at him.

'That's a big one,' she said, squeezing it. 'Thank you, Tino.' She picked up a large knife and cut the lemon in half.

Beside her, other women from the village were opening bottles of wine and lemonade, and breaking large blocks of ice wrapped up in towels. Albertino wondered if Papá would let him try a little sangria today.

He looked towards his parents. They were

standing together talking to his aunt and uncle. His papá looked healthy and well, despite leaning on a walking stick. His mother smiled and rubbed her husband's back gently as she listened to her sister talk.

When he had returned home after his trip with his grandfather, Albertino had been wary of going to the hospital for the first time. But instead of the silent, frightening Egyptian mummy, his father had been sitting up and talking. He still had some bandages on his head, but his face had been uncovered. Although swollen and discoloured, it was Papá.

On that first visit, his mamá had allowed him to sit very carefully on the edge of the bed and talk to his papá. His father listened with interest to Tino's account of their search for Apu's birthday, occasionally asking questions about who they had met, and what they had discovered.

Albertino had noticed that his father kept his hands under the covers. The boy's mother had told him Papá's hands were going to take a long time to recover. And she was right. His father had been through many operations as the surgeons tried to make his hands and arms better.

Rosa had explained to her son that the doctors had taken some skin from other parts of Papá's body and put it on the part that was burnt the worst. She said that the skin started to grow just like it was always supposed to be there, and soon it would look like new. These days, all these months on, Albertino thought his papá's hands looked much better than they did, but they still didn't look like before. His father's fine and dexterous fingers were now fat and clumsy. He watched his father struggle to do things that he used to do without thinking — Mamá even had to cut up his food for him like a baby.

His papá hadn't worked since the accident. His mother had taken more shifts at the factory, but the boy had heard his parents talk in hushed tones when they thought he wasn't listening, and he knew they were worried about money.

But today, it seemed that they had put their worries aside. Albertino thought his mother looked pretty in her best dress and his father very smart in his hat. He had to wear a hat all the time he was outside now, as his skin was sensitive to the sun, but his father said he would start a fashion for men's wide-brimmed hats that would spread across the country.

'So, little one,' said Señora Ortiz, 'would you like to see who wants sangria?'

The boy nodded and carefully picked up a

large earthenware jug, filled to the brim with the crimson liquid, slices of lemon and orange bobbing on the surface with the ice. Gingerly walking across the dried earth, he made his way towards a group of men. Tall and cheery, Andrés stood at the centre of them. The group were mainly men from the village, but after so many years looking after customers in Los Niños, Andrés was comfortable chatting with strangers.

Seeing the boy approach with the full sangria jug, Andrés stepped forward to help.

'Is this for us, Tino?' he asked.

When the boy nodded shyly, Andrés took the jug from him, saying, 'Let me — I'm a professional, you know.'

'Señores?' he said, holding the jug up to them.

Most of the men nodded happily and lifted their glasses. As he began to fill the mixture of plastic cups, wine glasses and mugs, Andrés began to sing.

'*And I say thank you to the Señor for the women. Yes, the women and the wine . . .* '

His voice was strong and melodic, and while some of the men joined in, others sipped their drinks and listened, smiling at the familiarity of the old song.

The boy smiled too as he watched Andrés raise his glass to the heavens and thank the

Lord one last time for the sangria. The men cheered with approval as he finished the song, and those standing around clapped appreciatively.

As Andrés started to sing another song, Albertino dashed over to his parents. His aunt and uncle had moved on to talk to some family friends, and his mother was talking quietly to his father.

'Mamá, Papá,' cried the boy, running up, 'Señor Andrés is singing!'

'Oh,' said his mother. 'So he is. He's very good, isn't he?'

'Yes,' replied his father, nodding. 'Remind me,' he asked — although he already knew the answer — 'where did you and Apu meet him?'

'At Los Niños — the restaurant. His mamá is Doña Isabel. She looked after Apu when he was in the orphanage,' said the boy excitedly.

'Ah, that's right. If he sings like that in his restaurant, maybe we should take a day out and go for lunch.'

Albertino nodded enthusiastically, but his mother said softly, 'Remember, Juan Carlos, we have to be careful with our money.'

'Pah,' said Juan Carlos. 'I'll be working again in no time and we'll have days out as often as we want.'

The boy noticed his mother's fleeting

glance at his papá's scarred hands leaning on his walking stick before smiling at her husband.

Suddenly, they heard the squealing of children, accompanied by the excited barking of a dog. Albertino looked towards the sound of the fun and grinned. His friends from school were playing with his cousins from the city. In the middle of the group was Bonita, his dog.

A few months after his father had come home from hospital, the family had gone to the local pound. There, his parents had let him choose a dog, although they guided him away from the dogs that were too big for their apartment and the puppies that were too little to be away from their mothers.

In the end, they had all fallen in love with a scruffy little bitch. Her dirty grey hair was matted, and she could barely see out of her gummed-up eyes. They had taken her straight to Rosa's friend who had a dog-grooming parlour and left the dog in her hands, returning an hour later to find a dog they didn't recognize. Her white fur was cropped short, even around her long, elegant tail and dainty feet, and her large dark eyes glowed with happiness.

As everyone gushed at the prettiness of the dog, her name had been decided. 'She is

Bonita,' announced the boy proudly. Bonita quickly settled into the family home and Albertino took her for a long walk every day after school. The dog slept at the foot of his bed at night, and Juan Carlos told him she sat by the door for half an hour before he came home from school.

Now she was barking excitedly as the children chased each other round the trees on the terraces. Thrilled at the thought of joining the game, Albertino was about to dash off towards them when he heard a familiar voice behind him.

'Good afternoon, Tino.'

The boy turned and saw Father Samuel approaching, smiling broadly.

'Hello, Father,' he replied.

'What a beautiful day for your grandfather's birthday party,' said the priest, holding out his hands and looking up to the spotlessly blue sky.

'Father,' said the boy's mother, holding out her hand to shake his and giving a respectful bob of her head. 'Thank you for coming. We're all so glad you could make it.'

'Thank you for the invitation,' said Father Samuel, shaking her hand graciously. 'You must be Albertino's parents.'

'Yes, this is my husband, Juan Carlos.'

The priest turned to the boy's father, his

hand outstretched. But Juan Carlos's hands remained resting on his walking stick, and after a brief glance at them, misshapen hands, the priest gently grasped the man's arm.

'Father,' Juan Carlos nodded at the priest.

'My apologies,' said Father Samuel. 'Doña Isabel told me of the accident. How is your recovery progressing?'

'Very well, thank you, Father,' replied Juan Carlos.

'I'm sure it has not been easy,' said the priest sincerely.

'No, Father, you're right,' said Rosa. 'But Juan Carlos has been very brave. All through the operations and therapy he has remained cheerful.'

'Excellent!' said the priest. 'Sometimes God sends us challenges and demands a great deal from us. It has always been my opinion that a positive attitude in the face of adversity is an asset.'

Juan Carlos nodded seriously. 'It's true what they say, Father, that being faced with death makes one appreciate life. Now I see things I may have missed before. And we are both determined not to waste our precious days.' He smiled at Rosa warmly.

'We should all count our blessings every day,' nodded Father Samuel. 'And may I add,' he continued, turning to Albertino, 'how sorry I was to hear the sad news of your grandfather. You must miss him very much,' he said gently.

The boy's breath caught as it always did when he remembered Apu was gone. Hot tears welled in his eyes as the image of his grandfather on that awful evening flashed in front of him.

Apu had come to his house for the evening. Albertino's father had only been home from the hospital for a few weeks, and was in bed. His mother had prepared *fideuà* — Apu's favourite, saffron-coloured noodles with lumps of fish and seafood nestled in its thick stock sauce. His grandfather told him it was what the fishermen cooked when they were out at sea, and it came from the part of Spain where they lived.

The three of them chatted, sopping up the rich, fishy juices with chunks of bread.

'And we should have fireworks for your birthday, Apu.'

The old man waved his hand, brushing away the idea.

'He's right, Papá,' his mother said. 'All those years you didn't have a birthday to celebrate — we should make this a real fiesta.'

'No, no. I don't want a fuss.'

'I do!' Tino declared.

His mother smiled, and as his grandfather

looked at him, he slowly nodded. He spoke quietly. 'Maybe just a few fireworks. Let's see what my pension can afford.'

'Well,' his mamá said, 'we have plenty of time to save up for it. And we clearly have a lot to plan.'

Albertino nodded forcefully. He was taking full responsibility for Apu's first birthday party. Aunt Mimi had said there had been celebrations for his birthday when he was a very young boy, but that was a whole lifetime ago. In a few months' time, he would have the best fiesta ever.

'Thank you, Rosa,' Alberto said, pushing away his empty plate.

'My pleasure, Papá,' his daughter replied, standing and crossing to the oven. She opened the door and took out the warming plate of food with a cloth. As she placed it on a waiting tray, she suggested, 'Tino, why don't you and Apu watch some television while I take Papá his meal?'

'Apu,' he said excitedly, 'maybe *Los Simpsons* will be on.'

His grandfather settled into the armchair in front of the television as the boy chattered away about his favourite show. But the evening news was on, so he picked up his toy car and drove it over the furniture, humming the noise of the engine.

'Albertino,' his grandfather said quietly.

'Yes?' he replied, driving the car up the leg of Apu's chair.

'I'd like to thank you,' the old man said gruffly.

The child stopped making the engine noise and, kneeling in front of him, looked at his grandfather. 'What for?'

Alberto took a deep breath and continued, 'Thank you for making me search for my birthday. I never expected to find it. But I did. And I found old friends. And memories that I thought had gone forever.'

He leant over and held his grandson's face in his large, leathery hand. 'And I would never have had that joy without you.'

The boy smiled up at his grandfather. Compliments from Apu were rare and he was pleased to receive these kind words.

'You're a very special boy. And I believe you will be a special man. Remember that. Your apu believes you will do wonderful things in your life.'

He placed a soft kiss on his grandson's forehead and smiled at him with tears in his eyes. Albertino smiled back, proud of his grandfather's words.

Then Apu's eyes narrowed and he rubbed his chest with his hand.

'Apu?'

His grandfather winced and, breathing out heavily, said to his grandson, 'I'm fine. Get me a brandy, will you?'

The boy dashed off into the kitchen, where he carefully took the bottle — the brandy his mamá kept especially for Apu — out of the cupboard and slowly measured out two fingers of the amber liquid as his grandfather had shown him many times.

When he had returned to the lounge, he'd seen Apu slumped forward, clutching his arm and letting out a grumbling groan.

'Mamá!' the boy shouted as he stood, rooted to the spot.

His mother came dashing into the room and, as soon as she saw her father leaning over in agony, rushed to his side.

'Papá!' she'd cried, as Tino edged towards them both, still holding the brandy.

'Sit with Apu,' his mother said to him loudly as she stood up and pushed past him.

Obediently, Tino sat on the floor beside his grandfather, placing the glass of brandy beside him. Looking up, he took in Apu's red, strained face, the muscles in his neck taut, veins throbbing visibly.

'Apu?' he said in a scared voice.

But his grandfather didn't reply.

The boy had heard his mother speak into the phone. Her father was having a heart attack, he had heard her say. She told whoever was on the other end to hurry. Please come quickly, she pleaded before slamming down the phone.

Then she had rejoined her son, sitting on the other side of Apu. As they watched, they saw his face start to relax. The muscles and veins softened, released of their intense strain, and his body slowly eased back into the chair. As it did, Apu gave a long, heavy sigh.

'Papá?' Rosa cried, shaking his arm violently.

But Apu had lain back, his face slack, his mouth open. As his mother frantically felt around her father's neck for a pulse, the boy looked at his grandfather's face. To Tino, Apu looked like he did when he dozed off in front of the television. He looked as though he were sleeping peacefully.

The ambulance had arrived not long after, and two men in uniforms rushed into the house. They quickly but gently pulled Apu onto the floor. Tino saw one of them knock over the glass of brandy, spilling his grandfather's drink on the floor. No one else noticed. While one of the medics pumped Apu's chest with his hands, the other opened a small case with what looked like a little machine in it.

'Tino!' his mother said sternly to him.

He wrenched his eyes away from the men leaning over his grandfather and looked at his mother, who was kneeling on the floor by Apu's head.

'Go to your papá,' she said. 'Now!'

He had wanted to stay and watch, but the tone of his mother's voice told him not to argue. He ran into his father's room, where his papá, worried, asked what was going on. Tino had explained as well as he could about the ambulance men, and about the machine, and that Apu just looked like he was asleep.

His father had lifted his bandaged hands up and opened his arms. Tino fell into his papá's body and his father hugged him tightly.

'Maybe he's just asleep, Papá,' he had said, as he fought back the scary feeling that fluttered in his stomach.

His father hadn't said anything, just held him. Perhaps it was then that Tino had realized that Apu was not sleeping.

But now, all these months on, he liked to think that he'd been right the first time, and that's what dying was like. It was like going to sleep, forever. Apu was having a lovely siesta — and was able to watch over his family in his dreams.

Rosa looked at her son, blinking away his tears, and placing a reassuring hand on his shoulder, said, 'Thank you, Father,' to the priest.

'Did your grandfather ever tell you what he did at my church?' asked Father Samuel with a wry smile.

The boy shook his head, swallowing hard.

'Well,' said the priest as Rosa and Juan Carlos leant in to hear the story, 'do you remember you got a bit dirty when you were climbing the tree and I took you into the church to clean up?'

The boy nodded seriously.

'Your grandfather and I had been talking about someone who was buried in the church graveyard. The burial had taken place a very long time ago, but the grave didn't have a headstone. It just had a simple wooden cross to mark the place. There wasn't even a name on the cross.

'I had been trying to get a headstone for the grave, but as I told your grandfather, things do not happen swiftly in an institution as large as the Church. Rightly, your grandfather considered this a poor excuse and took matters into his own hands.

'When you had gone, I went back into the churchyard. There, I found that your grandfather had carved the man's name into the wooden cross.' He looked at Rosa and Juan Carlos and smiled. 'Such a simple action, but it says a great deal about the compassion of Alberto.'

'What was his name?' asked the boy. 'The man who was buried?'

'Antonio,' replied the priest, 'Father Antonio.'

'A priest?' asked Rosa, surprised. 'How strange.'

Father Samuel nodded at her before continuing, 'I have taken a leaf out of your grandfather's book, Tino. In commemoration of your grandfather, I have had a headstone built for the grave. It will arrive and be placed next week. And I intend to say a few words — a blessing for the soul who is buried there.'

'What does it say?' asked Albertino. 'The headstone?'

'It's very simple. I didn't have any details other than a name. So it just says, 'Father Antonio. Commended to God. May he rest in peace.''

'That's very kind of you,' smiled Rosa. 'I wish my father could have known of your actions.'

'He knows,' said the boy clearly. When the three adults turned to him, he said confidently, 'Apu is always with us. You said so, Mamá. And now he knows about the gravestone.'

Smiling, Juan Carlos reached across to his

son and gently ruffled his hair with his thick-fingered hand.

'Father,' said Rosa, 'can I offer you something to eat? The whole village is here and everyone's brought something. We too could feed the five thousand, there's so much food.'

Grinning, Father Samuel let himself be led towards the trestle tables laden with food.

'Papá?' said the boy, looking up at his father.

'Yes?'

'Apu *is* here with us, isn't he?'

His father nodded. 'Yes. He is. He will always be with you and your mamá. And he will always be here on this land.'

Together, they looked across the small plot. The almond and lemon trees, the vines and the tiny corner of flowers. And now the patch of land was filled with people who had come to Alberto's birthday party.

Rosa had made copies of Albertino's hand-drawn poster and they had pinned the party invitation all over the village. She had also tracked down people the boy and his grandfather had met on their search for his birthday. And, as Señora Ortiz had predicted all that time ago, the whole village had come out for the occasion. Albertino was proud that Apu was such a well-liked person.

While the women had covered plates in

strips of sliced hams and chorizo, and prepared two large paellas to cook outdoors, the
men had brought beers and wines — many
home-made. The butcher had doñated a whole
pig — it was so big that the baker had cooked
it in his oven. And Rosa and her sisters had
ordered a huge birthday cake edged with nuts,
Alberto's name spelt out in blue icing.

Albertino wished his grandfather could be
here to appreciate it. Even if he was watching
from heaven, it wasn't the same as being here.
He imagined Apu standing with him,
embarrassed about the fuss, but secretly
pleased to see so many friends and
neighbours mixing happily with his family.

The boy's memory was broken by a frenzy
of barking. Turning quickly, he saw Bonita fly
past him, yapping madly. And there, tearing
towards her and yelping delightedly in return,
was Vito. The two dogs met joyously,
bouncing noisily around each other.

Grinning, the boy looked past the two dogs
and saw Mimi walking towards him.

'Aunt Mimi,' cried Albertino, running
towards her.

When she saw him, Mimi opened her arms.
He ran into them and she hugged him hard.

Rosa and Juan Carlos approached, smiling.

'Thank you so much for coming, Mimi,'
said Rosa.

'It's my pleasure,' replied Mimi, hugging her gently. 'How are you, Juan Carlos?' she asked as he limped towards them.

'Much better than the last time you saw me,' he grinned.

'Yes, you look much better than at the funeral, especially your walking,' she commented.

'It's the exercises I make him do,' teased Rosa.

'She's a tough boss,' grinned Juan Carlos, putting an arm around his wife, 'but I know all the hard work is paying off.'

'And your hands?' asked Mimi gently.

'Oh, you know,' replied Juan Carlos, lifting up one of his ugly hands to show her. 'Little by little.'

Mimi nodded sympathetically.

At that moment, Vito and Bonita ran up to them, jumping and slathering over them all.

Laughing, Albertino knelt down to their level and let them lick and nudge him. As he played with the two dogs, it was impossible to tell which of the three was happiest.

Leaning over the giggling child, Mimi handed Rosa a bag. It clinked loudly and she said, 'Just a few bottles. Not the best stuff, but perfectly good for sangria.'

Rosa kissed Mimi's cheek as she thanked her and delivered the bottles to Señora Ortiz.

'What a wonderful party!' Mimi said to Juan Carlos.

Across the stretch of land, children played noisily, a group of men sang, old women dressed in black and sitting on folding chairs gossiped loudly, and other people milled around the tables filled with plates of food and paella dishes.

'He was a very popular man.'

Mimi nodded. 'He was a wonderful friend when we were children,' she said sadly. 'I just wished I'd been able to spend time with him once we'd found each other again.'

'Rosa says he came back from that trip a different man. He had always been content with what he had, but she said it was as if he'd received a gift he'd never expected. And it was the best gift he could have wished for,' said Juan Carlos.

'I wish Rosa could have seen his face when he saw that bottle with the date of his birth on it. And, of course, as soon as he saw the date, he remembered it. He remembered the birthday parties we'd thrown him, and gifts his father had given him. He became quite emotional.'

'He was not a man who often showed his emotions.'

'May I ask what happened to the bottle of brandy?' asked Mimi.

'It's Tino's now,' replied Juan Carlos. 'It was his idea to search for his grandfather's birthday, so we all agreed he should have it. His mother and I will look after it for him until he's ready to take it. I don't know whether he will drink it or keep it somewhere safe; he's a bit young to think of things like that now.'

'When the time comes, he'll make the right decision, said Mimi. They both watched the child racing the dogs in circles. 'He's a wonderful child.'

'Thank you,' smiled Juan Carlos. 'Now, can I help you to a drink?'

Just then, the dogs barrelled past them, nearly knocking Juan Carlos off his feet.

'Tino!' cried Mimi. 'Don't excite those dogs any more than they already are!'

The boy grinned at Mimi and dashed after the barking dogs, who were heading for a group of people sitting chatting.

'Tino! There you are,' said a familiar voice.

The boy turned and saw among those seated an elderly woman with short white hair and glasses.

'Doña Isabel,' he said happily. Then the boy realized that sitting on either side of her were the gardener and his wife from Los Zorros.

They greeted him happily with kisses and smiles.

'You were playing when we arrived,' explained the gardener. 'I recognized Doña Isabel straight away and we have been catching up on old times.'

'See what you and your grandfather have done?' asked Isabel. 'You've brought together old friends. It's wonderful — I'm so pleased to have someone to talk to about the old days.'

'We do have some sad news, though,' said the gardener.

The boy turned to him, a worried look on his face.

'It's not such bad news,' smirked his wife. 'Old General García passed away last month.'

'Oh,' said the boy. He knew he should act as if this was very sad news, but he could not bring himself to do so, so he kept quiet.

'So what's happened to the old orphanage now?' asked Isabel.

'The government has bought the building,' said the gardener. 'It's not definite, but we believe they are planning to turn it into a care home for the elderly. We have already been approached about continuing to work there.'

'I was hoping they would turn the building into housing for immigrants,' chortled his wife. 'That evil old man would be rolling in his grave if they had!'

The boy smiled. He didn't know what an immigrant was, but anything that made the wizened, nasty man — the man who had been so horrid to Apu — spin in his grave seemed like a good thing to him.

★ ★ ★

Later in the evening, Albertino's uncles hung lanterns from the trees. A wind had picked up, and both the lanterns and the nearby rosemary bushes rustled in the breeze. The women wrapped their shawls tightly around them against the chill. Tired children dozed on their parents' laps, while the men continued to drink and sing and laugh.

The boy had been playing with his cousins and the other children when he saw Vito trotting back towards Mimi. Bonita followed her friend, and he, in turn, followed his dog.

Mimi was talking quietly with his parents, each of them nursing a glass of wine.

'No,' he heard his father say as he approached. 'It's not right.'

'I agree,' said his mother. 'It's too much, Mimi.'

'What's too much?' asked the boy.

The three adults fell silent in the flickering light.

Mimi was the first to speak. 'I have decided

I would like to give your parents a gift. It will help them while your father can't work, but it is also a gift to you — for your future.'

'What is it?' asked Albertino.

'My collection of wine,' replied Mimi.

'I don't like wine,' said the boy.

Despite himself, his father laughed. 'It's not for drinking,' he said.

'What's it for, then?'

'Such a large collection of special wines and brandies is worth a lot of money,' explained his mother.

'It's far too valuable a gift,' said his father firmly.

'Listen to me,' said Mimi. 'If it weren't for a stupid mistake my brother made, I believe Alberto would have stayed on and worked at Quintero's. I think he would have spent the rest of his life on the vineyard. It was a big part of his life as a child and it would have been a part of his future.'

'But what happened all those years ago, happened,' said Rosa. 'You owe us nothing now.'

'I know I don't,' said Mimi, sighing. 'But Tino brought Alberto back to me. He gave me a friend I thought I had lost forever. All the money in the world couldn't have done that. But a small boy with a big heart could. And now I'd like to do something for him.

Please,' she said simply, 'let me do this.'

'But it should go to your family,' said Juan Carlos.

'My family don't need it,' Mimi said firmly. 'Their father left me plenty of money, and I shall leave them that when I die. And, sad though it is, they're not interested in the history of the collection.'

'I don't know,' said Juan Carlos.

'Consider it not as a gift from me, but a gift from Alberto. I had decided to give him the collection after he left. I was planning to arrange it immediately and would have told him when I next saw him. But I never got the chance.'

'Really?' asked Rosa.

'Really,' said Mimi. 'And I can't believe Alberto would have done anything else but pass it on to the grandson who helped him find his birthday. Can you?'

The boy watched his mother and father as they looked at each other, unspoken words passing between them. Slowly, Juan Carlos nodded to Rosa.

The boy's mother turned to Mimi and smiled. Mimi smiled back and the women hugged.

Then it was Juan Carlos's turn to hug the elderly woman. He wiped tears from his eyes and said, 'I don't know what to say.'

'Why don't we raise a glass to Alberto?' said Mimi.

Albertino watched as the three of them silently lifted their glasses to the sky.

Suddenly, a whistle rang out and a light shot into the starry night. There was a moment's silence before a rainbow of colours filled the sky above them.

The children woke and cheered the fireworks, and the men — filled with beer and wine — joined them.

Bonita bounced up to the boy and leant against him, her soft fur warming his leg. Feeling her tremble slightly at the noisy explosions, he stroked her gently and she relaxed at his touch.

As the smoke cleared, and the crowd waited expectantly for the next volley of fireworks, Albertino noticed a tiny star glow a little more brightly in the black sky.

'Happy birthday, Apu,' he said quietly.

Acknowledgements

This book would not be in your hands if not for the following people:

The social workers, psychiatrists and teachers who believed that art could help children deal with the trauma of war. *They Still Draw Pictures*, a collection of drawings by children from all parts of Spain, gave me a unique and inspiring insight into life before, during and after the civil war.

The readers, reviewers and writers of Authonomy.com who encouraged me past the first few chapters. In particular Andrew, Fred, Steve, Geffordson, Jake, B Worm, Jeff, Mary, Jane and, by association, Judy Chilcote.

Diana Beaumont, my agent, who refused to give up on Alberto and me, despite the bumps in the road.

My publisher Sam Humphreys, who remembered this story, found it a nurturing home at Mantle, and held my hand through every edit.

All the friends and family who always believed this novel would be published.

John, who gave me all the loving support I needed and a surname that fits on the cover.

My parents Val and Tony who, through many happy family holidays, helped me fall in love with Spain.

María Luisa, whose big laugh and warm generosity always made our family feel at home in Spain, and her husband Pascual, now sadly passed. A gardener and man of few words, Pascual left an indelible impression on my seven-year-old self, who, like Tino, couldn't imagine a life without a birthday. Without him, neither this book nor Alberto would ever have existed.

We do hope that you have enjoyed reading this large print book.

Did you know that all of our titles are available for purchase?

We publish a wide range of high quality large print books including:
Romances, Mysteries, Classics
General Fiction
Non Fiction and Westerns

Special interest titles available in large print are:
The Little Oxford Dictionary
Music Book
Song Book
Hymn Book
Service Book

Also available from us courtesy of Oxford University Press:
Young Readers' Dictionary
(large print edition)
Young Readers' Thesaurus
(large print edition)

For further information or a free brochure, please contact us at:
Ulverscroft Large Print Books Ltd.,
The Green, Bradgate Road, Anstey,
Leicester, LE7 7FU, England.
Tel: (00 44) 0116 236 4325
Fax: (00 44) 0116 234 0205

Other titles published by Ulverscroft:

THE WACKY MAN

Lyn G. Farrell

Amanda secludes herself in her bedroom, no longer willing to face the outside world. Gradually, she pieces together the story of her life: her brothers have abandoned her, her mother scarcely speaks to her, and the Wacky Man could return any day to burn the house down. Just like he promised . . . As her family disintegrates, Amanda hopes for a better future, a way out from the violence and fear that has consumed her childhood. But can she cling to her sanity, before insanity itself is her only means of escape?

MONSIEUR LINH AND HIS CHILD

Philippe Claudel

Traumatized by memories of his war-ravaged country, his son and daughter-in-law dead, Monsieur Linh travels to a foreign land to bring the child in his arms to safety. To begin with, he is too afraid to leave the refugee centre — but the first time he braves the freezing cold to walk the streets of this strange, fast-moving town, he encounters Monsieur Bark, a widower whose dignified sorrow mirrors his own. Though they have no shared language, an instinctive friendship is forged between them . . .

THE MAKING OF MR BOLSOVER

Cornelius Medvei

NAME: Lynch, Andrew (b. 16.10.1958); a.k.a. 'Mr Bolsover'

CAREER: civil servant, librarian, columnist, local councillor, revolutionary

RECREATIONS: shooting squirrels, skinning rabbits, cooking with rats

ADDRESS: present whereabouts unknown; last sighted in South Downs woodland close to the A275

PROFESSIONAL INTERESTS: cataloguing systems, hermits, badger welfare, troglodytes, revolutionary politics

But a WHO'S WHO entry can reveal only so much. Like all the great political lives — Churchill, Disraeli, Gladstone, Genghis Khan — Bolsover's is one of incident, drama and passion: from the calm of Uckfield library to the demands of high office, a life on the run — and a final confrontation with the authorities . . .